Plumbing

Webster's Timeline History
2474 BC - 2007

Webster's Online Dictionary

(www.websters-online-dictionary.org)

Published by ICON Group International, Inc.
7404 Trade Street
San Diego, California 92121

www.icongrouponline.com

This edition published by ICON Group International, Inc. in 2009
Printed in the United States of America.

Plumbing: Webster's Timeline History, 2474 BC - 2007

ISBN 0-546-89452-6

PREFACE

Webster's bibliographic and event-based timelines are comprehensive in scope, covering virtually all topics, geographic locations and people. They do so from a linguistic point of view, and in the case of this book, the focus is on "plumbing," including when used in literature (e.g. all books that might have "plumbing" in their title). As such, this book represents the largest compilation of timeline events associated with "plumbing". Webster's timelines cover bibliographic citations, patented inventions, as well as non-conventional and alternative meanings which capture ambiguities in usage. These furthermore cover all parts of speech (possessive, institutional usage, geographic usage) and contexts, including pop culture, the arts, social sciences (linguistics, history, geography, economics, sociology, political science), business, computer science, literature, law, medicine, psychology, mathematics, chemistry, physics, biology and other physical sciences. The following keywords were used to build the timeline: plumbing, plomberie (French), rørarbejde (Danish), Wasserleitung (German). This "data dump" results in a comprehensive set of entries for a bibliographic and/or event-based timeline on the word "plumbing", since editorial decisions to include or exclude events is purely a linguistic process. The resulting entries are used under license or with permission, used under "fair use" conditions, used in agreement with the original authors, or are in the public domain. Across all of the Webster's timelines, at the end of some entries the following codes are used to identify certain sources: [WP] Wikipedia.org. All entries marked [WP] are adapted from articles created by contributors to Wikipedia.org, the free encyclopedia under a copyleft GNU Free Documentation License (GFDL) based on the headword. Please note that these entries are not full articles. For the full article associated with a given Wikipedia headword, the reader can simply go to www.wikipedia.org or www.websters-online-dictionary.org and type in the name of the topic to better understand the context of the entry; passages attributed to Wikipedia are exempt from any compilation or other copyright held by this book and can be freely used under the GFDL found at www.wikipedia.org. The full GFDL is reproduced at the end of the book before the index, and applies to each Wikipedia headword in any of the Webster's Timelines. For all of the sources, the original authors holding copyright retain any copyrights. Proceeds from this book are used to expand the content and coverage of Webster's Online Dictionary (www.websters-online-dictionary.org).

2474 BC

Inventions, discoveries, introductions: Indoor plumbing and sewage in the Indus Valley Civilization.

2000 BC

Women's History/General: According to Karen Greenspan, in The Timetables of Women's History, "Development of potter's wheel, bellows, and discovery of glass in Mesopotamia; bathroom plumbing in Crete."

7th Century

Aphrodisias: Evidence can be seen of emergency plumbing installed to combat this problem. Aphrodisias never fully recovered from the 7th century earthquake, and fell into disrepair. Part of the town was covered by the modern village of Geyre; some of the cottages were removed in the 20th century to reveal the older city. A new Geyre has been built a short distance away. [WP]

1823

Thomas Kelly: Publisher of "The new practical builder, and workman's companion: containing a full display and elucidation of the most skillful methods, pursued by architects and artificers, in the various departments of carpentry, joinery, bricklaying, masonry, slating, plumbing, painting, glazing, plastering..." Publisher: Thomas Kelly (London). Published in 1823.

1825

Nicholson, Peter: Born in 1765 and died in 1844, authored "The new practical builder, and workman's companion: containing a full display and elucidation of the most recent and skilful methods, pursued by architects and artificers, in the various departments of carpentry, joinery, bricklaying, masonry, slating, plumbing, painting, glazing, plastering, etc.. etc.. including, also, new treatises on geometry trigonometry, conic sections, perspective, shadows, and elevations copious accounts of building materials, strength of timber, cements, etc. ., a description of the tools used by the different workmen, an extensive glossary of the technical terms peculiar to each department, and the theory and practice of the five orders, as employed in decorative architecture." illustrated and embellished with numerous plates by Michael Angelo Nicholson, R. Elsam, W. Inwood, and other eminent architectural artists. Publisher: printed for Thomas Kelly (London). Published in 1825.

Partington, Charles Frederick: Author of "The builder's complete guide: comprehending the theory and practice of the various branches of architecture, bricklaying, masonry, carpentry, joinery, painting, plumbing, etc. etc." Publisher: printed for Sherwood, Gilbert, and Piper (London). Published in 1825.

1838

Edward Bulwer-Lytton Quotation: "Still, a foreboding, a warning instinct withheld Lucretia from plumbing farther into the deeps of her own fears." - Edward Bulwer-Lytton in Lucretia, vol 2.

Edward Bulwer-Lytton Quotation: "I was obstinately bent on plumbing the depth of my own fears." - Edward Bulwer-Lytton in The Caxtons, part 7.

1841

Charles Dickens Quotation: "Lights were shining from some of these casements, plumbing the depth of the black stream with their reflected rays, but all was profoundly silent." - Charles Dickens in Pictures From Italy.

1845

Edwin Lawrence Godkin Quotation: "He covers it with beautiful houses; he converts the scraggy, yellow pastures into smooth, green lawns; he fills the rock crevices with flowers; he introduces better food and neater clothing and the latest dodges in plumbing." - Edwin Lawrence Godkin in Reflections and Comments 1865-1895.

1851

Nicholson, Peter: Born in 1765 and died in 1844, authored "Practical masonry, bricklaying, and plastering, both plain and ornamental; containing a new and complete system of lines for stone-cutting; for the use of workmen; with an ample detail of the theory and practice of constructing arches, domes, groins, niches, stairs, columns, etc. Bond, foundations, walls, bridges, tunnels, light-houses, etc. Ovens, furnaces, etc. The formation of mortars and cements; including, also, practical treatises on slating, plumbing, glazing, etc. etc. and a full description of the various materials employed in all these arts." Illustrated by numerous engravings, by artists of first-rate talent. Published in 1851.

1864

Mississippi Valley Sanitary Fair: Publication of "Our appeal.: The Special Committee for Stoves, Tin Ware, Heaters, Gas Fitting and Plumbing, in connection with the Mississippi Valley Sanitary Fair, to be held at St. Louis, on the 17th of May next invite your attention, aid and favorable consideration.." Published in 1864.

1869

David Dunbar Buick: When he left school in 1869 he started working for a company which made plumbing goods and when it ran into trouble some years later in 1882, he and a partner took it over. At this time Buick began to show his promise as an inventor, producing many innovations including a lawn sprinkler, and a method for permanently coating cast iron with enamel which allowed the production of "white" baths at much reduced cost. Although cast iron baths are uncommon nowadays, the method is still in use for enamelling them. With the combination of Buick's innovation and his partner's sound business management the company became quite successful. [WP]

1873

Kohler Company: Kohler was founded in 1873 by Austrian immigrant John Michael Kohler with the purchase of the Sheboygan Union Iron and Steel Foundry. Early products included cast iron and steel farm implements, castings for furniture factories, and ornamental iron pieces including cemetery crosses and settees. A breakthrough came for the company when, in 1883, John Michael applied enamel to a cast iron horse trough to create the company's first bathtub. From this point on, the company has been primarily in the plumbing business, and became well known for high-quality plumbing fixtures. [WP]

Mulrein, James: Author of "Facts and hints in regard to plumbing ..." Published in 1873.

1876

Buchan, William Paton: Author of "Plumbing practice: a text-book to the practice of the art or craft of the plumber; with supplementary chapters upon house drainage; embodying the latest improvements." Publisher: C. Lockwood and Co (London). Published in 1876.

1877

Publication: Publication of "Hayden, Gere & co., brass founders, and manufacturers of every variety of brass work, for plumbers, steam engine builders, machinists, gas and steam fitters, &c., dealers in plumbing materials." Published in 1877.

1881

J. L. Mott Iron Works. Plumbing & Sanitary Dept: Publication of "Illustrated catalogue of the plumbing & sanitary department of the J.L. Mott Iron Works." Publisher: J.L. Mott Iron Works (New York, N.Y.). Published in 1881.

WATSON, GOW & CO.: Publication of

"Illustrated Catalogue of general Ironfoundry, Plumbing and Sanitary Goods." Published in 1881.

1882

Durham house drainage company, New York.: Publication of "Illustrations of the Durham patent system of house drainage construction, and a comparison with the ordinary methods of plumbing and drain-laying." Published in 1882.

Gerhard, William Paul: Born in 1854 and died in 1927, authored "House drainage and saintary plumbing. By Wm. Paul Gerhard. Reprinted from Van Nostrand's magazine." Published in 1882.

Hellyer, Samuel Stevens: Author of "Lectures on the science and art of Sanitary Plumbing." Published in 1882.

History of Seattle: Seattle in this era was an "open" and often relatively lawless town. Although it boasted newspapers and telephones, lynch law often prevailed (there were at least four lynchings in 1882), schools barely operated, and indoor plumbing was a rare novelty. In the low mud flats where much of the city was built, sewage was almost as likely to come in on the tide as to flow away. Potholes in the street were so bad as to cause at least one fatal drowning. [WP]

History of Seattle before 1900: As has been remarked, Seattle in this era was an "open" and often relatively lawless town. Although it boasted two English-language newspapers (and, for a while, a third in Norwegian), and telephones had arrived in town, lynch law sometimes prevailed (there were at least four lynchings in 1882), schools barely operated, and indoor plumbing was a rare novelty. In the low mud flats where much of the city was built, sewage was almost as likely to come in on the tide as to flow away. Potholes in the street were so bad as to cause at least one fatal drowning. [WP]

New York City. Health Dept.: Publication of "Registration of plumbers and the law and regulations governing the plumbing and drainage of buildings ..." Published in 1882.

1883

District of Columbia. Health de.. "Regulations governing plumbing, h... and the ventilation of house sewers, in the ... of Columbia." Published in 1883.

Dunedin cable tramway system: Opening on March 23, 1883, the Mornington line travelled 1 mile up High Street to Mornington. Cable Car House (now a plumbing business) is still clearly marked in the shopping area, having had little external changes since the line closed. The Mornington line was the last to close, on March 2, 1957, leaving San Francisco having the only cable cars in the world. [WP]

1884

Gerhard, William Paul: Born in 1854 and died in 1927, authored "House drainage and sanitary plumbing." Publisher: D. Van Nostrand (New York). Published in 1884.

Landis, H. G., builder: Publication of "(Builder's receipt book: receipts made out to H.G. Landis, Reading, PA, 1865-1884. Signed by tradesmen, etc., showing costs of carpentry, masonry, plumbing, mill work, lumber, terracotta, pipe, mantels, etc.)." Published in 1884.

PERIODICAL PUBLICATIONS. London: Publication of "Plumbing and Decorating Record and Gazette." Published in 1884.

1885-1904

Davies, Philip John: Author of "Standard practical plumbing." Publisher: E. & F.N. Spon (London). Published in 1885-1904.

Maguire, William R.: Author of "Plumbing. (Illustrated.)." Published in 1885.

Use in literature: "In towns, boys who begin to earn a living when they enter their teens may be taught in evening schools to practice the craft of carpentry, bricklaying, plastering, plumbing, gas fitting, etc." appears in Scientific American Supplement, No. 497 (July 11, 1885).

1886

Publication: Publication of "Plumbing problems; or, Questions, answers, and descriptions relating to house-drainage and plumbing, from the Sanitary Engineer. With one hundred and forty-six illustrations." Published in 1886.

1887

Gerhard, William Paul: Author of "Notes embodying recent practice in the sanitary drainage of buildings, with memoranda on the cost of plumbing work. By Wm. Paul Gerhard." Publisher: D. Van Nostrand (New York). Published in 1887.

Putnam, John Pickering: Born in 1847 and died in 1917, authored "Improved plumbing appliances, by J. Pickering Putnam, architect. With ninety-four illustrations." Published in 1887.

1888

Clarke, James Wright: Born in 1845 and died in 1912, authored "Plumbing practice." Publisher: The Engineering and Building Record (London; New York). Published in 1888.

J. L. Mott Iron Works: Publication of "Catalogue "G" illustrating the Plumbing and Sanitary Department of the J. L. Mott Iron Works." Publisher: E.D. Slater, Printer (New York). Published in 1888.

San Francisco: Publication of "Plumbing and drainage: rules and regulations adopted July 19th, 1888, by the Board of Health, City and County of San Francisco." Publisher: The Board (San Francisco, Calif). Published in 1888.

Standard Manufacturing Company, Pittsburgh: Publication of "Standard Manufacturing Company, Pittsburgh, manufacturers and enamelers of cast iron plumbing wares, sanitary goods and specialties." Published in 1888.

1889

Buchan, William Paton: Author of "Plumbing: a text book to the practice of the art or craft of the plumber, with supplementary chapters upon house drainage and ventilation embodying the latest improvements." Publisher: C. Lockwood & Son (London). Published in 1889.

Davies, Philip John: Author of "Standard practical plumbing." Published in 1889.

Vacher, Francis: Author of "Defects in Plumbing & Drainage Work. Illustrated, etc." Published in 1889.

1890

Bear Lake and River Water Works & Irrigation Company: Publication of "City water works, Ogden, Utah: rules, regulations, water rates and rules governing plumbing, 1890." Bear River Irrigation and Ogden Water Works Company. Published in 1890.

David Dunbar Buick: During the 1890s, Buick developed an interest in internal combustion engines and began to spend his time on experimenting with them. This meant that he was spending little time on the plumbing business and as a result his business partner became impatient with him. The result was that the partnership was dissolved and the company was sold. [WP]

Gerhard, William Paul: Author of "Recent practice in the sanitary drainage of buildings, with memoranda on the cost of plumbing work." Publisher: Van Nostrand (New York). Published in 1890-1949.

Hawkins, Nehemiah: Born in 1833, authored "Maxims and instructions for the boiler room Useful to engineers, fireman & mechanics, relating to steam generators, pumps, appliances, steam heating, practical plumbing, etc." Published in 1890.

Maguire, William R.: Author of "Domestic Sanitary Drainage and Plumbing, lecture on practical sanitation, etc." Published in 1890.

1891

Clarke, James Wright: Born in 1845 and died in 1912, authored "Plumbing practice." Publisher: Engineering and Building Record (London).

Published in 1891.

Davies, P. J.: Author of "Standard practical plumbing: being a complete encyclopædia for practical plumbers and guide for architects, builders, gas fitters, hot water fitters, ironmongers, lead burners, sanitary engineers, zinc workers; recommended by the Worshipful Company of Plumbers as a text book for registered plumbers, examinations, etc." Publisher: E. & F.N. Spon (London; New York). Published in 1891.

Hellyer, Samuel Stevens: Author of "Principles and practice of plumbing." Publisher: G. Bell: (London). Published in 1891.

Mary Wilkins Freeman Quotation: "It was ascertained that the house had cost a round sum only a few years ago; it was in perfect repair; nothing whatever was amiss with plumbing, furnace, anything." - Mary Wilkins Freeman in Stories Of The Supernatural.

National registration of plumbers council for Manch. and district. pre: Publication of "Lectures on sanitary plumbing, etc. ., Ser.1 (no.1)-10." Published in 1891-93.

1892

Engineering Record: Publisher of "Plumbing problems: or, Questions, answers, and descriptions relating to house-drainage and plumbing." Publisher: Engineering Record (New York). Published in 1892.

Garnett, William: Author of "The craft of plumbing: the work of the modern plumber: the needs and methods of instruction in sanitary plumbing, etc." Published in 1892.

Gee, William Winson Haldane: Author of "Electricity in its relation to Plumbing. Illustrated." Published in 1892.

1893

Greaves, H.: Author of "Manufactory and warerooms of Peck Bros. & Co: manufacturers of brass goods for water, gas and steam, and plumbing material, New Haven, Conn." H. Greaves, Concord, N.H., D.H. Hurd & Co., Boston. Published in 1893.

Hellyer, Samuel Stevens: Author of "Principles and practice of Plumbing. Second edition, revised." Published in 1893.

Jaffrey, William: Author of "The general practice of plumbing in Manchester and district." Published in 1893.

Peck bros. & co.: Publication of "Catalogue of plumbing and sanitary work manufactured by Peck bros. & co. General Offices ... New Haven, Conn. ..." Published in 1893.

Smeaton, John: Author of "Plumbing, drainage, water supply and hot water fitting." Publisher: Spon & Chamberlain (London: E. & F. N. Spon; New York). Published in 1893.

Tudor, Frederic: Author of "The pneumatic test; a system of inspecting plumbing and drainage." Publisher: San. Agency (Boston). Published in 1893.

1894

Capitol Construction: Completion of modern plumbing throughout building.

Dawes & Myler, New Brighton, Pa: Publication of "Porcelain-lined baths and sanitary plumbing supplies. Cataloque A." Published in 1894.

England, Miscellaneous Subheadings: Publication of "Model Regulations and bye-laws for the drainage and plumbing work of buildings. Prepared by a Committee of the Six District Councils in Scotland, etc." Published in 1894.

Publication: Publication of "Science and practice of heating, plumbing, lighting." Published in 1894.

Revill, Alfred: Author of "American plumbing: a complete compendium of practical plumbing, from solder making to high-class open work." Publisher: Excelsior Publishing House (New York). Published in 1894.

Smith & Winchester: Publication of "Smith & Winchester: illustrated catalogue of steam, water, gas and plumbing supplies, wind engines, pumps, artesian wells, tools, etc." Publisher: The Firm (Boston, Mass). Published in 1894.

Winston Churchill Quotation: "His chimneys don't smoke, his windows are tight, he knows what systems of heating are the best, and whom to go to: he knows what good plumbing is." - Winston Churchill in A Far Country, vol 3.

Winston Churchill Quotation: "Upstairs, the bedrooms were quite as unusual, the plumbing of the new pattern, heavy and imposing." - Winston Churchill in A Far Country, vol 2.

1895

Damrell, Charles Stanhope: Author of "A half century of Boston's building. The construction of buildings, the enactment of building laws and ordinances, sanitary laws, the ancient and modern building, building statistics, Boston's valuation, a chapter of Boston's big fire, fire losses, public lands account, prominent architects, contractors and builders, building materials and their source of supply, inspection of buildings, the building and plumbing associations. Written by Charles S. Damrell." Published in 1895.

1896

Dalton-Ingersoll Company: Publication of "Catalogue D: plumbing." Publisher: The Company (Boston). Published in 1896.

Jack London Quotation: "There was the matter of the plumbing." - Jack London in Burning Daylight.

Lawler, James J.: Author of "American sanitary plumbing. A practical work on the best methods of modern plumbing." Published in 1896.

Maguire, William R.: Author of "Domestic Sanitary Drainage and Plumbing. Second edition." Published in 1896.

Publication: Publication of "American plumbing practice. From the Engineering record (Prior to 1887 the sanitary engineer.) A selected reprint of articles describing notable plumbing installations in the United States, and questions and answers on problems arising in plumbing and house draining. With five hundred and thirty-six illustrations." Published in 1896.

The Engineering Record: Publisher of "American plumbing practice: From the Engineering record (Prior to 1887 the sanitary engineer.) A selected reprint of articles describing notable plumbing installations in the United States, and questions and answers on problems arising in plumbing and house draining. With five hundred and thirty-six illustrations." Publisher: The Engineering Record (New York). Published in 1896.

1897

Davis, George B.: Author of "Plumbing and sanitation: embracing drainage, hot and cold water supply, heating, ventilation, steam cooking, gas-fitting, etc." By George B. Davis and Frederick Dye. Publisher: Spon (London). Published in 1897.

Fawley, Fred: Author of "Rules and Tables specially arranged for students in Plumbing, etc." Published in 1897.

Gerhard, W. P.: Author of "Bibliography of house-drainage, plumbing work, and sewage-disposal for houses." Published in 1897.

International Correspondence Schools: Publication of "Mechanics' pocket memoranda. A convenient pocketbook for all persons interested in mechanical engineering, steam engineering, electrical engineering, railroad engineering, bridge engineering, architecture, plumbing, heating and ventilation, gas fitting, etc., etc. By the International Correspondence Schools, Scranton, Pa." Published in 1897.

J. L. Mott Iron Works: Publication of "J.L. Mott Iron Works plumbing and sanitary department catalogue "R"." Published in 1897.

L. Wolff Manufacturing Co: Publication of "General plumbing goods: catalogue E." Publisher: The Firm (Chicago, Ill). Published in 1897.

1898

Anthony Hope Quotation: "He would not have believed me, and would have done precisely what he proceeded to do, and that was to afford Miss Liston every chance of appraising his character and plumbing the depths of his soul." - Anthony Hope in Frivolous Cupid.

Publication: Publication of "(B. F. Finical's plumbing business in De Land) (graphic)."

Published in 1898.

United Association of Journeymen and Apprentices of the Plumbing and Pipe Fitting Industry. Local No. 75, Milwaukee: Publication of "By-laws, laws of sick, disability and death benefit, and rules of order of the Journeymen Plumbers' Benevolent and Protective Association of Milwaukee, Local No. 75 of the United States Association of Journeymen Plumbers, Gas and Steam Fitters, and Steam Fitters' Helpers of the United States and Canada." Published in 1898.

United States. Congress. Senate. Committee on the District of Columbia: Publication of "Plumbing: hearings before the United States Senate Committee on the District of Columbia, Fifty-Fifth Congress, second session, on Apr. 22, May 2, 1898." Published in 1898.

1899

Edith Wharton Quotation: "Might not the accumulated influences of such a house modify the lives within it in a manner unguessed by the inmates of a suburban villa with sanitary plumbing and a telephone?" - Edith Wharton in The Early Short Fiction of Edith Wharton Part One.

Edith Wharton Quotation: "Now at last Mrs. Hicks saw the possibility of being at once artistic and luxurious, of surrendering herself to the joys of modern plumbing and yet keeping the talk on the highest level." - Edith Wharton in The Glimpses of the Moon.

International correspondence schools, Scranton, Pa.: Publication of "School of plumbing, heating, and vetilation." Published in 1899.

The Colliery Engineer Co: Publisher of "The Building trades pocketbook: a handy manual of reference on building construction: including structural design, masonry, bricklaying, carpentry, joinery, roofing, plastering, painting, plumbing, lighting, heating, and ventilation." By the International Correspondence Schools, Scranton, Pa. Publisher: The Colliery Engineer Co (Scranton, Pa.). Published in 1899.

The Gresham Publishing Company: Publisher of "The principles and practice of modern house-construction: including water-supply and fittings, sanitary fittings and plumbing, drainage and sewage-disposal, warming ventiliation, lighting, sanitary aspects of furniture and decoration, climate and situation stables, sanitary law, etc." Written by F.W. Andrewes ... (et al.); edited by G. Lister Sutcliffe. Publisher: The Gresham Publishing Company (London). Published in 1899.

1900

Crook, Horner & Co: Publication of "(Catalogue): Crook, Horner & Co., manufacturers and jobbers of plumbing, steam, gas and water supplies, bath, closet and lavatory outfits: sanitary specialties brass pipe and fittings." Publisher: The Co (Baltimore, Md.). Published in 1900.

Gerhard, William Paul: Born in 1854 and died in 1927, authored "House-drainage and sanitary plumbing, by Wm. Paul Gerhard." Published in 1900.

H. & V. Pub. Co: Publisher of "Heating, ventilating & sanitary plumbing Heating, ventilating and sanitary plumbing." Publisher: H. & V. Pub. Co (New York). Published in 1900.

Hellyer, S. Stevens: Author of "The plumber and sanitary houses. A practical treatise on the principles of internal plumbing work, or The best means for effectually excluding noxious gases from our houses." Published in 1900.

Sosnin, H. A.: Author of "Procedures for pipewelding." Publisher: National Association of Plumbing, Heating, Cooling Contractors (Washington, D.C.). Published in 1900.

Starbuck, Robert Macy: Born in 1844 and died in 1927, authored "Modern plumbing illustrated." Publisher: R. M. Starbuck (Hartford, Conn). Published in 1900.

Vacher, Francis: Author of "Defects in Plumbing and Drainage Work. New and enlarged edition, etc." Published in 1900.

1901

Maguire, William R.: Author of "Domestic Sanitary Drainage and Plumbing. Third edition, revised and brought up to date." Published in 1901.

Sutcliffe, George Lister: Author of "Sanitary Fittings and Plumbing. With 212 illustrations." Published in 1901.

1902

Chaussé, Alcide, né 1868 Ritchie, J. William: Publication of "Building inspectors' hand book of the city of Montreal; containing the buildings by-laws and ordinances, plumbing and sanitaty by-laws rules and regulations, drainage, and sewerage laws engineers rules and regulations, and steam boiler inspector by-laws and rules, electric glossary of building and electric terms, and paragraphs of useful information." Compiled by Alcide Chaussé...; edited by J. William Ritchie = Manuel de l'inspecteur des bâtiments de la ville de Montréal; contenant les lois et règlements sur la construction, les lois, règles et règlements de plomberie sanitaire du drainage et des égoûts, les tables pour les ingénieurs, et les lois et règlements, pour l'inspecteur des chaudières à vapeur, un dictionnaire des termes électriques, et des lois et règlements de l'électricité, /compilé par Alcide Chaussé...; publié par J. William Ritchie Manuel de l'inspecteur des bâtiments de la ville de Montréal. Published in 1902.

Hart, John W.: Author of "External plumbing work: a treatise on lead work for roofs." By John W. Hart, with 180 illustrations. Publisher: Scott, Greenwood, & Co (London). Published in 1902.

Publication: Publication of "Haines, Jones & Cadbury company, manufacturers and dealers in sanitary plumbing fixtures and water, steam and gas supplies." Published in 1902.

1903

Arthur Christopher Benson Quotation: "I looked at the worn face and kind eyes of the man whose whole life is spent in plumbing abysses of human suffering." - Arthur Christopher Benson in The Altar Fire.

David Williams Co: Publisher of "The Metal worker: a weekly journal of the stove, roofing, cornice, tin, plumbing and heating trades." Publisher: David Williams Co (New York). Published in 1903.

International Textbook Co: Publisher of "Plumbing and gas-fitting. Heating and ventilation of buildings. Painting and decorating. Estimating and calculating quantities." Publisher: International Textbook Co (Scranton). Published in 1903.

Robert Herrick (1868-1938) Quotation: "They are too prosperous, too cosmopolitan to feel losses in national individuality. They realize merely the better hotels, the better railways, the improved plumbing in their country." - Robert Herrick (1868-1938) in The World Decision.

United Association of Journeymen and Apprentices of the Plumbing and Pipe Fitting Industry. Local No. 2, Brooklyn: Publication of "Constitution and by-laws of Local No. 2, United Association of Plumbers and Gas Fitters of the United States and Canada, adopted April 20th, 1903." Published in 1903.

1904-1905

Davies, Philip John: Author of "Standard practical plumbing." Philip John Davies. v. 2. Publisher: Spon. Published in 1904-1905.

Hart, John W.: Author of "Sanitary Plumbing and Draining, etc." Published in 1904.

Philadelphia: Publication of "Laws and ordinances relating to the bureau and to plumbing and house drainage and fire escapes." Published in 1904.

1905

Gerhard, William Paul: Born in 1854 and died in 1927, authored "House-drainage and sanitary plumbing." Published in 1905.

International Correspondence Schools, Scranton, Pa: Publication of "Plumbers and fitters' handbook; a convenient reference book for all persons interested in plumbing, steam heating, hot-air heating, hot-water heatng, ventilation, gas-fitting, drainage, and sewerage." Published in 1905.

Lucille Van Slyke Quotation: "You have not installed proper fire escapes or plumbing, you have not answered any of the notices that have been sent you." - Lucille Van Slyke in Little Miss By-The-Day.

Sutcliffe, George Lister: Author of "The principles and practice of modern house-construction: including water-supply and fittings - sanitary fittings and plumbing - drainage and sewage - disposal - warming, ventilation - lighting - sanitary aspects of furniture and decoration - climate and situation stables - sanitary law, etc." Written by F. W. Andrewes (and others). Publisher: Gresham Pub. Co (London). Published in 1905.

United Association of Journeymen and Apprentices of the Plumbing and Pipe Fitting Industry: Publication of "Information for steam fitters and all who are concerned in the differences between the United Association of Plumbers and Fitters and the so-called National Association of Steam Fitters." Publisher: General Office, United Association (Chicago). Published in 1905.

Zane Grey Quotation: "When the plumbing was all in and Carley saw verification of Hoyle's assurance that it would mean a gravity supply of water ample and continual, she lost her last concern as to the practicability of the work." - Zane Grey in The Call of the Canyon.

1906

Ball, Charles B.: Author of "Plumbing catechism: or, theory and practice of plumbing design in question and answer." By Chas. B. Ball and H.T. Sherriff. Publisher: Domestic Engineering (Chicago). Published in 1906.

Clow, George B.: Author of "Practical up-to-date plumbing." By George B. Clow; over 250 illustrations. Publisher: F.J. Drake (Chicago, Ill). Published in 1906.

Haines, Jones & Cadbury Co: Publication of "Illustrated catalog M: architect's edition sanitary plumbing fixtures and water, gas and steam supplies." Publisher: Haines, Jones & Cadbury Co (Philadelphia). Published in 1906.

John Simmons Co: Publication of "Illustrated catalogue and price list: wrought and cast iron pipe, brass and iron valves and fittings plumbing supplies, fixtures and tools and specialities of every description." Publisher: John Simmons Co (New York). Published in 1906.

Lawler, James Joseph: Author of "Modern plumbing, steam and hot water heating; a new practical work for the plumber, the heating engineer, the architect, and the builder, by James J. Lawler." Published in 1906.

Montreal: Publication of "Code of building laws and regulations of the city of Montreal: containing the by-laws relating to buildings, plumbing drainage and sewerage, streets and roads, hygiene." And a great amount of condensed informations and useful tables by Alcide Chausse´... Publisher: Guertin printing company (Montreal). Published in 1906.

Publication: Publication of "Plumbing and house drainage problems; a selection of articles for practical plumbers." Published in 1906.

Sayers, A., Lecturer on plumbing, Belfast: Publication of "Experiments on hot water systems, with prefatory statement by F.C. Forth, A.R.C.Sc.I.. Revised and reprinted from "The plumber and decorator."." Published in 1906.

Stephen Leacock Quotation: "In fact, the whole staging, including lights, plumbing and decorations was merely a matter of five hundred dollars." - Stephen Leacock in The Hohenzollerns in America.

1907

Booth Tarkington Quotation: "What he was proudest of was the plumbing and that Bay of Naples panorama in the hall." - Booth Tarkington in The Turmoil, A Novel.

Clow, George B.: Author of "Encyclopedia of plumbing, hot water, steam and gas fitting (by) Clow-Donaldson." Published in 1907.

Robert Hichens Quotation: "She was afraid of it, for it was black and profound beyond all plumbing. Often in her ten years of retirement she had felt melancholy." - Robert Hichens in December Love.

Starbuck, Robert Macy: Born in 1844 and died in 1927, authored "Practical wrinkles for the plumber: a collection of valuable and handy methods, devices and contrivances in plumbing work." Publisher: David Williams Co (New York). Published in 1907.

1908

James B. Clow & Sons: Publication of "The Clow catalog of plumbing apparatus: steam, gas and water supplies manufactured by James B. Clow & Sons." Publisher: The Company (Chicago). Published in 1908.

Tomlin, Decorator. I.: Author of "The New Decorator's Handbook. Painting, Polishing, Plumbing. 2000 new trade secrets. 25th edition. Rewritten and enlarged." Published in 1908.

1909

American School: Publication of "Plumbing: a complete working manual of approved American practice in the selection and installation of plumbing fixtures and piping systems, including the allied subjects of house drainage and modern methods of sanitation." By William Beall Gray and Charles B. Ball. Publisher: American school of correspondence (Chicago). Published in 1909.

Gerhard, William Paul: Born in 1854, authored "The water supply, sewerage and plumbing of modern city buildings; by Wm. Paul Gerhard." Published in 1909.

Gresham: Publisher of "The Modern plumber and sanitary engineer treating of plumbing, sanitary work." By sixteen specialist contributors; under the editorship of G. Lister Sutcliffe. Publisher: Gresham (London). Published in 1909.

Raynes, Frank W.: Author of "Domestic Sanitary Engineering and Plumbing. With 277 illustrations." Published in 1909.

Shaw, A. Herring-: Publication of "Domestic Sanitation and Plumbing." A. Herring-Shaw. V. 1. Publisher: Gurney & Jackson. Published in 1909-1911.

Stairs, Wm., Son & Morrow, Limited: Publication of "Catalogue "A": illustrated catalogue and price list: plumbing supplies: machinery supplies: tinners' supplies." Publisher: The Company (Halifax, N.S.). Published in 1909.

1910

Bennett, S. Barlow: Author of "12:A manual of technical plumbing and sanitary science." Publisher: Batsford (High Holborn). Published in 1910.

Cosgrove, John Joseph: Author of "Plumbing plans and specifications, by J. J Cosgrove." Publisher: Standard Sanitary Mfg. Co., (Pittsburgh). Published in 1910.

Gerhard, Wm. Paul: Born in 1854 and died in 1927, authored "Water supply, sewerage and plumbing of modern city buildings, by Wm. Paul Gerhard." Published in 1910.

Massachusetts Association of Plumbing Inspectors: Publication of "Compilation of all statutes of Massachusetts relative to the supervision of plumbing. Plumbing regulations of the city of Boston, taken from chapter 550, Acts of 1907, extracts from ordinances of all other cities, and from the by-laws or health rules of such towns as have plumbing regulations. Constitution and by-laws of the Massachusetts Assoc'n of Plumbing Inspectors. List of master plumbers engaged in business in Massachusetts." Published in 1910.

San Francisco: Publication of "The building law and the plumbing law of the City and County of San Francisco: the State Tenement House Act and Ordinance no. 746, Regulating the construction of buildings used as automobile garages, 1910." Publisher: Daily Pacific Builder (San Francisco, Calif). Published in 1910.

1911

Elwell, Fayette Herbert: Author of "Plumbing and house drain inspection." By Fayette H. Elwell; prepared under the direction of B.M. Rastall. Publisher: Keogh Press. Published in 1911.

Herring-Shaw, A.: Author of "Domestic sanitation and plumbing. Pt.2." Published in 1911.

Putnam, John Pickering: Born in 1847 and died in 1917, authored "Plumbing and household sanitation, by J. Pickering Putnam a course of lectures delivered before the plumbing school of the North end union, Boston." Published in 1911.

Shaw, A. Herring-: Publication of "Domestic

sanitation and plumbing. A treatise of the materials, designs, and methods used in sanitary engineering manufacture." Published in 1911.

Standard Sanitary Manufacturing Company: Publication of "Standard baths and plumbing fixtures." Publisher: Standard Sanitary Mfg. Co (Pittsburgh, Pa.). Published in 1911.

Sutcliffe, G. Lister: Author of "The modern plumber and sanitary engineer: treating of plumbing, sanitary work, ventilation, heating (electric and other), hot water services, gas-fitting, electric lighting, bell-work, glazing, etc. " By sixteen specialist contributors under the editorship of G. Lister Sutcliffe. Publisher: Gresham (London). Published in 1911.

1912

American Technical Society: Publication of "Cyclopedia of heating, plumbing and sanitation: a complete reference work on plumbing, gas fitting, sewers and drains heating and ventilating, steam fitting, chemistry, bacteriology and sanitation, hydraulics, water supply electric wiring, mechanical drawing, sheet metal work, etc." Prepared by a Corps of sanitary experts, consulting engineers, and specialists of the highest professional standing. Publisher: American Technical Society (Chicago, Ill). Published in 1912.

Edgar Rice Burroughs Quotation: "Still clutching his spear, he struck the water, and sank beneath its surface, plumbing the depths." - Edgar Rice Burroughs in Tarzan, Jewels of Opar.

Harris, Alton W.: Author of "Official building and plumbing ordinance, Hartford, New Haven, Waterbury and New Britain, 1912; and laws of Connecticut relating to factory inspection." Published in 1912.

International Correspondence Schools: Publication of "The building trades handbook: a convenient manual of reference on building construction, including structural design, masonry, bricklaying, carpentry, joinery, roofing, plastering, painting, plumbing, lighting, heating, and ventilation." By International Correspondence Schools, Scranton, Pa. Publisher: Internat. Textbook Co (Scranton). Published in 1912.

Mount Katmai: In June of 1912, the most spectacular Alaskan eruption in recorded history and the largest eruption in the world in the twentieth century resulted in the formation of a large summit caldera at Katmai volcano. The 60-hour-long eruption actually took place at a vent about 10 km to the west of Mt. Katmai (now marked by Novarupta dome) from which an estimated 30-35 km3 of ash flows and tephra were ejected rather than at Mt. Katmai itself. Based on geochemical and structural relationships, it has been suggested that magma drained from beneath Katmai Volcano to Novarupta via the plumbing system beneath Trident Volcano. The withdrawal of magma beneath Katmai resulted in the collapse of the summit area, forming the caldera. Following the subsidence, a small dacitic cinder cone was emplaced on the floor of the caldera; this is the only juvenile material erupted from Katmai caldera during the historical eruption. See: 1912 Novarupta eruption. [WP]

Sciota, Illinois: A grain elevator next to the single rail line is the only industry. Ross Newman was born in Sciota in 1912 and later rose to prominence in the oil industry. Sciota does have postal service, mostly indoor plumbing, and Northwestern High School is located on the outskirts. [WP]

Swannanoa, Virginia: Swannanoa is an imposing - if ecclectic - mansion of Georgian marble built by Richond millionaire and philantropist James H. Dooley above Rockfish Gap in eastern Augusta County, Virginia. Rockfish Gap is the southern end of the Skyline Drive through the Shenandoah National Park as well as the northern terminus of the Blue Ridge Parkway. Intended to be a 'summer place' for Dooley and his wife Sallie, it reportedly took over 300 artisans eight years to build the structure, complete with Tiffany windows, gold plumbing fixtures and terraced gardens. Despite the lavish expenditure, it was only ocupied for a few years following completion in 1912. The mansion stood empty through the Depression and World War II until it was leased in 1949 to the eccentric author and sculptor, Dr. William Russell for his "University of Science and Philosophy."

Today, the property is owned by J. F. Dulaney, Jr. of Richmond who has been attempting to restore the property to its former glory. [WP]

United Association of Journeymen and Apprentices of the Plumbing and Pipe Fitting Industry. Local 442, San Francisco: Publication of "Constitution and by-laws of Local Union No. 442, Journeymen Plumbers, Gas and Sprinkler Fitters of San Francisco. Adopted May 1, 1912." Published in 1912.

1913

Honolulu Iron Works Co: Publication of "Sugar factories and equipment, stationary, marine and traction engines, steam and mill supplies, sanitary plumbing fixtures and appliances." Publisher: Honolulu Iron Works Co (Honolulu and Hilo, T.H.). Published in 1913.

Jack London Quotation: "Edmund made it with his own hands even to the plumbing, though he did have a terrible time with that before he succeeded." - Jack London in The Valley of the Moon.

James, Builder. Alan G.: Author of "External Plumbing." Published in 1913.

Scout: Publication of "The Scout as Handyman. Practical instruction in painting, paperhanging, gasfitting, plumbing, upholstering, repairing locks, blinds, sash lines, etc. With hints about tools. Illustrated by 144 diagrams." Published in 1913.

Trane: Reuben Trane, James' son, earned a mechanical engineering degree at the University of Wisconsin in Madison, and joined his father's plumbing firm. In 1913, James and Reuben incorporated The Trane Company. [WP]

1914

Bruce, John W.: Author of "Necessity for uniform laws for sanitary plumbing." Published in 1914.

Clarke, J. Wright: Born in 1845 and died in 1912, authored "Modern plumbing practice. Volume I. An account of practical lead-working and plumbers' materials. By J. Wright Clarke. With upwards of 400 illustrations from the author's drawings and from photographs." Published in 1914.

Clow, George B.: Author of "Practical Up-to-Date Plumbing. Over 180 illustrations." Published in 1914.

Cosgrove, John Joseph: Author of "Principles and practice of plumbing, by J. J Cosgrove." Published in 1914.

Hutton, William: Author of "Country plumbing practice: design, installation and repair of systems of water supply and sewage disposal for country and suburban buildings; typical installations of plumbing work in new and old houses." Publisher: David Williams company (New York). Published in 1914.

Julian: Publication of "Illustrated catalog and price list cast iron heating and drainage fittings, heating and plumbing fixtures and specialties." Publisher: Priv. print (Tucson, Ariz). Published in 1914.

Montgomery Ward: Publication of "Building material: lighting systems, heating systems, paints, plumbing supplies, concrete machinery." Publisher: Montgomery Ward & Co (New York, N.Y.). Published in 1914.

Publication: Publication of "Plumbing fixtures and supplies: plumbers' & tinners' tools machines and supplies pumps: catalogue E n¿.140, Exposition edition 1914-1915." Published in 1914.

Trullinger, Robert William: Author of "Water supply, plumbing, and sewage disposal for country homes." Published in 1914.

Wisconsin State Board of Health, Plumbing Division: Publisher of "Tentative plumbing code." Publisher: Wisconsin State Board of Health, Plumbing Division (Madison, Wis). Published in 1914.

Wolverine Brass Works: Publication of "Illustrated catalogue H: high grade plumbing specialties." Publisher: The Works (Grand Rapids, Mich). Published in 1914.

1915

International Textbook Co: Publisher of "Gas making. Gas supply and distribution. Domestic uses of gas. Plumbing materials and tools. Soldering and wiping. Lead work. Pipework. Washing and drinking fixtures. Baths and urinals

Wiping. Lead work. Pipework. Washing and drinking fixtures. Baths and urinals." Publisher: International Textbook Co (Scranton). Published in 1915.

Lexington: Publication of "Rules and regulations of the City of Lexington, Ky. governing the construction, installation and inspection of plumbing and drainage." Published in 1915.

Price, George Moses: Born in 1864 and died in 1942, authored "Handbook on sanitation; a manual of theoretical and practical sanitation. For students and physicians, for health, sanitary, tenement-house, plumbing, factory, food, and other inspectors as well as for candidates for all municipal sanitary positions." Published in 1915.

Standard Sanitary Manufacturing Company: Publication of ""Standard" porcelain enameled vitreous china & brass plumbing goods. Catalogue "PF"." Publisher: Standard Sanitary Mfg. Co (Pittsburg, Pa.). Published in 1915.

1916

Cedar Rapids Pump Co: Publication of "Catalogue no. 12: wholesale plumbing, heating, mill, factory, water and well supplies, manufacturers of iron pumps and cylinders." Publisher: R.R. Donnelly & Sons Co (Chicago, Ill). Published in 1916.

Globe Machinery and Supply Co: Publication of "Globe Machinery and Supply Co. jobbers of plumbing, heating, factory and mill supplies." Publisher: R. R. Donnelley & Sons Co (Des Moines, Iowa). Published in 1916.

Gray, William Beall: Author of "Gray's plumbing design and installation; a veritable encyclopedia of modern practice based on work done by the author and other experts in every branch of the plumbing and allied trades and covering approved practice in every part of the country, by William Beall Gray." Published in 1916.

1917

Mary Roberts Rinehart Quotation: "What did he know of squalid city houses, with their insects and rats, their damp, moldy cellars, their hateful plumbing?" - Mary Roberts Rinehart in A Poor Wise Man.

Mary Roberts Rinehart Quotation: "Everything was in good order and repair; money had been spent lavishly on construction and plumbing." - Mary Roberts Rinehart in The Circular Staircase.

Mary Roberts Rinehart Quotation: "Indeed, new plumbing had been put in, and extra bathrooms installed." - Mary Roberts Rinehart in The Confession.

Pacific Pipe & Supply Company: Publication of "Plumbing goods: fixtures and supplies, heating supplies, steam fittings: catalog B, 1917." Pacific Pipe & Supply Company, successor to H.R. Boynton Company, Los Angeles, California. Publisher: The Company (Los Angeles). Published in 1917.

State Board of Health, Plumbing Division: Publisher of "List of licensed plumbers holding licenses issued by the Wisconsin State Board of Health from the passage of the Law in 1913 to August 1, 1917." Publisher: State Board of Health, Plumbing Division (Madison, Wis). Published in 1917.

1918

Dibble, Samuel Edward: Born in 1882, authored "Elements of plumbing." Publisher: McGraw-Hill (New York). Published in 1918.

Mary Grant Bruce Quotation: "It wouldn't take elaborate plumbing, and the pipes could discharge into an irrigation drain for your vegetable garden." - Mary Grant Bruce in Back To Billabong.

Sinclair Lewis Quotation: "He was the only person besides the repairman at Sam Clark's who understood plumbing." - Sinclair Lewis in Main Street.

United Association of Journeymen and Apprentices of the Plumbing and Pipe Fitting Industry. Local No. 597, Chicago: Publication of "Constitution and by-laws of the Steam Fitters Protective Association, Local Union No. 597, U. A., revised and adopted, 1918.." Published in 1918.

1919

Gray, William Beall: Author of "Plumbing; a working manual of American plumbing practice, including approved fixtures, piping systems, house drainage, and modern methods of sanitation, by William Beall Gray and Charles B. Ball." Published in 1919.

Leighton Supply Co: Publication of "Plumbing-heating, mill and auto supplies catalogue K." Publisher: Leighton Supply Co (Fort Dodge, Iowa). Published in 1919.

Standard Sanitary Manufacturing Company: Publication of "Standard plumbing goods." Publisher: Standard Sanitary Mfg. Co (Pittsburgh, Pa.). Published in 1919.

1920

Dishwasher: Models installed with permanent plumbing arrived in 1920s, and electric drying elements were added in 1940. [WP]

Massachusetts. Special Plumbing Board: Publication of "Report of the Special Plumbing Board of the Massachusetts Department of Public Health." Submitted to the Commissioner of Public Health and Public Health Council, January 3, 1920. Published in 1920.

Platt, Charles Adams: Born in 1861 and died in 1933, authored "Revised details of drinking fountain at Orford Parish (for the) Orford Parish Chapter, D.A.R., Manchester, Conn. (graphic): (full size elevation and section, with scale drawings showing construction and plumbing): order 608, sheet 1A." Charles A. Platt, Architect; drawn by W.A. Published in 1920.

Raynes, Frank W.: Author of "Domestic sanitary engineering and plumbing." Publisher: Longman, Green (London; New York). Published in 1920.

1921

Crane Co: Publication of "Crane plumbing, heating, plumbers' tools and supplies, water systems, etc. catalogue no. 142." Publisher: Crane Co (Chicago). Published in 1921.

Hansen, August E.: Author of "Plumbing fixture traps: an historical, statistical and experimental engineering research on vented and unvented traps." Publisher: Harper & brothers (New York). Published in 1921.

Harris Brothers Company: Publication of "Bargains: buildings material: lumber and millwork, plumbing and heating, hardware and paint, machinery and supplies, general equipment bought at government and forced sales." Publisher: Harris Brothers Co (Chicago (35th and Iron Streets, Chicago)). Published in 1921.

Kretschmer Mfg. Co: Publication of "Catalogue D: plumbing, heating, pump and mill supplies." Publisher: R.R. Donnelley & Sons Co (Chicago, Ill). Published in 1921.

Starbuck, Robert Macy: Author of "American Practical Plumbing, etc." Published in 1921.

Trenton Potteries Company: Publication of "The Blue Book of Plumbing. Catalogue R. July 1921." Published in 1921.

1922

Dallyn, Frederick Alfred, 1886- Berry, Albert Edward, 1894- Provincial Board of Health of Ontario. Division of Sanitary Engineering: Publication of "Rural and semi-urban sanitation; wells and domestic water supplies, fly control, dairy farm sanitation, plumbing instructions, methods of sewage disposal, rural school sanitation, suggested municipal sanitary by-law, revised statutes re water supply." Published in 1922.

International Textbook Co: Publisher of "Principles of mechanics. Hydromechanics. Pneumatics. Strength of materials. Contracts. Geometrical drawing. Principles of mechanical drawing. Plumbing and heating drawing. Reading architects' drawings Mechanical drawing. Plumbing and heating drawing." Publisher: International Textbook Co (Scranton). Published in 1922.

State Board of Health, Bureau of Plumbing and Domestic Sanitary Engineering: Publisher of "Master and journeymen plumbers license directory: list of plumbers holding state license in force March 15, 1922." Publisher: State Board of

Health, Bureau of Plumbing and Domestic Sanitary Engineering (Madison, Wis). Published in 1922.

1923

Hunting Company: Publication of "The Hunting Co. distributors of plumbing, heating, gas, steam, water and mill supplies." Publisher: R.R. Donnelley & Sons Co (Rochester, N.Y.). Published in 1923.

International Textbook Co: Publisher of "Water closets. House drains. Soil, waste, and vent stacks. Traps and vents. Drainage and sewerage. Sewage disposal. Sources of water supply. Water filtration. Cold-water supply. Hot-water supply. Plumbing inspection. Plumbing plans and specifications Sewage disposal. Sources of water supply. Water filtration. Cold-water supply. Hot-water supply." Publisher: International Textbook Co (Scranton). Published in 1923.

Kathleen Norris Quotation: "Anne had never kept house before, she had no eyes for obsolete plumbing, uneven floors, for the dark cellar sacred to cats and rubbish." - Kathleen Norris in Poor, Dear Margaret Kirby and Other Stories.

Starbuck, Robert Macy: Born in 1844, authored "Mechanical drawing for plumbers; a concise, comprehensive and practical treatise on the subject of mechanical drawing in its various modern applications to the work of all who are in any way connected with the plumbing trade." Published in 1923.

1924

Bew, Richard Henry: Author of "Principles of Sanitation and Plumbing." Published in 1924.

Blake, Ernest George: Author of "Plumbing. Based on the work of the same title by W. P. Buchan." Published in 1924.

Crane: Publication of "Plumbing suggestions for home builders." Publisher: Crane Co (Chicago). Published in 1924.

Mueller Co: Publication of "Plumbing, water and gas brass goods: catalog G." Publisher: Mueller Co (Decatur, Ill). Published in 1924.

Publication: Publication of "National plumbing and heating news." Published in 1924.

United States. Building Code Committee: Publication of "Recommended minimum requirements for plumbing in dwellings and similar buildings. Final report of subcommittee on plumbing of the Building Code Committee, July 23, 1923. Bureau of Standards." Published in 1924.

Warren, George Milton: Author of "Farm plumbing." Published in 1924.

1925

Harris Brothers Company: Publication of "Harris Brothers Co. building material, millwork, lumber, Harris homes, presto up garages, lakeside cottages, perfection plumbing and heating systems." Publisher: The Company (New York, N.Y.). Published in 1925.

Lehmann, Emil Wilhelm: Born in 1887, authored "Water and plumbing systems for farm homes." By E.W. Lehmann and F.P. Hanson. Publisher: University of Illinois Agricultural College and Experiment Station (Urbana, Ill). Published in 1925.

PHILIPPINE ISLANDS. Departments of State and Public Institutions: Publication of "Laws, Rules and Regulations and Tariff Rates for Water, Sewer, and Plumbing Services. (Leyes, reglas y reglamentos y tarifa de precios para el Servicio de Agua, Alcantarilla y Tuberías.) Eng. & Span." Published in 1925.

1926

Aladdin Company: Publication of "Aladdin heating, lighting, plumbing fixtures." Publisher: The Company (Bay City, Mich). Published in 1926.

City Council of Cedar Rapids, Iowa: Publisher of "Plumbing code of the City of Cedar Rapids." Publisher: City Council of Cedar Rapids, Iowa (Cedar Rapids, Iowa). Published in 1926.

Heaton, Arthur B.: Author of the image "(Washington Loan & Trust Company bank building (Washington, D.C.). Addition. Plumbing risers. Section. Rendering)." Published in 1926.

Starbuck, Robert Macy: Born in 1844 and died in 1927, authored "Modern plumbing illustrated; a comprehensive and thoroughly practical work on the modern and most approved methods of plumbing construction; the standard work for plumbers, architects, builders, property owners, boards of health and plumbing examiners, and for trade classes in plumbing, by R. M. Starbuck." Published in 1926.

United States. National bureau of standards: Publication of "United States government master specification for plumbing fixtures (for land use). Federal specifications board specification no. 448 ..." Published in 1926.

1927

Baker Manufacturing Company: Publication of "Catalog C. Baker Manufacturing Co. jobbers of plumbing and heating material. pipe, valves, fittings, mill and waterworks supplies." Publisher: Baker Manufacturing Co (Kansas City, Mo.). Published in 1927.

BRIDGEPORT BRASS COMPANY: Publication of "The History of Sanitation. Plumbing then and now, etc." Published in 1927.

Palmer, Jesse Joseph Webb: Born in 1902, authored "Foreign markets for plumbing supplies with notes on Water-supply systems in foreign countries, by J. Joseph W. Palmer, Iron and steel division." Published in 1927.

Plumbing and heating industries bureau. The apprenticeship service dept: Publication of "Standard text on steam-fitting, group one - eight." Published in 1927.

1928

Babbitt, Harold Eaton: Author of "Tests on the hydraulics and pneumatics of house plumbing, by Harold E. Babbitt." Publisher: University of Illinois (Urbana, Ill). Published in 1928.

Bureau of Business Research, Harvard University: Publisher of "Operating expenses of plumbing and heating supply wholesalers in the central states in 1927." Publisher: Bureau of Business Research, Harvard University (Boston, Mass). Published in 1928.

Hutton, William, Writer on Plumbing: Author of "Joint wiping and lead work: a practical treatise on the preparation of lead pipe and connections, and the wiping of joints in various positions." Publisher: Scientific book corporation (New York). Published in 1928.

Keystone Brass and Rubber Co: Publication of "Catalog no. 11: manufacturers & distributors of plumbing specialties: Keystone Brass & Rubber Co.. Philadelphia, Pa." Publisher: The Co (Philadelphia, Pa.). Published in 1928.

Kohler Company: Publication of "Color charm enters the bathroom: plumbing fixtures in color." Publisher: Kohler Co (Kohler, Wis). Published in 1928.

N. O. Nelson Manufacturing Co.: Publication of "Nonco plumbing fixtures." Publisher: The Company (St. Louis, Mo.). Published in 1928.

National Joint Industrial Council for the Plumbing Trade: Publication of "Schedule of plumbers' work." Published in 1928.

Nugey, Anthony L.: Author of "Plumbing design; a practical handbook for architects, designers, draftsman, plumbers and students, by A. L. Nugey, 248 illustrations." Published in 1928.

Partington, Ernest Bicknell: Author of "Chemical Plumbing and Leadburning." Published in 1928.

Raynes, Frank W.: Author of "Domestic sanitary engineering and plumbing, dealing with domestic water supplies, pump & hydraulic ram work, hydraulics, sanitary work, heating by low pressure, hot water, & external plumbing work, by Frank W. Raynes, with 277 illustrations." Published in 1928.

Starbuck, Robert Macy: Born in 1844 and died in 1927, authored "Standard practical plumbing; an exhaustive treatise on all branches of plumbing construction, including drainage and venting, ventilation, hot and cold water supply and circulation; showing the latest and best plumbing practice, special attention being given to the skilled work of the plumber, and to the theory underlying plumbing devices and operations, including a chapter on examinations for plumbers and fitters, and features of government plumbing, by R. M.Starbuck." Published in 1928.

Swensrud, Sidney A.: Born in 1900, authored "Methods of departmentizing merchandise and expense figures for plumbing and heating supply wholesalers." Publisher: Harvard University, Graduate School of Business Administration, Bureau of Business Research, (Boston). Published in 1928.

Thomas, Minor Wine: Born in 1890 and died in 1966, authored "Public school plumbing equipment, by Minor Wine Thomas." Publisher: Teachers College, Columbia University (New York). Published in 1928.

Wisconsin State Board of Vocational Education: Publisher of "Plumbing and domestic sanitary engineering." Prepared by F.O. Maeder ... (et al.). Publisher: Wisconsin State Board of Vocational Education (Madison, Wis). Published in 1928.

1929

Detroit association of sanitary and heating contractors: Publication of "Authorized dealership plan for the plumbing and heating industries." Published in 1929.

Manser, Percy: Author of "Plumbing and gasfitting: a complete work by practical specialists describing modern practice in the work of the plumber and the gasfitter." Published in 1929.

New Orleans: Publication of "Building, electrical and plumbing code of the city of New Orleans, La." Published in 1929.

United States. Dept. of Commerce. Building code committee: Publication of "Recommended minimum requirements for plumbing Report of subcommittee on plumbing of the Building code committee. Rev. August 30, 1928. Bureau of standards." Published in 1929.

1930

Canada. Dept. of Justice: Publication of "Combines Investigation Act: investigation into the Amalgamated Builders' Council and related organizations: an alleged combine of plumbing and heating contractors and others in the province of Ontario: reports of commissioner, October 31 and December 18, 1929." Publisher: Acland (Ottawa). Published in 1930.

Hutton, William. Author of "Country Plumbing Practice.": Publication of "Joint Wiping and Lead Work. Third edition, revised and enlarged." Published in 1930.

Phoenix Brass Fittings: Publication of "Phoenix Brass Fittings Corp., Irvington, New Jersey: manufacturers of the P.B.F. brass fittings, founders and finishers of plumbing brass goods and specialties. catalogue "D"." Publisher: Phoenix Brass Fittings (Irvington, N.J.). Published in 1930.

Publication: Publication of "Superior sanitary plumbing fixtures: catalogue J The Louis Lipp Company." Published in 1930.

Stairs, Wm., Son & Morrow, Limited: Publication of "Scotia brand want book and index of hardware, machinery, auto accessories, plumbing and heating supplies." Publisher: The Company (Halifax). Published in 1930.

United States. National Bureau of Standards: Publication of "Staple vitreous china plumbing fixtures." U.S Department of Commerce, Bureau of Standards. Publisher: United States Government Printing Office; For sale by the Superintendent of Documents (Washington). Published in 1930.

1931

Davenport: Publication of "Building, electrical and plumbing code including zoning ordinance, smoke ordinance, fire prevention." Published in 1931.

Schaefer, Clemens Thomas: Born in 1886, authored "The handy man's handbook; a handbook on general mechanical operations, including wood, metal, electrical, and plumbing work.-Tools, their use and abuse, for the handy man in the home, apartment, or public buildings, on the farm, and in the factory. By C. T. Schaefer." Published in 1931.

Trane: By 1916, the Tranes were no longer in the plumbing business, but rather were focusing their attention on manufacturing heating products. Trane's first air conditioning unit was developed in 1931. [WP]

Virginia Polytechnic Institute, Blacksburg. Engineering Extension Division: Publication of "Gantt installment payment chart; its adaptation to the uses of the plumbing and heating contractor."

Published in 1931.

Whitman, Roger Bradbury: Born in 1875 and died in 1942, authored "The American home book of heating, plumbing, and wiring, by Roger B. Whitman; illustrated with diagrams; edited by Reginald T. Townsend." Published in 1931.

Wisconsin State Board of Vocational Education: Publisher of "Adult trade extension: plumbing: repair service, Wisconsin City Vocational Schools." Publisher: Wisconsin State Board of Vocational Education (Madison, Wis). Published in 1931.

1932

Lambert, Roger: Author of "A.T. Cheaney Plumbing Company collection." Published in 1932.

Murphy, Howard G.: Author of "Consumer demand for plumbing fixtures,- its relation to plumbing shop merchandising." Published in 1932.

Strohm, Rufus Tracy: Author of "Plumbing drawing, by Rufus T. Strohm." Publisher: International textbook company, (Scranton, Pa.). Published in 1932.

United States. Bureau of Standards. Building Code Committee. Subcommittee on Plumbing: Publication of "Recommended minimum requirements for plumbing (with supplement containing progress revision to May, 1931): report." Of subcommittee on plumbing of the Building Code Committee. Published in 1932.

1933

Martin, Albert Charles: Author of "The Use of Copper in Plumbing. Edited by Frank Herod." Published in 1933.

United States. National Recovery Administration: Publication of "Code of fair competition for the contracting and retail division of the plumbing and heating industry." Published in 1933.

1934

Brett, Thomas J.: Author of "Engineer-custodians manual: examination questions and answers for engineers, custodians, firemen, building superintendents, etc. including boilers and combustion engines, heating and ventilating, air conditioning, pumps, sanitation and plumbing, electrical machinery, mechanics, technical formulas, tables and general information." Publisher: American Technical Society (Chicago). Published in 1934.

Domestic Engineering Company, Chicago: Publication of "Domestic engineering plumbing and heating catalogue 1934." Published in 1934.

Movie Release: The movie "Plumbing for Gold" is released.

Roth, Emery: Born in 1871 and died in 1948, authored "20 story & pent house apartment hotel on the NE cor. of University Place & Waverly Place, New York City (graphic): (plumbing and electrical diagrams)." Published in 1934.

United States. National Recovery Administration: Publication of "Supplementary code of fair competition for the plumbing contracting industry: (a division of the construction industry) as approved on May 15, 1934 by President Roosevelt." Published in 1934.

1935

Blake, E. G.: Author of "Plumbing: a textbook to the practice of the art of craft of the plumber." based on the work of the same title by W. P. Buchan. Published in 1935.

Lower East Side Tenement National Historic Site: Lower East Side Tenement National Historic Site preserves a six-story brick tenement building that was home to an estimated 7,000 people, from over 20 nations, between 1863 and 1935. Located at 97 Orchard Street in the Lower East Side neighborhood of Manhattan in New York, New York, the structure was opened by Lukas Glockner and was modified several times to conform with the city's developing housing laws. The top two floors contain rooms, wallpaper, plumbing, and lighting preserved as they were left in 1935, when they were boarded up and sealed until their discovery in 1988. The building is able to convey a vivid sense of the deplorable living conditions experienced by its tenants. [WP]

Swinson, E. Thomas: Author of "Plumbing & Domestic Engineering. Advisory editor: E. T. Swinson." Published in 1935.

United States. Rural Electrification Administration: Publication of "Master plumbing for American farms." Published in 1935.

1936

Publication: Publication of "Federal standard stock catalog. Section IV, part 5, Federal specification for gaskets: plumbing-fixture-setting." Published in 1936.

1937

Cleverdon, Walter Sherman Lyle: Born in 1877, authored "Plumbing engineering for architects, engineers, plumbers, building superintendents, students and others interested in the sanitation of buildings and their surroundings, by Walter S. L. Cleverdon." Published in 1937.

Dawson, Francis Murray: Born in 1889, authored "Report on hydraulics and pneumatics of plumbing drainage systems." By F.M. Dawson and A.A. Kalinske. Publisher: The University (Iowa City, Ia.). Published in 1937.

Dundee: Publication of "Bye-laws with respect to the drainage and plumbing work of buildings." Published in 1937.

Luff, Willard J.: Author of "Organization of a farm water system and plumbing program." Published in 1937.

United States. Public Health Service: Author of "Public health hazards in plumbing; a summary of the inspection of plumbing in Federal buildings in New York City, N. Y., and Detroit, Michigan made by United States Public Health Service and Works Progress Administration, May 1936-June 1937." Published in 1937.

Warren, Henry G.: Author of "Plumbing." Publisher: Crosby Lockwood & Son (London). Published in 1937.

1938

Bew, Richard Henry: Author of "Principles of Sanitation and Plumbing. Second edition." Published in 1938.

Day, Louis J.: Author of "Standard Plumbing Details for Architects, Engineers, Contractors, Plumbers and Students. Plans." Published in 1938.

Fuller, Charles Arthur: Born in 1880, authored "Air conditioning handbook; a modern, authoritative treatise for plumbing and heating contractors on the subject of air conditioning, air distribution, refrigeration, comfort cooling, humidification and air purification, by Charles A. Fuller with the collaboration of David Snow." Published in 1938.

HENDERSON BUSINESS SERVICE: Publication of "Henderson's Resale Price Service. Suggested resale prices on plumbing and heating material. Published and revised as market prices change. With an explanatory confidential booklet." Published in 1938.

Movie Release: The movie "Plumbing Is a 'Pipe'" is released.

1939

Domestic Engineering Company, inc., Chicago: Publication of "Engineer's fact finder; a reference manual for the man who designs and installs plumbing, heating and air conditioning." Published in 1939.

Foster, Milton A.: Author of "Labor and material, by Milton A. Foster. A reference book for estimating plumbing and heating jobs." Published in 1939.

Miller, Arthur Patterson: Born in 1896, authored "Plumbing and public health; a bibliography." Published in 1939.

Standards association of Australia. Pipes and plumbing committee: Publication of "Australian standard specifications for water supply and sanitary fittings ..." Published in 1939.

United States. Rural electrification administration: Publication of "Planning for farm plumbing. Rural electrification administration." Published in 1939.

1941.

1940

Carolyn Wells Quotation: "Oxidized silver plumbing exposure." - Carolyn Wells in Ptomaine Street.

Cosgrove, John Joseph: Born in 1869, authored "Sanitary plumbing fixtures, by J. J. Cosgrove." Published in 1940.

Cronkright, Arthur Bradford: Born in 1911, authored "Plumbing and public health, by Arthur B Cronkright and Arthur P. Miller." Published in 1940.

Harftord Plumbing Apprenticeship Committee: Publication of "Hartford, Connecticut, plumbing apprenticeship standards." Formulated by the Hartford Plumbing Apprenticeship Committee, representing the Hartford Master Plumbers' Association and the United Association of Journeymen Plumbers and Steamfitters, Local Union No. 76, in cooperation with the Connecticut State Apprenticeship Council. Published in 1940.

Johnson, John Weeks: Author of "Johnson's new handy manual on plumbing, domestic and sanitary engineering, drainage, sewerage, and streamline." Published in 1940.

National Research Council of Canada: Publication of "National building code: a standard plumbing by-law. --." Publisher: N.R.C., Codes and Specifications Section (Ottawa). Published in 1940.

Thomson, Thomas N.: Born in 1867, authored "Brass pipe, by T. N. Thomson. A handbook on plumbing and heating for the architect, engineer and the plumbing and heating contractor." Published in 1940.

1941

Kalinske, Anton Adam: Born in 1911, authored "Cross-connections in plumbing and water-supply systems." By A.A. Kalinske under the direction of F.M. Dawson and Walter Spencer. Published in 1941.

Partington, Ernest Bicknell: Author of "Chemical plumbing, leadburning and oxy-acetylene welding for plumbers and heating engineers." Published in 1941.

1942

Eddie Slovik: He was paroled in April 1942, after which he got a job at Montella Plumbing Co. in Dearborn, where he met his wife Antoinette Wisniewski. On November 7, 1942, they got married and moved in with her parents. Shortly after their first aniversary, in November 1943, Slovik was reclassified to 1-A and drafted by the army. He was sent to Camp Wolters in Texas on January 24, 1944 for basic military training. In August of 1944 his training was finished and he sailed to France, arriving on the 20th of the same month. [WP]

Harper, Herbert Druery: Author of "Plumbing, heating, and air conditioning; shop mathematics." Publisher: D. Van Nostrand Co (New York). Published in 1942.

Publication: Publication of "The war-time guide book, prepared by the editorial staff of Popular science monthly. In two parts: I. Make it yourself; formulas, recipes, methods and secret processes for the handy man in meeting a multitude of household needs. II. Fix it yourself; home maintenance and repairs in carpentry, plumbing, electrical equipment, concrete, metal work and automobiles." Published in 1942.

United States. Office for Emergency Management Division of Defense Housing Coordination: Publication of "Emergency plumbing standards for defense housing: (plans)." Published in 1942.

1943

Detroit. Ordinances, etc.: Publication of "Official plumbing code of Detroit, Michigan ..." Published in 1943.

Killam, Edward R.: Author of "Plumbing and heating equipment, a statistical handbook, by Edward R. Killam." Published in 1943.

New Zealand: Publication of "Drainage and plumbing." Publisher: Govt. Printer (Wellington (N.Z.)). Published in 1943.

Publication: Publication of "Plumbing practice and design by Svend Plum." Published in 1943.

Spottswood, John Gordon: Author of "(R.L. Slauter Plumbing and Heating office building) (picture)." Published in 1943.

1944

Blake, Ernest George: Author of "Plumbing. Third edition revised and enlarged." Published in 1944.

England, Departments of State and Official Bodies: Publication of "Plumbing. By the Plumbing Committee of the Building Research Board, etc." Published in 1944.

Warren, George M.: Author of "Farm plumbing (by George M. Warren). --." Published in 1944.

1945

Publication: Publication of "Building, estimating and contracting; a home-study course and general reference work on carpentry, steel square, mechanical drawing, blueprint reading, strength of materials, architectural drawing and detailing, sheet metal work, stair building, painting and decorating, concrete, plumbing, furnaces and unit heaters, heating and ventilating, planning house wiring, how to plan a house, how to remodel a house, estimating." Published in 1945.

United States. Rural Electrification Administration: Publication of "New loan program for consumers; simplified lowcost financing of wiring, plumbing, and farm and home electrical equipment." Published in 1945.

Woolgar, W. J.: Author of "The practical plumber and sanitary engineer: an authoritative guide to accepted methods of plumbing and allied sanitation, with special reference to the modern trends in technique." Edited by W. J. Woolgar. Publisher: Odhams Press (London). Published in 1945.

1946

Great Britain. Dept. of Scientific and Industrial Research: Publication of "Some common defects in plumbing designs for post-war repetition dwellings." Publisher: Dept. of Scientific and Industrial Research, (London). Published in 1946.

McCarron Bird: Publisher of "Roof plumbing." Commonwealth of Australia, Department of Labour and National Service, Industrial Training Division. Publisher: McCarron Bird (Melbourne). Published in 1946.

Miller, John Guthrie: Author of "Plumbing. A handbook of tools, materials, methods and directions." Published in 1946.

Molloy, Edward: Author of "Plumbing and Gas-Fitting. Written by master craftsmen for the practical man. General Editor, E. Molloy, etc." Published in 1946.

Mutter, Lawrence P.: Author of "Establishing and Operating a Heating and Plumbing Contracting Business, etc." Published in 1946.

Nash, G. J.: Author of "Plumbing and hot-water fitting." Publisher: George Allen & Unwin (London). Published in 1946.

Plum, Svend: Author of "Plumbing Practice and Design." Published in 1946.

Winder, Richard Henry: Born in 1896, authored "Plumbing." By R. H. Winder; with 64 drawings by the author. Publisher: Longmans, Green and Co (London; New York). Published in 1946.

1947

Alt, Harold Lynn: Author of "Practical plumbing: a book for the plumbing contractor and sanitary designer, containing the fundamentals of American plumbing practice and helpful design data, which may be applied to any plumbing installation." Publisher: Domestic Engineering Co., (Chicago). Published in 1947.

Duncan, Kenneth: Born in 1890, authored "Funk & Wagnalls' standard primer for home builders and home buyers; blueprint for happy home ownership. Illus., technical data, and chapters covering construction, plumbing, heating, modernizing, and all allied subjects, produced under the direction of Douglas Tuomey." Publisher: Funk & Wagnall's Co (New York). Published in 1947.

England, Miscellaneous Subheadings: Publication of "PTU. Journal of the Plumbing Trades' Union. vol. 1. no. 2, etc. Sept. 1947, etc." Published in

1947.

Great Britain. Dept. of Scientific and Industrial Research. Building Research Board: Publication of "Domestic drainage." By the Plumbing Committee of the Building Research Board of the Department of Scientific and Industrial Research. Publisher: H.M.S.O (London). Published in 1947.

His Majesty's Stationery Office: Publisher of "Domestic drainage: by the Plumbing Committee of the Building Research Board of the Department of Scientific and Industrial Research." Publisher: His Majesty's Stationery Office (London). Published in 1947.

Odhams Press: Publisher of "Odhams practical and technical encyclopædia; covering terms used in mechanical engineering, automobile engineering, electrical engineering, aeronautical engineering, building, painting and decorating, plumbing, carpentry and joinery, chemistry and physics, metallurgy, sheet metal work, foundry work, radio, printing and bookbinding." Publisher: Odhams Press (London). Published in 1947.

1948

American Radiator & Standard Sanitary Corporation: Publication of "American-Standard heating, plumbing for hospitals." Publisher: The Corporation (Pittsburgh). Published in 1948.

Barrow, Frank Leslie: Author of "Plumbing in America. A report on a visit to U.S.A. and Canada on plumbing." Published in 1948.

Blake, Ernest George: Author of "Plumbing. A textbook based on the work of the same title by W.P. Buchan. With illustrations." Published in 1948.

Chatsworth House: The 10th Duke was pessimistic about the future of houses like Chatsworth, and made no plans to move back in after the war. After Penrhos College left in 1945 the only people who slept in the house were two housemaids, but over the winter of 1948-49 the house was cleaned and tidied for reopening to the public by two Hungarian women who had been Kathleen Kennedy's cook and housemaid in London and a team of their compatriots. In the mid-1950s, perhaps encouraged by the election and re-election of a Conservative Party Conservative government, which suggested that country houses might not be doomed after all, the new Andrew Cavendish, 11th Duke of Duke and Deborah Duchess began to think about moving back in. The pre-war house had relied entirely on a large staff for its comforts, and lacked modern facilities. The house was rewired, the plumbing and heating was overhauled, and six self-contained staff flats were created to replace the small staff bedrooms and communal servants hall. Including those in the staff flats, seventeen bathrooms were added to the handful which had existed before. The 6th Duke's cavernous kitchen was abandoned and a new one was created closer to the family dining room. The family rooms were repainted, carpets were brought out of store, and curtains were repaired or replaced. The Duke and Duchess and their three children moved across the park from Edensor House in 1959. [WP]

H. R. Haldeman: Bob Haldeman was born in Los Angeles, California the son of socially prominent parents. His father, a prosperous plumbing contractor, gave time and financial support to local Republican Party (United Republican causes, while mother Betty was a longtime volunteer with the Salvation Army and other philanthropic organizations. Young Bob and his siblings Tom and Betsy were raised in the strict Church of Christ, Christian Science faith. Known to his peers as a "straight arrow," he sported his trademark flat-top haircut from early childhood, enjoyed discussions of ethics, and achieved the rank of Eagle Scout. He married his childhood friend Jo (Joanne) Horton in 1948. [WP]

Tennessee Valley Authority. Commerce Dept: Publication of "Pumps and plumbing for the farmstead, prepared by G. E. Henderson, Associate Agricultural Engineer in cooperation with Jane A. Roberts, Associate Specialist in Home Electrification. Illustrator, L. H. Poole. Agricultural Engineering Development Division, Commerce Dept., Tennessee Valley Authority, Nov. 1940." Published in 1948.

United Association of Journeymen and Apprentices of the Plumbing and Pipefitting Industry of the United States and Canada:

Publisher of "Journeymen and apprentices of the plumbing and pipe fitting industry journal." Publisher: United Association of Journeymen and Apprentices of the Plumbing and Pipefitting Industry of the United States and Canada (Washington, D.C.). Published in 1948.

United States. Office of Price Administration Economic Data Analysis Branch: Publication of "Survey of retail lumber dealers, wholesale stock millwork distributors, and plumbing and heating equipment jobbers and dealers: summary of mark-ups and operating data for various periods, 1936-1946." Published in 1948.

Warren, George Milton: Author of "Simple plumbing repairs in the home (by George M Warren). --." Published in 1948.

1949

American Standards Association. Sectional Committee on Minimum Requirements for Plumbing Equipment, A.: Publication of "American standard plumbing code: minimum requirements for plumbing." Sponsors: The American public health association; the American society of mechanical engineers. Publisher: American society of mechanical engineers (New York). Published in 1949.

Buffalo: Publication of "Buffalo building laws: building ordinances and regulations relating to building and zoning, heating, plumbing, gas, electricity, elevator, wiring, excavations, foundations, piling, walls, loads, stresses, water, sanitation, drainage, floors, roofs, signs, boilers and furnaces, fireproofing, fire protection, etc., in all factory, industrial, residential, mercantile buildings, 1949." Publisher: Building Laws Co (Buffalo). Published in 1949.

Forster, Percy M.: Author of "Forster's practical lay-out book: this book is presented to the plumbing trade and allied pipe trades, architects and mechanical engineers, it shows the different ways and the closest approximate measurements for assembling cast iron pipe fittings." Compiled and published by Percy M. Forster. Publisher: P.M. Forster (Berkeley). Published in 1949.

Louisiana. Board of Health: Publication of "Water supply, sewerage and plumbing, chapters 8, 10 and 10A. Sanitary code, state of Louisiana. Prepared and promulgated by the Louisiana State Board of Health in accordance with Act 79, of 1921, as amended." Published in 1949.

Uniform Plumbing Code Committee: Publication of "Uniform plumbing code, report." Issued jointly by United States Dept. of Commerce, Office of Domestic Commerce, Construction Division (and) Housing and Home Finance Agency, Office of the Administrator, Division of Standardized Building Codes and Materials. Publisher: U.S.G.P.O (Washington). Published in 1949.

1950

American Radiator & Standard Sanitary Corp: Publication of "American-Standard plumbing fixtures." Published in 1950.

Babbitt, Harold Eaton: Publication of "Plumbing." Publisher: McGraw-Hill (New York). Published in 1950.

Blayton, Joseph W.: Author of "Plumbing apprentice training." Published in 1950-51.

Foster, Milton A.: Author of "Labor and material; a reference book for estimating plumbing and heating jobs." Published in 1950.

French, John L.: Author of "Wet venting of plumbing fixtures." By John L French, Herbert N. Eaton, and Robert S. Wyly. Publisher: G.P.O (Washington). Published in 1950.

Martin, A. C., Writer on Plumbing: Publication of "The modern practical plumber." With sections on heating and ventilation by L.C.C. Rayner and special contributions by other experts. Published in 1950.

Pennington, Herbert: Author of "Plumbing for Secondary Technical Schools of Building." Published in 1950.

University of Michigan. School of Public Health: Publication of "Proceedings of Inservice training course in plumbing problems, Sept. 15 and 16, 1950." Published in 1950.

W. H. Cunningham and Hill: Publication of "Quality guaranteed specialties, tools and equipment for the plumbing, heating, electrical and sheet metal trades: (catalogue "C" 1950)

Specialties, tools and equipment for the plumbing, heating electrical and sheet metal trades General catalogue "C." Tool catalogue "C."." Publisher: W.H. Cunningham and Hill (Toronto). Published in 1950.

Woolgar, William Joseph: Author of "Questions and Answers on Plumbing and Sanitary Fittings, etc." Published in 1950.

1951

Arkansas: Publication of "Arkansas State plumbing code; rules and regulations of the State Board of Health governing the construction, installation and inspection of plumbing and drainage." Publisher: State Board of Health; (Little Rock). Published in 1951.

Burkhardt, Charles H.: Author of "Domestic oil burners: installation and servicing. Based on the series of articles, Principles of Automatic Oil Heating, which appeared in Sheet Metal Worker and Plumbing and Heating Journal, 1947-1950. by Charles H. Burkhardt." Publisher: McGraw-Hill (New York). Published in 1951.

Coordinating Committee for a National Plumbing Code: Publication of "Report." Issued jointly by U.S. Dept. of Commerce, National Production Authority, Housing and Home Finance Agency, Office of the Administrator. Published in 1951.

Deshpande, Raghunath Shripad: Born in 1889, authored "A text-book of sanitary engineering (including plumbing)." Published in 1951.

Eaton, Herbert Nelson: Author of "Fixture Unit Ratings as used in Plumbing System Design, etc." Published in 1951.

Hutton, William: Author of "Hot water supply, residential, commercial, industrial; installation and maintenance." William Hutton and Wendell M. Dillon. Publisher: Plumbing and Heating Journal (New York). Published in 1951.

Ingerslev, Fritz, 1912- Petersen, Jørgen Akademiet for de tekniske videnskaber: Publication of "Plumbing noises Støj fra vandinstallationer." Af Fritz Ingerslev og Jørgen Petersen. Publisher: Akademiet for de Tekniske Videnskaber, Lydteknisk Laboratorium (København). Published in 1951.

James Robertson Company: Publication of "Plumbing, heating, mill supplies: catalogue 51." Publisher: J. Robertson Co (Montreal; Toronto). Published in 1951.

Krause, Ernest W.: Author of "From wood to steel. The story of Ernest W. Krause as told at a meeting of his associates of Wheeling Machine Products Company, Wheeling Plumbing & Industrial Supply, Trimble & Lutz Supply Company, and Krause Stamping and Manufacturing Company. Edited and prepared for publication by Andrew R. McClure." Published in 1951.

UNITED STATES OF AMERICA. Departments of State and Public Institutions: Publication of "Report of the Coordinating Committee for a National Plumbing Code. Issued jointly by U.S. Department of Commerce, National Production Authority. Housing and Home Finance Agency, Office of the Administrator." Published in 1951.

1952

Arco: Publisher of "Handy man's plumbing and heating guide." Publisher: Arco (New York, N.Y.). Published in 1952.

Borcina, David M.: Author of "Lead work for modern plumbing." Publisher: Lead Industries Association (New York). Published in 1952.

De Rougemont, J. and L. Meyer: "Extraperiostous acrylic plumbing; collapse therapy in limited cases" appears in Lyon Chirurgical written by J. De Rougemont and L. Meyer. Published in July 1952.

H.M.S.O: Publisher of "One-pipe (single stack) plumbing for housing. Part II. Principles of design." Publisher: H.M.S.O (London). Published in 1952.

Innes, John Hosking: Author of "Plumbing." Publisher: English Universities Press (London). Published in 1952.

Matthias, Arthur John: Author of "How to design and instal Plumbing. Revised by Esles Smith. Third edition. Illustrated. With plans." Published in 1952.

McElroy, Frank Shafer: Author of "Injuries and accident causes in plumbing operation. (A detailed analysis of accidents experienced by plumbers during 1948-1949, by Frank S. McElroy, George R. McCormack, and Francis J. Rafferty)." Published in 1952.

Wolf, Ralph J.: Author of "The Wise handbook of home plumbing." Published in 1952.

Wyly, Robert S.: Author of "Capacities of plumbing stacks in buildings." Robert S. Wyly and Herbert N. Eaton. Publisher: G.P.O (Washington). Published in 1952.

1953

Buffalo: Publication of "Buffalo building laws. Buffalo building code and the Multiple dwelling law of the State of New York. Ordinances-laws-regulations relating to building and zoning, heating, plumbing, gas, electricity, elevator, wiring, excavations, foundations, piling, walls, loads, stresses, water, sanitation, drainage, floors, roofs, signs, boilers and furnaces, fireproofing, fire protection, etc., in all factory, industrial, residential, mercantile buildings and structures. 1953-1954." Published in 1953.

Encyclopaedias: Publication of "The Encyclopedia of Plumbing, Heating and Sanitary Engineering. The Encyclopedia of Sanitary Engineering, Heating & Plumbing. General editor: S. G. Blaxland Stubbs. Third edition, revised and enlarged." Published in 1953.

Haan, Enno R.: Born in 1899, authored "Popular mechanics home plumbing guide: complete detailed information on the requirements, design, installation, operation, maintenance and repair of home plumbing systems, including the proper use of tools and materials." Published in 1953.

Hann, Enno R.: Author of "Popular mechanics home plumbing guide." Published in 1953.

Manas Publications: Publisher of "National plumbing code, illustrated." Publisher: Manas Publishers (Washington, D.C.). Published in 1953.

Publication: Publication of "Operating results of plumbing and heating supplies wholesalers. (Microfiche)." Published in 1953.

Stubbs, S. G. Blaxland: Author of "The encyclopedia of sanitary engineering, heating & plumbing: a handbook of modern practice for the craftsman, tradesman & engineer." Publisher: Waverley (London). Published in 1953.

1954

Angus Co: Publisher of "Plumbing and heating journal." Publisher: Angus Co (New York, N.Y.). Published in 1954.

Durand, Germain: Author of "Manuel de tracés de plomberie = Plumbing sketches manual." Germain Durand Plumbing sketches manual. Published in 1954.

Eaton, Herbert N.: Author of "Frost closure of roof vents in plumbing systems." Herbert N. Eaton and Robert S. Wyly. Publisher: G.P.O (Washington). Published in 1954.

Housing and Home Finance Agency, Office of the Administrator, Division of Housing Research: Publisher of "Performance of plumbing fixtures and drainage stacks." Publisher: Housing and Home Finance Agency, Office of the Administrator, Division of Housing Research (Washington, D.C.). Published in 1954.

Institute for Research: Publication of "Careers in plumbing and plumbing contracting." Published in 1954.

Manly, Harold Phillips: Author of "How-to-do-it plumbing guide; a guide to selection, installation, and repair of plumbing fixtures and connections in the home." Published in 1954.

Sherlock, George L.: Author of "Blue book of plumbing estimating; a practical reference book for plumbing contractors and journeymen." Published in 1954.

1955

American Standards Association: Publication of "American standard national plumbing code minimum requirements for plumbing." Sponsors: The American Public Health Association (and) the American Society of Mechanical Engineers. Publisher: American Society of Mechanical Engineers (New York). Published in 1955.

Miller, Leslie Avinal: Born in 1887, authored "Plumbing and pipe-fitting layout job sheets." Publisher: Goodheart-Willcox Co (Chicago). Published in 1955.

National Association of Plumbing Contractors MacArthur, R. M Sellers, C. W.: Publication of "Law primer for plumbing-heating contractors: a manual for the guidance of plumbing-heating contractors in forming, reorganizing, and conducting the affairs of local and state associations." Rev. by C. W. Sellers and R. M. MacArthur. Published in 1955.

Reid, Maurice H.: Author of "Handyman's plumbing and heating guide." (by Maurice H. Reid and Byron B. Courtney). Publisher: Arco (New York). Published in 1955.

Scott-Choate: Publisher of "The Journal of plumbing, heating, & air conditioning." Publisher: Scott-Choate (Tarrytown, N.Y.). Published in 1955.

Townsend, Gilbert: Born in 1880, authored "How to estimate carpentry, masonry, lath and plaster, marble and tile, air conditioning, electrical wiring, sheet metal, plumbing, linoleum, glass, painting, hardware." By Gilbert Townsend, J. Ralph Dalzell, James McKinney. Publisher: American Technical Society (Chicago Ill). Published in 1955.

1956

Bulbar polio: Polio is highly contagious caused by a virus that has three distinct strains, called types I, II and III. It is noteworthy to recognize that exposure and a resulting immunity to one type doesn't confer immunity to the other two. Type I causes the most paralysis and is the frequent cause of most of the polio epidemics of the first half of the 20th century. The poliovirus enters the body through the mouth, either by contaminated hands or contaminated food or water after coming into contact with expelled fasces, which contains the poliovirus. Polio epidemics occurred usually in the summer and early fall because the poliovirus flourishes in warm weather. Children were more often affected than adults were which is why the disease carried the moniker infantile paralysis. Two famous adults have been stricken with polio, and each had a different outcome. Franklin D. Roosevelt contracted polio in the 1920s and recovered enough to lead a semi-normal life, but never gained full use of his legs, and Evangelist Jack Coe contracted Bulbar Polio in 1956 and died due to complications. Before the 20th century, there were cases of polio, but they were few and no major outbreaks occurred. The question then is how did polio emerged from centuries of obscurity to becoming a killer just a few decades? The answer lies in a major change sanitation practices. Before the advent of modern indoor plumbing and sewage systems, many cities had open sewers that were no more than gutters and outhouses stood in the backyard. Almost everyone had, at one time or another, been exposed to polio, and with open sewers and outhouses the norm--there was ample opportunity to contract polio. Polioviruses infected generation of babies, who were protected in part by antibodies passed on to them by their mothers. When a child became infected with the poliovirus the results were flu like or cold like symptoms. The diagnosis of polio was rare because the symptoms were often indistinguishable from other childhood diseases. [WP]

D'Arcangelo, Bartholomew: Author of "Blueprint reading and sketching: plumbing trades, residential, commercial." By Bartholomew d'Arcangelo, Benjamin d'Arcangelo and J. Russell Guest. Publisher: Delmar Publishers (Albany). Published in 1956.

Gill, Ray: Author of "How to make Plumbing Repairs. R. Gill, editor.With illustrations." Published in 1956.

National Research Council: Publication of "What's new in plumbing. Fifth annual meeting of the Building Research Institute, Niagra Falls, Ontario, May 20-22, 1956." Published in 1956.

Thor (rocket): Douglas further refined the design by choosing bolted tank bulkheads (as opposed to the initially suggested welded ones) and a tapered fuel tank for improved aerodynamics. The engine was developed as a direct descendant of the Atlas MA-3 booster engine. Changes involved removal of one thrust chamber and a rerouting of the plumbing to allow the engine to fit within the smaller Thor boat-tail. Engine tests where being performed as of March 1956. The first engineering model engine was available in June, followed by the first flight engine in September. Engine development was complicated by serious turbopump problems. Early Thor engines suffered from what was known as "Bearing Walking', whereby the turbopump bearings shift axially within their housing, causing rapid wear and the bearings to seize. [WP]

1957

Domestic engineering company, Chicago: Publication of "Domestic engineering catalog directory: industrial, commercial, residential, heating plumbing, air conditioning, refrigeration." Publisher: The Company (Chicago). Published in 1957.

Manas, Vincent Thomas: Born in 1895, authored "National plumbing code, illustrated; minimum requirements for plumbing. (Illustrating: American Standards Association, A.S.A. A40.8-1955, National plumbing code and Report of the Coordinating Committee.)." Published in 1957.

Martin, Albert Charles: Author of "Plumbing Data Booklet. Revised by H. Ryland." Published in 1957.

McGraw-Hill: Publisher of "National plumbing code handbook: standards and design information." Chapters relating to research and special technical material by Herbert N. Eaton. Publisher: McGraw-Hill (New York). Published in 1957.

Plumbing Trades' Union: Publication of "General rules. As amended 1957." Published in 1957.

Webster, Sydney: Author of "Plumbing in building." Publisher: B. T. Batsford (London). Published in 1957.

1958

Gubitz, Myron Bertram: Author of "Handy Man's Handbook. Plumbing, heating and air conditioning. M. B. Gubitz, editor. With illustrations." Published in 1958.

Milwaukee Plumbing Contractors Association: Publication of "75th anniversary, 1883-1958." Published in 1958.

Plumbing Trades Union: Publication of "Annual report." Published in 1958.

Slater, Harry: Author of "Plumbing: related information." Published in 1958.

1959

Blendermann, Louis: Author of "Design of Plumbing and Drainage Systems." Published in 1959.

Canadian Standards Association: Publication of "B45.1-1959. specification for vitreous china plumbing fixtures." Published in 1959.

Domestic Engineering Co: Publication of "Domestic engineering catalog directory: purchasing references for plumbing, heating, ventilating, air conditioning, refrigeration; industrial, commercial, domestic." Publisher: The Company (Chicago). Published in 1959.

H.M.S.O: Publisher of "Questions and answers: heat pumps for domestic heating, short bored piles-costs, shrinkage cracking while houses dry out, dry construction for partition walling, single-stack plumbing for two-story houses." Publisher: H.M.S.O (London). Published in 1959.

Ontario Water Resources Commission: Publication of "Illustrations for the regulations on plumbing and sewers." Publisher: The Commission (Toronto). Published in 1959.

Stanford University. School Planning Laboratory: Publication of "Plumbing fixtures for educational facilities, prepared for the Plumbing Fixture Manufactures Association by James D. MacConnell, professor of education (and) William R. Odell, professor of education. Staff: Jon S. Peters (and others)." Published in 1959.

Webster, Sydney: Author of "Plumbing materials and techniques." Publisher: B. T. Batsford (London). Published in 1959.

1960

Anderson, Edwin P.: Born in 1895, authored "Audels domestic water supply and sewage disposal guide: a practical treatise covering construction of wells, modern pumping systems, pump controls, pumphouses, pump installation & maintenance, hydraulic rams, water treatment methods, also modern sewage disposal systems, septic tanks, drainage, plumbing, water heaters, basement drainage, pumps, useful tables and data." Published in 1960.

Babbitt, Harold Eaton: Author of "Plumbing.. Third edition." Published in 1960.

Bachmann, George Kirsten: Author of "Pipefitter's and Plumber's Vest Pocket Reference Book. Compiled by G. K. Bachmann.. Section on Estimating Piping and Plumbing Costs by Frank Murray." Published in 1960.

Berry, Evan: Author of "An illustrated dictionary of plumbing terms." By Evan Berry; with a foreward by G.J. Nash. Published in 1960.

Davis, Paul G.: Author of "Plumbing, Heating, and Piping Estimators' Guide." Published in 1960.

Government of Peru: Decree 98-60-DGS of 10/7/1960, approves 45 articles dealing with sanitary conditions and requirements for public beaches and establishments connected therewith. This applies both to public and privately owned seashore, and covers aspects of cleanliness of the sand, separation of men and women in bathing and restrooms, plumbing, drinking water, trash disposal, etc. Published in El peruano on October 07, 1960.

Leonard Rudling: Originally from Pietermaritzburg, South Africa, Len immigrated to Canada with his wife and children in 1960. He first developed his plumbing techniques in the challenging Canadian climate, later becoming a collegiate lecturer and administrator. [WP]

Manners, David X.: Author of "Plumbing and Heating Handbook. With illustrations." Published in 1960.

Preston North End F.C.: Preston's most famous player is the legendary Tom Finney, one of England's finest ever forwards who combined playing throughout his long career for his home town club with running a successful plumbing business. Finney scored 30 times for England, in the company of such greats as Stanley Matthews who starred for local rivals Blackpool F.C. Finney retired as a player in 1960 but remains close to the club and still serves as Club President. [WP]

The Bureau,: Publisher of "Facts for industry, M34E. Plumbing fixtures." U.S. Dept. of Commerce, Bureau of the Census. Publisher: The Bureau, (Washington, D.C.). Published in 1960.

Vuorelainen, Olavi: Author of "Thermal conditions in the ground from the viewpoint of foundation work, heating and plumbing installations and draining." Published in 1960.

1961

Haig, James Muir: Author of "The Practical Plumbing Guide." Published in 1961.

HALL, A.M.I.P.H.E. Fred.: Publication of "Plumbing. Illustrated by A. L. Moseley." Published in 1961.

Mobile Homes Manufacturers Association: Publication of "Mobile homes standards for plumbing, heating and electrical systems, approved by Mobile homes manufactures association (and) Trailer coach association, July 10, 1959." Published in 1961.

Tulsa: Publication of "Plumbing code." Publisher: The City (Tulsa, Okla). Published in 1961.

1962

British Columbia. Dept. of Education. Vocational Curriculum Development Division: Publication of "Plumbing course outline for five year night school programme." Publisher: Dept. of Education (Victoria, B.C.). Published in 1962.

Bucknell, Barry: Author of "Simple plumbing." Publisher: Cassell (London; Melbourne). Published in 1962.

Canadian Standards Association: Publication of "Stainless steel plumbing fixtures." Published in 1962.

Colorado. State Dept. of Public Health: Publication of "Plumbing: (technical plumbing code) regulations (effective October 28, 1953) (amended June 14, 1954) (amended April 9, 1956) (amended October 9 and November 13, 1961)." Issued by the Colorado State Dept. of Public Health. Publisher: The Dept (Denver). Published in 1962.

Inspiration Consolidated Copper Company: Publication of "Agreement between Inspiration Consolidated Copper Company and International Brotherhood of Boilermakers, Blacksmiths, Iron

Ship Builders, Forgers and Helpers, Local no. 187, A.F.L.-C.I.O.; United Association of Journeymen & Apprentices of the Plumbing and Pipe Fitting Industry of the United States and Canada, Local no. 808, A.F.L.-C.I.O.; (and) United Brotherhood of Carpenters and Joiners of America, Local no. 1538, A.F.L.-C.I.O., affiliated with Globe-Miami Trades Council." Published in 1962.

Kentucky: Publication of "Kentucky state plumbing law, regulation & code, 1962." Issued by the State Department of Health, Division of Plumbing. Publisher: The Division (Frankfort, Ky.). Published in 1962.

Maddock, Archibald M.: Author of "The polished earth; a history of the pottery plumbing fixture industry in the United States." Published in 1962.

Miller, Perrin C.: Author of "Continental cans, etc: a tourists guide to European plumbing." By Perrin C. Miller and Ruth Willock, drawings by Milda Vizbar. Publisher: George Allen & Unwin (London). Published in 1962.

Plumbing Trade Journal Company, Limited: Publisher of "The plumbing trade journal." Publisher: Plumbing Trade Journal Company, Limited (Manchester). Published in 1962.

Ron Todd: After completing his national service, Todd returned to plumbing and then worked in the Ford factory in Dagenham, where he joined the TGWU. He became a shop steward and then deputy convenor, before becoming a full-time district officer in 1962. In 1969, he became the first group secretary of the Region One Vehicle Building and Automotive Trade Group. He became regional secretary for Region One (London, the Southeast and East Anglia) in 1975, before being promoted to national organiser in 1978. [WP]

SEWERAGE AND WATER BOARD OF NEW ORLEANS: Publication of "RULES OF THE SEWERAGE AND WATER BOARD OF NEW ORLEANS: GOVERNING USE OF SEWERAGE, WATER AND DRAINAGE SYSTEMS AND PLUMBING." Publisher: SEWERAGE AND WATER BOARD OF NEW ORLEANS (NEW ORLEANS). Published in 1962.

Taylor, Lieberfeld and Heldman, inc., New York: Publication of "Plumbing fixture requirements in university instructional and research buildings." Published in 1962.

Townsend, A L.: Author of "Plumbing: first year." Published in 1962.

United States. Public Health Service. Technical Committee on Plumbing Standards: Publication of "Report of Public Health Service Technical Committee on Plumbing Standards: a proposed revision of the National Plumbing Code ASA A40. 8-1955." Published in 1962.

1963

American Standards Association: Publication of "American standard installations of plumbing, heating, and electrical systems in mobil homes. Sponsors: Mobil Homes Manufacturers Association and Trailer Coach Association. Approved March 12, 1963." Published in 1963.

Bureau of the Census: Publisher of "States and small areas: United States Summary data on tenure, rent, value, equipment, condition, plumbing, etc." Publisher: Bureau of the Census (Washington, DC). Published in 1963.

Canada. Dept. of Justice: Publication of "Report of the Canada Restrictive Trade Practices Commission concerning the distribution, supply and sale of plumbing supplies and related products." Published in 1963.

Delaware. Laws, statutes, etc: Author of "Sanitary plumbing code for the State of Delaware (adopted by the State Board of Health May 1, 1950; amended April 5, 1963)." Published in 1963.

Geiser, Charles J.: Author of "Practical information: care and repair of the plumbing and heating system in your home." Published in 1963.

Great Britain. National Incomes Commission: Publication of "Minutes of proceedings at a hearing with reference to the 40-hour settlements in the Scottish building and plumbing industries 13th February (-6th March), 1963." Published in 1963.

H.M.S.O: Publisher of "Simplified plumbing for housing." Publisher: H.M.S.O (London). Published in 1963.

1964

Nielsen, Louis S.: Author of "Standard plumbing engineering design." Publisher: McGraw-Hill Book Company (New York). Published in 1963.

North Carolina. Building Code Council North Carolina. Laws, statutes, etc: Publication of "North Carolina State building code: Article xx, plumbing." Published in 1963.

Toney Anaya: Toney Anaya was born in Moriarty, New Mexico, and grew up in a small dirt-floored adobe house with no electricity or indoor plumbing. After attending public school in Moriarity and a brief stint at New Mexico Highlands University in the late 1950's, Anaya transferred to Washington D.C., where he graduated from Georgetown University in 1963 with a B.A. in Economics/Political Science. He received his J.D. from Washington College of Law at American University in Washington D.C. in 1967. [WP]

United States. Public Health Service. Division of Environmental Engineering and Food Protection: Author of "Water supply and plumbing cross connections: hazards in household and community supply systems; a manual of recommended control practices, including a recommended ordinance." Published in 1963.

Woolgar, William Joseph: Author of "Plastics in plumbing." Publisher: Hutchinson Technical Education (London). Published in 1963.

1964

Canada. Restrictive Trade Practices Commission: Publication of "Report concerning the distribution, supply and sale of plumbing supplies and related products: Combines Investigation Act." Publisher: R. Duhamel, Queen's Printer (Ottawa). Published in 1964.

Canadian Plumbing and Mechanical Contractors Association. National Apprenticeship Committee: Publication of "Steam fitting information sheets." Published in 1964.

Gladstone, Bernard: Author of "The How-to-Book of Plumbing and Heating. With illustrations." Published in 1964.

Govt.Print: Publisher of "Plumbing in New Zealand, written and prepared." The New Zealand Technical Correspondence Institute, Department of Education. Publisher: Govt.Print (Wellington). Published in 1964.

Louisiana: Publication of "Rules and regulations, Louisiana State Plumbing Board, Act 498." Published in 1964.

New Zealand Technical Correspondence Institute: Publication of "Plumbing in New Zealand." Written and prepared by the New Zealand Technical Correspondence Institute, Department of Education. Publisher: Govt.Printer (Wellington). Published in 1964.

NEW ZEALAND. Departments of State and Public Institutions: Publication of "Plumbing in New Zealand, etc." Published in 1964.

United States. Bureau of Yards and Docks: Publication of "Building maintenance: plumbing, heating, and ventilation." Published in 1964.

Western Plumbing Officials Association: Publication of "Uniform plumbing code." Publisher: The Association (Los Angeles, Calif). Published in 1964.

Wyly, Robert S.: Author of "Investigation of the Hydraulics of Horizontal Drains in Plumbing Systems." Published in 1964.

1965

Jonathan Myrick Daniels: On August 13, 1965, Daniels went with a group to picket whites-only stores in the small town of Fort Deposit, Alabama. The next day, all the protestors were arrested and taken to jail in the nearby town of Hayneville, where they were held for six days, having refused to accept bail until bail was made for all the arrested protestors. Daniels' fellow prisoners have recorded that the cell had barely enough room for all the men to fit in (the women were in a separate area), that it was without air conditioning or adequate plumbing (the temperature was regularly over 100 degrees Fahrenheit, and the toilet quickly backed up and began dumping sewage on the floor), and that the little food they were given was often overcooked, uncooked, or full of vermin. Finally, on August 20, all the prisoners were released, without explanation and without transport back to Fort Deposit. Several of the group went to find a payphone with which to call for help, while Daniels and a few others went down the street to get a cold soft drink at Varner's Cash Store, one of the few local stores that would serve nonwhites. They were met on the front steps by an unemployed highway construction worker, Tom Coleman, who was wielding a shotgun. The man threatened the group, and finally leveled his gun at sixteen-year-old Ruby Sales. Daniels pushed Sales out of the way and caught the full blast of the gun. He was killed instantly. [WP]

Markowitz, Isadore: Author of "Design & estimating guide for plumbing." Publisher: Technical Guide Publications (Miami, Fla). Published in 1965.

Robinson, Geoffrey James: Author of "Home Plumbing and Heating. With plates." Published in 1965.

Stairs, Wm., Son & Morrow Ltd. Pluming and Heating Division: Publication of "Catalogue." Wm. Stairs Son & Morrow Plumbing & Heating Division. Published in 1965.

Townsend, A. L.: Author of "Plumbing: second year." Publisher: Hutchinson (London). Published in 1965.

1966

Atlanta Region Metropolitan Planning Commission: Publication of "Building, plumbing, electrical, housing, fire prevention code study." Published in 1966.

Department of Health, Education and Welfare: Publisher of "Water supply and plumbing cross-connections, hazards in househald and community supply systems: a manual of recommended ordinance." U.S. Departament of Health Education and Walfere. Publisher: Department of Health, Education and Welfare (Washington, D.C.). Published in 1966.

Garver, Harry L.: Born in 1891, authored "Plumbing for the home and farmstead (by H. L Garver and J. W. Rockey." Published in 1966.

Lenow, Martin: Author of "Inventory control for small plumbing and heating wholesalers." Published in 1966.

Maccreary, Andrew: Author of "Elementary plumbing. Ordinary Craft Certificate." Published in 1966.

Metropolitan Washington Council of Governments: Publication of "Model plumbing code proposed for the Washington metropolitan area." Published in 1966.

Ontario. Laws, etc Ontario Water Resources Commission: Publication of "Regulation 471 of Revised regulations of Ontario, 1960 as amended by O. Reg. 178/64, O. Reg. 246-66, respecting plumbing." Made under The Ontario Water Resources Commission act Plumbing. Publisher: Ontario Water Resources Commission (Toronto). Published in 1966.

Plumbing Conference: Publication of "Selected papers of the second Missouri Plumbing Conference; January 12 & 13, 1966, University of Missouri, Columbia." Edited by Lindon J. Murphy. Publisher: University of Missouri (Columbia). Published in 1966.

Québec: Publication of "Code de plomberie de la province de Québec; arrêté en conseil no 1189 du 19 juillet 1963: publié dans la Gazette officielle de Québec du 26 octobre 1963 = Plumbing code of the province of Quebec; Order in council, No 1189 of July 19, 1963: published in the Quebec Official Gazette of October 26, 1963 Loi concernant les mécaniciens en tuyauterie Plumbing code of the province of Quebec Order in council no 1189 of July 19, 1963 Pipe-Mechanics act Arrêté en conseil no 1189 du 19 juillet 1963." Publisher: Ministère du travail (Québec). Published in 1966.

Wisconsin. Legislature. Legislative Council Plumbing License Law Committee: Publication of "Report to the 1965 Wisconsin Legislature on Senate Bill 657 relative to the licensing of plumbers." Publisher: Legislative Council (Madison, Wis). Published in 1966.

1967

Brann, Donald R.: Author of "Plumbing repairs simplified, by Donald R. Brann." Published in 1967.

California. Division of Building and Housing Standards: Publication of "Rules and regulations for plumbing, heat-producing, and electrical equipment in mobilehomes, travel trailers, trailer coaches, and camp cars: California administrative code, title 8, part 2, chapter 2, article 2.1; effective May 25, 1967." Published in 1967.

Canadian Institute of Plumbing and Heating: Publication of "Plumbing and heating in Canada; 1966 review." Published in 1967.

The Association: Publisher of "United Association of Journeymen and Apprentices of the Plumbing and Pipe Fitting Industry journal." Publisher: The Association (Washington, D.C.). Published in 1967.

United Association of Journeymen and Apprentices of the Plumbing and Pipe Fitting Industry of United States and Canada: Publisher of "UA journal." Publisher: United Association of Journeymen and Apprentices of the Plumbing and Pipe Fitting Industry of United States and Canada (Washington, D.C.). Published in 1967.

Veenstra & Kimm, Engineers and Planners: Publisher of "Building code, plumbing code, electrical code, fire prevention code Adopted June 19, 1967 City of Belmond, Iowa Prepared by Veenstra & Kimm." Publisher: Veenstra & Kimm, Engineers and Planners (West Des Moines, Iowa). Published in 1967.

Villiard, Paul: Author of "Handy man's plumbing and heating guide." Joseph Piazza, editor Mechanix illustrated. Publisher: Fawcett Publications (Greenwich, Conn). Published in 1967.

1968

Bahamas: Publication of "Plumbing code." Publisher: GPO (Nassau). Published in 1968.

Beeman, Carl E Florida. University, Gainesville. Agricultural Education Dept. Instructional Materials Service Mississippi State University. Agricultural Education Dept. Subject Matter Service: Publication of "Plumbing job operation sheets." Prepared by Carl E. Beeman. Publisher: Agricultural Education Dept., Instructional Materials Service, University of Florida, (Tallahassee). Published in 1968.

Canal Zone: Publication of "Plumbing regulations for the Canal Zone, effective March 1, 1958." Published in 1968.

Central Supply Association: Publication of "Report of operating costs, plumbing, heating piping wholesalers." Published in 1968.

Day, Richard: Born in 1928, authored "The practical guide to plumbing and heating Plumbing and heating." Publisher: Fawcett Publications (Greenwich, Conn). Published in 1968.

Harris, W. L.: Author of "Modernisation of plumbing." Published in 1968.

Lendrum, J. T.: Author of "Plumbing." Publisher: Small Homes Council-Building Research Council (Champaign, Ill). Published in 1968.

New Zealand Trades Certification Board: Publication of "Examinations in plumbing." Publisher: New Zealand Trades Certification Board (Wellington (N.Z.)). Published in 1968.

Ontario. Dept. of Labour. Research Branch: Publication of "Working conditions in the plumbing and heating industry in London, Ontario." Publisher: The Branch (Toronto). Published in 1968.

Royal Melbourne Institute of Technology: Publication of "Plumbing (S. & G.) and gasfitting, grade IV." Published in 1968.

The Bureau,: Publisher of "Current industrial reports. M34E, Plumbing fixtures." U.S. Department of Commerce, Bureau of the Census. Publisher: The Bureau, (Washington, D.C.). Published in 1968.

The Office: Publisher of "Audit report: Board of Plumbing, Michigan Department of Licensing and Regulation." Prepared by Office of the Auditor General. Publisher: The Office (Lansing, Mich). Published in 1968.

1969

Bureau of the Census: Publisher of "1967 census of manufacturers. Preliminary report Industry series. Vitreous plumbing fixtures SIC Code 3261." Publisher: Bureau of the Census (Washington, D.C.). Published in 1969.

Central Mortgage and Housing Corporation: Publication of "Installation of electrical, plumbing and heating in one-storey wood frame house construction." Published in 1969.

Day, Richard: Born in 1928, authored "The practical handbook of plumbing and heating." Publisher: Fawcett Publications (New York). Published in 1969.

Electrical, Electronic, Telecommunication, and Plumbing Union: Publication of "Contact (Electrical, Electronic, Telecommunication, and Plumbing Union (Great Britain)) Contact." Electrical, Electronic & Telecommunication Union-Plumbing Trades Union. Publisher: The Union (Bromley, England). Published in 1969.

Illinois. Division of Sanitary Engineering: Publication of "Illinois State plumbing code, 1969." Published in 1969.

Kendrick, Lee: Author of "Specifications manual for heating, ventilation, air conditioning and plumbing." Published in 1969.

Publication: Publication of "The plumbing trade journal and heating review." Publisher: National Federation of Plumbers and Domestic Engineers (Employers) (Southport). Published in 1969.

Saveker, David Richard: Author of "Mass production urban housing: the design and applications of a structural system employing explosive formed elements to allow integral plumbing and electrical services." (by) David R. Saveker (and) J. Handel Evans. Published in 1969.

Swinburne College of Technology. Plumbing Dept: Publication of "Plumbing practice grade IV." Publisher: Swinburne College of Technology (Melbourne). Published in 1969.

Townsend, A. L.: Author of "Plumbing 1." Publisher: Hutchinson (London). Published in 1969.

Turner, David Reuben, 1915- Arco Publishing Company: Publication of "Maintainer's helper group D: structures, sheet metal, masonry, plumbing, electricity, painting." Publisher: Arco (New York). Published in 1969.

United States of America Standards Institute: Publication of "Standard for mobile homes; body and frame design and construction, installation of plumbing, heating, and electrical systems. Sponsored by: Mobile Homes Manufacturers Association, National Fire Protection Association (and) Trailer Coach Association." Published in 1969.

Virginia Municipal League: Publication of "Fees for building, plumbing and electrical permits and inspections in Virginia municipalities." Published in 1969.

1970

American National Standards Institute. Committee on Mobile Homes and Recreational Vehicles, A.: Publication of "Standard for recreational vehicles, travel trailers, camping trailers, truck campers, motor homes; installation of plumbing, heating, and electrical systems." Published in 1970.

Associate Committee on the National Building Code, National Research Council of Canada: Publisher of "Canadian plumbing code. --." Publisher: Associate Committee on the National Building Code, National Research Council of Canada (Ottawa). Published in 1970.

Building Officials and Code Administrators International: Publication of "The BOCA basic plumbing code: as recommended and maintained by the active membership." Of Building Officials & Code Administrators International, Inc. Publisher: The International (Chicago). Published in 1970.

Canadian Institute of Plumbing and Heating: Publication of "Plumbing and heating in Canada. Statistical review: 1960-70." Published in 1970.

Canadian Standards Association: Publication of "Plumbing requirements for recreational vehicles." Published in 1970.

Hall, Fred: Born in 1924, authored "Plumbing by F. Hall illustrated by A. L. Moseley." Published in 1970.

Institute for Applied Technology: Publication of "Investigation of performance characteristics for sanitary plumbing fixtures." Published in 1970.

National Plumbing Symposium, London: Publication of "Papers." Publisher: Houston Junior Chamber of Commerce (Houston, Tex). Published in 1970.

National Research Council of Canada. Canadian

Commission on Building and Fire Codes: Publication of "National Plumbing Code of Canada." Publisher: The Committee (Ottawa). Published in 1970.

Papua-New Guinea: Publication of "Plumbing syllabus: practical training for school leavers: Length of course: 36 weeks 12 hours per week." Published in 1970.

Publication: Publication of "1967 census of manufactures. Industry series Heating apparatus (except electric) and plumbing fixtures." Published in 1970.

R. Fowler Ltd: Publisher of "Fowler's plumbing trade news." Publisher: R. Fowler Ltd (Marrickville, N.S.W.). Published in 1970.

Saskatchewan. Family Farm Improvement Branch: Publication of "Farm house plumbing." Publisher: Saskatchewan Department of Agriculture, Family Farm Improvement Branch (Regina, SK). Published in 1970.

Studor: STUDOR is a specialist manufacturer of Air Admittance Valves. AAVs are devices designed to remove problems associated with inadequate Plumbing drainage venting. Headquartered in the United Kingdom, with subsidiaries around the world. The company was founded in 1970s by STUre and DORis Ericson and has become a world leader in Air Admittance Technology through continuous research in association with Heriot-Watt University and other academic and professional bodies. [WP]

1971

Almond, Joseph P.: Author of "Plumbers' handbook: a plumbing guide with illustrations and diagrams." (by) Joseph P. Almond, Sr. Publisher: Harper Print. Co (Norcross, Ga.). Published in 1971.

American Society of Sanitary Engineering. Code Committee: Publication of "Plumbing code reference guide, 1971." A.S.S.E Code Committee; Robert L. Wallace, chairman. --. Publisher: The Committee (Cleveland). Published in 1971.

Brann, Donald R.: Author of "How to add an extra bathroom; a complete guide to home plumbing, by Donald R. Brann." Published in 1971.

Canadian Institute of Plumbing and Heating: Publication of "Plumbing and heating in Canada; 1969-70 statistical review." Published in 1971.

England, Departments of State and Official Bodies: Publication of "European plumbing notes. By A. Sobolev." Published in 1971.

Garfield Dunlop: Dunlop was educated at the University of Waterloo. Before entering public life, he was involved with a family business, Glen Dunlop Plumbing, Heating and Supplies (which he first joined in 1971). [WP]

Innes, John H.: Author of "Plumbing." Publisher: English Universities Press; dist. by St. Paul's House (London). Published in 1971.

Institute of Plumbing: Publication of "Pipe sizing to hot and cold water installations, in SI units." Publisher: Institute of Plumbing (London). Published in 1971.

Lent, Samuel N.: Author of "Plumbing code of New York City: guide and interpretation." Publisher: Industrial Press (New York). Published in 1971.

National Association of Plumbing-Heating-Cooling Contractors: Publication of "National standard plumbing code." As suggested by National Association of Plumbing-Heating-Cooling Contractors. Publisher: NAPHCC (Washington, D.C.). Published in 1971.

National Research Council of Canada. Associate Committee on the National Building Code: Publication of "Canadian plumbing code, 1970: based on the National building code of Canada, 1970." Publisher: National Research Council of Canada (Ottawa). Published in 1971.

New England Patriots: The first event held at the new Schaefer Stadium was a preseason game against the New York Giants on August 15, 1971. In a sign of things to come, in the days leading up to the game there was great concern with the plumbing at the facility. To ensure the proper functioning of the plumbing a "flush-off" was conducted, where every toilet in the stadium was flushed at the same time, to ensure that the plumbing could withstand the heaviest use. [WP]

Nova Scotia. Dept. of Labour: Publication of "Plumbing." Nova Scotia Dept. of Labour. Publisher: Dept. of Labour (Halifax). Published in 1971.

Southam Business Publications: Publisher of "Heating, plumbing, air conditioning. HPAC annual buyer's guide." Publisher: Southam Business Publishers (Don Mills, Ont). Published in 1971.

Southern Building Code Congress: Publication of "Southern standard plumbing code. Adopted November 6th, 1955, annual congress, Birmingham, Ala. With revisions and changes officially approved at annual congress." Published in 1971.

1972

American National Standards Institute: Publication of "American national standard supports for off-the-floor plumbing fixtures for public use." Publisher: American Society of Mechanical Engineers (New York). Published in 1972.

American Society of Plumbing Engineers: Publication of "1971 data book." American Society of Plumbing Engineers. Publisher: ASPE (Encino, Calif). Published in 1972.

Association canadienne de normalisation *Canadian Standards Association: Publication of "Polyester composite plumbing fixtures/ Canadian Standards Association." Published in 1972.

British Columbia. Laws, etc: Publication of "Handbook of plumbing sketches: supplement to the British Columbia plumbing code, 1972. --." Publisher: Queen's Printer (Victoria). Published in 1972.

Canadian Institute of Plumbing and Heating. Marketing Services Committee: Publication of "Plumbing and heating in Canada, 1961-1972 statistical review." Published in 1972.

Colorado. Dept. of Health: Publication of "1972 plumbing code: (technical plumbing code) regulations (amended March 15, 1972)." Issued by the Colorado Dept. of Health. Publisher: The Dept (Denver). Published in 1972.

Construction Industry Training Board: Publication of "Metal-arc welding practice in mechanical engineering services (heating and ventilating and plumbing industries) Construction Industry Training Board." Published in 1972.

Disch, Thomas M.: Author of "The right way to figure plumbing, by Thomas M Disch." Published in 1972.

Institute of Plumbing: Publication of "The sizing of sanitary pipework the Institute of Plumbing (prepared by H.A. Howick)." Published in 1972.

Kaussner, John C.: Author of "Sanitary plumbing fixtures." Publisher: ICS (Scranton, Pa.). Published in 1972.

Miller, Russell: Author of "All you need to know about basic home repairs including plumbing, gas, electricity, furniture, repairs, damp and draught proofing." Publisher: Marshall Cavendish Ltd (London (58 Old Compton St., W1V 5PA)). Published in 1972.

National Federation of Plumbers and Domestic Heating Engineers: Publisher of "Plumbing & heating journal." Publisher: National Federation of Plumbers and Domestic Heating Engineers (London). Published in 1972.

Publication: Publication of "Characteristics of occupied housing units by plumbing facilities and tenure for the United States: 1970; supplementary report." Published in 1972.

Thomas, Minor Wine: Born in 1890 and died in 1966, authored "Public school plumbing equipment." New York, Bureau of Publications, Teachers College, Columbia University, 1928. Publisher: AMS Press (New York). Published in 1972.

United Association of Journeymen and Apprentices of the Plumbing and Pipe Fitting Industry of the United States and Canada: Publisher of "General officers' weekly newsletter." Publisher: United Association of Journeymen and Apprentices of the Plumbing and Pipe Fitting Industry of the United States and Canada (Washington, D.C.). Published in 1972.

1973

Association canadienne de normalisation *Canadian Standards Association: Publication of "Vitreous china plumbing fixtures." Publisher: Canadian Standards Association (Rexdale, Ont). Published in 1973.

1973

British Columbia. Laws, etc: Publication of "British Columbia plumbing code: 1972. --." Publisher: Queen's Printer (Victoria). Published in 1973.

California Community Colleges. Board of Governors: Publication of "Construction, supervision, and inspection plumbing and piping." Published in 1973.

Canadian Standards Association: Publication of "Plumbing requirements for mobile homes." Publisher: Canadian Standards Association (Rexdale, Ont). Published in 1973.

Daniels, George Emery: Born in 1914, authored "Home guide to plumbing, heating, and air conditioning by George Daniels." Published in 1973.

Fala, Mario J.: Author of "Residential plumbing inspector's manual principles of residential plumbing inspection." Publisher: American Society of Sanitary Engineering (Bay Village, OH). Published in 1973.

H.M.S.O.: Publisher of "Plumbing with stainless steel." Publisher: H.M.S.O. (London). Published in 1973.

Idaho. Legislature. Legislative Auditor's Office: Publication of "An audit report of Idaho State Plumbing Board." Publisher: Office of Legislative Auditor (Boise). Published in 1973.

King, Harold: Born in 1927, authored "Do your own home plumbing." Publisher: Foulsham (London (etc.)). Published in 1973.

Modern Productions: Publisher of "N.Z. plumbing heating & ventilation review: a monthly magazine serving plumbers, contractors, sheetmetal and ducting fabricators, drainlayers and manufacturers." Publisher: Modern Productions (Auckland, N.Z.). Published in 1973.

Morton Research Corporation: Publication of "The market for plumbing fixtures: an economic, marketing and financial investigation." Published in 1973.

National Research Council of Canada. Associate Committee on the National Building Code: Publication of "Revisions to the Canadian plumbing code, 1970." Associate Committee on the National Building Code, National Research Council of Canada Plumbing. Publisher: Associate Committee on the National Building Code, National Research Council of Canada (Ottawa). Published in 1973.

National Sanitation Foundation: Publication of "Standard no. 24 for plumbing system components for mobile homes and recreational vehicles." As prepared by the NSF Advisory Committee on Plumbing System Components for Mobile Homes and Recreational Vehicles. Publisher: The National Sanitation Foundation (Ann Arbor). Published in 1973.

Ohio State University. Building Research Laboratory Plastics Pipe Institute: Publication of "Report of a standard ASTM fire endurance test and fire and hose stream test on duplicate non-load bearing poly (vinyl chloride) (PVC) plumbing wall assemblies Standard ASTM fire endurance test and fire and hose stream test on duplicate non-load bearing poly (vinyl chloride) (PVC) plumbing wall assemblies." Publisher: Engineering Experiment Station, Ohio State University (Columbus, Ohio). Published in 1973.

Québec: Publication of "(Loi des mécaniciens en tuyauterie) Code de plomberie. Plumbing code: Croquis explicatifs relatifs à certaines règles du code de plomberie du Québec (1973) Croquis explicatifs à certaines règles du code de plomberie du Québec (1973) Explanatory diagrams respecting certain regulations of the Québec plumbing code (1973)." Publisher: Editeur officiel du Québec (Québec). Published in 1973.

Saskatchewan. Court of Appeal: Publication of "In the Court of Appeal for Saskatchewan on appeal from in the Queen's Bench for Saskatchewan (in chambers), Judicial Centre of Regina between Flint Construction (1970) Ltd., and Ken Busch, representing himself and all other members of the United Association of Journeymen and Apprentices of the Plumbing and Pipefitting Industry of the United States and Canada, Local 179: judgement of the court." Publisher: court of Appeal (Regina). Published in 1973.

Scottish Plumbing and Mechanical Services Employers' Federation: Publication of "Jubilee directory, 1923-1973." Publisher: S.P. Technical Publications (Edinburgh). Published in 1973.

Sitka National Historical Park: In 1973, the Park

Service embarked on a 16-year restoration project to return the property to its former glory. Modern plumbing, heating, and electrical systems were installed, while at the same time keeping the structure as authentic as possible. The second floor was restored to its 1853 appearance, based on archaeological evidence and early diaries and drawings. Today, numerous exhibits and lavish icons in the "Chapel of the Annunciation" convey the legacy of Russian America. [WP]

Spanner, D. C.: Author of "Problems of vegetable plumbing: an inaugural lecture given by." Publisher: Bedford College (London). Published in 1973.

U. S. Bureau of the Census: Publication of "Plumbing facilities and estimates of dilapidated housing." Published in 1973.

United States. Bureau of the Census: Publication of "1970 census of housing: plumbing facilities and estimates of dilapidated housing." Published in 1973.

Urquhart, David Inglis: Author of "Plumbing and how it works." David Inglis Urquhart; illustrated by Allan Eitzen. Publisher: H.Z. Walck (New York). Published in 1973.

1974

Alberta. Plumbing Inspection Branch: Publication of "Private sewage disposal." Dept. of Labour, Plumbing Inspection Branch. Publisher: Dept. of Labour, Plumbing Inspection Branch, (Edmonton). Published in 1974.

Clement, John T.: Author of "Towards a provincial warranty on housing; notes for an address to Canadian Institute of Plumbing and Heating (Ontario Region)." Published in 1974.

Crane Canada Limited: Publication of "Roughing-in for plumbing fixtures = Dimensions pour la plomberie brute Dimensions pour la plomberie brûte Trade catalogues (NLC), Building materials, part 3 Catalogues commerciaux (BNC), matériaux de construction, partie 3." Publisher: Crane Canada (Montreal). Published in 1974.

Day, Richard: Born in 1928, authored "The home owner handbook of plumbing and heating." Illustrated by Henry Clark Plumbing and heating. Publisher: Bounty Books (New York). Published in 1974.

Elrod, Larry: Author of "Home plumbing repairs." Publisher: T. Audel (Indianapolis). Published in 1974.

Hadlock, Paul: Author of "Occupational employment: plumbing and heating, except electric, industry, June 1971." Published in 1974.

Haig, James Muir: Author of "The practical plumbing guide. The householder's guide to plumbing." Published in 1974.

Innes, John Hosking: Author of "Plumbing. (Third impression.)." Published in 1974.

Johnson, Albert: Author of "Questions and answers on plumbing." Publisher: Newnes-Butterworths (London). Published in 1974.

Kukichowa Kyuhaisui Eiseikoji no Jitsumu Hensan Iinkai: Publication of "Kukichowa kyuhaisui eiseikoji no jitsumu. (Manual for air-conditioning, plumbing, and sanitary engineering." Published in 1974.

Marshall Cavendish: Publisher of "Central heating, plumbing, electricity." Publisher: Marshall Cavendish (London). Published in 1974.

McGuire, J. H.: Author of "A full-scale fire test of a wall penetrated by plumbing facilities." Publisher: National Research Council Canada, Division of Building Research (Ottawa, Ont). Published in 1974.

New Zealand Technical Correspondence Institute: Publication of "Plumbing in New Zealand." .;. written and prepared for publication by the New Zealand Technical Correspondence Institute, Department of Education. Publisher: A. R. Shearer, Govt. Printer (Wellington, N.Z.). Published in 1974.

Ontario. Ministry of Colleges and Universities Industrial Training Branch: Publication of "An analysis of the plumbing and steamfitting trades." Prepared by a Sub-Committee of the Provincial Advisory Committee. Publisher: The Branch (Toronto). Published in 1974.

R.E.M. Publications: Publisher of "The journal." Institute of N.Z. Plumbing & Drainage Inspectors. Publisher: R.E.M. Publishers (Auckland). Published in 1974.

Scottish Plumbing Employers' Federation:

Publisher of "Scottish plumbing and heating monthly." Publisher: Scottish Plumbing Employers' Federation (Edinburgh). Published in 1974.

Sobol, Donald J.: Born in 1924, authored "Encyclopedia Brown: the case of the exploding plumbing and other mysteries." Donald J. Sobol; illustrated by Leonard Shortall. Publisher: Scholastic (New York). Published in 1974.

Spanner, Douglas Clement: Author of "Problems of vegetable plumbing." Publisher: Bedford College ((London) ((Regent's Park, NW1 4NS))). Published in 1974.

Traister, John E.: Author of "Practical plumbing drafting." Publisher: H. W. Sams (Indianapolis). Published in 1974.

Winnipeg: Publication of "The Winnipeg plumbing by-law. --." Published in 1974.

Wyly, Robert S.: Publication of "Laboratory studies of the hydraulic performance of one-story and split-level residential plumbing systems with reduced-size vents." (by) Robert S. Wyly, Grover C. Sherlin, and Robert W. Beausoliel. Published in 1974.

Wyoming State Capitol: In 1974 the 42nd State Legislature authorized funds for the first phase of a renovation of the building. The renovation was completed in 1980 at a total cost of $7.6 million. It included stripping and staining all woodwork, painting walls in the original design, replacing wooden floor beams with steel and concrete, as well as modernizing the wiring, heating, plumbing, and air conditioning. [WP]

Zim, Herbert Spencer: Born in 1909 and died in 1994, authored "Pipes and plumbing systems." By Herbert S. Zim and James R. Skelly; illustrated with drawings by Lee J. Ames and Mel Erikson. Publisher: Morrow (New York). Published in 1974.

1975

Alth, Max: Born in 1927, authored "Do-it-yourself plumbing." Max Alth; drawings by Carl J. De Groote. Publisher: Popular Science (New York). Published in 1975.

Australia. Dept. of Employment and Industrial Relations. Training Development Branch: Publication of "Sanitary plumbing." (Training Development Branch of the Department of Employment and Industrial Relations). Publisher: Australian Government Publishing Service (Canberra). Published in 1975.

Australian Water and Sewerage Authorities Standing Committee Plumbing and Drainage: Publication of "Draft national plumbing code, October, 1975." By the Australian Water and Sewerage Authorities Standing Committee Plumbing and Drainage. Published in 1975.

Building Officials and Code Administrators International: Publication of "The BOCA basic plumbing code." Published in 1975.

Canada. Employment and Immigration Canada: Publication of "Manpower needs in the Mechanical construction industry: a joint study of the Department of Manpower and Immigration, the United Association of the Plumbing & Pipefitting Industry of the U S A and Canada and the Mechanical Contractors Association of Canada = (Les besoins de main-d'oeuvre dans l'industrie des entreprises en mécanique: une étude conjointe du Ministère de la main d'oeuvre et de l'immigration, l'Association unie des compagnons et apprentis de l'industrie de la plomberie et de la tuyanterie (sic) des Etats-Unis et du Canada et l'Association des entrepreneurs en mécanique du Canada) Les besoins de main-d'oeuvre dans l'industrie des entreprises en mécanique." Publisher: Mechanical Contractors Association of Canada ((Ottawa): Manpower and Immigration; (Winnipeg): United Association of Journeymen and Apprentices of the Plumbing & Pipefitting Industry of the U.S.A. & Canada; (Ottawa)). Published in 1975.

Cassels, David: Author of "Services for housing, sanitary plumbing and drainage (author David Cassels) (for the Housing Development Directorate)." Published in 1975.

Demske, Dick: Born in 1930, authored "Plumbing." Publisher: Grosset & Dunlap (New York). Published in 1975.

Georgia. State Building Administrative Board: Publication of "Georgia State plumbing code." Publisher: State Building Administrative Board

(Atlanta). Published in 1975.

Green, Philip Palmer: Born in 1922, authored "Legal responsibilities of the local plumbing inspector in North Carolina." By Philip P. Green, Jr. Published in 1975.

Hagiwara, Akinobu: Author of "Kyuhaisui eiseisetsubi. (Plumbing and sanitary engineering, by Akinobu Hagiwara, et al." Published in 1975.

Hoovler, Whitney: Author of "Plumbing." By Whitney Hoovler and Jeffrey Pulis. Publisher: castle Books (Secaucus, N.J.). Published in 1975.

International Association of Plumbing and Mechanical Officials: Publication of "Uniform plumbing code: 1976 edition, adopted at the forty-sixth annual conference, September, 1975." International Association of Plumbing and Mechanical Officials. --. Publisher: The Association (Los Angeles). Published in 1975.

Jacobson, I. D American Society of Sanitary Engineering: Publication of "Plumbing dictionary." Publisher: American Society of Sanitary Engineering, (Cleveland). Published in 1975.

Koons, Richard A.; Evans, Leonard A.: Author of "Plumbing & general principles (slide)." R. A. Koons, L. A. Evans. Publisher: National Audiovisual Center (Washington). Published in 1975.

Lo Schiavo, Joseph V.: Author of "You fix it, plumbing." Joseph V. Lo Schiavo, Jr in association with A. R. Squittieri, Carmine C. Castellano, and Clifford P. Seitz. Publisher: Arco (New York). Published in 1975.

LoSchiavo, Joseph V.: Author of "Plumbing repairs made easy." Joseph V. LoSchiavo, Jr.; in association with A. R. Squittieri, Carmine C. Castellano, and Clifford P. Seitz. --. Publisher: Coles (Toronto). Published in 1975.

Minnesota Mining and Manufacturing Company. Automotive-Hardware Trades Division: Publication of "The home pro plumbing guide." (Automotive-Hardware Trades Division, 3M Company). --. Publisher: The Division (St. Paul). Published in 1975.

Morton Research Corporation Goldberg, D.: Publication of "The plumbing fixture industry: an economic, financial and marketing analysis." Published in 1975.

National Audiovisual Center: Publisher of "Plumbing & general principles (slide)." R. A Koons, L. A. Evans. Publisher: National Audiovisual Center (Washington). Published in 1975.

National Bureau of Standards: Publisher of "Review of performance characteristics, standards and regulatory restrictions relating to the use of thermoplastic piping in residential plumbing." Publisher: National Bureau of Standards (Washington, D.C.). Published in 1975.

National Institute for Occupational Safety and Health: Publication of "Health and safety for plumbing, heating and air conditioning contractors." Publisher: NIOSH (Cincinnati, OH). Published in 1975.

National Research Council Canada. Associate Committee on the National Building Code: Publication of "National plumbing code, 1975." Issued by the Associate Committee on the National Building Code, National Research Council of Canada, Ottawa Canadian plumbing code, 1975. Publisher: National Research Council of Canada (Ottawa). Published in 1975.

Ontario. Ministère de la santé *Ontario. Ministry of Health: Publication of "Regulation 701, Revised regulations of Ontario, 1970, camps in unorganized territory; Regulation 715, Revised regulations of Ontario, 1970, plumbing in unorganized territory; Regulation 718, Revised regulations of Ontario, 1970 as amended by O. Reg. 228/74, sanitary code for unorganized territory." Publisher: Queen's Printer (Toronto). Published in 1975.

Parker, William James: Born in 1926, authored "Fire endurance of gypsum board walls and chases containing plastic an metallic drain, waste, and vent plumbing systems." W. J. Parker ... (et. al.). Published in 1975.

Plumbing Trade Journal Co. Ltd: Publisher of "International plumbing & heating journal." Publisher: Plumbing Trade Journal Co. Ltd (Southport). Published in 1975.

Reader's Digest Association: Publisher of "Home plumbing." Publisher: Reader's Digest Association (London). Published in 1975.

Richard Fulton: In 1975, the only mayor Nashville had ever had since its consoldiation with Davidson County, Beverly Briley, could not run for a fourth term. A secretive group of Nashville business leaders known as "Watauga" (after the area in East Tennessee from which the original white settlers of Nashville had migrated), was not impressed with the prospective successors that they saw among local political leaders. They approached Fulton and promised him that he would almost certainly win if he ran. This proved prophetic, as Fulton won the race that year with almost a two-thirds majority. His only major opponent, Criminal Court Clerk Earl Hawkins, received about 25%. (In contrast the third-place finisher, plumbing-supply store operator Ralph Cohen, received only about 6%.) He was again succeeded by Clifford Allen, this time as Congressman. [WP]

Rogers, Keith: Born in 1925, authored "Fix it yourself, plumbing basic repairs and maintenance by Keith Rogers." Published in 1975.

Scottish and Northern Ireland Plumbing Employers' Federation: Publisher of "Scottish and Northern Ireland plumbing and heating." Publisher: Scottish and Northern Ireland Plumbing Employers' Federation (Edinburgh). Published in 1975.

Slater, Harry: Publication of "Plumbing." Harry Slater; Robert Voorhees, reviser; Richard P. Walsh, technical consultant. Publisher: Delmar Publishers (Albany). Published in 1975.

Southern Building Code Congress International: Publication of "Standard plumbing code." Publisher: Southern Building Code Congress (Birmingham, Ala). Published in 1975.

Standards Association of Australia: Publication of "Welded stainless steel tubes for plumbing applications." By Standards Association of Australia. Publisher: Standards Association of Australia (North Sydney). Published in 1975.

Sunset Books: Publication of "Basic plumbing illustrated/ by the Editors of Sunset Books and Sunset Magazine." Publisher: Lane Pub. Co (Menlo Park, Calif). Published in 1975.

1976

Australia. Dept. of Employment and Industrial Relations. Training Development Branch: Publication of "Sanitary plumbing. 3." (Training Development Branch of the Department of Employment and Industrial Relations). Publisher: Australian Government Publishing Service (Canberra). Published in 1976.

Bierman, Elenore C.: Author of "There's an iguana in my plumbing." Publisher: Ashley Books (Port Washington, N.Y.). Published in 1976.

Clarke, Robin: Author of "Building for self-sufficiency: tools, materials, building, heat, insulation, solar energy, wind power, water & plumbing, waste & compost, methane, transport, food." Robin Clarke; (ill. by Janine Clarke). --. Publisher: Universe Books (New York). Published in 1976.

Clifford, Martin: Born in 1910, authored "The encyclopedia of household plumbing installation and repair." Publisher: Bonanza Books (New York). Published in 1976.

Day, Roy: Author of "All about plumbing and central heating." Publisher: Hamlyn (London; New York). Published in 1976.

Defense Logistics Services Center: Publication of "Plumbing fixtures and accessories." Publisher: Battle Creek, Mich.: U.S. Dept. of Defense, Defense Supply Agency, Defense Logistics Services Center. Published in 1976.

Demske, Dick: Born in 1930, authored "Plumbing." Written by Dick Demske; illustrated by James E. Barry. Publisher: Consolidated Book Publishers (New York). Published in 1976.

Galeno, Joseph J.: Author of "Plumbing estimating handbook." Publisher: Van Nostrand Reinhold Co (New York). Published in 1976.

Indiana. Administrative Building Council. cn: Publication of "Plumbing rules and regulations." Promulgated by the Administrative Building Council of Indiana. Publisher: The Council (Indianapolis). Published in 1976.

Kohler Company: Publication of "Kohler Plumbing Products: Catalog K200." Publisher: Kohler (Kohler, Wis). Published in 1976.

Melbourne and Metropolitan Boards of Works: Publisher of "Plumbing code and sewerage regulations 1976." Melbourne and Metropolitan Board of Works. Publisher: Melbourne and Metropolitan Boards of Works (Melbourne). Published in 1976.

Nunn, Richard V.: Author of "Easy home plumbing." Publisher: Oxmoor House (Birmingham, Ala). Published in 1976.

Québec: Publication of "Code de plomberie adopté en vertu de la Loi des mécaniciens en tuyauterie (S.R. 1964, c.154) = Plumbing Code made under the Pipe-Mechanics Act (R.S. 1964, c.154) Plumbing Code made under the Pipe-Mechanics Act." Publisher: Éditeur officiel du Québec (Québec). Published in 1976.

Southern Building Code Congress International: Publication of "Plumbing inspector manual." Publisher: The Congress (Birmingham, Ala). Published in 1976.

Waite, Diana S., comp: Publication of "Architectural elements: the technological revolution; galvanized iron roof plates and corrugated sheets; cast iron facades, columns, door and window caps, sills and lintels; galvanized cornices; marbleized slate mantels; plumbing and heating supplies and fixtures; staircases, balconies, newels and balusters in wood and iron; cut and etched glass transoms and sidelights. Edited, and with an introd. by Diana S. Waite." Published in 1976.

Western Australian Industrial Commission: Publication of "Apprentices syllabus of training: plumbing." Publisher: Govt. Pr (Perth). Published in 1976.

1977

Adams, Jeannette T.: Author of "Complete home plumbing & heating handbook." Publisher: Arco Pub. Co (New York). Published in 1977.

Aleotti, Luciano: Translator of "Plumbing" by Fred Hall into Italian ("Come sustituirsi all'idraulico"). Publisher: Rizzoli (Milano). Published in 1977.

American National Standards Institute: Publication of "Graphic symbols for plumbing fixtures for diagrams used in architecture and building construction." Publisher: American Society of Mechanical Engineers (New York). Published in 1977.

Australia. Dept. of the Capital Territory: Publication of "Draft A.C.T. plumbing code." Dept. of the Capital Territory. Publisher: Australian Govt. Printing Service (Canberra, A.C.T.). Published in 1977.

Australian Water and Sewerage Authorities Standing Committee Plumbing and Drainage: Publication of "Australian model plumbing code: sanitary drainage, October 1977." By the Australian Water and Sewerage Authorities Standing Committee Plumbing and Drainage. Publisher: Australian Govt. Pub. Service (Canberra). Published in 1977.

Bragdon, Allen D Day, Doug Foley, Joseph H.: Publication of "Plumbing & heating." (editorial director, Allen D. Bragdon; text originated by Doug Day, Joseph H. Foley) Fixit yourself book of plumbing & heating. Publisher: Petersen Pub. Co (Los Angeles). Published in 1977.

Burman, N. P. and J. S. Colbourne: "Techniques for the assessment of growth of micro-organisms on plumbing materials used in contact with potable water supplies" appears in The Journal of Applied Bacteriology written by N. P. Burman and J. S. Colbourne. Published in August 1977.

California Energy Commission. Conservation Division: Publication of "Proposed energy efficiency regulations for space heaters, water heaters, and plumbing fittings: final environmental impact report." California State Energy Resources Conservation and Development Commission. Publisher: The Commission (Sacramento). Published in 1977.

Canadian Standards Association: Publication of "Porcelain enamelled steel plumbing fixtures." Publisher: Canadian Standards Association (Rexdale, Ont). Published in 1977.

Day, Richard, 1928- Genova, Inc: Publication of "Plumb-it-yourself: it's easy with Genova: the complete guide to do-it-yourself home plumbing, from simple fix-up jobs to plumbing a whole house!." Written for Genova by Richard Day. Publisher: Genova (Davison, Mich). Published in 1977.

Hall, Fred: Author of "Plumbing." Translated into Italian, titled "Come sustituirsi all'idraulico" (translator: Luciano Aleotti). Publisher: Rizzoli (Milano). Published in 1977.

Institute of Plumbing: Publication of "Plumbing services design guide." Compiled by the Institute of Plumbing. Publisher: The Institute (Hornchurch, Essex: Scottish Mutual House, North St., Hornchurch, Essex RM11 1RU). Published in 1977.

Leber, Jonathan P.: Author of "The California appliance efficiency program revised staff report, November, 1977, relating to space heaters, storage type water heaters and plumbing fixtures." Publisher: California Energy Resources Conservation and Development Commission, Conservation Division (Sacramento). Published in 1977.

Matthias, Arthur John: Author of "How to design and install plumbing." By A. J. Matthias, Jr.; contributor, Robert J. Volland. Publisher: American Technical Society, c1960, printing (Chicago). Published in 1977.

National Association of Plumbing, Heating and Mechanical Services Contractors: Publication of "Members reference book & list of members." National Association of Plumbing, Heating and Mechanical Services Contractors. Publisher: The Association (London). Published in 1977.

National Joint Plumbing Apprentice and Journeyman Training Committee: Publication of "National apprenticeship standards for plumbing and steamfitting-pipefitting." (established by the National Joint Plumbing Apprentice and Journeyman Training Committee and the National Joint Steamfitter-Pipe-fitter Apprenticeship Committee in cooperation with the Bureau of Apprenticeship and Training, U.S. Dept. of Labor). Publisher: Dept. of Labor, Employment and Training Administration, Bureau of Apprenticeship and Training (Washington). Published in 1977.

National Research Council of Canada. Associate Committee on the National Building Code: Publication of "Metric values for use with the National plumbing code, 1977." Issued by the Associate Committee on the National Building Code, National Research Council of Canada. Publisher: National Research Council of Canada (Ottawa). Published in 1977.

New Zealand Trades Certification Board: Publication of "Examinations in plumbing and gasfitting." Publisher: New Zealand Trades Certification Board (Wellington (N.Z.)). Published in 1977.

Petersen Pub. Co: Publisher of "Plumbing & heating." (editorial director, Allen D. Bragdon; text originated by Doug Day, Joseph H. Foley). Publisher: Petersen Pub. Co (Los Angeles). Published in 1977.

Philbin, Tom: Born in 1934, authored "Basic plumbing." Publisher: reston Pub. Co (Reston, Va.). Published in 1977.

Plumbing Information Bureau: Publisher of "Plumbing guide book." Publisher: Plumbing Information Bureau (Wellington). Published in 1977.

Plumbing Symposium 1976 Bristol: Publication of "1976 Plumbing Symposium, Grand Hotel, Bristol, Saturday, 5th June, 1976." Publisher: Institute of Plumbing (Bristol). Published in 1977.

Sewerage Branch: Publisher of "Sanitary plumbing and drainage directions." Engineering and Water Supply Department, Sewerage Branch. Publisher: Sewerage Branch (Adelaide). Published in 1977.

Sidal, Cavit: Translator of "How to design and install plumbing" by Arthur John Matthias into Turkish ("Sihhi tesisat nasil planlanir ve yapilir"). Publisher: s. n. (Ankara). Published in 1977.

Steele, Alfred: Author of "Engineered plumbing design." Publisher: Miramar Publishing Co (Los Angeles, Ca.). Published in 1977.

Victoria: Publication of "Uniform plumbing and sewerage regulations 1977." Melbourne and Metropolitan Board of Works. Publisher: Govt. Printer (Melbourne). Published in 1977.

1978

Adams, Jeannette T.: Author of "The complete encyclopedia of home plumbing and heating." Jeannette T. Adams Encyclopedia of home plumbing and heating Home plumbing and heating. Publisher: Coles (Toronto). Published in

1978.

Alberta. Plumbing Inspection Branch: Publication of "Private sewage disposal systems: instructions to installers 1978." Alberta Labour, General Safety Services Division, Plumbing Inspection Branch. Publisher: Plumbing Inspection Branch (Edmonton). Published in 1978.

Canadian Institute of Plumbing and Heating: Publication of "Statistical review: plumbing & heating in Canada, 1960-1976 = Résumé statistique: plomberie & chauffage au Canada, (1960-1976)." Canadian Institute of Plumbing and Heating. Publisher: CIPH (Montreal). Published in 1978.

Canadian Standards Association: Publication of "Plumbing, drainage and other piping systems in health care facilities." Publisher: Canadian Standards Association (Rexdale, Ont). Published in 1978.

Coe, Arnold L.: Born in 1940, authored "Water supply and plumbing practices in continental Europe." Publisher: Hutchinson (London). Published in 1978.

Dunhall & Associates: Publisher of "Plumbing, heating and ventilation review." Publisher: Dunhall & Associates (Melbourne). Published in 1978.

Goddard, Haynes C.: Author of "Planning water supply: cost-rate differentials and plumbing permits." By Haynes C. Goddard, Richard G. Stevie, and Gregory D. Trygg. Publisher: Available from the National Technical Information Service (Cincinnati, Ohio: Environmental Protection Agency, Office of Research and Development, Municipal Environmental Research Laboratory; Springfield, Va.). Published in 1978.

Government Printer: Publisher of "Plumbing." written and prepared for publication by the New Zealand Technical Correspondence Institute. Publisher: Government Printer (Wellington, N.Z.). Published in 1978.

Gundrey, Elizabeth: Author of "Simple plumbing Elizabeth Gundrey." Published in 1978.

Institute of Plumbing: Publication of "List of members and register of plumbers the Institute of Plumbing." Published in 1978.

International Association Of Plumbing And Mechanical Officials: Publication of "Uniform solar energy code: 1979 edition, adopted at the 49th annual Conference, September 1978." Publisher: The Association (Los Angeles). Published in 1978.

International Conference of Building Officals: Publication of "Plumbing code, 1978." International Conference of Building Officials. Publisher: International Conference of Building Officials (Whittier, Calif). Published in 1978.

Lawrence Livermore Laboratory. Technology Applications Group: Publication of "Plumbing engineers solar energy handbook: Southern California region." Published in 1978.

Leavy, Herbert T.: Author of "Parker's illustrated home guide to plumbing." Publisher: Parker Pub. Co (West Nyack, N.Y.). Published in 1978.

Morton Research Corporation La Rosa, John: Publication of "The United States plumbing fixture industry." Publisher: Morton Research Corp (Merrick, N.Y.). Published in 1978.

New York: Publication of "1978 amendment program for the State Building Construction Code: applicable to one- and two-family dwellings, multiple dwellings, general building construction, and plumbing." Publisher: State of New York, Executive Dept., Division of Housing and Community Renewal, State Building Code Council (New York, N.Y.). Published in 1978.

New Zealand Technical Correspondence Institute: Publication of "Plumbing: (Reprinted and metricated with two supplements)." Publisher: Govt Print (Wellington). Published in 1978.

Ontario Securities Commission: Publication of "In the matter of the Securities Act and the matter of Plumbing Mart Corporation: order." Publisher: The Commission (Toronto). Published in 1978.

Orloski, M J.: Author of "Performance criteria and plumbing system design." M. J. Orloski and R. S. Wyly. Published in 1978.

Page, John S.: Author of "Estimator's man-hour manual on heating, air conditioning, ventilating, and plumbing." Publisher: Gulf Pub. Co., Book Division (Houston (Tex.)). Published in 1978.

Sessions, Ken W.: Author of "The homeowner's handbook of plumbing and repair." Publisher:

Wiley (New York). Published in 1978.

Snyder, Milton: Author of "Snyder on plumbing: volume 1." Published in 1978.

1979

American Society of Sanitary Engineering: Publisher of "Plumbing dictionary." Editor, I.D. Jacobson; associate editors, Amy Harris, Sanford Schwartz. Publisher: American Society of Sanitary Engineering (Cleveland, Ohio). Published in 1979.

Brann, Donald R.: Author of "Plumbing repairs simplified." Publisher: Directions Simplified (Briarcliff Manor, N.Y.). Published in 1979.

Church, James C.: Author of "Practical plumbing design guide." Publisher: McGraw-Hill (New York; London (etc.)). Published in 1979.

Cipriano, Anthony Vincent: Author of "A comparison of the perceptions of indentured apprentices and their employers of selected aspects of work-related instruction in the plumbing trade in Massachusetts." Published in 1979.

Greer, Lou: Author of "Your personal plumber." By Lou Greer; (artist, Ann Carroll). Publisher: Plumbing Publications (Midland, Tex). Published in 1979.

Hall, Ernest: Author of "Plumbing Ernest Hall." Published in 1979.

Hedden, Jay W.: Author of "Modern plumbing for old and new homes." Publisher: Creative Homeowner Press (Milwaukee). Published in 1979.

Hunter District Water Board: Publication of "Interim plumbing code, sanitary drainage, May 1979." Publisher: Hunter District Water Board (Newcastle, N.S.W.). Published in 1979.

International Association of Plumbing and Mechanical Officials: Publication of "Uniform solar energy code: adopted at the forty-ninth annual conference, September, 1978." International Association of Plumbing and Mechanical Officials. Publisher: The Association (Los Angeles). Published in 1979.

International Conference of Building Officials: Publication of "ICBO plumbing code." Publisher: International Conference of Building Officials, (Whittier, Calif). Published in 1979.

Jacobson, I. D American Society of Sanitary Engineering: Publication of "Plumbing dictionary." Editor, I.D. Jacobson; associate editors, Amy Harris, Sanford Schwartz. Publisher: American Society of Sanitary Engineering (Cleveland, Ohio). Published in 1979.

Master Plumbers Association of Western Australia: Publisher of "Construction & plumbing." Publisher: Master Plumbers Association of Western Australia (West Perth, W.A). Published in 1979.

New Zealand. Division of Public Health: Publication of "Explanatory commentary: the Drainage and Plumbing Regulations, 1978." Prepared by the Division of Public Health, Department of Health. Publisher: The Division (Wellington). Published in 1979.

Plumbing, Gas and Drainlaying Industry Training Board: Publication of "Instructing and training plumbing and gasfitting appreatices: a guide to on-the-job apprentice training." Plumbing, Gas and Drainlaying Industry Training Board. Publisher: The Board (Wellington). Published in 1979.

Prentice-Hall Media: Publisher of "Basic carpentry and building construction Segment 6, Rough plumbing and heating. (Filmstrip)." Prentice-Hall Media, inc.; made by Joel Fried Audiovisuals, inc. Publisher: Prentice-Hall Media (Tarrytown, N.Y.). Published in 1979.

Publication: Publication of "Camp Konocti 1979." Publisher: Local Union No. 38, United Association of Journeymen and Apprentices of the Plumbing and Pipe Fitting Industry in San Francisco, Marin, Sonoma, Mendocino and Lake Counties of California (San Francisco, Calif). Published in 1979.

Quebec: Publication of "Code de plomberie: (A.C. 4028-72 de 1972 1227 (1973) G.O. II, 525; erratum (1974) G.O. II, 2339; modifié par A.C. 1578-74 de 1974 0501 (1974) G.O. II, 2235; A.C. 4386-76 de 1976 1222 (1977) G.O. II, 243) = Plumbing code: (O.C. 4028-72 of 1972 1227 (1973) O.G. II, 525: erratum (1974) O.G. II, 2339; amended by O.C. 1578-74 of 1974 0501 (1974) O.G. II, 2235; O.C. 4386-76 of 1976 1222 (1977) O.G. II, 243) Plumbing code." Publisher: Editeur officiel (Québec). Published in 1979.

Sibbison, Ron: Author of "Proposed year 11 building technical (plumbing) leaving certificate course: gas." (syllabus developed by Ron Sibbison, Ken Wulf and Alan Cross). Publisher: Technical Division, Education Dept of Victoria (Melbourne). Published in 1979.

Slater, Harry: Author of "Basic plumbing." Publisher: Van Nostrand Reinhold (New York; Toronto). Published in 1979.

Southern Building Code Congress International: Publication of "Standard plumbing code." Southern Building Code Congress International, Inc. Publisher: The Congress (Birmingham, Ala). Published in 1979.

State Board of Examiners of Plumbing and Heating Contractors: Publisher of "Register of licensees serial)." Publisher: State Board of Examiners of Plumbing and Heating Contractors (Raleigh, N.C.). Published in 1979.

Stone, M. N.: "The plumbing paradox: American attitudes toward late nineteenth-century domestic sanitary arrangements" appears in Winterthur Portfolio written by M. N. Stone. Published in 1979.

Time-Life Books: Publication of "Plumbing." By the editors of Time-Life Books. Publisher: Time-Life Books (Alexandria, Va.). Published in 1979.

United States. Bureau of the Census: Publication of "1977 census of construction industries: industry series, plumbing, heating (except electric), and air conditioning special trade contractors, SIC 1711." Publisher: Washington: Dept. of Commerce, Bureau of the Census: for sale by the Subscribers Services (Publications), Bureau of the Census. Published in 1979.

1980

American Society of Plumbing Engineers: Publisher of "ASPE data book, 1979-1980." Publisher: American Society of Plumbing Engineers (Sherman Oaks, CA). Published in 1980.

Australia. Dept. of Employment and Youth Affairs: Publication of "Roof plumbing: introduction and downpipes." Department of Employment and Youth Affairs. Publisher: A.G.P.S (Canberra). Published in 1980.

Australian Govt. Pub. Service: Publisher of "Basic training manual. 12, Roof plumbing." Department of Employment and Youth Affairs. Publisher: Australian Govt. Pub. Service (Canberra). Published in 1980.

Blackwell, S. Duncan: Author of "Plumbing with plastic." Publisher: tab Books (Blue Ridge Summit, Pa.). Published in 1980.

Burney Lamar: Burney Lamar, from West Sacramento, CA was born on August 21st, 1980. He drives the 33 HPS Plumbing Chevrolet in the NASCAR West Series for Kevin Harvick Incorporated. [WP]

California Energy Commission: Publication of "Regulations for appliance efficiency standards (including requirements for intermittent ignition devices): relating to refrigerators and freezers, room air conditioners, central air conditioners, gas space heaters, water heaters, plumbing fittings, gas clothes dryers, and gas cooking appliances." Published in 1980.

Coppersmith: Coppersmiths started to be phased out in the late 1970's early 1980's and the trade is now generally taken over by the sheetmetal trade, and the practises used can sometimes be close to the plumbing trade. There are very few coppersmiths left in the trade. Most have found other occupations and many have converted to sheetmetal workers. [WP]

Elkis, William Jack: Author of "The effect of insulation on energy losses in domestic plumbing." Publisher: Building Research Association of New Zealand (Wellington, N.Z.). Published in 1980.

Gurley, George H.: Author of "Fugues in the plumbing." Publisher: BkMk Press (Kansas City, Mo.). Published in 1980.

Hall, Fred: Born in 1924, authored "Plumbing and heating." F. Hall; illustrated by A.L. Moseley. Publisher: Macmillan (London (etc)). Published in 1980.

Hedden, Jay W.: Author of "Plumbing for old and new houses: projects for building and installing bathrooms, faucet, piping and toilet repairs, passive solar collectors and lawn sprinklers." Publisher: Creative Homeowner Press (Upper

Saddle River, NJ). Published in 1980.

Institute of Plumbing: Publication of "Business directory of plumbers." Publisher: Institute of Plumbing (Hornchurch). Published in 1980.

International Conference of Building Officials: Publication of "Accumulative supplement to the Uniform building code, U.B.C. standards, Uniform mechanical code, ICBO plumbing code, Uniform administrative code, Uniform building security code, Uniform fire code, Uniform fire code standards." International Conference of Building Officials International Conference of Building Officials. Uniform building code. Publisher: International Conference of Building Officials (Whittier, Calif). Published in 1980.

Jones, Peter: Born in 1934, authored "Homeowner's guide to plumbing, heating, wiring, and air conditioning." Publisher: reston Pub Co (Reston, Va.). Published in 1980.

Lansing: Publication of "Lansing uniform plumbing code, ordinance nos 569, chapter 9C, building code plumbing." Publisher: City of Lansing (Lansing, Mich). Published in 1980.

Legg, Andrew P.: Author of "Innovations for courses in plumbing." Andrew P Legg, L.H. Pyke. Publisher: Technical Education Division (West Perth, W.A.). Published in 1980.

Lerchen, Frank H.: Author of "Selected methods for condition assessment of structural, HVAC, plumbing and electrical systems in existing buildings." Frank H. Lerchen, James H. Pielert, Thomas K. Faison; sponsored by the Energy, Building Technology and Standards Division, Office of Policy Development and Research, Department of Housing and Urban Development and Center for Building Technology, National Engineering Laboratory, National Bureau of Standards. Published in 1980.

Massey, Howard C.: Author of "Basic plumbing with illustrations." Howard C Massey; (illustrations by Mike Aten and the author). Publisher: Craftsman Book Co (Carlsbad, Calif). Published in 1980.

McGraw-Hill: Publisher of "Guide to plumbing." Publisher: McGraw-Hill (New York). Published in 1980.

Miller, William Charles: Born in 1927, authored "Estimating and cost control in plumbing design." William C. Miller, Leonard Gallina. Publisher: Van Nostrand Reinhold (New York). Published in 1980.

National Association of Plumbing-Heating-Cooling Contractors: Publication of "National standard plumbing code--illustrated, based upon the National standard plumbing code 1978 and 1979 supplement." National Association of Plumbing-Heating-Cooling Contractors. Publisher: The Association (Washington, D.C.). Published in 1980.

National Institute of Building Sciences: Publication of "Rehabilitation guidelines 1980. 7, Plumbing DWV guideline for residential rehabilitation." (prepared by the National Institute of Building Sciences, for the U.S. Department of Housing and Urban Development, Office of Policy Development and Research). Published in 1980.

National Research Council of Canada. Associate Committee on the National Building Code: Publication of "Canadian plumbing code, 1980." Issued by the Associate Committee on the National Building Code, National Research Council of Canada. --. Publisher: The Council (Ottawa, Ont). Published in 1980.

New Mexico. Mechanical Bureau: Publication of "New Mexico uniform plumbing code, 1979." Commerce and Industry Department, Construction Industries Division, Mechanical Bureau. Publisher: The Bureau (Santa Fe, N.M.). Published in 1980.

Prentice-Hall Media: Publisher of "Rough plumbing and heating." Publisher: Prentice-Hall Media (Tarrytown, N.Y.). Published in 1980.

Queen's Printer for Ontario: Publisher of "Regulation 647: Revised regulations of Ontario, 1970 as amended to O. Reg. 295/79; Plumbing code under the Ontario water resources act." Publisher: Queen's Printer for Ontario (Toronto). Published in 1980.

Scharff, Robert: Author of "Successful plumbing." Publisher: Structures Pub. Co (Farmington, MI). Published in 1980.

Selenium: Growth in selenium consumption was driven by the development of new uses, including applications in rubber compounding, steel alloying, and selenium rectifiers. By 1970, selenium in rectifiers had largely been replaced by silicon, but its use as a photoconductor in plain paper copiers had become its leading application. During the 1980s, the photoconductor application declined (although it was still a large end-use) as more and more copiers using organic photoconductors were produced. In 1996, continuing research showed a positive correlation between selenium supplementation and cancer prevention in humans, but widespread direct application of this important finding would not add significantly to demand owing to the small doses required. In the late 1990s, the use of selenium (usually with bismuth) as an additive to plumbing brasses to meet no-lead environmental standards became important. [WP]

Slater, Harry: Publication of "Advanced plumbing." Publisher: Delmar Publishers (Albany, N.Y.). Published in 1980.

Smith, Frederick C.: Author of "Plumbing: mechanical services." Building Industries Division, Technical College, Royal Melbourne Institute of Technology. Publisher: RMIT (Melbourne). Published in 1980.

SMRB: Publisher of "Home furnishings & home improvements: bathroom plumbing fixtures, bedding, linens & towels, carpeting & flooring." Simmons Market Research Bureau, Inc. --. Publisher: SMRB (New York, N.Y.). Published in 1980.

U.S. Dept. of Housing and Urban Development, Office of Policy Development and Research: Publisher of "Rehabilitation guidelines 1980. 7, Plumbing DWV guideline for residential rehabilitation." Publisher: U.S. Dept. of Housing and Urban Development, Office of Policy Development and Research (Washington). Published in 1980.

Victoria. Education Dept. Support Services Unit: Publication of "Introductory plumbing skills program, trial copy; plumbing course - 32 C.D.A. fabricating a 90 internal angle in quadrant spouting: sheetmetal practices unit no.1.10.2.4." (Support Services Unit, Planning Services, Education Department of Victoria). Publisher: Planning Services, Education Dept of Victoria (Melbourne). Published in 1980.

W.E. Rack: Publisher of "Cranwells plumbing, hardware and electrical buyers catalogue." Publisher: W.E. Rack (Auckland). Published in 1980.

Woudhuysen, Jan: Author of "The pocket book of plumbing Jan Woudhuysen." Published in 1980.

1981

Astor Row: The houses were not maintained as Harlem decayed from 1930 - 1990, and the porches were gradually lost. In 1981, New York City declared the entire row to be landmarks and raised funds to restore their facades, and improve their plumbing, heating systems, and electrical lines where needed. The group overseeing and financing the work included the Landmarks Conservancy, Landmarks Preservation Commission, Vincent Astor Foundation, Community Board 10, Abyssian Development Corporation, the Commonwealth Fund, the New York City Department of Housing Preservation and Development, and several local banks. In 1992, Ella Fitzgerald performed at a benefit at Radio City Music Hall to raise money for the restoration. By the end of the 1990s, the porches and other decorative elements had been restored to almost all the buildings on the block. [WP]

Australia. Dept. of Employment and Youth Affairs: Publication of "Roof plumbing: deck fixing and materials." Department of Employment and Youth Affairs. Publisher: A.G.P.S (Canberra). Published in 1981.

Blankenbaker, E. Keith: Author of "Modern plumbing." Publisher: Goodheart-Willcox Co (South Holland, Ill). Published in 1981.

Building Officials and Code Administrators International: Publication of "The BOCA basic plumbing code." Publisher: Building Officials and Code Administrators International (Chicago). Published in 1981.

Butler, Harry; Zanelli, Leo: Authors of "Basic home repairs:central heating plumbing electricity." Translated into Spanish, titled "Manual doméstico de las reparaciones" (translator: Diorki). Publisher: Vidorama (Barcelona). Published in 1981.

Dept. of Further Education: Publisher of "Building services A: resource pack, topic 6, sanitary plumbing." By J. Norton, L.D. Riley, R. Pillion. Publisher: Dept. of Further Education (Adelaide). Published in 1981.

Equiptment News: Publisher of "Domestic heating + plumbing, bathrooms, kitchens." Publisher: Equiptment News (London). Published in 1981.

Hall, Fred: Author of "Plumbing and heating." Publisher: Macmillan (London). Published in 1981.

Hedden, Jay W.: Author of "Modern plumbing for new and old houses: solar collectors, plastic and metal pipe, repairs." Publisher: Creative Homeowner Press (Passiac, NJ). Published in 1981.

Institute of Plumbing, Australia: Publisher of "Australian plumbing engineer." Publisher: Institute of Plumbing, Australia (West Leederville, W.A.). Published in 1981.

International Conference of Building Officials: Publisher of "1981 accumulative supplement to the Uniform Building Code, U.B.C. Standards, Uniform Mechanical Code, ICBO Plumbing Code, Uniform Administrative Code, Uniform Building Security Code, Uniform Fire Code, Uniform Fire Code Standards." Publisher: International Conference of Building Officials (Whittier, Calif). Published in 1981.

Leonardini and Fathy: Publisher of "Health hazards associated with plastic pipe: a status report of the California Pipe Trades Council of the United Association of Journeymen and Apprentices of the Plumbing and Pipe Fitting Industry of the United States and Canada." Prepared by Leonardini and Fathy. Publisher: Leonardini and Fathy (Sacramento, Calif). Published in 1981.

Meikle, Hugh E.: Author of "Plumbing from the ground up." Publisher: Holt, Rinehart & Winston of Canada (Toronto, Ont). Published in 1981.

Sanderson, Barbara: Author of "Getting down to business: plumbing business." Publisher: American Institutes for Research in the Behavioral Sciences (Palo Alto, Calif). Published in 1981.

Scharff, Robert: Author of "Homeowner's guide to plumbing." Publisher: Ideals Pub. Corp (Milwaukee, Wis). Published in 1981.

Technical and Further Education, Western Australia: Publisher of "Course innovations for plumbing training: a paper presented to the sixth National Convention of the Institute of Plumbing, Australia in Hobart, Tasmania, October 1981." F.J. Juracich, L.H. Pyke. Publisher: Technical and Further Education, Western Australia (Perth, W.A.). Published in 1981.

Technical Publications Trust: Publisher of "Plumbing calculations (supplement)." Publisher: Technical Publishers Trust (Perth, W.A.). Published in 1981.

Thiesse, James L.: Author of "Plumbing fundamentals." Publisher: Gregg Division, McGraw-Hill (New York). Published in 1981.

Willers, L. J.: Author of "Report on plumbing industry survey." Publisher: TAFE (Perth, WA.). Published in 1981.

1982

A.G.P.S: Publisher of "Sanitary plumbing Introduction." Department of Employment and Industrial Relations. Publisher: A.G.P.S (Canberra). Published in 1982.

American Society of Plumbing Engineers: Publisher of "ASPE 1982 Convention proceedings: technical papers presented at the eighth biennial convention." Publisher: American Society of Plumbing Engineers (Sherman Oaks, Calif). Published in 1982.

ASPE Convention: Publication of "ASPE 1982 Convention proceedings: technical papers presented at the eighth biennial convention." Publisher: American Society of Plumbing Engineers (Sherman Oaks, Calif). Published in 1982.

Australia. Department Of Employment And Industrial Relations: Publication of "Sanitary plumbing: introduction." Publisher: Australian Gov. Publish. Services (Canberra). Published in 1982.

Australian Govt. Pub. Service: Publisher of "Basic training manual. 10, Sanitary plumbing." Department of Employment and Industrial

Relations. Publisher: Australian Govt. Pub. Service (Canberra). Published in 1982.

Blower, G. J.: Author of "Plumbing: mechanical services." G.J. Blower. Bk 1. Publisher: Longman Scientific & Technical (Harlow). Published in 1982.

Building Officials and Code Administrators International: Publication of "1983 proposed changes to the BOCA basic codes containing proposed changes to the BOCA basic property maintenance code/1981, basic fire prevention code/1981, basic plumbing code/1981, basic mechanical code/1981 (as amended by 1983 supplement)." Publisher: Building Officials and Code Administrators International (Homewood, Ill). Published in 1982.

Construction Industry Press: Publisher of "... 8th biennial ASPE Convention and Engineered Plumbing Exposition." Publisher: Construction Industry Press (Elmhurst, Ill). Published in 1982.

Dept. of Technical and Further Education: Publisher of "1426 - plumbing advanced post trade course syllabus: module 7: 14037 - water supply II." Publisher: Dept. of Technical and Further Education (Sydney). Published in 1982.

Florida. Legislature. Senate. Economic, Community, and Consumer Affairs Committee: Publication of "1982 changes in the definition of plumbing contractor." By staff of the Senate Economic, Community, and Consumer Affairs Committee. Publisher: The Committee (Tallahassee). Published in 1982.

Hall, Ernest: Author of "The David & Charles manual of home plumbing." Ernest Hall; line illustrations by Calvin Brett. Publisher: David & Charles (Newton Abbot). Published in 1982.

Hildebrand, Ron: Author of "Basic plumbing techniques." Created and designed by the editorial staff of Ortho Books; writer (and) illustrator, Ron Hildebrand; photographer, Fred Lyon. Publisher: Ortho Books (San Francisco, CA.). Published in 1982.

Hornung, William J.: Author of "Plumbing and heating." Publisher: Prentice-Hall (Englewood Cliffs, N.J.). Published in 1982.

Institute of Plumbing: Publication of "The pursuit of better standards." Publisher: Institute of Plumbing (London). Published in 1982.

International Association of Plumbing and Mechanical Officials: Publication of "Uniform plumbing code: adopted at the fifty-second annual conference, October, 1981." International Association of Plumbing and Mechanical Officials. Publisher: The Association (Los Angeles). Published in 1982.

International Conference of Building Officials: Publication of "1982 Accumulative supplement to the ICBO plumbing code." Publisher: International Conference of Building Officials (Whittier, Calif). Published in 1982.

International Reference Centre for Community Water Supply and Sanitation: Publication of "Guidelines on health aspects of plumbing." Publisher: IRC (The Hague). Published in 1982.

MacArthur, Colin: Author of "A little poetry, a little plumbing." Publisher: Jewel Books (Miami). Published in 1982.

Massachusetts. Board of State Examiners of Plumbers and Gas Fitters: Publication of "The Commonwealth of Massachusetts fuel gas and plumbing codes: 1982." Board of State Examiners of Plumbers and Gas Fitters. Publisher: Office of the Secretary of the Commonwealtyh (Boston). Published in 1982.

Massey, Howard C.: Author of "Estimating plumbing costs." Publisher: Craftsman Book Co (Carlsbad, Calif). Published in 1982.

Morgan, Robert E.: Author of "The complete handbook of plumbing." Publisher: TAB Books (Blue Ridge Summit, Pa.). Published in 1982.

Mulcahy, Sean: Author of "Architecting the plumbing (slide)." Publisher: Pidgeon Audio Visual (London). Published in 1982.

New York: Publication of "State building construction code applicable to plumbing: including factory manufactured homes." Publisher: New York State Division of Housing and Community Renewal (New York). Published in 1982.

Province of British Columbia: Publisher of "Plumbing: manual of instruction for the plumbing trade." Developed by the Ministry of Education in cooperation with the Ministry of Labour. Publisher: Province of British Columbia

(Victoria). Published in 1982.

Sherry, Gerald B.: Author of "Vocational plumbing." Publisher: Prentice-Hall (Englewood Cliffs, N.J.). Published in 1982.

Technical Publications Trust: Publisher of "Plumbing notes, stage 3B." Publisher: Technical Publishers Trust (Perth, W.A.). Published in 1982.

Wadowsky, R. M., et al.: "Hot water systems as sources of Legionella pneumophila in hospital and nonhospital plumbing fixtures" appears in Applied and Environmental Microbiology written by R. M. Wadowsky, R. B. Yee, L. Mezmar, E. J. Wing and J. N. Dowling. Published in May 1982.

Winter, Fred: Author of "Experimental evaluation of circulation loop drain and vent plumbing modifications for building rehabilitation." Published in 1982.

1983

American Society of Plumbing Engineers,: Publisher of "Fundamentals of plumbing design." Publisher: American Society of Plumbing Engineers, (Sherman Oaks, CA). Published in 1983.

Australia. Department Of Employment And Industrial Relations: Publication of "Sanitary plumbing: connection systems & special disposal." Publisher: Australian Government Publishing Service (Canberra). Published in 1983.

BOCA: Publisher of "The BOCA basic/national plumbing code." Publisher: BOCA (Country Club Hills, IL.). Published in 1983.

Building Officials and Code Administrators International: Publication of "The BOCA basic/national plumbing code." Publisher: Building Officials & Code Administrators International, Inc (Country Club Hills, IL.). Published in 1983.

Canada. Mortgage and Housing Corporation. Technical Research Division: Publication of "Canadian single stack plumbing demonstration project. (Microfiche)." Published in 1983.

Fredriksson, Don: Author of "Plumbing for dummies: a guide to the maintenance and repair of everything including the kitchen sink." By Don Fredriksson; illustrations by Holly Evans Sammons. Publisher: Bobbs-Merrill (Indianapolis). Published in 1983.

Hall, Ernest: Author of "Plumbing in the home Ernest Hall." Published in 1983.

International Conference of Building Officials: Publication of "1983 supplement to the Uniform building code, U.B.C. standards, Uniform mechanical code, Uniform fire code, and the ICBO plumbing code." Publisher: International Conference of Building Officials (Whittier, Calif). Published in 1983.

Ireland, V.: Author of "Survey of the plumbing industry 1983." Publisher: The Board. Published in 1983.

Lane Pub. Co: Publisher of "Sunset Basic plumbing, illustrated." By the editors of Sunset books and Sunset magazine. Publisher: Lane Pub. Co (Menlo Park, Calif). Published in 1983.

National Research Council Canada. Associate Committee on the National Building Code: Publication of "Proposed changes for inclusion in the Canadian Plumbing Code 1985: issued for public review and comment." National Research Council of Canada, Associate Committee on the National Building Code. Publisher: The Committee (Ottawa, Ont). Published in 1983.

New South Wales. Metropolitan Water, Sewerage and Drainage Board: Publication of "Routine instruction 1983/5: approved plumbing and drainage practice: fully vented and fully vented modified systems." M.W.S.D.B. Publisher: The Board (Sydney). Published in 1983.

New Zealand Society of Master Plumbers and Gasfitters: Publisher of "Homeowner plumbing report." Publisher: New Zealand Society of Master Plumbers and Gasfitters (Auckland, N.Z.). Published in 1983.

Pates, Andrew: Author of "Skills for plumbing (written by Andrew Pates with help from Hilary Rosenberg and Ann Freeman) (produced by Basic Skills Unit)." Published in 1983.

Poole, K. A.: Author of "Evaluation of the implementation of the nationally common curricular content and practices in plumbing, gasfitting and draining. paper 5, South Australian findings." Prepared by K.A. Poole. Publisher: Department of Technical and Further Education,

South Australia (Adelaide). Published in 1983.

Queen's Printer: Publisher of "An Act to Amend the Plumbing Installation and Inspection Act = Loi modifiant la Loi sur le montage et l'inspection des installations de plomberie Plumbing Installation and Inspection Act Loi modifiant la Loi sur le montage et l'inspection des installations de plomberie." Publisher: Queen's Printer (Fredericton, N.B.). Published in 1983.

Schuler, Stanley: Author of "The complete home mechanic: a homeowner's guide to plumbing, heating, cooling, and electrical repairs and improvements." Publisher: reston Pub. Co (Reston, Va.). Published in 1983.

Section of Plumbing & Fire Protection Systems, Bureau of Environmental Health, Division of Health, Dept. of Health and Social Services: Publisher of "Drain, waste & vent." Publisher: Section of Plumbing & Fire Protection Systems, Bureau of Environmental Health, Division of Health, Dept. of Health and Social Services (Madison, Wis). Published in 1983.

State of Wisconsin, Dept. of Industry, Labor and Human Relations, Division of Safety and Buildings, Bureau of Plumbing: Publisher of "Initial adverse determination: section ILHR 83.11, Wisconsin administrative code." Publisher: State of Wisconsin, Dept. of Industry, Labor and Human Relations, Division of Safety and Buildings, Bureau of Plumbing (Madison, Wis). Published in 1983.

The Bureau: Publisher of "Excavation & trenching." Developed and distributed by Wisconsin Department of Industry, Labor and Human Relations, Division of Safety and Buildings, Bureau of Plumbing. Publisher: The Bureau (Madison, Wis). Published in 1983.

The Department: Publisher of "Explanatory commentary: the Drainage and Plumbing Regulations 1978." Prepared by the Division of Public Health, Department of Health. Publisher: The Department (Wellington, N.Z.). Published in 1983.

The Section: Publisher of "Back-siphonage, cross-connection, potability control." Wisconsin Division of Health, Bureau of Environmental Health, Plumbing and Fire Protection. Publisher: The Section (Madison, Wis). Published in 1983.

Traister, John E.: Author of "Planning & designing plumbing systems." Publisher: Craftsman Book Co (Carlsbad, CA). Published in 1983.

UPVC Pipe and Fitting Manufacturers Divison: Publisher of "UPVC in plumbing and drainage: training reference manual." Publisher: UPVC Pipe and Fitting Manufacturers Divison (Melbourne). Published in 1983.

Wisconsin Dept. of Industry, Labor & Human Relations, Division of Safety & Buildings, Bureau of Plumbing: Publisher of "Bucky wonders: is the grass greener over your septic system?." Publisher: Wisconsin Dept. of Industry, Labor & Human Relations, Division of Safety & Buildings, Bureau of Plumbing (Madison, Wis). Published in 1983.

1984

Blower, G. J.: Author of "Plumbing: mechanical services." Publisher: Macdonald Evans (Plymouth). Published in 1984.

California. Governor: Publication of "California's water future: policy and plumbing go hand in hand: a special message to the legislature." By Governor George Deukmejian, Thursday, April 5, 1984. Publisher: The Governor? (Sacramento). Published in 1984.

Ciesielski, C. A., et al.: "Role of stagnation and obstruction of water flow in isolation of Legionella pneumophila from hospital plumbing" appears in Applied and Environmental Microbiology written by C. A. Ciesielski, M. J. Blaser and W. L. Wang. Published in November 1984.

Cranwell Publishing Co: Publication of "Cranwells plumbing & hardware: buyers catalogue." Publisher: Cranwell Publishing Co (Auckland (N.Z.)). Published in 1984.

Dept. of Industry and Human Relations, Bureau of Plumbing, Division of Safety and Buildings: Publisher of "Soil tester manual." Publisher: Dept. of Industry and Human Relations, Bureau of Plumbing, Division of Safety and Buildings (Madison, Wis). Published in 1984.

Dumdei, Terrence S.: Author of "Plumbing

technician (AFSC 55275)." (prepared by Terrence S. Dumdei; edited by Naomi E. Combs). Publisher: Extension Course Institute, Air University (Gunter Air Force Station, Ala). Published in 1984.

Hall, Ernest: Author of "Home plumbing Ernest Hall." Published in 1984.

Hartigan, Gerry: Author of "Country plumbing: Living with a septic system." Gerry Hartigan; illustrations by Bob Vogel. Publisher: Alan C. Hood & Company, Inc (Putney, Vt.). Published in 1984.

Henry Francis du Pont Winterthur Museum: Publication of "Plumbing, heating, and cooling.)." Publisher: Clearwater Pub. Co (New York). Published in 1984.

International Association of Plumbing and Mechanical Officials: Publication of "IAPMO installation standards." Published in 1984.

Masterman, Arnold: Author of "Plumbing and mechanical services." Published in 1984.

National Association of Plumbing-Heating-Cooling Contractors: Publisher of "National standard plumbing code, illustrated based upon the 1983 National standard plumbing code." Publisher: National Association of Plumbing-Heating-Cooling Contractors (Washington). Published in 1984.

Plumbing Information Bureau: Publisher of "Complete bathroom kit." Publisher: Plumbing Information Bureau (Wellington, N.Z.). Published in 1984.

Smith, Arthur J.: Author of "Professional plumbing techniques illustrated & simplified." Publisher: tab Books (Blue Ridge Summit, Penn). Published in 1984.

United States. Bureau of the Census: Publication of "1982 census of wholesale trade. Preliminary report. Industry series. Plumbing and heating equipment and supplies (hydronics) (industry 5074)." Publisher: USGPO (Washington, D.C.). Published in 1984.

Worthington, Julian: Author of "Home plumbing: repairs and maintenance." Julian Worthington and David Knight. Publisher: Foulsham (London). Published in 1984.

Wyly, Robert S.: Author of "Field hydraulic performance of one- and two-story residential plumbing systems with reduced-size vents." Robert S. Wyly and Lawrence S. Galowin; sponsored by Tri Services, Department of Defense and Department of Housing and Urban Development. Publisher: National Technical Information Service, distributor. Published in 1984.

1985

Bergwall Productions: Publisher of "Basic plumbing: plastic piping Bergwall Productions." Publisher: Bergwall Productions (Uniondale, N.Y.). Published in 1985.

Bisby, Roger: Author of "Home plumbing (Roger Bisby)." Published in 1985.

Canada. Dept. of National Health and Welfare Social Service Programs Branch: Publication of "Plumbing fixtures." Published in 1985.

D.I.Y: Publisher of "Plumbing (videocassette)." Do-It-Yourself Show; produced by Dan Ellithorpe; directed by Bill Heitz. Publisher: D.I.Y (Charlotte, NC). Published in 1985.

Division of Plumbing: Publisher of "Kentucky state plumbing law, regulations & code, 1985-1986." Publisher: Division of Plumbing (Frankfort, Ky.). Published in 1985.

Fala, Mario J International Association of Plumbing and Mechanical Officials: Publication of "Uniform plumbing code study guide." Published in 1985.

Gregory, Margaret R.: Author of "V-tecs guide for plumbing." Prepared by Margaret R. Gregory, Robert T. Benson. Publisher: Office of Vocational Education, South Carolina Dept. of Education (Columbia, S.C.). Published in 1985.

Gundrey, Walter: Author of "Plumbing, floors and flooring, insulation Walter Gundrey." Published in 1985.

Hall, Ernest: Author of "Home plumbing." Translated into Spanish, titled "Fontanería en el hogar" (translator: Jaime Gavaldá Posiello). Publisher: Marcombo (Barcelona). Published in 1985.

Houston: Publication of "Plumbing code, city of Houston: based on the 1985 edition of the Uniform plumbing code." Publisher: The City (Houston, Tex). Published in 1985.

International Conference of Building Officials: Publisher of "1985 Annual report of the Code Development Committees and 1984 recommendations of the International Association of Plumbing and Mechanical Officials on proposed changes to the Uniform Plumbing Code." Publisher: International Conference of Building Officials (Whittier, Calif). Published in 1985.

James T. Piechowiak: "Polybutylene plumbing fittings and method and apparatus for assembly thereof" is is patented by James T. Piechowiak.

McConnell, Charles: Author of "Home plumbing handbook." Publisher: T. Audel (Boston). Published in 1985.

Millet, Rita: Author of "The plumbing leaks when you sneeze: or, How to laugh at rheumatism, retirement, and geriatric sex." By Rita Millet; (cartoon illustrations by E. Millet). Publisher: La Cote Publishers (French Settlement, LA). Published in 1985.

National Research Council Canada. Associate Committee on the National Building Code: Publication of "Canadian plumbing code, 1985." Issued by the Associate Committee on the National Building Code, National Research Council of Canada. Publisher: NRCC (Ottawa). Published in 1985.

New Zealand Trades Certification Board: Publication of "Examinations for craftsman registration in plumbing & gasfitting." New Zealand Trades Certificate Board. Publisher: New Zealand Trades Certification Board (Wellington (N.Z.)). Published in 1985.

New Zealand. Division of Public Health: Publication of "Code of recommended practice for the design, installation, testing and maintenance of sanitary plumbing and drainage in multi-storey, commercial and industrial premises." Prepared by Division of Public Health, Department of Health. Publisher: The Division (Wellington, N.Z.). Published in 1985.

Posiello, Jaime Gavaldá: Translator of "Home plumbing" by Ernest Hall into Spanish ("Fontanería en el hogar"). Publisher: Marcombo (Barcelona). Published in 1985.

Standards Association of Australia: Publication of "Australian standards for plumbing students." (prepared by the Standards Association of Australia ...). Publisher: Standards Association of Australia (North Sydney, N.S.W.). Published in 1985.

The Centre: Publisher of "Plumbing." Produced by Instructional Design Centre, Educational Resources Branch, N.S.W. Department of Technical and Further Education. Publisher: The Centre (Sydney). Published in 1985.

The Laboratory: Publisher of "Plumbing materials and drinking water quality: proceedings of a seminar, Cincinnati, Ohio May 16-17, 1984." Co-sponsored by Office of Drinking Water, U.S. Environmental Protection Agency and Drinking Water Research Division, Water Engineering Research Laboratory, Office of Research and Development, U.S. Environmental Protection Agency; coordinated by Eastern Research Group, Inc. Publisher: The Laboratory (Cincinnati, Ohio). Published in 1985.

US Army Engineer School: Publisher of "Prepare a plumbing takeoff list. Phase II, Elbows, tees and faucets." Publisher: US Army Engineer School (Fort Belvoir, Va.). Published in 1985.

1986

Alfonso T. Lubrano, et al.: "Low toxicity corrosion resistant solder" is patented by Alfonso T. Lubrano, Thomas S. Bannos, Malcolm Warren and Robert A. Dorvel. Abstract: An article of manufacture, such as is used in plumbing, is formed by soldering copper workpieces together with a lead-free solder having a tin content of from about 92 to 99%, a copper content of from about 0.7 to 6% and a silver content of from about 0.05-3%, by weight.

Australian Building Industry Specifications: Publisher of "NATSPEC: 730 sanitary plumbing: a document of the National Building Industry Specification System (NBISS)." Publisher: Australian Building Industry Specifications (Milsons Point, N.S.W.). Published in 1986.

Butler, Harry; Zanelli, Leo: Authors of "Basic

home repairs: central heating, plumbing and electricity." Translated into Spanish, titled "Manual doméstico de las reparaciones" (translator: Diorki). Publisher: Jaimes Libros (Barcelona). Published in 1986.

Diorki: Translator of "Basic home repairs: central heating, plumbing and electricity" by Harry Butler and Leo Zanelli into Spanish ("Manual doméstico de las reparaciones"). Publisher: Jaimes Libros (Barcelona). Published in 1986.

Hall, Fred: Born in 1924, authored "Plumbing cold water supplies, drainage and sanitation F. Hall." Published in 1986.

Hearst Direct: Publisher of "Popular Mechanics do-it-yourself encyclopedia Volume 19: Plumbing to Power Tools." Publisher: Hearst Direct (New York). Published in 1986.

Illinois: Publication of "Plumbing license law." Publisher: State of Illinois, Dept. of Public Health (Springfield, Ill). Published in 1986.

Lead Development Association: Publication of "Control of lead at work: guidelines for plumbers and plumbing lecturers." Publisher: Lead Development Association (London). Published in 1986.

Mass deacidification: One technique proposed was to place books in an evacuated chamber, then introduce diethyl zinc (DEZ). In theory, the diethyl zinc would react with acidic residues in the paper, leaving an alkaline residue that would protect the paper against further degradation. In practice, the heating required to remove trace water from the books before reaction (DEZ reacts violently with water) caused an accelerated degradation of the paper, and a range of other chemical reactions between DEZ and other components of the book (glues, bindings) caused further damage and the production of unpleasant smells. Regardless, in the 1980s, a pilot plant for mass deacidification using this process was constructed by NASA, but it was discovered in 1986 that the DEZ had not been removed in one of the deacidification runs and was pooled in the bottom of the chamber, and probably remained within some of the plumbing. DEZ is violently flammable in contact with oxygen, so the vacuum chamber could not be opened to remove the books within. Eventually, explosives were used to rupture the suspect plumbing: suspicions of the presence of residual DEZ were confirmed by the subsequent fire that destroyed the plant. [WP]

Master Plumbers' and Mechanical Services Association of Victoria: Publisher of "Victorian plumbing industry journal." Publisher: Master Plumbers' and Mechanical Services Association of Victoria (West Melbourne). Published in 1986.

McGraw-Hill: Publisher of "Plumbing services." Project coordinators: R.J Puffett, L.J. Hossack. Publisher: McGraw-Hill (Sydney). Published in 1986.

National Institute of Building Sciences: Publication of "Plumbing DWV guideline for residential rehabilitation." (prepared by the National Institute of Building Sciences, for the U.S. Department of Housing and Urban Development, Office of Policy Development and Research). Published in 1986.

Plumbing Information Bureau: Publisher of "New Zealand home & plumbing: practical plumbing information, decor and design for New Zealand homes." Publisher: Plumbing Information Bureau (Wellington, N.Z.). Published in 1986.

Puffett, R. J.: Author of "Plumbing services. Volume 4. Mechanical services, air conditioning." Publisher: Mcgraw-Hill (Sydney). Published in 1986.

Queensbridge, Queens: Within last few years elevators have been rebuilt and now stop at floors 1-2-3-4-5. Kitchens have been completely renovated and now have frost free-fridges. 3000 bathrooms were renovated with new tubs, toilets, vanities, floor tile and lighting in 2000+. This followed a renovation in 1986 where 1000 of the bathrooms were renovated by Arc Plumbing, a firm for which the salesman to NYCHA was John Gotti. [WP]

State Building Standards Commission, State and Consumer Services Agency: Publisher of "Annual supplement to the State plumbing code." Publisher: State Building Standards Commission, State and Consumer Services Agency (Sacramento). Published in 1986.

The Bureau: Publisher of "Blueprint & drafting. One." Developed and distributed by Wisconsin

Department of Industry, Labor and Human Relations, Division of Safety and Buildings, Bureau of Plumbing. Publisher: The Bureau (Madison, Wis). Published in 1986.

US Army Engineer School: Publisher of "Student workbook: military plumbing systems." Publisher: US Army Engineer School (Fort Belvoir, Va.). Published in 1986.

1987

Alberta. Alberta Environment. Standards and Approvals Division. Municipal Engineering Branch Alberta. Plumbing and Gas Safety Services Branch Stanley Associates Engineering: Publication of "Standards and recommended design practices for subsurface wastewater treatment and disposal: draft." Prepared by: Stanley Associates Engineering Ltd. Publisher: The Company (Alberta). Published in 1987.

Alth, Max: Born in 1927, authored "Do-it-yourself plumbing." Publisher: Sterling Pub. Co (New York). Published in 1987.

Armpriester, Kate: Born in 1947, authored "Do your own plumbing." Publisher: Popular Science Books (New York, N.Y.). Published in 1987.

Arthur L. Smalley III: "Building construction utilizing plastic components" is patented by Arthur L. Smalley III. Abstract: In a building system, extruded plastic panel components are joined together to form a building structure. External and internal connectors adhesively join the panel components together to form a completed structure. The panel components are internally ribbed and may be partially or fully insulated. Internal conduits in the panel components provide passageways for electrical wiring, plumbing and other required utilities.

Blankenbaker, E. Keith: Author of "Modern plumbing." Publisher: Goodheart-Willcox (South Holland, Ill). Published in 1987.

BRANZ: Publisher of "The Acorn push-fit plumbing system." Publisher: BRANZ (Porirua, N.Z.). Published in 1987.

Building Officials and Code Administrators International. cn: Publication of "The BOCA national plumbing code." Publisher: Building Officials & Code Administrators International (Country Club Hills, Ill). Published in 1987.

California Energy Commission: Publisher of "Directory of plumbing fittings." Publisher: California Energy Commission (Sacramento). Published in 1987.

Canadian Hydronics Council Canadian Institute of Plumbing and Heating: Publication of "Hydronic heating." Publisher: Canadian Hydronics Council. Canadian Institute of Plumbing and Heating. Published in 1987.

Christians, K.: Author of "Validation of plumbing course 32 CDA 1984." Prepared by K. Christians for the TAFE Board of Victoria. Publisher: Victorian TAFE Clearinghouse (Melbourne). Published in 1987.

Donald J. Klein: "Swivel joint" is patented by Donald J. Klein. Abstract: A swivel joint assembly for plumbing systems includes a first fitting having a receptacle end and a second fitting having a plug end positionable in the receptacle end. The plug end and receptacle end having cooperating mating surfaces, one of which has a locking groove divided into first and second portions, the more distal of which is shallower than the other. The other surface has a groove to receive a locking ring also positioned in the locking groove. A barrel end of the plug receives a seal member to seal against the inner surface of the receptical end.

Gerold J. Harbeke: "Plumbing Concrete Form Accessory" is is patented by Gerold J. Harbeke.

Harrison, Gilbert: Author of "Plumbing services water supply." Publisher: Technical Publications Trust (Perth, W.A.). Published in 1987.

Hohhertz, Durwin: Author of "General construction trades. Plumbing: teacher's guide." Prepared by Durwin Hohhertz; revisions by Shelia I. Grant. Publisher: Occupational Curriculum Laboratory, Secondary and Higher Education, East Texas State University (Commerce, Tex). Published in 1987.

Isaev, Vjaceslav Nikolaevic; Sasin, Vitalij Ivanovic; Cistjakov, Nikolaj Nikolaevic: Authors of "Ustrojstvo i montaž sanitarno-tehniceskih sistem zdanij." Translated into English, titled "Plumbing systems" (translator:

Alexander Kuznetsov). Publisher: Mir (Moskva). Published in 1987.

J. L. Mott Iron Works: Publication of "Mott's illustrated catalog of Victorian plumbing fixtures for bathrooms and kitchens." By the J.L. Mott Iron Works. Publisher: Dover Publications; London Constable (New York). Published in 1987.

Joseph D. Cohen: "Full flow multiport butterfly valve" is patented by Joseph D. Cohen. Abstract: A multiport valve with union plumbing connections utilizing a disc diverter of diameter larger than the valve's flow port diameter permanently housed in a spherical two piece welded housing that yields a nonserviceable but easily replaced multiport valve with low resistance. With removable plugs having surfaces shaped to correspond with the interior of the valve, the valve configuration can be changed from four ports to three or two ports at any time. Two external valve coupling flanges located normal to the ports together with clamps and a drop through actuator shaft allow multiple valve operation by a common shaft.

Kish, George R.: Author of "Trace-metal leaching from plumbing materials exposed to acidic ground water in three areas of the coastal plain of New Jersey." By George R. Kish, Jo Ann Macy, and Robert T. Mueller; prepared in cooperation with the New Jersey Department of Environmental Protection, Office of Science and Research. Publisher: Books and Open-File Reports (distributor) (West Trenton, N.J. Dept. of the Interior, U.S Geological Survey; Denver, Colo). Published in 1987.

Kittle, James L.: Born in 1913, authored "Home plumbing made easy: an illustrated manual." James L. Kittle; some illustrations by Gary Mckinney. Publisher: tab Books (Blue Ridge Summit, PA). Published in 1987.

Kuznetsov, Alexander: Translator of "Ustrojstvo i montaž sanitarno-tehniceskih sistem zdanij" by Vjaceslav Nikolaevic Isaev, Vitalij Ivanovic Sasin and Nikolaj Nikolaevic Cistjakov into English ("Plumbing systems"). Publisher: Mir (Moskva). Published in 1987.

Mueller, Jerome F. cn: Author of "Plumbing design and installation details." Publisher: McGraw-Hill (New York). Published in 1987.

Naval Facilities Engineering Command: Publisher of "Plumbing systems." Publisher: Naval Facilities Engineering Command (Alexandria, Va.). Published in 1987.

Neff, Chester H.: Author of "Relationships between water quality and corrosion of plumbing materials in buildings." By Chester H. Neff, Michael R. Schock, and John I. Marden. Published in 1987.

Pays-Bas. Centraal Bureau voor de Statistiek. Hoofdafdeling statistieken van industrie en bouwnijverheid: Publication of "Loodgieters, fitters en sanitairinstallatiebedrijven ... = Building installation: plumbing, fitting." Centraal Bureau voor de Statistiek. Hoofdafdeling statistieken van industrie en bouwnijverheid. Publisher: CBS (Voorburg). Published in 1987.

Peter U. Graefe and Karl T. Kuszaj: "Lightweight, Durable Plumbing Fixture Fabricated from a Delamination-Resistant Multilayer Polymeric Composite" is is patented by Peter U. Graefe and Karl T. Kuszaj.

Raymond J. Lepine Jr. and Eginald F. Roberts Jr: "Safety mechanism for hot-water dispenser" is patented by Raymond J. Lepine Jr. and Eginald F. Roberts Jr. Abstract: Safety mechanisms for a plumbing fixture supplying hot and cold water through a common line. One mechanism is mechanical and the other electrical. The mechanical mechanism makes use of a mechanical linkage between the hot-water valve and an auxiliary cold-water valve to flush residual hot water out of the common line with an excess of cold water. The electrical mechanism uses a microprocessor to activate the cold-water valve when the hot-water valve is shut of, this flushing the residual hot water out of the line with an excess of cold water.

Richard A. Rosen: "Method and means for adapting plumbing valve stems to desired trim" is is patented by Richard A. Rosen.

Rodolfo J. Viegener: "Faucet Assembly Plumbing Fixture" is is patented by Rodolfo J. Viegener.

S.P. Technical Publications: Publisher of "Plumbing & heating." Publisher: S.P. Technical Publishers (Edinburgh). Published in 1987.

Stanley M. Paul: "Valve for Spread Set Plumbing

Fixture and Method of Installation" is is patented by Stanley M. Paul.

Stanton W. Kerr: "Transmission Device for Plumbing Snakes" is is patented by Stanton W. Kerr.

Statistics Canada: Publication of "Metal plumbing fixtures and fittings industry = Industrie des garnitures et raccords de plomberie en métal." Publisher: Statistics Canada (Ottawa). Published in 1987.

The Bureau: Publisher of "Basic & applied math. Appliance." Developed and distributed by Wisconsin Department of Industry, Labor and Human Relations, Division of Safety and Buildings, Bureau of Plumbing. Publisher: The Bureau (Madison, Wis). Published in 1987.

Time-Life Books: Publication of "Kitchen & bathroom plumbing Kitchen and bathroom plumbing." Publisher: Time-Life Books (Alexandria, Va.). Published in 1987.

Trust Publication: Publisher of "29-087 plumbing services water supply. Sections 1-15, 14 assignments." Publisher: Trust Publisher (Perth). Published in 1987.

Victorian TAFE Clearinghouse: Publisher of "Plumbing course 32 CDA assessment issues." For Holmesglen College of TAFE by IBIS-DH & S. Publisher: Victorian TAFE Clearinghouse (Melbourne). Published in 1987.

Wakeford, Alan: Author of "Plumbing Alan Wakeford." Published in 1987.

Wilhelm Hegler and Ralph-Peter Hegler: "Double tubing comprising two protective tubes integrally joined to one another by a web" is patented by Wilhelm Hegler and Ralph-Peter Hegler. Abstract: Double tubing comprises two flexible plastic protective tubes (1, 2), integrally joined with one another via a web (5), which are embodied as corrugated tubes. For installing the double tubing without damage and to prevent deformation of the protective tubes, and in this manner to make them particularly suitable for plumbing applications, fastening holes (11) for fastening screws (17) are embodied in the web (5). Each fastening hole (11) is embodied between two corrugation crests (3) disposed opposite one another in pairs, and in the area of the respective fastening hole (11) the crests (3) are deformed into secant-like defining walls (12) of the respective fastening hole (11).

1988

American Society of Sanitary Engineering: Publisher of "Plumbing dictionary." Published by American Society of Sanitary Engineering; edited by A.S.S.E. Plumbing Nomenclature Committee, J. Russell Boates, Chairman. Publisher: American Society of Sanitary Engineering (Bay Village, OH). Published in 1988.

Black Cat: Publisher of "Home plumbing." Publisher: Black Cat (London). Published in 1988.

California Energy Commission: Publication of "Regulations for appliance efficiency standards relating to refrigerators and freezers, room air conditioners, central air conditioners, gas space heaters, water heaters, plumbing fittings, fluorescent lamp ballasts, luminaires, gas cooking appliances and gas pool heaters." Publisher: California Energy Commission (Sacramento). Published in 1988.

Callow, N.: Author of "From smudge pot to computer: teaching plumbing at RMIT: the first hundred years 1888-1988." Publisher: Royal Melbourne Institute of Technology (Melbourne). Published in 1988.

Canadian Standards Association Standards Council of Canada: Publication of "CSA standards on plumbing fixtures: (including standards on fixtures for use in recreational vehicles)." Prepared by Canadian Standards Association; approved by Standards Council of Canada. Publisher: The Association (Rexdale, Ont). Published in 1988.

Central Wholesalers: Publication of "Central Wholesalers, Inc. plumbing, heating/air conditioning, automotive ... (et al.)." Published in 1988.

Centre scientifique et technique du bâtiment: Publication of "Appareils sanitaires en matériaux de synthèse: guide technique spécialisé pour la constitution d'une demande d'avis technique Sanitary plumbing fixtures made of synthetic materials: specialized technical guide for the constitution of a request for a technical assessment." Publisher: Centre scientifique et technique du bâtiment, (Paris). Published in 1988.

Dept. of the Army, Office of the Chief of Engineers: Publisher of "Plumbing, hospital." Publisher: Dept. of the Army, Office of the Chief of Engineers (Washington, D.C.). Published in 1988.

Donald P. Miller: "TRIPOD STAND FOR A SURVEYOR'S ROD" is patented by Donald P. Miller. Abstract: A portable stand having a frictionally adjustable receiver for a surveyor's rod permits plumbing of the rod and maintains the rod vertical and stationary with respect to a point on the ground.

Doyle, Kenneth M.: Author of "Plumbing and gasfitting. Volume 1, Trade practice and skills." Prepared and edited by Kenneth M. Doyle. Publisher: GP Books (Wellington, N.Z.). Published in 1988.

Ernst Blattler: "Electrically Controlled Plumbing Fixture of a Hot and Cold Water Dispenser" is is patented by Ernst Blattler.

Giorgio Scanferla: "WALL-MOUNTED HOT WATER BOILER OF THE INSTANT TYPE" is patented by Giorgio Scanferla. Abstract: A wall-mounted hot water boiler of the instant type comprises a plurality of plumbing components in fluid communication with one another by plumbing lines preformed on a wall member, which wall member forms a hanging frame for the wall-mounted boiler; the plumbing lines are defined between two juxtaposed metal sheets and provided with fittings for connecting and supporting mechanically respective ones of the plumbing components.

Hall, Fred: Born in 1924, authored "Design calculations for plumbing and heating engineers." Publisher: Longman Scientific & Technical (Harlow). Published in 1988.

Harold Perry: "Plumbing Tool" is is patented by Harold Perry.

Hoffmann, John P.: Author of "Statistical and geodetic approach to monitoring the formation and evolution of the shallow plumbing system at Puu Oo, Kilauea Hawaii." Published in 1988.

Hugo Byers and Tracy H. Lang: "Plumbing Fixture with Interior Insulating and Adhesive Foam" is is patented by Hugo Byers and Tracy H. Lang.

Illiam W. Conger IV: "VIBRATION DAMPENED BLOWER" is patented by Illiam W. Conger IV. Abstract: An air blower for a therapy pool has its motor blower assembly resiliently mounted to the housing for decreased transmission of noise and vibration to the case and attached plumbing. A resilient, elastomeric annulus, reinforced at its inner edge, connects the motor to the blower housing by means of an improved connection between the flexible annulus and the housing. The outer peripheral edge of the flexible annulus is formed with a pair of circumferential locking ribs and a number of circumferentially spaced holes, and this edge is permanently secured to the housing by being molded to and integrally embedded within a housing mounting ring that forms part of the blower housing.

Institute of Plumbing: Publication of "Plumbing engineering services design guide." Compiled and published by the Institute of Plumbing. Publisher: Institute of Plumbing (Hornchurch). Published in 1988.

International Association of Plumbing and Mechanical Officials: Publisher of "Uniform plumbing code: adopted at the fifty-seventh annual conference, September, 1986." Publisher: International Association of Plumbing and Mechanical Officials (Los Angeles, Calif). Published in 1988.

Jackson, Albert: Born in 1943, authored "Plumbing and central heating Albert Jackson and David Day." Published in 1988.

John A. Barclay, et al.: "Slush hydrogen production method and apparatus" is patented by John A. Barclay, Steven R. Jaeger, Peter J. Claybaker, Carl B. Zimm and Steven F. Kral. Abstract: A slush hydrogen production device (10) utilizes a hydrogen slushifier magnetic refrigerator (30) having a wheel (50) of material exhibiting the magnetocaloric effect. The wheel is rotated through a magnetic field of varying intensity around the circumference of a wheel housing (36) created by the windings of superconductive magnets (56). The material of the wheel (50) follows a magnetic Carnot cycle as the wheel rotates (36) through regions of low temperature heat transfer and high temperature heat transfer.

John J. Grasseschi: "Plumbing Sealing System" is is patented by John J. Grasseschi.

Joseph E. Gold/Dalg and Larry G. Mckinney: "AUTOMATED CASTING APPARATUS" is patented by Joseph E. Gold/Dalg and Larry G. Mckinney. Abstract: An apparatus for automated casting of an item such as a plumbing fixture is disclosed. Female and male mold portions provide the spacing for molding the desired item between them. A fluid activated release mechanism is operatively positioned on one of the mold portions so as to assist in separating the formed item from a mold portion in a controlled and uniform manner so as to minimize damage to the cast item. In a preferred manner, there is also a fluid activated holding mechanism for temporarily holding all of the mold portions together as well as an additional fluid activated mechanism to separate the mold halves. The apparatus and method herein described is especially well suited to multiple or battery-type casting operations.

Konrad Bergmann: "ELECTRONIC TEMPERATURE CONTROL SYSTEM" is patented by Konrad Bergmann. Abstract: An electronic temperature control method and apparatus unit for a mixing valve for plumbing fixtures. The loop gain in the control unit is at least approximately inversely proportional to the instantaneous slope of the characteristic curve of the mixing valve, and the slope of the characteristic curve is determined from the instantaneous conditions of valve opening, hot and cold supply temperatures and mix temperatures.

Louie P. Ruiz: "Pressure Test Cap for Plumbing Drain Pipes" is is patented by Louie P. Ruiz.

Luigi F. Bartella: "FLUSH CONTROL SYSTEM FOR PLUMBING FIXTURE" is is patented by Luigi F. Bartella.

Martin J. Laverty Jr: "Disabler and Activation System for Plumbing Fixture" is is patented by Martin J. Laverty Jr.

McConnell, Charles: Author of "Home plumbing handbook." Publisher: Macmillan (New York). Published in 1988.

Means: Publisher of "Means plumbing cost data." Publisher: Means (Kingston, MA). Published in 1988.

Michael M. Lewy: "Apparatus and Method for Polishing a Plumbing or Electrical Fixture" is is patented by Michael M. Lewy.

Oliver, Nicholas Harrie Stuart: Born in 1960, authored "A metamorphic plumbing system (manuscript): the Mary Kathleen Fold Belt, Northwest Queensland, Australia." By Nicholas H.S. Oliver. Published in 1988.

Robert E. Harrington: "CLOSET SPUD TOOL" is patented by Robert E. Harrington. Abstract: A four-way closet spud insertion tool for inserting a spud into a inlet/outlet hole of a plumbing fixture. The closet spud includes a couple having at least one lug protruding inwardly therefrom and a gasket circumscribing the couple, the gasket having a flared portion that is to be inserted into the inlet/outlet hole of the fixture with a portion of the couple, the diameter of the flared portion being greater than the diameter of the hole.

Ronald J. Mrugala, et al.: "BOTTLED WATER COOLER HAVING VENT ON DEMAND DELIVERY SYSTEM" is patented by Ronald J. Mrugala, Doyle Raymer, Dipak J. Negandhi and Robert L. Latzko. Abstract: The vent on demand system for bottled water coolers employs a suction wand having water suction tube, vent tube and air pressure tube for sensing the water level within the bottle. The plumbing system is only exposed to atmospheric air during water dispensing. Air pressure trapped within a bulb well located at the lowermost end of the wand responds to water level within the bottle by changing air pressure which is sensed by a pressure switch employed to disengage the pump when water levels approach empty. A check valve prevents air from entering the water suction tube during bottle replacement and the vent tube is coupled through a vent valve which maintains the water delivery system in a sealed state, only venting to atmosphere during actual water delivery.

Rudy Rosa: "HAND SANITIZING STATION" is patented by Rudy Rosa. Abstract: A sanitizing station suitable for use in institutional kitchens and the like includes a plumbing cabinet, a sink mounted on top of the cabinet and a spray manifold for spraying a sanitizing solution mounted above the sink. The solution is a mixture of water and a sanitizing chemical. A pump is used to inject the sanitizing chemical into a water pipe that is connected to the spray manifold. Tubing connects an outlet of this pump to the pipe. An infrared proximity switch mounted above the sink operates both the pump and a solenoid valve located in the water pipe for a preset period of time upon placement of the user's hands at a predetermined location above or in the sink. A covering hood can be mounted above the sink and it can provide support for the spray manifold and the switch.

Scott E. Moore: "FILTER PUMP HEAD ASSEMBLY IMPROVEMENTS" is patented by Scott E. Moore. Abstract: Valve and channeling improvements in a filter pump head assembly used for dispensing photoresist in a semiconductor manufacturing facility.

Texas State Board of Plumbing Examiners: Publication of "Examination plumbing code and study guide." Texas State Board of Plumbing Examiners. Publisher: The Board (Austin, Tex). Published in 1988.

The Association: Publisher of "Uniform plumbing code illustrated training manual." International Association of Plumbing and Mechanical Officials. Publisher: The Association (Los Angeles). Published in 1988.

The Bureau: Publisher of "Sizing the water supply system." (prepared by the staff of the Bureau of Plumbing). Publisher: The Bureau (Madison, WI). Published in 1988.

The Institute: Publisher of "Plumbing engineering services design guide." Compiled by The Institute of Plumbing. Publisher: The Institute (Hornchurch, Essex). Published in 1988.

1989

Alexander Barenburg: "METHOD OF INSTALLING PIPING, DUCTS AND CONDUITS IN A PREFABRICATED FRAMED WALL FOR A BUILDING STRUCTURE AND PARTITION MADE THEREBY" is patented by Alexander Barenburg. Abstract: A method of making a partition for a prefabricated framed wall to be mounted into a building structure under construction has several steps: cutting at least one hole through each of a plurality of frame studs, a top frame plate, and a bottom frame plate; aligning the plurality of frame studs; securing tops of the frame studs to the top frame plate; securing bottoms of the frame studs to the bottom frame plate; installing plumbing pipes between the frame studs; and inserting either a sanitary tee or a waste pipe connector or a heating/cooling duct through the holes in the bottom frame plate so that they depend therebelow. The sanitary tees connect below a bathroom floor to either a toilet fixture or a bathtub or a shower.

Alfons Rundzaitis, et al.: "HOUSING WITH REPLACEABLE FILTER CARTRIDGE FOR USE WITH SHOWER HEAD" is patented by Alfons Rundzaitis, Jefferson L. Gentry and John R. Jiambalvo. Abstract: A shower filter is adapted to be installed between a plumbing pipe and a shower head. The filter includes a changeable filter cartridge. A three position valve in the appliance is able to (a) block all flow of water, (b) deliver filtered water, or (c) deliver unfiltered water. An adapter may be used to enable the appliance to receive different types of filter cartridges.

Andrew T. Kornylak: "VIBRATION RESISTANT BUILDING CONSTRUCTION" is patented by Andrew T. Kornylak. Abstract: A building that can be constructed quickly in a wide variety of configurations has a sill beam that runs along the perimeter of the building. The plumbing, electrical and other utility needs for the building are channeled through a cavity provided for in the sill beam. Columns are removably mounted on the sill beam according to the desired configuration with exterior and interior panels extending between the columns. Overhead, roof beams extend between columns with roof panels extending between the roof beams. Similarly, the floor is constructed of a plurality of floor panels. The panels forming the exterior walls of the building are pre-finished on both sides.

Annis, William H.: Author of "Basic plumbing skills." Publisher: American Association for

Vocational Instructional Materials (Athens, Ga.). Published in 1989.

Australian Govt. Pub. Service: Publisher of "Roof plumbing: stormwater drainage." Prepared by the Manuals Unit of the Industry Training Services Branch of the Department of Employment and Youth Affairs (DEYA); editor J.R.M. Jentzema. Publisher: Australian Govt. Pub. Service (Canberra). Published in 1989.

Bailey, Thomas Melville: Born in 1912, authored "Organized for action and pride in performance: the history of Local 67, Hamilton, of the United Association of Journeymen and Apprentices of the Plumbing and Pipefitters Industry of the United States and Canada, 1899-1989." By Thomas Melville Bailey History of Local 67, Hamilton. Publisher: United Association, Local 67, Plumbers and Steamfitters (Hamilton, Ont). Published in 1989.

Barlow, Ronald S.: Author of "Vanishing American outhouse: a history of country plumbing." Published in 1989.

Bellarosa, James M.: Born in 1939, authored "A problem of plumbing and other stories." Publisher: distributed by Texas Monthly Press (Santa Barbara, Calif. J. Daniel; Austin, Tex). Published in 1989.

Blower, G. J.: Author of "Plumbing: mechanical services." Published in 1989.

Boy Scouts of America: Publication of "PLUMBING." Publisher: BOY SCOUTS OF AMERICA (IRVING, TEX). Published in 1989.

Bradley Corporation: Publication of "Bradley: security plumbing fixtures." Publisher: The Company (Menomonee Falls, Wi.). Published in 1989.

Bruce E. Wrenn: "JET PROPELLED WATERCRAFT LOADING AND STORING APPARATUS" is patented by Bruce E. Wrenn. Abstract: An apparatus for loading, unloading and storing a jet propelled water vehicle comprising a first pair of tubes made of relatively smooth surfaced plastic plumbing pipe or the like, a second pair of tubes of similar construction which telescope within and extend from the first pair of tubes and devices to adjustably support and space the first pair of tubes on a truck bed, mini-van floor, trailer frame, elevated rack or the like.

Bureau of the Census: Publisher of "Housing: plumbing, equipment, and fuels." Publisher: Bureau of the Census (Washington, DC). Published in 1989.

Connie H. Houghton: "SYSTEM OF CONSERVING WATER IN A BUILDING" is patented by Connie H. Houghton. Abstract: A system of conserving water using non-electrically operated, readily available plumbing equipment. The water to be saved with the system is water once heated which has cooled due to heat loss in a hot water line. This normally wasted cold water in the hot water line is often directed down the drain prior to dispensing of the hot water from a fixture. The system is adapted to divert the normally wasted cold water in the hot water line to a remotely positioned storage tank. The diverting process begins upon manual activation of a by-pass valve positioned slightly upstream of the hot water valve of a typical hot water dispensing fixture. The cold water to be saved is diverted by the manual by-pass valve through by-pass piping leading into the storage tank.

D. William Giroux: "METHOD AND APPARATUS FOR INSTALLATION AND ALIGNMENT OF A SERIES OF POSTS" is patented by D. William Giroux. Abstract: An apparatus for plumbing a series of posts includes a generally vertical frame supported on three operable jacks mounted to form a three-point support for the frame. Each jack is operable to raise or lower that support and thereby align and plumb the frame. The frame includes upper, intermediate and lower horizontal members, vertically spaced-apart and parallel. The horizontal members are comprised of a pair of telescoping halves, so as to be selectively and adjustably extensible. A winch and strap is affixed proximal to each end of each horizontal member, which is operable to hang a post against each end of the frame.

David D. Boyd and Michael W. Johnson: "HOT BEVERAGE PREPARATION AND DISPENSING CART" is patented by David D. Boyd and Michael W. Johnson. Abstract: A portable cabinet is provided for facilitating the operation of espresso and coffe-making machines and for the merchandising of espresso and coffee. The cabinet includes a counter top with at least two beverage preparation stations at different levels, one for preparing espresso and the other for preparing coffee. An internal fresh water supply and plumbing system enables the cabinet to be used at locations where a continuous supply of fresh water is unavailable. Filtered water from a holding tank is supplied to both beverage preparation stations on the top counter. A power distribution system built into the cabinet supplies electric power to both beverage preparation stations and to built-in lighting within the canopy which extends over the top counter.

Delta Communications: Publisher of "DE, domestic engineering magazine for plumbing, piping, hydronics." Publisher: Delta Communications (Elmhurst, Il). Published in 1989.

Domingo Tovar: "WATER PURIFICATION DEVICE" is patented by Domingo Tovar. Abstract: The water purification device includes a hollow casing split into a pair of mating sections releasably connected together for easy access to the inside of the casing. A water pipe is disposed in the casing, extends out opposite ends thereof and bears connectors for connection to water-bearing plumbing and the like. A non-rotating removable and replaceable water impeller having a spaced number of blade segments is disposed longitudinally on the water pipe to control mixing and the residence time of water passing through the pipe.

EBSCO Curriculum Materials: Publisher of "Victorian-era Indoor Plumbing. ca. 1890. (slide) --." Publisher: EBSCO Curriculum Materials (Birmingham, Alabama). Published in 1989.

Eric C. Peterman and John S. Lindstedt: "METHOD OF DECORATING AN EXPANSIVE SURFACE OF A METALLIC FAUCET SPOUT OR OTHER PLUMBING FIXTURE" is is patented by Eric C. Peterman and John S. Lindstedt.

Fernand Bertrand: "FOLDING BUILDING STRUCTURE" is patented by Fernand Bertrand. Abstract: A refoldable and transportable rigid building which requires no load bearing interior walls and further permits the permanent placement of plumbing and plumbing fixtures almost anywhere within the periphery of the exterior walls. Upon unfolding, the structural components of the building become fast on one another providing a rigid building which is capable of resisting substantial racking and compression stresses without loss of integrity. Folding and unfolding of the building may be accomplished with the use of hand tools only. A sixty per cent volume reduction is achieved on folding and when folded the structure may be handled by a forklift and/or supported on a pair of dollies.

Florida. Legislature. Senate. Committee on Health Care: Publication of "A Review of the Advisory Council for Uniform Interpretation of the State Plumbing Code; prepared pursuant to the Sundown Act." By staff of the Florida Senate Committee on Health Care. Publisher: The Committee (Tallahassee, Fla). Published in 1989.

Frozen Dead Guy Days: In 1989, a Norwegian citizen, Trygve Bauge, brought the corpse of his recently-dead grandfather, Bredo Morstel, to the town of Nederland. When Trygve was deported from the United States for overstaying his visa, his mother, Aud, continued on in the shack, keeping her father's body cryogenically frozen in a shack behind her unfinished house. Aud was eventually evicted from her home for living in a house with no electricity and plumbing, in violation of local ordinances. At that time, she told a local reporter about her father's body, and the reporter went to the local city hall in order to let them know about Aud's fears that her eviction would cause her father's body to thaw out. [WP]

Gary George: "FIRE EXTINGUISHING DEVICE FOR THE HOME HEATING PLANT UTILIZING AN EXISTING SPIGOT AS THE WATER SOURCE" is patented by Gary George. Abstract: An automatic fire sprinkler of commercial grade is installed in a domestic dwelling independent of existing plumbing and without alteration of the plumbing in the dwelling. The automatic sprinkler head is connected to one end of a flexible hose. The opposite end of the hose is connected to an existing spigot to the water supply of a central heating unit, hot water heater or the like. The spigot may be a drain outlet or other outlet. The opposite end of the hose may also be connected to a water faucet which provides water to the domestic clothes washing machine. The fire sprinkler head is hung above the heat system or clothes washer/dryer. In response to a fire the sprinkler automatically sprays water from the existing water supply to the immediate area.

George L. Fuller: "HEMISPHERICAL SUNDIAL WITH INSTALLATION INDICIA" is patented by George L. Fuller. Abstract: A sundial with a concave hemispherical body and top surface generally horizontal has longitude displacement, latitude, sun declination, and time indicia originating at the spherical gnomon located at the spherical center of the hemisphere. Site set up is accomplished by plumbing the gnomon over the site latitude and longitude displacement indicia and then rotating on a horizontal surface until the correct time is indicated by the shadow of the gnomon from the sun. Two six-month sundials or two removably attachable inserts are used for indication of watch time for complete years.

Gilbert J. Rietsch: "CAR WASH WASHER INSTALLATION" is patented by Gilbert J. Rietsch. Abstract: A side washer installation for an automatic car wash line in which each side washer is bottom mounted on a mounting arrangement comprised of a swing arm having upwardly extending drive shaft over which the washer is mounted. An internal web plate is secured within each washer cylinder which rests atop a flange attached to the drive shaft, the flange bolted to the web plate at assembly. The drive motor and associated hardware are located beneath each side washer to remove this componentry from the field of view of the occupants of vehicles passing down the wash line.

Harold D. Waltenburg: "FLUID SUPPLY LINE FLOW CONTROL DEVICE" is patented by Harold D. Waltenburg. Abstract: The present invention deals broadly with the field of plumbing. ore narrowly, however, it deals with apparatus for controlling flow through a fluid supply line. The preferred embodiment of the invention is directed to a mechanism for automatically terminating flow through a fluid supply line when flow through the line continues for a period of time greater than a defined time, such as when a break in the line occurs.

Harvey Rodstein: "CARTRIDGE VALVE" is patented by Harvey Rodstein. Abstract: A faucet valve is operated by a rotatable stem which is inserted in a tube-shaped housing. The valve, preferably composed of brass, is screwed into a standard size plumbing fixture. The body of the stem is disposed between a washer preferably made of teflon and an "O" ring, which exerts a pressure between said body of the stem and the tube. The pressure does not generally vary according to the fluid pressure therein or fluid flow therethrough enabling the valve to be used in high pressure applications. A stationary valving member within the housing mates with a cooperating rotatable valving member which is driven by the stem.

Iain M. Smith: "KNOCKDOWN BATHING ENCLOSURE" is patented by Iain M. Smith. Abstract: A knockdown type bathing enclosure is disclosed. It can be manufactured as a one-piece plumbing fixture, cut into portions for transportation, and assembled at the installation site. The bathing enclosure has a joining strip attached to an external side of a wall structure. The joining strip has an attachment surface for abutting the wall structure, and an outer tubular bulge. The joining strip and the wall structure are cut into portions along a plane passing through the tubular bulge. A plurality of locator members are then inserted into an internal slot formed in each portion of the cut tubular bulge. Guided into proper alignment by the locator members, the cut portions are then fastened together using a clamp member.

Institute of New Zealand Plumbing & Drainage Inspectors. Conference: Publication of "Institute of New Zealand Plumbing and Drainage Inspectors Inc. Conference '89: addresses, items of interest from conference, 6th to 9th March 1989." Publisher: The Institute (Palmerston North?, N.Z.). Published in 1989.

James F. Helderman: "IMMEDIATELY ACCESSIBLE WALL AND CEILING SYSTEM" is patented by James F. Helderman. Abstract: A wall and ceiling furring and panel system for an interior side or ceiling wall of a building utilizes parallel furring strips and other panel supporting components which are fixed to the frame members of the wall and which provide panel support surfaces one of which is of relatively narrow width and the other of which is of relatively wide width. Immediate access to plumbing, wiring or other utilities behind the wall or above the ceiling is gained by sliding or lifting a panel to provide an opening at the desired point of entry. The system is adaptable for use with any conventional wallboard and with wood or metal studs.

John F. Whiteside: "TUBULAR TAILPIECE FOR A FLUSH VALVE" is patented by John F. Whiteside. Abstract: A tubular connection for a plumbing fixture such as a flush valve includes a conduit, one end of which is formed and adapted to extend within an opening in the plumbing fixture. The plumbing fixture opening includes an exterior peripheral stop. The conduit has a peripheral recess spaced from the end within the plumbing fixture opening, with a seal ring being positioned within the recess and in sealing contact with the opening and the conduit. The conduit has an outward peripheral projection, adjacent the recess, which projection is positioned against the peripheral stop of the plumbing fixture.

John M. Garrison: "RUNOFF WATER TRAP" is patented by John M. Garrison. Abstract: A device for collecting liquid samples of runoff water. The device is configured such that it does not collect any sample until a predetermined amount of runoff water has flowed. At that time, a predetermined water quantity is allowed to enter a water storage area. Once this water storage area is full, a closure occurs, and further water cannot be trapped. In the most preferred embodiment of this invention, the entire structure is formed of PVC plumbing materials. A first embodiment of the invention is adapted to be mounted vertically and uses a check valve and a float. A second embodiment of the invention is adapted for use in a runoff sewer, and collects water when the water flow is above a certain height.

Joseph A. Giametta: "WASTE PIPE CONNECTOR" is patented by Joseph A. Giametta. Abstract: A plumbing fitting for coupling a urinal or water closet to the drain waste pipe whether it be copper, PVC, steel or cast iron pipe without using any adapters, threaded pipe or glue. The fitting having a cylindrical body divided longitudinally into two arcuate members having a pipe receiving socket, and a pair of horizontal bars extending perpendicularly from the longitudinal sides of the cylindrical body. The fitting also consists of a protrusion extending from the receiving socket and a flexible gasket positioned on the inside of the cylindrical body having a lip that envelopes the protrusion.

Kathie K. Jones: "URINAL FOR USE BY FEMALE INDIVIDUALS" is patented by Kathie K. Jones. Abstract: A plumbing fixture for installation in women's rooms that enables female individuals to urinate from a standing position. An elongate flexible hose has a urine-collecting funnel at its top end and its bottom end is in communication with a water-holding bowl that is flushed by a siphoning action. A sanitary cuff lines the rim of the funnel so that the funnel does not contact the body of the user, and the cuff is knocked off the funnel after use by a passive ejector arm when the funnel is suspended between the arms of a hanger member.

Kay L. Tucker and Ulysses Ma: "LOW TOXICITY ALLOY COMPOSITIONS FOR JOINING AND SEALING" is patented by Kay L. Tucker and Ulysses Ma. Abstract: A lead-free alloy for joining and sealing which is useful as a plumbing solder comprises from 0.08 to 20% by weight of bismuth, from 0.02 to 1.5% by weight of copper, from 0.01 to 1.5% by weight of silver, from 0 to 0.10 percent by weight of phosphorus, from 0 to 0.20% of a rare earth mixture and the balance tin, together with incidental impurities. The alloy has a similar pasty range (i.e. melting temperature and melting range) to the traditional tin-lead plumbing solders.

Kenneth R. Jerkins: "BACKWATER ESCAPE VALVE" is patented by Kenneth R. Jerkins. Abstract: A backwater escape valve for plumbing systems comprising a cylindrical body adapted to be coupled to a drainpipe system at the opening normally occupied by a sealing plug, and having a vertically disposed outflow opening covered with a hinged, spring-loaded cover which is adapted to be forced open when the associated sewer becomes blocked and water rises in the associated vertical drainpipe to or near the lowest sink or bathtub coupled thereto.

Konrad Bergmann and Axel Enthoven: "COMBINATION SANITARYWARE AND FITTING" is patented by Konrad Bergmann and Axel Enthoven. Abstract: A sanitary fitting and plumbing fixture, such as a sink, bathtub or lavatory, are so arranged such that the actuating lever and spout are disposed in recesses formed in the plumbing fitting, the spout being constructed so that when water is flowing through the fitting, it is discharged from the spout in a waterfall-like fashion.

M. R. Gill: "WATER CONSERVATOR SYSTEM AND METHOD" is patented by M. R. Gill. Abstract: A water conserving system for plumbing installations in buildings, for instance in homes, institutions, industry, etc., facilitates saving of water during adjustment of volume and temperature and precludes the need for water shut-off and subsequent readjustment to accomodate suspensions of actual water use while saving, for reuse, the water that otherwise flows unused to drain and into the sewer system.

McReynolds, Ray: Author of "Home plumbing: a step-by-step guide." Publisher: Self-Counsel Press (North Vancouver, B.C.). Published in 1989.

Minnesota Association of Plumbing-Heating-Cooling Contractors: Publisher of "Minnesota plumbing, heating, cooling contractor." Publisher: Minnesota Association of Plumbing-Heating-Cooling Contractors (Minneapolis, MN). Published in 1989.

PBS HOME VIDEO: Publisher of "CREATING A NEW KITCHEN, PART 1. PLUMBING AND ELECTRICITY (VIDEO)." Publisher: PBS HOME VIDEO (BEVERLY HILLS, CA). Published in 1989.

Pietro Rollini and Domenic Luisi: "VALVE ASSEMBLY FOR PLUMBING FIXTURE" is is patented by Pietro Rollini and Domenic Luisi.

Plumbers, Gasfitters & Drainlayers Board: Publisher of "Plumbing and gasfitting: a career with a future." Publisher: Plumbers, Gasfitters & Drainlayers Board (Wellington, N.Z.). Published in 1989.

Ray Imhoff and Sadraddin Seif: "WATER CONSERVATION DEVICE" is patented by Ray Imhoff and Sadraddin Seif. Abstract: Herein described is a compact and self-contained circular water conservation device which can be easily installed in conjunction with existing and non-existing plumbing systems and fixtures having a source of pressurized water, a hot water supply line, a cold water supply line, a hot water heater, and outlet fixtures coupled to the hot and cold water supply lines. The water conservation device includes essentially an elecric water pump for pumping water from the hot water supply line into a solenoid valve. The solenoid valve prevents the mixture of hot and cold water systems. The solenoid valve is coupled to the cold water line directly leading to and coupled to an outlet fixture.

Richard W. Grabenkort, et al.: "METHOD OF PACKAGING FOR A STERILIZABLE CALIBRATABLE MEDICAL DEVICE" is patented by Richard W. Grabenkort, Scott P. Huntley and Sheldon M. Wecker. Abstract: The present invention provides a package for and method of packaging a sterilizable calibratable medical device including a hydratable sensor component. The device is maintained in a sterile environment during storage and in a clean environment during the calibration procedure. The package includes a manifold connected to the sensor component by plumbing. The plumbing establishes fluid communication between the manifold and the sensor component and/or between the sensor component and the ambient environment of the plumbing. The manifold, plumbing and medical device are sealed in a wrap including a gas-permeable surface.

Ronald C. Zentner and Steven A. Smith: "MECHANIZED FLUID CONNECTOR AND ASSEMBLY TOOL SYSTEM WITH BALL DETENTS" is patented by Ronald C. Zentner and Steven A. Smith. Abstract: A fluid connector system including a modified plumbing union having a rotatable member for drawing said union into a fluid tight condition. A drive tool is electric motor actuated and includes a reduction gear train providing an output gear engaging an integral peripheral spur gear on the rotatable member. A housing member attached to the connector assembly provides coaxial alignment for an interface socket on the drive tool. A hand lever actuated latching system includes a plurality of circumferentially spaced latching balls selectively wedged against the housing member attached to the connector assembly or to secure the drive tool to the connector assembly with its output gear in mesh with the integral peripheral spur gear. The drive motor is torque, spped and direction controllable.

The Association: Publisher of "Dwelling requirements of the Uniform plumbing code." International Association of Plumbing and Mechanical Officials. Publisher: The Association (Walnut, Calif). Published in 1989.

The Bureau: Publisher of "Builder's level." Developed and distributed by Wisconsin Department of Industry, Labor and Human Relations, Division of Safety and Buildings, Bureau of Plumbing. Publisher: The Bureau (Madison, Wis). Published in 1989.

Thomas E. Nelson: "TRUSS SETTING SYSTEM" is patented by Thomas E. Nelson. Abstract: Prefabricated metal truss units have depending set wedges and lateral notches to rapidly center them and snap them into predetermined positions over underlying substructure made up of prefabricated metal wall panels having U-shaped channel truss locks along their upper surfaces. Diagonal members centnrally pivoted to the king posts of prefabricated roof truss units have angularly oriented plumb lock elements that interconnect with king posts of adjacent units to quickly establish vertical plumbing. The tail ends of top chords are provided with soffit framework for rapid soffit plate and fascia attachment. The upper surfaces of top chords are marked to locate the first run of roof sheathing.

Thurman J. Carmody, et al.: "REUSABLE PLUMBING TEST PIPE" is is patented by Thurman J. Carmody, Arthur D. Mcwilliams and James S. Bauer.

Treloar, R. D.: Author of "Mechanical engineering services: a plumbing encyclopaedia." Publisher: BSP (Oxford). Published in 1989.

United Association of Journeymen and Apprentices of the Plumbing and Pipe Fitting Industry of the United States and Canada: Publisher of "100 years of pride, UA, 1889-1989." Publisher: United Association of Journeymen and Apprentices of the Plumbing and Pipe Fitting Industry of the United States and Canada (Washington, D.C.). Published in 1989.

Vincent Lo Guidici: "PREFABRICATED DWELLING UNIT" is patented by Vincent Lo Guidici. Abstract: There is disclosed a prefabricated dwelling capable of being employed on a single dwelling unit or in cooperative relationship with one or more like dwelling units, the dwelling unit having a body member provided with a wooden floor, a pair of corrugated side walls attached to the floor around the periphery thereof and enclosing the area above the floor, a cover member attached to the side walls opposite the floor and a door at level one and at least one window located in the side walls, the corrugations of the side walls facing toward the interior of the dwelling unit and forming supporting and strengthening studs therefor.

William J. Lund: "ACCELERATED HOT WATER DELIVERY SYSTEM" is patented by William J. Lund. Abstract: A plumbing system in accordance with the present invention provides for accelerated hot water delivery to a plurality of plumbing fixtures from a hot water source. Flow switch means are provided to enable a pump to circulate hot water to the plumbing fixtures in response to water being withdrawn from a plumbing fixture. In addition, the hot water source may include a hot water recovery apparatus for withdrawing hot water from circulation pipes subsequent to cessation of water flow from a plumbing fixture.

1990

Alexander Barenburg: "FRAMED WALL WITH A PREFABRICATED UNDERFLOOR DRAIN LINE AND METHOD OF MANUFACTURE" is patented by Alexander Barenburg. Abstract: A method of manufacturing a prefabricated framed wall to be mounted in a floor of a building structure under construction has several steps: cutting at least one hole through all but one of a plurality of frame studs, a top frame plate, and a bottom frame plate; aligning the plurality of frame studs; securing tops of the frame studs to the top frame plate; securing bottoms of the frame studs to the bottom frame plate; installing plumbing and other pipes between the frame studs; and inserting at least one sanitary tee through the hole in the bottom frame plate so that it depends therebelow. The one sanitary tee connects below the floor to either a bathtub or a shower. An underfloor drain line is connected to at least one fixture, such as a bathtub/shower, a toilet and a lavatory.

Alvie E. Everhart: "Plumb-align device" is patented by Alvie E. Everhart. Abstract: An apparatus for conveniently plumb-aligning walls is provided. The apparatus includes an anchor for pivotally attaching the device to the ground. The anchor is attached to a support member for positioning a tubular member at a convenient height for manual manipulation. Extending upwardly from the tubular member is an extender. Attached to the end of the extender is a bracket member for clasping the top of the wall which is to be plumbed. The tubular member is equipped with a threaded rod disposed therein.

Bureau of Mines: Sponsored research "Minerals Yearbook, 1990: Feldspar, Nepheline Syenite, and Aplite. - Annual rept." Sponsored by: Bureau of Mines, Washington, DC. Written by M. J. Potter. Abstract: Feldspars are major components in most igneous rocks and constitute a large part of at least the outer layers of the Earth and its moon. Feldspar, usually of the potash or soda type or in mixtures of the two, finds its principal end uses in the manufacture of glass and ceramics. Feldspar acts as a flux and lowers the melting temperature of a ceramic mixture. In glassmaking, feldspar provides a source of alumina, which enhances the workability of the product and increases its chemical stability. Feldspar consumption in glass containers and pottery remained flat during the first half of 1990 and decreased in the second half of the year.

Bureau of the Census: Sponsored research "Census of Manufactures, 1987. Industry Series: Heating Apparatus (Except Electric and Warm Air Furnaces) and Plumbing Fixtures. Industries 3431, 3432, and 3433." Sponsored by: Bureau of the Census, Washington, DC. Abstract: The report shows 1987 Census of Manufactures statistics for establishments classified in each of the following industries: Metal Sanitary Ware; Plumbing Fixture Fittings and Trim; and Heating Equipment, Except Electric. The industry statistics (employment, payroll, cost of materials, value of shipments, inventories, etc.) are reported for each establishment as a whole. Aggregates of such data for an industry reflect not only the primary activities of the establishments but also their activities in the manufacture of secondary products as well as their miscellaneous activities (contract work on materials owned by others, repair work, etc.).

California Energy Commission: Publication of "Appliance efficiency standards for refrigerators and freezers, room air conditioners, central air conditioners, gas space heaters, water heaters, plumbing fittings, fluorescent lamp ballasts, luminaires, gas cooking appliances and gas pool heaters." Publisher: California Energy Commission, ? (Sacramento). Published in 1990.

Carlton L. Whiteford: "ILLUMINATED LEVEL" is patented by Carlton L. Whiteford. Abstract: The bubble vials of a carpenter's level are individually illuminated by a respective light emitting diode (LED) energized from a battery supported within the body of the level. Charge on the batteries is maintained by one or more solar cells mounted on an exterior surface of the body, and the LED's are energized by a control circuit including a normally open manually actuable switch and a pair of mercury switches supported within the body at different fixed orientations relative thereto such that one of them closes when the body is horizontally oriented to apply voltage to the LED for the horizontal bubble vial, and the other closes when the body of the level is vertically oriented and connects the battery to the LED for the bubble vials of the plumbing levels.

1990

Consumers Union: Publisher of "Preventive home maintenance: how to detect and prevent structural, electrical, plumbing, and other common problems in your home." The American Society of Home Inspectors and the editors of Consumer Reports Books. Publisher: Consumers Union (Mount Vernon, N.Y.). Published in 1990.

Cowgate Communications: Publisher of "HPAC, Heating plumbing air conditioning magazine buyer's guide & wholesale directory." Publisher: Cowgate Communications (Don Mills, Ont). Published in 1990.

David E. Gayton: "BACKFLOW PREVENTER AND VACUUM BREAKER" is patented by David E. Gayton. Abstract: An omnidirectional backflow preventer and vacuum breaker for use with a plumbing fixture in which the discharge may be moved to a position within a body of water includes a body having an inlet and an outlet, a chamber connecting the inlet and outlet and an air vent opening into the chamber. There is a diaphragm positioned within the chamber which normally closes communication between the inlet and outlet. The diaphram prevents water seepage from the outlet from reaching the air vent and has an integral one-way check valve positioned at the inlet which permits air from the vent to pass to the inlet to remove a vacuum condition therein.

David G. Lewandowski and Edward J. Guard: "URINAL FOR CONVENIENCE AND TRAINING OF JUVENILE MALES" is patented by David G. Lewandowski and Edward J. Guard. Abstract: A urinal provided for the convenience and training of juvenile boys in accordance with this invention requires no plumbing, and comprises a support means having front and rear surfaces. The rear surface is adapted for attachment to a vertical surface, and the front surface has a receptacle-receiving lower portion. A dish shaped urine-receiving receptacle is utilized, with its lower portion having a configuration closely complementary to the lower portion of the support means. The receptacle has a full height rear wall and a front wall of abbreviated height, with the upper portions of the wall portions terminating in a generally oval front opening.

Donald K. Pollard: "PLUMBING SLEEVE" is patented by Donald K. Pollard. Abstract: A pipe coupling is described suitable for joining together drainage, or other, plastic piping through a poured concrete layer, typically a floor. The coupling permits precise location of fittings, such as a toilet flange, after the concrete has been poured and set.

Donald N. Jursich and Jefferson L. Gentry: "SHOWER SHAVER" is patented by Donald N. Jursich and Jefferson L. Gentry. Abstract: A shower shaver is made from two plastic piece parts. A first part is a handle in the nature of a pipe terminating in a fan-shaped or flared, tray like top surface. The other piece part is a cover or top which fits over and cooperates with the tray top to form a cavity which delivers a flared sheet of water toward orifices which cause the water to strike to a broad surfaces of said blade and then exits under the cutting edge of the blade with enough force to wash debris away from the blade. A notch beneath the flaired surface delivers a stream of water to the skin in advance of the cutting edge. A tubing or hose attached to the shower shaver razor leads to a nipple which may be interposed between a shower head and a plumbing pipe.

Donald R. Grunwald: "PLUMBING ELBOWS OR BENDS" is patented by Donald R. Grunwald. Abstract: A plumbling fitting in the form of an elbow or bend is formed of standard radius at the extrados in order to provide a fitting of minimal size, and, is expanded outwardly intermediate its ends at positions other than at the extrados, in order to increase the internal cross-sectional area of the elbow or bend intermediate the ends thereof and minimize pressure losses in the elbow or bend. A major portion of the cross sectional area is located in the vicinity of the extrados, thus positioning the centroid of that area and the longitudinal axis of the elbow or bend at a location displaced towards the extrados and displaced radially outwardly along the radius of the extrados, thus providing a reduced pressure loss comparable to an elbow or fitting of larger size.

Doyle, Kenneth M.: Author of "Plumbing and gasfitting. Vol. 2, Services and roofing." Prepared and edited by Kenneth M. Doyle. Publisher: Plumbing, Gas & Drainlaying Training

Foundation (Wellington, N.Z.). Published in 1990.

EG and G Mound Applied Technologies: Sponsored research "Corrosion of copper in Mound's single-pass potable water systems." Sponsored by: EG and G Mound Applied Technologies, Miamisburg, OH.; Department of Energy, Washington, DC. Written by P. M. Schleitweiler and P. S. Miller. Abstract: An increase in the number of copper plumbing failures at Mound prompted a thorough analysis of the failed components. Most of the components were elbow joints. All of these parts exhibited the same type of accelerated deterioration. The failed parts were analyzed optically and by scanning electron microscopy. Water chemistry, solder, and soldering fluxes were evaluated to determine their possible roles in the accelerated attack. Cross-sectioning of the elbow joints revealed residual soldering flux and cutting burrs on the inside of the elbows. Water analysis showed Mound's water was rated as corrosive. Recommendations for improved workmanship and design are presented. Testing of potable water at a regular basis was also recommended. 8 refs., 10 figs., 3 tabs.

Energy Concepts Co.: Sponsored research "Intermittent Solar Ammonia Absorption Cycle (ISAAC) refrigeration for lesser developed countries. Final report, April 23, 1987-October 22, 1989. - Progress rept." Sponsored by: Energy Concepts Co., Annapolis, MD.; Department of Energy, Washington, DC. Written by D. C. Erickson. Abstract: The Intermittent Solar Ammonia Absorption Cycle (ISAAC) refrigerator is a solar thermal technology which provides low cost, efficient, reliable ice-making to areas without ready access to electricity. An ISAAC refrigeration system consists of a compound parabolic solar collector, two pressure vessels, a condenser, a cold box or refrigerated space, and simple connective piping -- no moving parts or electrical components. Most parts are simple construction or plumbing grade materials, locally available in many remote areas. This technology has numerous potential benefits in lesser developed countries both by providing a cheap, reliable source of ice, and, since manufacture requires only semi-skilled labor, a source of employment to the local economy.

F. Budd Ferre, et al.: "MANUAL, SELF-CONTAINED, FREE-STANDING, VEHICLE WASHING/CLEANING CENTER" is patented by F. Budd Ferre, Rowell Sims, Vibert L. Kesler and James B. Mayfield. Abstract: A transportable, self-contained work site, designed specifically to facilitate manual vehicle washing and engine cleaning, comprising a rigid skeletal structure which is constructed of preformed, connectable modules and a lightweight raised platform or flooring which slopes inwardly to capture liquids for recycling.

Francis C. Bauer: "FORAGE TREATMENT, GRANULAR MATERIAL DISTRIBUTOR" is patented by Francis C. Bauer. Abstract: A distributor of granular material for the treatment of forage is disclosed including an air manifold suspended by a parallelogram system from a dispenser. The lower ends of the arms of the parallelogram system are pivotably and slideably mounted to the manifold by bolts extending from the air manifold through apertures formed in the arms to allow the air manifold to slide as the metering rate of the dispenser is adjusted. The discharge tubes for the granular material terminate beyond and below the air tubes of the air manifold.

Francis J. Fuoco: "MODULAR COOLING FIXTURE FOR POWER TRANSISTORS" is patented by Francis J. Fuoco. Abstract: A modular cooling fixture for power transistors include a carrier plate. Transistors are mounted to the plate and insulated transistor leads pass through openings formed in the plate for connection to a printed circuit board. Spacers fasten the board to the carrier plate so that a removable assembly for the transistors is created. A chill plate is juxtaposed in contact with the carrier plate and recesses are formed in the chill plate so that the hat portions of the transistors project into the chill plate, thereby enabling thermal juxtaposed contact between the chill plate and the carrier plate. Passageways are formed through the chill plate to enable the circulation of cooling liquid therethrough.

Frank S. Fischer: "MIXING FAUCET ROTARY BRAKE" is patented by Frank S. Fischer.

Abstract: A control valve for use in plumbing fittings such as shower control valves or the like includes a housing, a valve member within the housing, and a handle attached to the rotatable stem of the valve member. The handle and valve stem are rotatable relative to the housing to control discharge from the valve. There are cooperating stops on the handle and housing limiting rotation of the valve stem. The improvement comprises a device for retarding rotational movement of the handle and stem relative to the housing.

Fred J. Meyer and Samuel L. Jacks: "DRAIN AUGER" is patented by Fred J. Meyer and Samuel L. Jacks. Abstract: A storage container for a drain cleaning plumbing tool such as a snake or auger having an apertured rear wall is provided with a closure member rotatably mounted to the portion of the rear wall surrounding the aperture. The closure member includes a lever arm and a hook member attached to the radially outer end of the lever arm and a drive rod fixed to said closure member along an axis of rotation. A handle radially offset from said axis of rotation extends axially rearward from said apertured wall.

Fred Sparling and Wilfred Maloney: "Remote nozzle unit" is patented by Fred Sparling and Wilfred Maloney. Abstract: There is described a portable water monitor for fire fighting, irrigating or other watering purposes. The water invention is of compact, stable, light-weight configuration. The device has a base unit which may be filled with water to increase the weight of the unit when deployed in the field. Compact plumbing is provided which permits the monitor nozzle to be rotated 360.degree. in the horizontal direction about a vertical axis swivel coupling and to be elevated and depressed in a ball and socket coupling. The ball and socket coupling additionally provides that the monitor nozzle may be offset relative to the swivel action coupling on the ball and socket coupling.

Frederick Prue: "Additive injection unit for a marine toilet system" is patented by Frederick Prue. Abstract: A unit for injecting a disinfectant, deodorant or the like into the inlet stream of flushing water as it is pumped into the bowl of a tankless marine toilet. The injection unit is preferably constructed of commercially-available plastic plumbing components. The main body of the unit provides an additive reservoir which surrounds the flush water inlet pipe and is formed from a conventional plastic sanitary tee jointed fitted at each end with plastic size-reduction bushings. The two bushings connect the injection unit to the flush water inlet tubing and also support an interior flow pipe.

George R. Hubbard: "SECURE SUPPORT PIPE FASTENER" is patented by George R. Hubbard. Abstract: A metal pipe bracket is disclosed for firmly securing a plumbing pipe within a stud bay. The metal pipe bracket has a U-channel that is slipped over a steel strap nailed between the two studs of a stud bay. Locking tabs located on the pipe bracket aligned with and snapped into locking holes on the steel strap. A metallic plumbing pipe either extending horizontally within the stud bay or vertically within the stud bay is then soldered to the pipe bracket thereby providing a secure attachment between the plumbing pipe and the stud bay structure. Secured in this manner, the plumbing pipe is held secure against vertical, horizontal, and axial movement. A pipe secured in this manner can be attached to a shower head or a shower water mixer valve.

Gordon L. Love: "DEVICE FOR ERECTING AND PLUMBING A WALL FRAME UNIT" is is patented by Gordon L. Love.

Hans-Jurgen Jensen: "MOUNTING ASSEMBLY FOR IN-THE-WALL PLUMBING FITTING" is is patented by Hans-Jurgen Jensen.

Haskell, Jennifer A.: Author of "Plumbing at the Highlands, Fort Washington, Pennsylvania, 1845-1904." Published in 1990.

Heinrich Monch: "Sanitary faucet for surface attachment" is patented by Heinrich Monch. Abstract: A domestic plumbing installation of a generally simple design which is easy to manufacture, is obtained in the following manner: a connecting end of the water-conduit element is merely pushed into a connection-receiving part and includes at least one locking notch, which extends generally perpendicularly to the direction of insertion, preferably approximately tangentially, the valve housing includes at least one locking bore extending generally perpendicularly to the direction of insertion preferably approximately tangentially to the connection-receiving part and ending in the connection-receiving part.

Henry Francis du Pont Winterthur Museum: Publication of "Plumbing, heating, and cooling trade catalogues at Winterthur." Publisher: Clearwater Pub. Co (Frederick, MD). Published in 1990.

International Association of Plumbing and Mechanical Officials: Publication of "IAPMO installation standards." Publisher: International Association of Plumbing and Mechanical Officials (Walnut, Calif). Published in 1990.

Jefferson L. Gentry, et al.: "SHOWER SHAVER" is patented by Jefferson L. Gentry, Alfons Rundzaitis and Ronald O. Hilger. Abstract: A shower shaver is made from two plastic piece parts. A first part is a handle in the nature of a pipe terminating in a fan-shaped or flared, tray like top surface. The other piece part is a cover or top which fits over and cooperates with the tray top to form a cavity which delivers a flared sheet of water toward an orifice which strikes to broad surfaces of said blade and then exits under the cutting edge of the blade. The tubing or hose attached to the shower shaver razor leads to a nipple which may be interposed between a shower head and a plumbing pipe. A valve on the nipple provides a continuously variable control over the flow of water to the shaver and/or the shower head. A bracket or hanger is attached to the nipple to receive and support the razor when it is not in use.

John A. Barclay, et al.: "Rotary dipole active magnetic regenerative refrigerator" is patented by John A. Barclay, Joseph A. Waynert, Anthony J. DeGregoria, Joseph W. Johnson and Peter J. Claybaker. Abstract: The rotary dipole active magnetic regenerative refrigerator (10) of the present invention comprises a stationary first regenerative magnetic bed (12) positioned within a stationary first inner dipole magnet (14), a stationary second regenerative magnetic material bed (16) positioned within a stationary second inner dipole magnet (18), an outer dipole magnet (20) that rotates on a longitudinal axis and encloses the inner dipole magnets (14, 18), a cold heat exchanger (22), hot heat exchangers (24, 26), a fluid displacer (28), and connective plumbing through which a heat transfer fluid is conveyed.

John D. Jeter: "ACCELERATION COMPENSATING SYSTEM" is patented by John D. Jeter. Abstract: In the preferred application, an acceleration compensation mass is supported in a downhole drilling related housing for independent movement along an axis in response to acceleration of the housing. A control member that moves relative to the housing in a direction parallel the axis to carry out the function of the housed apparatus is connected to a piston in a cooperating bore in the housing to displace fluid when the member moves. A second piston and cooperating bore in the housing is arranged to displace fluid when the mass moves. Fluid plumbing is arranged to connect the two hydraulic cylinders such that the mass and the member, if they move, must move in unison in opposite directions.

Joseph Skvaril: "Prefabricated compact sevice core" is patented by Joseph Skvaril. Abstract: Walls of the prefabricated compact service core structure are higher than the total height of the floor, wall and ceiling structure of an ordinary one-storey residental building, but lower than the total height of a two-storey building of any kind. The height of the walls is large enough to e.g. accommodate the serviced fixtures of complete main floor bathroom, kitchen, and possibly laundry and utility rooms, as well as lower parts of the same rooms of the second storey of a two-storey structure. On the other hand, the height is small enough to make the prefabricated compact service core structure possible to ship on standard low trailers anywhere in the world.

Karsten A. Laing and Nikolaus J. Laing: "Pump for secondary circulation" is patented by Karsten A. Laing and Nikolaus J. Laing. Abstract: In a plumbing installation wherein hot water is piped from a water heater or reservoir to a plurality of taps by a distribution conduit, an improved recirculation circuit of limited power consumption to continually pump small amounts of hot water from said conduit back into said reservoir which comprises a low power radial pump unprotected by a check valve against backflow, but having a rotary impeller with linear radial vanes leading to an annular output channel larger than necessary for maximum pumping throughput. The oversized annular channel and linear vanes limit the impact of any backflow upon the impeller and prevents its operating as a tubine as the pump is subjected to back pressure when a large amount of water is being drawn through the taps.

Kelly, George: Author of "Manipulating consumers means plumbing motivational depths." Published in 1990.

Kenneth Graham: "Plumbing drainage system" is patented by Kenneth Graham. Abstract: A plumbing drainage system has a plumbing stack with a clean-out hole formed therein. A drainage device for controlled drainage of the plumbing stack includes a device for connecting the drainage device to a plumbing stack at the clean-out hole formed in the plumbing stack. A shut-off valve is connected downstream of the first connecting device. A second connecting device is connected downstream of the shut-off valve for connection to a drainage hose.

Manfred Pawelzik and Rudolf Haufe: "CONVERTIBLE FAUCET/HAND-SHOWER FITTING" is patented by Manfred Pawelzik and Rudolf Haufe. Abstract: A plumbing fitting has a flexible hose suppliable with water under pressure and having an outer end, an upstream end piece having an upstream side connected to the outer end and a downstream side, and a downstream end piece having a downstream side and an upstream side. An outer sleeve has an upstream end and a downstream end and respective couplings releasably connect the upstream end of the sleeve to the downstream side of the upstream end piece and the downstream end of the sleeve to the upstream side of the downstream end piece. An inner tube having a downstream end connected to the upstream side of the downstream end piece and an upstream end connected to the downstream side of the upstream end piece forms a flow conduit therebetween.

Masterman, Arnold H.: Author of "Plumbing and mechanical services. Bk. 2." A.H Masterman and R.M. Boyce. Published in 1990.

Moore, Alan A.: Author of "Effects of ozone and Photozone on waterborne bacteria, fish survival, and plumbing equipment." Publisher: Iowa Dept. of Natural Resources (Des Moines, IA). Published in 1990.

Mouse Trap (board game): A children's gameshow of the same name was transmitted on the British channel ITV in the early 1990s as part of the Saturday morning entertainment show "MotorMouth". The game featured a scaled-up version of the board game's contraption, and contestants had to complete small activities round the outside of the trap (such as completing a mathematical puzzle, crawling through a tube or throwing objects into buckets to lower a drawbridge. At any point during the game a siren would sound, meaning that the trap had been activated. One team member would then have to run round the exterior of the trap and tag the other player who would attempt to turn the trap off before the ball-bearing hit the plumbing. If they failed, the grand prize would be "trapped" and replaced with a prize of lesser value. In the final part of the show, the contestants had the time it took the trap to run to answer 5 general knowledge questions to win the prize. It is often possible to note the cage slowing down as it made its descent, in an attempt to ensure that the contestants won the prize! There is also a keychain version of Mousetrap, which is similar, except all the pieces are miniature. [WP]

National Research Council of Canada: Publication of "Canadian Plumbing Code, 1990." Issued by the Associate Committee on the National Building Code, National Research Council of Canada. Publisher: Associate Committee on the National Building Code, National Research Council of Canada (Ottawa). Published in 1990.

Paul Panella: "CONNECTORS FOR PLUMBING LINES" is patented by Paul Panella. Abstract: The present invention comprises couplings which require no adhesives or cold welding or similar techniques for joining lengths of pipe of any known composition. The couplings, in their various shapes, are molded from Ultra high olecular Weight Polyethylene (UHWP). Within each end of each coupling form there are a plurality of spaced apart inwardly extending flexible rings, each ring terminating in an angular tip portion which is deformed in the direction of the inserted pipe end and forms a plurality of locking annular seals around the inserted pipe end portion, UHWP has an inherent self-lubricity which facilitates the insertion of the pipe end portion. UHWP is chemically inert.

Puffett, R. J.: Author of "Plumbing services Volume 2 Waste disposal, roof plumbing." Project co-ordinators R. J. Puffett, L.J. Hossack. Publisher: McGraw-Hill (Sydney). Published in 1990.

Raymond P. Gore and James E. Park: "Apparatus and method for in situ calibration of a metering device" is patented by Raymond P. Gore and James E. Park. Abstract: An apparatus and method for in situ calibration of a metering device (21) in a gas manifold or plumbing system. A calibrated gas source and inlet (17) are provided. Connected to the calibrated gas source is a first three way valve. The first three way valve is connected to an inlet of the metering device (21) with an outlet connected to a second three way valve. The second three way valve is connected to both a reaction chamber or an exhaust. A calibration gas is allowed to flow through the calibration inlet (17), through the first three way valve, through the metering device (21), and through the second three way valve so as to calibrate the metering device to the calibrated gas source.

Richard C. Spencer: "System for improving the appearance of plumbing fixtures" is is patented by Richard C. Spencer.

Richard H. Conrad: "METHOD FOR PREVENTING BIOFILM IN SPAS" is patented by Richard H. Conrad. Abstract: A method for preventing stagnation and biofilm formation in the jet pump circuit of a spa, therapy pool or bath employing separate pumps or plumbing circuits for circulation and for pressure jet/massaging functions.

Richard W. Grabenkort, et al.: "Packaging system for a sterilizable calbratable medical device" is patented by Richard W. Grabenkort, Conrad T. Fong and Cheryl D. Germany. Abstract: An improved package for a medical device includes an inner wrap that envelopes the medical device, the inner wrap including a gas-permeable surface, and a chamber defined in the inner wrap to store a hydratable sensor of the medical device. Plumbing for the package controls fluid flow into and within the inner wrap, to selectively establish, without breaching a portion of the inner wrap surrounding the sensor, fluid communication between the gas-permeable surface and the sensor, to sterilize the sensor and the inner wrap with a gaseous sterilant, or to hydrate the sensor with hydration fluid obtained from a source of hydration fluid connected to the chamber, or to equilibrate the hydration fluid in the chamber with an external source of gas, to calibrate the sensor within the inner wrap.

Rick D. Erhardt: "PLUMBING LEAK TESTING APPARATUS" is patented by Rick D. Erhardt. Abstract: An apparatus for pressure testing a plumbing system having a fluid inlet assembly having an inlet connection, a pressure-actuated flow regulator valve, and a fluid inlet, all made from or lined with corrosion resistant materials. A paddle shaped member is coaxially coupled to a freely rotatable threaded cap member which removably engages the tee fitting in the plumbing system. O-rings along the outer edges of a paddle-shaped member serve to seat the paddle-shaped member into the inner diameter of the tee-fitting and seal the downstream portion of the Y or tee fitting from the upstream portion.

Robert L. Duke: "PLUMBING TOOL" is patented by Robert L. Duke. Abstract: A plumbing tool having a suction producing effect allows for the convenient installation of plumbing components which are mounted on barriers such as within sinks which cannot be conveniently held in place by a lone individual during installation. The suction device acts as an extra "band" to allow the plumber to install and assemble components on opposite sides of sinks in a quick, safe efficient manner.

Rudolph R. Ceccucci Jr: "MECHANICAL TOOL FOR MANIPULATING FITTINGS AND CAPS" is patented by Rudolph R. Ceccucci Jr. Abstract: A mechanical tool for facilitating coupling and decoupling of home fittings and caps to a plumbing outlet, such as septic drain outlet on a recreational vehicle is disclosed. The tool includes a handle and two opposed branches extending from one end thereof. The free end of each branch has a slot therein sized to engageably receive one of the two diametrically opposed outwardly projecting lugs existing on a conventional drain hose fitting or drain cap. The branches are roughly spaced such that when in use the slotted free ends of the branches are capable of being adjusted to engagably receive the lugs. An adjustable biasing member susposed between the branches and a position so its not to interfere with the operation of the tool when used to manipulate the fitting or cap.

Scottish and Northern Ireland Plumbing Employers' Federation: Publisher of "Plumbing in the 1990's: a guide to the plumbing and heating industry in Scotland and Northern Ireland." Publisher: Scottish and Northern Ireland Plumbing Employers' Federation (Edinburgh). Published in 1990.

Sergio Capilli and Anna D. Capilli: "PRECAST WALL WITH THERMIC REGULATION ELEMENTS" is patented by Sergio Capilli and Anna D. Capilli. Abstract: A prefabricated wall is constructed of pre-cast concrete in such a way as to have embedded therein (1) a plurality of heat-accumulator elements and (2) channels adapted to receive, after installation of the prefabricated wall element, suitable pipes and plumbing connectors for the conveyance of heated water. Each heat-accumulator element is substantially filled with water prior to being embedded in the concrete of the wall element. Each heat accumulator element is positioned so that at least one channel passes close thereto, so that heat flows from the heated water to the water in the heat accumulator element through membranes which separate the heated water from the water in the heat accumulator element.

Southern Research Inst.: Sponsored research "What About When Sub-Slab Depressurization Doesn't Work Well." Sponsored by: Southern Research Inst., Birmingham, AL.; Environmental Protection Agency, Research Triangle Park, NC. Air and Energy Engineering Research Lab. Written by B. E. Pyle, A. D. Williamson and M. C. Osborne. Abstract: The paper discusses the mitigation of radon levels in basement houses when sub-slab depressurization (SSD), a widely used mitigation technique, is not a viable option. For example, in some houses the slab is poured directly on the soil, resulting in poor-to-nonexistent communication under the slab. To apply SSD requires elaborate plumbing and multiple suction holes in the slab. To develop viable alternatives, EPA has funded research to explore other radon mitigation options. Case studies include: basement pressurization with and without heat extraction, and filtration using charcoal. In the first, air from the upper portion of the house was forced into the basement, producing a pressure barrier at the slab/soil interface.

SRI International: Publisher of "Environmental impact report, expanded uses of plastic plumbing pipe. Part 1." SRI International; prepared for State of California, Department of Housing & Community Development. Publisher: SRI International (Menlo Park, CA). Published in 1990.

Teknologisk Inst.: Sponsored research "VVS og energi. Det Indre Markeds tekniske krav. (Plumbing and energy. The Single Market's specifications for technology)." Sponsored by: Teknologisk Inst., Tastrup (Denmark). Energiteknologi. Written by I. L. Clausen and K. L. Bryder. Abstract: The Commission for the European Communities gives directives founded on concrete requirements expressed in basic documents, produced by committees of specialists, on standards regarding the technological niveau of imported goods within the Single Market. The structure of the European standardization organizations dealing with directives concerning building materials, plumbing and energy-technological installations, and these organizations' relation to the Danish ones, is described. The organizations shall cooperate with the European testing and certifying organization to ensure the working-out of marking and certification procedures. A list of sources of further information and of the relevant organizations is included.(AB).

1991

The Bureau: Publisher of "Blueprint & drafting. Two, Appliance." Developed and distributed by Wisconsin Department of Industry, Labor and Human Relations, Division of Safety and Buildings, Bureau of Plumbing. Publisher: The Bureau (Madison, Wis). Published in 1990.

Thomas E. Nelson: "WATER HEATER CONSTRUCTION" is patented by Thomas E. Nelson. Abstract: A water heater construction and method includes arranging the inner water tank and the surrounding outer shell in an inverted orientation and positioning the outer shell into a cover which is arranged with clearance openings for the plumbing connections extending from the top of the tank to extend therethrough. With the tank, shell and cover in an inverted and assembled condition, the annular clearance space defined between the tank and shell is filled, at least the majority, with liquid, foam-in-place insulation.

United States. Congress. Senate. Committee on Commerce, Science, and Transportation. Subcommittee on the Consumer: Publication of "National Plumbing Products Efficiency Act of 1989: hearing before the Subcommittee on the Consumer of the Committee on Commerce, Science, and Transportation, United States Senate, One Hundred First Congress, first session, on S. 583 to establish national standards for the manufacture and labeling of certain plumbing products in order to conserve and protect water resources. October 4, 1989." Published in 1990.

William A. Scott: "Sanitary drain adaptor" is patented by William A. Scott. Abstract: A hollowed platform mountable between a toilet stool and floor and permitting one or more above-grade waste plumbing connections. Each take-off port is recessed from a primary flow channel and a vacuum break groove interconnects each port with the other.

Wilton J. Pino: "FLUSH CONTROL ASSEMBLY FOR PRESSURE FLUSH VALVES" is patented by Wilton J. Pino. Abstract: A flush control assembly for delaying the flush cycle of pressure flush valves for use on plumbing fixtures. The flush control assembly attaches to, and becomes an integral working part of the flush valve and contains a delaying means which is actuated by water pressure differentials in the flush valve.

Wisconsin Dept. of Industry, Labor and Human Relations, Safety and Buildings Division, Plumbing Product Review: Publisher of "Plumbing product review under Wisconsin's uniform plumbing code." Publisher: Wisconsin Dept. of Industry, Labor and Human Relations, Safety and Buildings Division, Plumbing Product Review (Madison, Wis). Published in 1990.

1991

Acorn Engineering Company: Publication of "Acorn: stainless steel plumbing fixtures." Publisher: The Company (Industry, Ca.). Published in 1991.

Alexander Brucker: "Golf club and plumbing device thereof" is is patented by Alexander Brucker.

Armpriester, Kate: Born in 1947, authored "Do your own plumbing." Publisher: Sterling Pub. Co (New York). Published in 1991.

Association canadienne de normalisation: Publication of "Polyethylene/aluminum/polyethylene composite pressure pipe systems: (plumbing products and materials)." Prepared by Canadian Standards Association; approved by Standards Council of Canada. Publisher: Canadian Standards Association (Rexdale, Ont). Published in 1991.

Bocchino, Anthony J.: Author of "Drury Plumbing Construction Company v. Gordon Plastics, Inc." Publisher: National Institute for Trial Advocacy (Notre Dame, Ind). Published in 1991.

British Columbia. Building Standards Branch: Publication of "British Columbia Plumbing Code change process: challenges/amendments to the British Columbia Plumbing Code Advisory Committee recommendations for the 1990 B.C. Plumbing Code." Publisher: Ministry of Municipal Affairs, Recreation and Culture, Building Standards Branch (Victoria). Published in 1991.

California Energy Commission: Publication of "Appliance efficiency regulations for refrigerators and freezers, room air conditioners, central air conditioners, gas space heaters, water heaters, plumbing fittings, fluorescent lamp ballasts, luminaires, gas cooking appliances, and gas pool heaters." Energy Efficiency & Local Assistance Division, Building & Appliance Efficiency Office. Publisher: California Energy Commission (Sacramento). Published in 1991.

Canada. Industrie, sciences et technologie Canada: Publication of "Plumbing products." Publisher: Industrie, Sciences et Technologie Canada, (Ottawa). Published in 1991.

Charles C. Hill: "Fluid fractionator" is patented by Charles C. Hill. Abstract: An improved apparatus for fractionating fluid mixtures by pressure swing molecular adsorption employing a rotary distributor valve and an array of adsorber columns. The columns are contained within a product holding tank. The valve sequences to provide a quasi steady-state flow, allowing optimization of adsorption/desorption cycles, and eliminating most of the valves, switches and plumbing usually required.

Charles E. Hallum: "Integrated valve assembly" is patented by Charles E. Hallum. Abstract: An improvement to an integrated valve assembly which generally consists of a cluster of two poppet valves, four electric-solenoid-operated flapper valves, and four thrust nozzles and interconnecting plumbing. The improvement to the integrated valve assembly reduces the force required to operate the flapper valves thereby minimizing solenoid size, weight, and power consumption. The improvement consists of a modified flapper valve tip having a hole bored through the tip in the direction of tip motion, and a free-fitting piston located therein and suitably axially restrained relative to the flapper valve body.

Christopher J. Engler and Michael W. Johnson: "AUTOMATIC FLOW CONTROL SYSTEM AND FLOOD PROTECTOR" is patented by Christopher J. Engler and Michael W. Johnson. Abstract: An automatic fluid-flow control system is provided for controlling the quantity of fluid allowed to flow uninterrupted through a conduit. It is particularly useful in controlling potentially damaging floods caused by breakage in a branch plumbing line used to supply water to beverage dispensing appliances, ice-making machines and similar devices which repeatedly consume limited quantities of water in relatively short flow cycles. The fluid-flow control system includes a flow meter which emits a signal containing information about the flow of fluid and also indicating when fluid is flowing and when it is not. The preferred metering device emits pulses at a rate proportional to the flow rate. A counter accumulates a pulse count during each period of fluid flow.

Construction Engineering Research Lab.: Sponsored research "Maintenance Task Data Base for Buildings: Plumbing Systems. - Final rept." Sponsored by: Construction Engineering Research Lab. (Army), Champaign, IL. Written by E. S. Neely, R. D. Neathammer, J. R. Stirn and R. P. Winkler. Abstract: This research project has provided improved maintenance resource data for use during facility planning, design, and maintenance activities. Data bases and computer systems have been developed to assist planners in preparing DD Form 1391 documentation, designers in life-cycle cost component selection, and maintainers in resource planning. The data bases and computer systems are being used by U.S. Army Corps of Engineers (USACE) designers at the District and installation levels and by resource programmers at USACE Headquarters, and Army Major Commands and installations. These research products may also be useful to other Government agencies and the private sector. This report describes the building task maintenance and repair data base development and gives examples of its application.

Daniel J. Haughian: "Pipe ring crimping tool" is patented by Daniel J. Haughian. Abstract: This invention is directed to a novel pipe ring crimping tool which is adapted for crimping a ring over plastic plumbing pipe onto a plastic fitting.

David Gozikowski and Falls PA Box 279: "Fireplace furnace heating system" is patented by David Gozikowski and Falls PA Box 279. Abstract: A fireplace furnace heating system for a structure having a firebox for combustion of fuel, preferably coal. A heating unit is disposed proximately to, and preferably surrounds the firebox. Conduits carry interior air from remote locations to the heating unit. The heating unit is preferably a multi-walled, chambered structure to define numerous air passageways. Air delivered from the conduits to the heating unit must travel through the air passageways. The proximate disposition of the heating unit to the firebox heats the heating unit and the air travelling therethrough. The heating unit has vents for returning the heated air to the interior of the structure. A blower is included for forcible moving the air through the heating unit and back to the interior.

Dennis J. Downs and Jeffrey C. Coburn: "Appliance waste water drought relief system" is patented by Dennis J. Downs and Jeffrey C. Coburn. Abstract: A drought relief system employs waste water as normally discharged from an appliance into a plumbing drain. A dual valve assembly is mounted in series within an existing appliance discharge line, usually exteriorly of the appliance and includes a first valve allowing for the distribution of waste water to the normal discharge line. By shutting off this first valve and opening a second valve, waste water is directed into a drought diversion conduit passing through the building wall and communicating with an appropriate distribution line. The latter may comprise a single conduit or a manifold network of conduits such as perforated pipes or hoses and thus permits utilization of water that otherwise would be discharged into the user's septic system or municipal waste system.

Dwight B. Stephenson and Dennis R. Marks: "FLUID CONTROLLER WITH LOAD SENSING PRIORITY FLOW CONTROL CAPABILITY" is patented by Dwight B. Stephenson and Dennis R. Marks. Abstract: A fluid controller (15) is provided of the type which controls the flow of fluid from a source (11) to a priority device (19) and an auxiliary device (21). The controller includes a valving arrangement (33) comprising a primary, rotatable spool valve (51), and a cooperating, relatively rotatable follow-up sleeve valve member (53). The spool and sleeve cooperate to define controller valving (35) while the sleeve and housing cooperate to define load sensing, priority flow control valving (37). In a preferred embodiment, the controller valving is defined by relative rotation between the spool and the sleeve, while the priority flow control valving is defined by relative axial movement between the sleeve and the housing.

Galeno, Joseph J.: Author of "Means plumbing estimating: practical methods for contractors, includes fire protection and medical gas." Joseph J. Galeno and Sheldon T. Greene. Publisher: Construction Consultants & Publishers. Published in 1991.

George Nugent: "Remote water shut-off module for use by disabled and infirm" is patented by George Nugent. Abstract: A single-unit, remote shut-off module for use by the disabled and infirm has a single-unit module attached by clamps to external water source and outflow connector pipes and housing a shaft which itself houses a plunger with a rubber ball seal which is guided through a shaft guide by electrical current from an electrical motor unit, which is fitably attached above the external water source connector pipe to direct the plunger into the seal of the mouth of the outflow connector pipe, and thereby to interrupt the communication of water from the external water source connector pipe through the module into the outflow connector pipe during a plumbing emergency at the discretion of the user.

Government of Colombia: Decree 1842 of 7/22/91 approves the National Statute of Users of Public Services in Domiciles, which covers use of water, plumbing, electricity, local and long distance telephones, garbage collection, transportation, gas, and waste and waste disposal. Provides for access to these services, consumption, billing, installation and periodic inspection of meters, procedures for consumer complaints, and many other related subjects. Published in Diario Oficial on July 22, 1991.

Great Britain. Scottish Office: Publication of "Lead plumbing in Scottish Homes." Publisher: Scottish Office (Edinburgh). Published in 1991.

Hank Walraven: "Plumbing fixture" is patented by Hank Walraven. Abstract: Disclosed is plumbing fixture integrated with the side of a sink and the like having an elongated compartment extending lengthwise along at least a portion of the height of the side wall or piece. The compartment has a bottom with a drain and an open side which allows liquid from a sink to flow into the compartment. A removable strainer is placed in position at the open side of the compartment, and a standpipe is placed in the drain. There is a catch connected to the strainer which is manually movable between a latched position to hold the strainer in position and an unlatched position which allows the strainer to be removed from the open side of the compartment.

Harald I. Eggen: "Extender for a plumbing mount with spring loaded sealing piston" is is patented by Harald I. Eggen.

Harold L. Hull and David M. Bates: "Prefabricated concrete wall" is patented by Harold L. Hull and David M. Bates. Abstract: A prefabricated concrete wall with outer and inner wall panels seperated by a rigid insulation panel and air cavities, that allows each wall to expand and contract independently. Mounting brackets are embedded in the panels to allow the inner panel to be raised and dropped into place and openings for doors and windows are provided as well as cavities for electrical service panels, plumbing, electrical boxes, etc. The outer panels are joined together by pins and the base mounting brackets have slotted holes to allow the panels to expand and contract. Also, the outer surfaces of both the inner and outer panels may have finished surfaces to take the appearance of stucco, bricks, stones, or wood panels, etc.

Harry E. Thomason: "THERMOSYPHON HEAT-STORAGE AND BACKUP HEAT APPARATUS" is patented by Harry E. Thomason. Abstract: Prior inventions in 2-tank solar heat-storage systems, generally speaking, provide for solar-produced heat stored in a first tank. Therefore STORED solar heat is limited to that one tank. Backup heat is produced and stored in a second tank. In the present invention, SOLAR-PRODUCED heat from said first tank flows to said second tank. No pump is used. No pump-control is used. No valve is used. Flow is automatic, by natural thermosyphon action when the temperature in said first tank exceeds the temperature in said second tank. AND, the EFFECTIVE storage of solar-produced heat is much greater. oreover, heat from said second tank, which usually contains the backup heater(s), does not flow from said second tank back to said first tank.

Harry J. Molligan: "Back water trap" is patented by Harry J. Molligan. Abstract: The invention relates to a device for preventing communication through pipe lines of high security institutions. A flapper valve is provided with a valve seat having a plurality of teeth extending into the center of the opening formed in the valve seat. A pivotal flapper opens or closes the valve by abutting a seating face of the valve seat or moving away, under the force of a fluid flow, and allowing passage of waste water from a plumbing fixture to the main waste conduit. A water trap seal is optionally and/or separately mounted for delivering an additional amount of water into the conventional waste trap to fill in the waste trap with fluid and prevent undesirable communication.

Industry, Science and Technology Canada: Publisher of "Industry profile 1990-1991: plumbing products." Publisher: Industry, Science and Technology Canada (Ottawa). Published in 1991.

Institute of New Zealand Plumbing and Drainage Inspectors. Conference: Publication of "22nd conference I.N.Z.P.D. Inc, 4th-7th March 1991." Publisher: The Institute (Rotorua?, N.Z.). Published in 1991.

International Association of Plumbing and Mechanical Officials: Publication of "Uniform swimming pool, spa, and hot tub code." International Association of Plumbing and Mechanical Officials. Publisher: The Association (Walnut, CA). Published in 1991.

International Conference of Building Officials: Publication of "Dwelling construction under the Uniform mechanical code." Publisher: International Association of Plumbing & Mechanical Officials (Whittier, Calif. International Conference of Building Officials; Walnut, Calif). Published in 1991.

John W. Sunderland: "Compression boiler drain" is patented by John W. Sunderland. Abstract: A compression boiler drain is provided which is integrally form with a plumbing fitting having inwardly tapered external threads and an outwardly tapered bore. This construction permits the user to choose which ever of two methods he/she decides is more desirable when installing the associated plumbing fitting that is: 1) using an appropriate sized compression ferrule and compression nut to connect to tubing; or 2) alternatively using an ordinary thread conventional plumbing coupling to connect to threaded pipe.

Joseph P. Terreta: "PLANTER EDGING LANDSCAPING SYSTEM" is patented by Joseph P. Terreta. Abstract: The present invention relates to an improved planter edging landscaping system. In a first embodiment, the planter edging landscaping system includes a planter wall edging member which may be installed along wall structures or the like to create a planter area as well as provide an edging lip for ease of grass trimming or shearing. In a second embodiment, the present invention includes a flexible wall structure which is combinable with an edging cap to create an edging system which is adaptable to varying terrain. In addition, the edging cap may have channels therein to facilitate the installation of plumbing, wiring or drainage channels in outside environments.

Jurgen Humpert: "Escutcheon for recessed plumbing fixture" is is patented by Jurgen Humpert.

Kathie K. Jones: "Urinals" is patented by Kathie K. Jones. Abstract: A plumbing fixture for installation in restrooms that enables female individuals to urinate from a standing position. An elongate flexible hose has a urine collecting funnel at one end and the other end communicates with a bowl of the fixture. A sanitary liner is received by the rim of the funnel so that the funnel does not contact the body of the user. The liner is knocked off the funnel after use by a passive ejector arm when the funnel is suspended between a pair of hanger arms. The hanger arms each include a pair of arm members that guide and receive the funnel. Also, the fixture includes a trough formed in an upper portion of an inside surface to direct flushing water supplied to the fixture onto the suspended funnel for cleaning.

MacGregor, John Monroe: Author of "Plumbing the depths." Publisher: art & Antiques (New York). Published in 1991.

McGraw-Hill: Publisher of "Practical plumbing engineering." Cyril M. Harris, editor in chief. Publisher: McGraw-Hill (New York). Published in 1991.

Michael J. Pyzik: "Flexible mount header for engine mounted fuel filter" is patented by Michael J. Pyzik. Abstract: A flexible header mounting for an engine mounted fuel filter includes structure for dependingly engaging a fuel filter and its associated plumbing and a planar base member by means of which the header is mounted to the engine supporting structure. Flexible engagement of the base member to the engine is accomplished by means of bolts, each of which has a compression spring mounted thereon over the shaft thereof, between the base member and the bolt head. The free threaded end of the bolt extends through a bore drilled into the base member and engages within a threaded bore in the engine housing.

Nahapetian, K., et al.: "The intracellular multiplication of Legionella pneumophila in protozoa from hospital plumbing systems" appears in Research in Microbiology written by K. Nahapetian, O. Challemel, D. Beurtin, S. Dubrou, P. Gounon and F. Squinazi. Published in July - August 1991.

National Association of Plumbing, Heating and Mechanical Services Contractors: Publisher of "Members' reference book and buyers' guide." National Association of Plumbing, Heating and Mechanical Services Contractors. Publisher: National Association of Plumbing, Heating and Mechanical Services Contractors (London). Published in 1991.

National Inst. for Occupational Safety and Health: Sponsored research "Health Hazard Evaluation Report HETA 91-290-2131, New England Lead Burning Co. (NELCo), Eaton Metals, Salt Lake City, Utah." Sponsored by: National Inst. for Occupational Safety and Health, Cincinnati, OH. Hazard Evaluations and Technical Assistance Branch. Written by C. S. McCammon, W. J. Daniels, T. R. Hales and S. A. Lee. Abstract: In response to a request from the Director of Safety and Health of the United Association of the

Plumbing and Pipe Fitting Industry, an investigation was undertaken at the New England Lead Burning Company (SIC-3443) project at Eaton Metals, Salt Lake City, Utah because of concerns about lead (7439921) exposure. The company contracted for jobs throughout the United States that involved the use of lead. The particular job involved the lining of two 85 foot long, 14.5 foot diameter steel tanks with lead sheets. Time weighted average exposures for lead ranged from 141 to 307 micrograms of lead per cubic meters of air (microg/cum).

Paul E. Terry: "FLOW SENSITIVE FLUID SHUTOFF SAFETY DEVICE" is patented by Paul E. Terry. Abstract: A fluid shutoff device for use as a safety device to cut off the water supply to a building in the event of overly high water consumption due to a leak or break in the plumbing in the building is provided with a motor that is responsive to remote actuation to rotate a three position selector valve to a desired flow setting. The selector valve is settable in a position which allows water to flow freely through the safety flow control device as if it were not there, a position which diverts water through a safety flow pathway, or a position that prevents water flow into the main water line entrance of the building, thereby allowing the invention to act as a shutoff valve.

Paul H. Johnson: "Cellular landfill process and apparatus" is patented by Paul H. Johnson. Abstract: The present invention is directed to a process and apparatus wherein municipal refuse, and many other types of solid waste, are disposed of in a landfill repository that maintains them in a dry state indefinitely. This eliminates most environmental and many cost problems. The principal design feature of this landfill is its cellular internal structure, which has rows of contiguous, rectangular water- and gas-tight cells that are built on top of one another to form a high, multi-layered structure. These cells are simultaneously constructed and filled with solid waste in a series of short, incremental wall berm construction and filling steps on a one-cell-at-a-time basis in the top layer of the landfill.

Princeton Univ.: Sponsored research "Operation of a TFTR ion source with a ground potential gas feed into the neutralizer." Sponsored by: Princeton Univ., NJ. Plasma Physics Lab.; Department of Energy, Washington, DC. Written by J. H. Kamperschroer, L. E. Dudek, L. R. Grisham, R. A. Newman and T. E. O'Conner. Abstract: TFTR long pulse ion sources have been operated with gas fed only into the neutralizer. Gas for the plasma generator entered through the accelerator rather than directly into the arc chamber. This modification has been proposed for tritium beam operation to locate control electronics at ground potential and to simplify tritium plumbing. Source operation with this configuration and with the nominal gas system which feeds gas into both the ion source and the center of the neutralizer are compared. Comparison is based upon accelerator grid currents, beam composition, and neutral power delivered to the calorimeter. Charge exchange in the accelerator can be a significant loss mechanism in both systems at high throughput.

Robert E. Saadi, et al.: "ON DEMAND SENSOR FLUSH VALVE" is patented by Robert E. Saadi, Allen R. Becker, Christopher J. Ball and John Steffan. Abstract: An on demand, non-contact sensor controlled flush valve actuation system includes a flush valve between a water supply and a plumbing fixture. An actuator for the flush valve includes a moveable piston in fluid communication with a control water inlet, with a control water conduit carrying water from the flush valve through a solenoid operated control valve to the actuator assembly. A radiation sensing/detecting unit generates a first control signal in response to the return reflection of infrared radiation. A timer receives the first control signal and, in response thereto, generates a second control signal of a predetermined duration which activates the solenoid.

Samuel G. Zaccone: "Shelving system and method of installation" is patented by Samuel G. Zaccone. Abstract: There is disclosed a system for the installation of one or more shelves in a cabinet. Included in the system are a pair of shelf guide rail assemblies which are adapted to be respectively mounted to the side walls of a cabinet for slidably receiving the shelves. The shelves are each of two-piece construction and adjustable in length. The shelves may be provided with a rearwardly disposed slot for receiving the plumbing when the system is installed in a cabinet into which a sink has been installed. A number of precut filler pieces are provided for the filling the spaces between the top surfaces of the respective sections of the shelves.

Sandia National Labs.: Sponsored research "Experimental techniques in high-pressure research on elastomeric O-ring seal designs." Sponsored by: Sandia National Labs., Livermore, CA.; Department of Energy, Washington, DC. Written by B. A. Meyer, C. A. LaJeunesse, J. T. Carrell and M. Kelley. Abstract: Gas transfer systems store and deliver isotopes of hydrogen in nuclear weapon systems. Pressure vessels, explosive valves, and associated plumbing are the main components of the gas transfer system. There are many ways to couple the pressure vessels to the valve housing. Some systems use metal to metal seals, welded integral designs, or O-ring designs. In this paper we present a simple methodology for experimentally evaluating and theoretically predicting the performance or failure point of O-ring designs during transient pressure excursions at high-pressure. A good understanding of seal performance is demonstrated by comparing a model of seal failure with experimental data. Agreement between the model and experiment is within 10% at pressures up to 31 ksi. 3 refs., 8 figs.

Sanjeev Madan, et al.: "Polyurethanes comprising the reaction of an isocyanate terminated prepolymer and a polyol mixture comprising triols and an organic diamine" is patented by Sanjeev Madan, Hans-Joachim Kogelnik, Majid Daneshvar, Richard S. Pantone and Jan L. Clatty. Abstract: A novel polyurethane prepared by reacting a) a specific polyol or specific polyol blend, b) an organic diamine, c) fillers, and d) a specific polyisocyanate is described. The invention also relates to the use of the polyurethane in the preparation of a composite structure wherein the polyurethane is applied to an adhesive coated ceramic enamel layer. The composites are eminently suitable for use in plumbing applications (e.g. as a bathtub).

Standards Association of Australia: Publication of "Australian standards for plumbing students. Part 1, Trade course." Publisher: Standards Australia (North Sydney, N.S.W.). Published in 1991.

Stanford Linear Accelerator Center: Sponsored research "Proceedings of the REXX Symposium for developers and users." Sponsored by: Stanford Linear Accelerator Center, CA.; Department of Energy, Washington, DC. Abstract: This report contains papers and viewgraphs on the following topics: the design of REXX; REXX Oracle Interface; issues in the specification of REXX; REXXLIB; platform-specific standards for REXX; REXXoids; pipelines: how CMS got its plumbing fixed; expert system design in REXX; review of ANSI and other language discussions; IBM REXX compiler; practical application of REXX in the UNIX environment; REXX language parsing capabilities; and using REXX to teach programming.

Stark, Patty: Author of "Sex is more than a plumbing lesson: a parents' guide to sexuality education for infants through the teen years." Publisher: Preston Hollow Enterprises (Dallas, Texas). Published in 1991.

Timothy H. Nurse: "Building entrance boot drain" is patented by Timothy H. Nurse. Abstract: The building entrance boot drain is similar in function to a shower-base, but is recessed into the floor inside an entrance to a house or building. An expanded metal grate is supported by the receptacle. At the center of the base of the receptacle, an opening leads to suitable plumbing fixtures which form a water-trap and thence a drain to the building's water-waste system. Snow and ice, melting off winter boots placed on the building entrance boot drain, forms water which is conveniently drained away into the building's water-waste system.

Todd Mcintosh: "GRAY-WATER RECLAMATION AND REUSE SYSTEM" is patented by Todd Mcintosh. Abstract: A gray-water reclamation and reuse system for collecting, filtering and storing waste water (i.e., gray-water) for reuse where potable quality water is not required comprises a sump for collecting the waste water; a filter connected for filtering the waste water collected in the sump; a tank for holding the filtered filtered waste water; and plumbing and electrically-operated valves for providing waste water to said sump from one or more waste water sources, including shower stalls, bathtubs, sinks and/or clothes washers, the valves being operable by electric controls for diverting the waste water from the sources between the sump and a conventional waste water drain pipe to a sewer, septic tank or the like.

Tzeng-Shyang Chiou: "Automatic flushing device" is patented by Tzeng-Shyang Chiou. Abstract: A water and energy efficient automatic flushing device is used to control water flow from a water inlet pipe to a flushing conduit of a plumbing fixture, such as a toilet bowl. The automatic flushing device includes an electromagnetic valve unit and a control unit to control opening and closing action of the electromagnetic valve unit. The control unit includes a programmed central processing unit (CPU), a transmitter circuit, a detecting unit to detect the presence of a person using the plumbing fixture, a receiver circuit and a valve control circuit.

Virginia Polytechnic Inst. and State Univ.: Sponsored research "Process development unit testing of microbubble flotation. Technical progress report for the sixth quarter (December 1, 1987-February 29, 1988)." Sponsored by: Virginia Polytechnic Inst. and State Univ., Blacksburg. Dept. of Mining and Minerals Engineering.; Department of Energy, Washington, DC. Written by G. T. Adel, G. H. Luttrell, D. J. Boron and R. H. Yoon. Abstract: Activities this past quarter focused primarily on preparation of the PDU for operation. Scale-up testing was also initiated for the in-line bubble generation system to be used in the PDU. Construction work on the PDU was completed in February. Virginia Tech Physical Plant engineers and safety personnel inspected the facility soon after completion and gave approval to start moving equipment into the building. Efforts since then have focused on installation of major equipment items including the Drais ball mill, Denver cells, columns, pumps and sumps. All wiring and plumbing work associated with this equipment is also underway. Completion of these efforts is anticipated by the end of March.

Walker, P. M., et al.: "Signal-to-noise improvement in mid-field MRI surface coils: a degree in plumbing?" appears in Magnetic Resonance Imaging written by P. M. Walker, B. Robin-Lherbier, J. M. Escanye and J. Robert. Published in 1991.

Werner Gnauert and Hans-Jurgen Jensen: "BACKFLOW PREVENTER FOR HAND SPRAY" is patented by Werner Gnauert and Hans-Jurgen Jensen. Abstract: A backflow preventer used in combination with a plumbing fixture has a pressurizable supply line, an output hose that can be equipped with a sprayer or shower, and a drain. It further has a valve casing having an inlet valve seat forming an inlet port connected to the supply line, a vent valve seat forming a vent port opening to the atmosphere, and an outlet port opening laterally between the seats and connected to the supply hose. A valve body is movable in the casing between a normal-flow position on the vent seat blocking the vent and permitting flow between the inlet and outlet ports and a backflow-preventing position on the inlet seat blocking the inlet port and permitting flow between the outlet and vent ports.

William J. Lund: "Hot water demand system suitable for retrofit" is patented by William J. Lund. Abstract: A hot water recovery system includes a hot water source; a hot water delivery line connected between said hot water source and at least one plumbing fixture along with a cold water delivery line connection between said plumbing fixture, a cold water source and said hot water source; a pump, interconnected between said hot and cold water delivery lines, enables circulation of water from the hot water delivery line through the cold water delivery line and into the hot water source, thus eliminating the need for a separate recirculation system.

Yardley, Thompson: Born in 1952, authored "Down the plughole: explore your plumbing." Publisher: Cassell (London). Published in 1991.

1992

Alberta. Plumbing and Gas Safety Standards: Publication of "Handbook supplement to the Alberta private sewage treatment and disposal regulations." Publisher: Alberta Labour, Plumbing and Gas Safety Standards (Edmonton). Published in 1992.

American Society of Mechanical Engineers: Publication of "Air gaps in plumbing systems." Publisher: American Society of Mechanical Engineers (New York). Published in 1992.

Anthony S. Bonacci: "Adjustable flange for plumbing fixtures" is is patented by Anthony S. Bonacci.

Army Engineer Waterways Experiment Station: Sponsored research "Control Strategies for Zebra Mussel Infestations at Public Facilities. - Final rept." Sponsored by: Army Engineer Waterways Experiment Station, Vicksburg, MS. Environmental Lab. Written by A. C. Miller, B. S. Payne, F. Neilson and R. F. McMahon. Abstract: On September 16-18, 1991, the U.S. Army Corps of Engineers held a meeting in Ft. Mitchell, KY (near Cincinnati, OH), to develop strategies for the detection and control of zebra mussels. More than 50 scientists and engineers prepared a preliminary list of strategies to deal with zebra mussel infestations at public facilities.

Barlow, Ronald S.: Author of "The vanishing American outhouse: a history of country plumbing." Publisher: Windmill Pub. Co (El Cajon, Calif). Published in 1992.

Billie W. Childers: "Prefabricated water plumbing station" is patented by Billie W. Childers. Abstract: A prefabricated water plumbing station is provided that is a time saving component for installer because it may be installed as a single unit in a wall cavity between two vertical studs. The unit consists of a housing mountable between studs having plumbing hardware (valves and drain connection) for connecting a building's hot and cold water supply and drain lines to a fixture/appliance. A front panel on the housing is provided with a choice of a plurality of alignment lugs for properly positioning the unit from the studs to allow for the installation of paneling and similar materials to the studs about and beneath the front panel after installation thereof.

Bradley Corporation: Publication of "Bradley: security plumbing fixtures: 1992." Published in 1992.

Brian E. Appelwick: "T-connector for use in plumbing" is is patented by Brian E. Appelwick.

British Columbia: Publication of "The British Columbia Plumbing Code, 1992." Publisher: Building Standards Branch (Victoria, B.C.). Published in 1992.

California Building Standards Commission: Publication of "Uniform plumbing code. State of California 1989 amendments." Publisher: California Building Standards Commission (Sacramento, CA). Published in 1992.

Charles D. Wood: "Variable compression piston" is patented by Charles D. Wood. Abstract: An engine having a variable piston capable of adjusting an engine's compression ratio while cranking or operating throughout an engine's speed/load range. Control may be obtained through varying the volume of lubricating fluid supplied to an inertia operated pump/accumulator device located in each multi-element piston. Fluid is supplied to said pump/accumulator device by means of a low pressure jet directed into an opening in the accumulator. No direct plumbing connection is required between the fluid source and the pump/accumulator device. Each piston includes an inner element conventionally mounted on a connecting rod and an outer element slidably mounted above and around said inner element.

Charles H. Perrott: "Multiple drain trap primer valve assembly for sewer lines" is patented by Charles H. Perrott. Abstract: A multiple drain trap primer valve assembly. The assembly comprises a plumbing conduit system including a house line 10 carrying water under pressure and a plurality of branch lines 12 each serving the drain trap 14 of a particular plumbing fixture. A manifold 26 having multiple discharge openings is connected into the house line. Coupling means 30 couple the branch lines to the manifold, one to each opening. Each coupling means includes a flow orifice 44 of size predetermined to equalize the flow of priming water to the branch line. Time-clock controlled valve means 20 is positioned in the house line to open it to the flow of water at predetermined time intervals.

Consumers' Association & Hodder & Stoughton: Publisher of "The Which? book of plumbing and central heating." Publisher: Consumers' Association & Hodder & Stoughton (London). Published in 1992.

Dean Christian: "Simulated log and panel prefabricated house structure" is patented by Dean Christian. Abstract: Simulated logs for home construction are formed from PVC pipe which is filled with hard cast foam. The pipes are precast with a simulated log design to include knots, cracks and wood grain, and the bottom of each log contains a one inch groove to hold a longitudinally extending rubber gasket. The logs are attached together by threaded rod fasteners which utilize doubleended nuts, and caps are used to close off the ends of the log. Plumbing, electrical conduits, and the like may be retained within the tubing, and T-bolts are used to attach the initial log to a concrete foundation.

Demcy L. Burwell: "Aerobic septic system" is patented by Demcy L. Burwell. Abstract: An aerobic septic system having a conventional tank, conical separator or clarifier, and air injection system has an air header discharging air around the entire periphery of the tank. Substantially all solids suspended in wastewater are therefore mechanically agitated and aerated, greatly increasing system efficiency. Wastewater rises along the tank walls and spills over the top of the separator. It then descends in the separator. A vent pipe has an egress port in the roof of the tank, and rises to join an incoming sewage line from a residential plumbing system, which in turn communicates with a vent stack.

Dept. of Defense, Defense Logistics Agency, Defense Logistics Services Center: Publisher of "Consolidated federal supply catalog identification list. FSC 4500. Plumbing, heating, and sanitation equipment." Publisher: Dept. of Defense, Defense Logistics Agency, Defense Logistics Services Center (Battle Creek, Mich). Published in 1992.

Dietrick C. Jones and Glenda M. Jones: "Prefabricated bay window conservatory enclosure for recyclable waste receptacles" is patented by Dietrick C. Jones and Glenda M. Jones. Abstract: A prefabricated conservatory enclosure for a waste recycling center to be attached to a building includes an upper bay window recess having a bottom counter and a lower housing for enclosing one or more receptacles for recyclable material, the counter having openings for deposit of waste into the receptacles from the upper recess, and the lower portion of the enclosure having an integrating wall fitted with plumbing for a kitchen sink and adapted to be integrated with the structure of a building to which the enclosure is annexed.

Duane R. Condon: "Plumbing leakage test apparatus and method of use" is is patented by Duane R. Condon.

Floyd E. Bigelow Jr. and William H. Bigelow: "Two story building collapsed for shipping" is patented by Floyd E. Bigelow Jr. and William H. Bigelow. Abstract: A two story building provided by modules which may be shipped with one or both stories collapsed and with plumbing manifolds factory installed in the base frame and in the ceiling-floor between stories.

Francis J. Horrigan: "Apparatus for mounting a tubular safety stanchion-vent element through a roof" is patented by Francis J. Horrigan. Abstract: There is disclosed an apparatus, for mounting a combined roof plumbing vent, and a safety stanchion element, on a roof with its roof covering, the elements having a mounting bracket, in conjunction with the roof beam element, being formed by fixedly connecting with a least one roof beam or rafter element, a substantially vertical tubular element, and having a fixably attached in a known manner, a roof covering.

Gregory A. Mosbrucker: "Multi-purpose square" is patented by Gregory A. Mosbrucker. Abstract: A layout square having a handle and two legs that extend away from the handle in the same direction, both perpendicular to the handle. The handle includes a level to allow angular measurements against level, as well as for plumbing and leveling purposes. The legs correspond in width to standard dimensions of construction materials to facilitate the measuring and marking of those dimensions on materials.

One leg is marked along its edges with linear and angular measurement marks for measuring and marking lines and angles, and has holes disposed selectively along its length for receiving a marker, such as a carpentry pencil.

H. Michael Von Hoene: "Integral regenerative fluid system" is patented by H. Michael Von Hoene. Abstract: This integral regenerative system is particularly well suited for retrofitting to standard hydraulic systems which did not originally employ regeneration circuitry. To reduce the amount of external plumbing and valving normally associated with retrofitting, the invention utilizes the integration of uniquely directed flow paths and specially configured valves into its housing components. The valves provide fluid flow control within the system and automatically prevent undesirable drainage of fluid from the system.

Hooshang Kashani: "Fastening assembly for a sink trap having a removable bottom portion" is patented by Hooshang Kashani. Abstract: A trap for a sink, or the like, having an easily removable bottom portion by which to permit the trap to be cleaned and lost articles removed. The bottom portion of the trap is detachably connected to a dip portion by a plurality of locking clips. The dip portion includes a plurality of locking receptacles and the bottom portion includes a plurality of locking tabs that are axially aligned with respective locking receptacles. Each locking clip extends between an axially aligned receptacle and tab so as to apply a clamping force to the trap to prevent the separation of the bottom portion from the dip portion. The locking clips may be removed from the trap, whereby the trap may be opened without any special tools or plumbing skills.

Iain M. Smith: "Alignment system for bathing enclosure" is patented by Iain M. Smith. Abstract: A knock down type bathing enclosure is disclosed which is manufactured as a one-piece plumbing fixture, cut into two or more portions for transportation, and assembled at an installation site. In addition to having a clamping system to clamp an upper and lower portion together vertically, there is provided a corner web structure which provides for horizontal alignment through the use of a C-shaped clip and aligned ribs.

Institute for Research: Publisher of "Your career as a plumber, plumbing contractor pipefitter, HVAC mechanic, new installations, maintenance." Publisher: Institute for Research (Chicago, Ill). Published in 1992.

Institute of Plumbing: Publisher of "Plumbing magazine." Publisher: Institute of Plumbing (Hornchurch). Published in 1992.

International Association of Plumbing and Mechanical Officials International Conference of Building Officials: Publication of "Handbook to the Uniform mechanical code: an illustrative commentary." Publisher: International Association of Plumbing and Mechanical Officials (Whittier, Calif. International Conference of Building Officials; Walnut, Calif). Published in 1992.

International Trade Administration: Sponsored research "Franchising (Brazil). Franchising Services, March 1992. - Export trade information." Sponsored by: International Trade Administration, Washington, DC. Office of Latin America. Abstract: The report covers franchising services such as: education and training, cleaning and maintenance services, and specialized services (automobile repair and services, computer maintenance and repair, quick printing, etc.). Segments supposed to have the highest growth rate in the next three years include: education and training (especially the ones related to computer training); cleaning and maintenance, such as residential and office cleaning; laundromats; electric, plumbing, and home appliances repair; and specialized services, such as automobile repair and services, parking, computer maintenance and repair, clothes remodeling, and quick printing. The restrictive legislation for the remittance of profits and dividends has been relaxed in Brazil.

Jackson, Albert: Born in 1943, authored "Plumbing & central heating." Publisher: HarperCollins (London). Published in 1992.

James A. Millett and Robert R. Foresman: "Through-hull valve and mounting unit" is patented by James A. Millett and Robert R. Foresman. Abstract: An integrated plumbing system comprising a plurality of interchangeable and interengagable parts which is especially useful in conjunction with boats or other marine vessels.

The plumbing system includes a through-hull unit, a mounting unit, a ball valve and a plurality of components useful therewith. The components, including the valve, are made of a strong, non-corrosive, non-metallic material, in particular, a plastic-type material known as MARELON. The valve and associated components and fittings provide various configurations of units which are adapted to numerous plumbing requirements. The mounting unit permits close-coupling of the system to provide enhanced lever ratios in the event accidental side loads are applied to the system.

James J. Reidy: "Portable air-water generator" is patented by James J. Reidy. Abstract: A water generating device for obtaining portable water from ambient air inside or outside a structure or dwelling. There is an air filter for filtering the air prior to processing of the air. The air filter may include a one-time sensing element which renders it unusable when removed from the generator. A condenser is provided for extracting water vapor in the air.

James S. Jaffe: "Portable cleaning device for clogged fluid conduits" is patented by James S. Jaffe. Abstract: A disengageable, portable, self-contained fluid conduit cleaning device for unclogging fuel lines, plumbing lines or similar fluid conduits has a pneumatic pump, and a pressure delivery tank chamber. Controls alternatively connect the pump to supply either a pressure charge or a partial vacuum to the chamber. A delivery valve connects the chamber to the fluid conduit, to provide sudden pneumatic or hydraulic shocks to impact and break loose clogging material from the fluid conduit.

Jeffrey D. Baldwin, et al.: "Cooling arrangement and method for offset gearbox" is patented by Jeffrey D. Baldwin, Ellen J. Wagle and Jude C. Lai. Abstract: An offset gearbox of an aircraft has a sump for a lubricant. A heat exchanger core extends through the sump in contact with the lubricant. A fluid coolant for cooling an accessory such as an electrical power generating unit drivingly connected to the offset gearbox is circulated through the core in thermal communication but not mixed with the lubricant of the offset gearbox for cooling the lubricant. The cooling arrangement for the offset gearbox advantageously does not require a separate or dedicated heat exchanger which reduces system weight and cost. The single pump of the accessory can also be used for circulating the coolant.

John C. Wright: "Spacer for mounting plumbing to a wall" is is patented by John C. Wright.

John F. Hanlon: "Water extraction device" is patented by John F. Hanlon. Abstract: A water extraction device for partially drying wet hair surrounding a perm rod disposed in a person's hair includes a housing having an inlet and an outlet. The inlet includes a shroud which is dimensioned to closely encompass the perm rod. A motor and fan are provided for producing a substantial vacuum at the inlet and a flow of air from the inlet to the outlet. The substantial vacuum pulls water from the wet hair and the flow of air transports the water toward the outlet. The device further includes one or more water separators for removing the water from the flow of air. The water separated from the air is stored in a holding tank or communicated directly to a plumbing drain.

John Gurowitz: "Multi-port angle stop type of shut-off valve" is patented by John Gurowitz. Abstract: A multi-port shut-off valve assembly of the type known to the plumbing industry as an angle stop. The valve has a body shaped as a solid rectangle, with an internally threaded port in each face of the body. A shut-off valve is received in one of the ports, and it controls the flow of water entering the body from another of the ports to the remaining ports. A number of fittings are threaded into the remaining ports, the fittings being either compression unions or compression reducing unions, and each of the fittings has external threads at each end thereof. Water-carrying tubes are respectively coupled to the fittings by compression nuts threaded thereto.

Joseph A. Wolney and Thomas A. Wolney Sr: "Front-loading washing machine drain system" is patented by Joseph A. Wolney and Thomas A. Wolney Sr. Abstract: A drain system for adapting the drain/extraction plumbing of a front-loading washing machine which includes an agitator drum mounted for rotation about a generally horizontal axis, means for driving the drum in rotation about the axis during the various cycles of the machine, and a drain pipe extending downward from the agitator drum and disposed to convey a water/suds mixture vacated from the agitator drum away from the drum. The system includes a conduit into which the water/suds mixture is conveyed from the drain pipe. The conduit is oriented generally horizontally with a first end of the conduit intersecting, and being in fluid communication with, the distal end of the drain pipe.

Joseph P. Santoli: "In-line static water conditioner and method for inhibiting scale formation" is patented by Joseph P. Santoli. Abstract: An in-line static water conditioning device is provided for inhibiting scale formation in plumbing containing hard water. The water conditioning device is a housing containing a core to define a flow annulus. Water flowing through the annulus contacts the core surface comprising predominately copper and lesser amounts of tin, nickel and zinc to inhibit scale formation in the plumbing downstream of the device.

Kurt Martin: "Plumbing system with connector between a flexible pipe conduit laid underneath plaster and a fitting to be arranged outside the plaster" is is patented by Kurt Martin.

Lester B. Jacobi, et al.: "Double bulb mercury vapor lamp apparatus" is patented by Lester B. Jacobi, Arthur B. Jacobi, Keith E. Brown, Daniel E. Cunningham and James B. Woodsmall. Abstract: A two bulb mercury vapor lamp apparatus includes a housing with a bottom whose cross-section forms a curved "M" shape. A pair of reflectors are attached to the bottom of the housing with each reflector positioned in one-half of the "m". The reflectors direct light from the bulbs onto a focal plane where a photosensitive material is located. A plurality of quartz liquid coolant circulating tubes are positioned between the bulbs and the photosensitive material which tubes both cool the lamp and filter out infrared rays. The coolant tubes are attached to a pair of end blocks which are removably secured to the housing. The end blocks, connected plumbing lines and coolant tubes can be lowered from the housing intact, thus greatly facilitating maintenance access to the bulbs and reflectors.

Louisiana. State Plumbing Board: Publication of "State plumbing law: LA. R.S. 37:1361 et seq rules and regulations." Publisher: The Board (Baton Rouge, La.). Published in 1992.

Manfred Pawelzik and Heinz Brandebusemeyer: "Battery-powered temperature indicator for faucet" is patented by Manfred Pawelzik and Heinz Brandebusemeyer. Abstract: A temperature indicator for use in combination with a plumbing fitting through which water passes has a core assembly including a display, a circuit module fixed to and driving the display, a temperature sensor connected to the circuit module, a pair of long battery contacts connected to the module, a finger extending from the module and carrying the long contacts, and a pair of short battery contacts connected to the module in parallel with the long contacts. An inner housing part interfitting with the fitting and traversed by the water is formed with a recess in which the sensor is engageable. A battery is connected to one of the pairs of contacts and the other pair is unused. An outer housing part mounted on the inner housing part carries the core assembly.

Manitoba Manitoba. Building Standards Board Manitoba. Manitoba Labour: Publication of "Manitoba Plumbing Code Canadian plumbing code." Publisher: Manitoba Labour (Winnipeg). Published in 1992.

Manitoba. Manitoba Labour: Publication of "Manitoba plumbing code 1992." Publisher: National Research Council Canada (Ottawa). Published in 1992.

McConnell, Charles: Author of "The home plumbing handbook." Publisher: Maxwell Macmillan International (New York: Macmillan; Toronto: Maxwell Macmillan Canada; New York). Published in 1992.

Mechanical Contractors Association of Alberta Mechanical Contractors Association of British Columbia Mechanical Contractors Association of Saskatchewan: Publication of "Mechanical, piping, plumbing journal Mechanical, piping, plumbing journal." Publisher: Naylor Communications. Published in 1992.

Michael Schiller: "Freeze safety box organization"

is patented by Michael Schiller. Abstract: A plumbing box mounted in fluid communication with fluid pipes within wall structure is arranged to provide for threaded bores for securement of the pipes thereto, with a front wall of the box or housing structure having a plug member frictionally retained within a front wall smooth bore. Upon freezing of fluid within the box structure, the plug member is displaced relative to the box indicating pipe freezing, with the plug member arranged with its cap portion coplanar with a wall surface for visual indication of a freezing condition within the pipe structure directed into the box.

Ministry of Municipal Affairs Recreation & Housing: Publisher of "The British Columbia plumbing code, 1992." Ministry of Municipal Affairs, Recreation and Housing, Building Standards Branch. --. Publisher: Ministry of Municipal Affairs Recreation & Housing (Victoria, B.C.). Published in 1992.

National Inst. for Occupational Safety and Health: Sponsored research "Modification and Evaluation of a Microwave Plasma/Atomic Emission Detector System." Sponsored by: National Inst. for Occupational Safety and Health, Cincinnati, OH. Div. of Physical Sciences and Engineering. Written by M. E. Birch. Abstract: Modifications made to an Applied Chromatography Systems plasma emission detector and the evaluation of the performance of the modified instrument were described. The detector modified was the MPD-850. The overall performance of the modified equipment was much improved for carbon (7440440) determination relative to that found for the original instrument. Limits of detection were somewhat higher for the other elements examined in the study including hydrogen (1333740), fluorine (778414), chlorine (7782505), bromine (7726956) and iodine (7553562). The carbon response for seven of the compounds examined in the study did not appear to be compound dependent when the helium flow rate was 70 milliliters/minute. Toluene (108883) and 2-chlorobutane (78864) responses were lower than expected.

Paul J. Barker: "Quick shut-off valve for in-line installation with a defective valve" is patented by Paul J. Barker. Abstract: A trouble-shooting, one-quarter-turn quick shut-off valve is mountable directly to a compression-type fitting outlet of a defective shut-off valve in series with the defective valve so that the quick shut-off valve becomes located immediately downstream from the defective valve. Projecting from an inlet end of a housing of the quick shut-off valve is an inlet-tail-tube having an inlet passage extending axially through the inlet-tail-tube. This inlet-tail-tube is adapted for insertion directly into a socket in a compression-type fitting outlet of a shut-off valve.

Paul L. Traylor: "Air gap apparatus" is patented by Paul L. Traylor. Abstract: An air gap apparatus for plumbing applications such as reverse osmosis (RO) units and other systems in which reject water empties at a relatively slow rate into a drain line. The apparatus can be incorporated in an under-the-counter unit or in a countertop embodiment which eliminates umbilical connections between the RO unit and the kitchen faucet and sink drain. The apparatus has a conventional air gap to protect against back siphoning and against high velocity backflow from the drainage line. It uses a deflector wall in combination with a supplemental opening and one or more backflow restrictors to slow and shunt any backflow to atmosphere. Different styles of countertop and wall mount installations are disclosed, as well as various deflector walls and back flow devices.

Publication: Publication of "Assessment of on-site graywater and combined wastewater treatment and recycling systems." Submitted to U.S. Environmental Protection Agency by National Association of Plumbing-Heating-Cooling Contractors and Enviro-Management & Research, Inc. Published in 1992.

Richard Eisfeller and Gerard Vachon: "Method for making bright trim articles" is patented by Richard Eisfeller and Gerard Vachon. Abstract: A bright trim article is manufactured by a process including applying a primer coat material to the outer surface of a raw part and thereafter applying a dielectric substrate basecoat by rotation and spray painting to prevent orange peel; thereafter vacuum metallizing a corrosion prone metal, namely indium, on the dielectric substrate basecoat to form "islands" of the indium that are etched following the growth of the metal as it is deposited after the nucleation stage and the stage of channelization but before the formation of an electrically conductive film.

Rickey A. Daniels and Thomas R. Daniels: "Liquid dispensing apparatus" is patented by Rickey A. Daniels and Thomas R. Daniels. Abstract: Liquid dispensing apparatus includes a tank for storing liquid to be dispensed, a fill line communicating with an interior of the tank and adapted to be coupled to a source of the liquid, a heating element for heating the liquid, a heating control device for controlling the heating element to heat the liquid to a predetermined temperature, a dispensing device for dispensing liquid from the tank under pressure and a dispensing control device for selectively controlling the dispensing of the liquid by the dispensing device. The fill line is adapted to be connected to existing plumbing, such as a toilet water supply line behind a wall adjacent the toilet.

Rodney Griffin: "Cutting tool for machining a plumbing nipple" is is patented by Rodney Griffin.

Sacramento County: Publication of "The County of Sacramento plumbing trade competency: Ordinance no. SCC 647 (2/18/86) amended by Ordinances SCC--670, --671, --697, and --728." Publisher: Building Inspection Division (Sacramento, Calif). Published in 1992.

Sanjiv K. Basseen, et al.: "Oil/water separator" is patented by Sanjiv K. Basseen, Devendra K. Sahu and Masoud Zarif. Abstract: A separator for removing oil-like substances from water using vertical columns of coalescing media to then enhance separation of the two phases. The coalescing media is an inert packing material having surfaces to enhance coalescing without significant resistance to flow. Final oil removal is achieved by a vertical column of charcoal pellets. The separator is of particular value in the processing of oil/water discharges from air compressing systems. This produces water that can be discharged in an environmentally safe manner to conventional sewers, etc. The oil is held in a convenient storage vessel for ultimate disposal. No pumping devices are needed in the separator as flow is provided either by the pressure in the outlet from the compressor system, or by gravity from a feed tank.

Softdesk, Inc: Publication of "AdCADD architectural: plumbing application guide." Published in 1992.

Standards Australia: Publisher of "National plumbing and drainage code. Part 1, Water supply." Publisher: Standards Australia (Homebush, N.S.W.). Published in 1992.

Steven D. Hiebert: "Fish egg and larvae collection system" is patented by Steven D. Hiebert. Abstract: A system for continuously collecting and preserving fish eggs and larvae by pumping, concentrating, separating, and preserving samples for a specific period of time or volume. Water containing fish eggs and larvae is pumped by a centrifugal pump through smooth-walled plumbing into a headbox. Water flows out of the headbox over a sheet-metal ogee crest down over an inclined panel and then across a wedge-wire screen. Water with retained material drops through smooth-walled plumbing and a swing-joint union into a diverter arm. The swing-joint union is coupled through a chain and sprocket to a stepper motor programmable to position the diverter arm over each of the sample buckets.

STS-45: Launch: March 24, 1992, 8:13 a.m. EST. Launch originally scheduled for March 23, but was delayed one day because of higher-than-allowable concentrations of liquid hydrogen and liquid oxygen in the orbiter's aft compartment during tanking operations. During troubleshooting, the leaks could not be reproduced, leading engineers to believe that they were the result of plumbing in the main propulsion system not thermally conditioned to the supercold propellants. Launch was rescheduled for March 24. Launch weight: 233,650 lb (105,982 kg). [WP]

Sunset Pub. Corp: Publisher of "Basic plumbing illustrated." By the editors of Sunset and Southern living; (book editors, Lynne Gilberg, Don Vandervort). Publisher: Sunset Pub. Corp (Menlo Park, CA). Published in 1992.

Thomas E. Nelson: "Water heater construction and method of making same" is patented by Thomas E.

Nelson. Abstract: A water heater construction and method includes arranging the inner water tank and the surrounding outer shell in an inverted orientation and positioning the outer shell into a cover which is arranged with clearance openings for the plumbing connections extending from the top of the tank to extend therethrough. With the tank, shell and cover in an inverted and assembled condition, the annular clearance space defined between the tank and shell is filled, at least the majority, with liquid, foam-in-place insulation.

Tom E. Robbins: "Plumbing spout" is patented by Tom E. Robbins. Abstract: A plumbing spout is disclosed that discharges a hollow cylinder of water. In one form, the inside of the cylinder can be viewed from the top of the spout. Concentric walls are provided in a spout body to equalize the pressure of the entering water around the spout circumference. An inner wall extends below an outer wall when the fluid discharges from the spout to assist in cylinder formation. The portion of the inner wall that extends below the outer wall preferably also flares outwardly.

Willi Schutz and Ferdinand Hochstrasser: "Anti-siphoning valve assembly and plumbing fixture including same" is is patented by Willi Schutz and Ferdinand Hochstrasser.

Wood, Robert W.: Born in 1933, authored "All thumbs guide to home plumbing." Robert W Wood; illustrations by Steve Hoeft. Publisher: tab Books (Blue Ridge Summit, PA). Published in 1992.

Woodson, Roger Dodge: Born in 1955, authored "The complete guide to home plumbing repair and replacement: a practical guide to (almost always) doing it yourself." Publisher: Betterway Books (Cincinnati, Ohio). Published in 1992.

1993

Amar K. Burayez and Nathan H. Noe: "Liquid heater using electrical oscillations" is patented by Amar K. Burayez and Nathan H. Noe. Abstract: A diathermal water heater for the rapid and controlled heating of water and like fluids. A diathermal heating chamber uses electrical oscillations to heat liquids flowing through it. By means of feedback circuitry, the electrical oscillations are controlled to provide liquids at a constant temperature. Household and industrial quantities of hot water, wet steam and dry steam may be generated by the water heater. The heater itself is compact and can be used to provide one pipe plumbing to provide water at controlled heated temperatures.

American Society of Plumbing Engineers: Publisher of "Technical proceedings of the 1992 ASPE Convention: November 14-18, 1992, Washington, D.C." Publisher: American Society of Plumbing Engineers (Westlake, CA). Published in 1993.

Bradley C. Burgess and Joseph D. Esker: "Prism pole for a surveying system" is patented by Bradley C. Burgess and Joseph D. Esker. Abstract: The prism pole consists of an extensible aluminum pole that can be adjusted between a length of 30 and 47 inches. The pole has a hardened steel point on one end thereof and a prism assembly on its opposite end. The prism pole also has a steel point mounted to the prism assembly such that the pole can be turned "upside down" placing the prism assembly approximately 4 inches from the point being measured. To assist in plumbing the prism pole, two level vials are provided, the first being observable when the pole is in the upright position and the second being observable when the pole is in the upside down position.

Bruce Mulholland: "Polymeric acetals resistant to mineral deposition" is patented by Bruce Mulholland. Abstract: Polymeric compositions characterized by containing polymeric acetals and zinc-containing inorganic fillers exhibiting improved resistance to the formation and adhesion of mineral deposits when used in applications wherein the composition is exposed to water containing dissolved minerals for extended periods of time. The composition may be prepared into shaped articles which are useful as mineral resistant, plumbing fixtures.

Building Dept., City and County of Honolulu, State of Hawaii: Publisher of "Building code of the City and County of Honolulu, and fees and permits for building, electrical, plumbing and sidewalk codes." Publisher: Building Dept., City and County of Honolulu, State of Hawaii (Honolulu). Published in 1993.

Building Officials and Code Administrators International: Publication of "The BOCA national plumbing code / 1993: model building regulations for the protection of public health, safety and welfare." As recommended and maintained by the voting membership of Building Officials & Code Administrators International, Inc. Publisher: Building Officials & Code Administrators International, Inc (Country Club Hills, Ill). Published in 1993.

Bureau of the Census: Publisher of "We asked--: you told us: complete plumbing and kitchen facilities." Publisher: Bureau of the Census (Washington, D.C.). Published in 1993.

California Energy Commission: Publisher of "Directory of certified plumbing fittings and plumbing fixtures." Building & Appliance Efficiency Office, Energy Efficiency & Local Assistance Division. Publisher: California Energy Commission (Sacramento, Calif). Published in 1993.

Canada. Industrie, sciences et technologie Canada: Publication of "Profil de l'industrie: produits de plomberie = Industry profile: plumbing products Plumbing products Produits de plomberie Industry profile: plumbing products." Publisher: Industrie, sciences et technologie Canada, (Ottawa). Published in 1993.

Canadian Commission on Building and Fire Codes: Publication of "Canadian plumbing code 1990: first series of proposed changes = Code canadien de la plomberie 1990: premières modifications proposées Code canadien de la plomberie 1990: premières modifications proposées." Publisher: Canadian Commission on Building and Fire Codes (Ottawa). Published in 1993.

Canadian Standards Association: Publication of "Polypropylene (PP-R) pipe and fittings for pressure applications: plumbing products and materials." Canadian Standards Association; (Technical editor: Jim Carnegie; Managing editor: Bernard Kelly). Publisher: Canadian Standards Association (Rexdale, Ont). Published in 1993.

Clifford B. Cordy: "Solar powered high pressure steam generator" is patented by Clifford B. Cordy. Abstract: A point focus distributed receiver system for generating high-pressure steam by means of solar energy collection is disclosed. The cradle within which a gimbal mounted concentrator dish rotates is designed to withstand high wind forces by delivering all forces along the polar axis to the equatorial end of the cradle, requires only one structural member to withstand flexural forces and provides an unobstructed volume behind the axis of rotation for the concentrator dish to rotate in. The concentrator dish comprises a plurality of segments whose bracing forms a tee-pee-like structure behind the dish.

Dan R. Howell: "Adjustable surface mount plumbing adapter" is is patented by Dan R. Howell.

Daniel C. Shaw and Donald F. Bush: "Push button assembly for control of plumbing fixtures in prisons and the like" is is patented by Daniel C. Shaw and Donald F. Bush.

David R. Livingston: "Method of insulating a spa using a flexible insulation blanket" is patented by David R. Livingston. Abstract: A portable type spa is insulated by a sequence of steps involving initially the preparation of an insulation blanket having a metal foil heat reflective surface on one side with orthogonal dimensions of the blanket sized larger than the orthogonal dimensions of the spa shell. The spa shell is placed on top of the insulation blanket in a preferred method, with the metal foil heat reflective surface facing the exterior of the spa shell. The spa shell foot well is leveled by shims placed between the bottom of the spa shell and the underlying support surface such as a floor. The periphery of the insulation blanket is preferably sandwiched between the underside of a spa rim and a top edge of wood skirt panels surrounding the exterior of the spa shell.

David Sol: "Water plumbing instrumentation and control system for recreational vehicles and marine vessels" is is patented by David Sol.

Delta Communications: Publisher of "Plumbing, heating, piping." Publisher: Delta Communications (Chicago, IL). Published in 1993.

Department of Energy: Sponsored research

"Technical support document: Energy efficiency standards for consumer products: Room air conditioners, water heaters, direct heating equipment, mobile home furnaces, kitchen ranges and ovens, pool heaters, fluorescent lamp ballasts and television sets. Volume 3, Water heaters, pool heaters, direct heating equipment, and mobile home furnaces." Sponsored by: Department of Energy, Washington, DC. Office of Codes and Standards. Abstract: This is Volume 3 in a series of documents on energy efficiency of consumer products. This volume discusses energy efficiency of water heaters. Water heaters are defined by NAECA as products that utilize oil, gas, or electricity to heat potable water for use outside the heater upon demand. These are major appliances, which use a large portion (18% on average) of total energy consumed per household (1). They differ from most other appliances in that they are usually installed in obscure locations as part of the plumbing and are ignored until they fail. Residential water heaters are capable of heating water up to 180(degrees)F, although the setpoints are usually set lower.

Dixon, Graham: Born in 1950, authored "The washerdrier & tumbledrier manual: DIY plumbing, maintenance, repair." Publisher: Haynes (Sparkford). Published in 1993.

Donnie R. Fell Sr: "Plumbing test and trap fitting" is is patented by Donnie R. Fell Sr.

Dragon's World, Ltd.; New York Smithmark Pub., Inc: Publisher of "Plumbing: a step-by-step guide." Publisher: Dragon's World, Ltd.; New York Smithmark Pub., Inc (London). Published in 1993.

Dwight N. Johnson: "Plumbing hookup kit" is patented by Dwight N. Johnson. Abstract: A plumbing hookup kit includes a length of flexible tubing having terminals mounted on each end; different sized brass compression nuts; a brass ferrule; a pair of identical plastic sealing sleeves of one size and a pair of identical plastic sealing sleeves of another size; four identical split locking ring components, pairs of which are adapted to be combined into a locking ring; a pair of identical sealing rings of one size and another larger sealing ring. Different components of the plumbing hookup kit enable the establishment of a fluid tight connection between any of a number of different male threaded fittings in 3/8", 7/16" and 1/2" sizes, each of the type that cooperates with a corresponding one of a plurality of coupling nuts.

Erik W. Peterson: "Aspiration system having pressure-controlled and flow-controlled modes" is patented by Erik W. Peterson. Abstract: An aspiration system (10) having pressure-controlled and flow-controlled modes comprises connective plumbing (26), a collector (14), a pump (12), a variable flow resistor (20), a pressure sensor (18).

G. Robert Goss, et al.: "Animal litter with galactomannan gum clumping agent and carrageenan gum extender" is patented by G. Robert Goss, Olga I. Spaldon and Nancy L. Nolan. Abstract: A composition for a clumping animal litter forms agglomerates upon contact with relatively small amounts of an aqueous liquid, such as an animal body fluid, yet rapidly disperses upon disposal in a household plumbing system to produce only non-swelling clay particles and biodegradable end products. The animal litter composition is substantially dust-free, and can be safely ingested by pets. The composition includes non-swelling clay and/or diatomaceous earth particles and a galactomannan gum that has been distributed in a non-toxic liquid vehicle on the surface of the free-flowing clay particles. The galactomannan gum may be a guar gum or a locust bean gum, or an ether derivative of guar gum or locust bean gum.

Gerhard Fischer: "Plumbing fixture" is patented by Gerhard Fischer. Abstract: The plumbing fixture, which can be actuated without physical contact, has a water line that is connected to a source of water and has a water outlet. A shut-off valve is disposed in the water line downstream of a mixer valve. A control unit controls the shut-off valve as a function of control signals from a proximity-sensitive sensor. A turbine is disposed in the water line for supplying electrical energy to the control unit. Permanent magnets are distributed equidistantly about an outer periphery of a wheel of the turbine. At the level of the permanent magnets, at least two magnet coils are provided in a tubular section of the water line. The coils cooperate with the permanent magnets to form a generator.

Government of Venezuela: Decree 3133 of 9/9/93 contains Partial Regulation 6 of the Organic Law to Decentralize, Limit, and Transfer Jurisdictions of the Public Power to a Council of Government for the Metropolitan Area of Caracas. Provides for the membership of the Council of Government of the Caracas Metropolitan Area. Creates committees for the Council to cover the areas of urban planning; transportation and traffic; security and urban police; urban cleanliness; aqueducts and plumbing; public health; and urban maintenance. Articles 18 and 19 deal with the sharing of information on local government matters. Published in Gaceta Oficial on September 09, 1993.

Henri D. Limet, et al.: "Thermostatic mixing device" is patented by Henri D. Limet, Francois P. Vogt, Jacques R. Debaecker and Kathleen S. DeKeyser. Abstract: A fluid mixing device which can adjust for temperature fluctuations of fluids wherein a thermal expansion element drives a reciprocating member and has a portion extending into and through a fluid inlet. In a preferred embodiment, the inlet is a common inlet for both hot and cold fluids and the flow of fluid is controlled as it exits from the mixing device. A fluid mixing device which is highly responsive to fluid temperatures results and is particularly suited for use in plumbing fixtures of various types.

Industry Training and Apprenticeship Commission: Publisher of "Plumbing apprenticeship: training record book." Publisher: Industry Training and Apprenticeship Commission (Victoria). Published in 1993.

Institute of New Zealand Plumbing & Drainage Inspectors. Conference: Publication of "It's all right here: 1993 Dunedin Conference, Institute of N.Z. Plumbing & Drainage Inspectors Inc., March 1st - 3rd, Dunedin Town Hall." Publisher: The Institute (Palmerston North?, N.Z.). Published in 1993.

International Centre for Theoretical Physics: Sponsored research "Pinching and plumbing deformations of quadratic rational maps." Sponsored by: International Centre for Theoretical Physics, Trieste (Italy). Written by P. Makienko. Abstract: We apply the pinching, plumbing constructions to study the boundaries of spaces quasiconformal deformations of rational maps. (author). 26 refs, 3 pictures.

Jeffery A. Humber: "Washing machine or ice maker outlet box installation with torque inhibiting water supply connection" is patented by Jeffery A. Humber. Abstract: A plumbing installation is provided which includes an outlet box, at least one water supply pipe extending into the box and a torque inhibiting connection between the pipe and a boiler drain valve positioned in the interior of the box. A compression nut is screwed over a male threaded lower shank of the boiler drain valve to compress a ferrule around the upper end of the water supply pipe. A male threaded cylindrical adapter is connected to, and extends downwardly from, the compression nut through a water supply hole in a bottom wall of the outlet box. The adapter surrounds the water supply pipe. A lock nut is screwed over the adapter and squeezes the bottom wall between the compression nut and the lock nut.

Jeffrey D. Cohen: "Water flow monitoring system for determining the presence of leaks and stopping flow in plumbing pipes" is is patented by Jeffrey D. Cohen.

Jerry B. Monroe, et al.: "Counter top reverse osmosis system" is patented by Jerry B. Monroe, Wayne T. Widenburg, Jon S. Ford and James A. Monroe. Abstract: A reverse osmosis (RO) unit uses a membrane permitting operation at abnormally low water pressures, typically as low as 10 PSI. Because any requirement for a pump to boost inlet water pressure is obviated, the RO unit makes do with only one, small and compact, outlet pump. An optional single, or a dual-channel dual-pass, ultraviolet (UV) light source sterilizes filtered inlet, and/or the purified output, water flows. Purified water is stored at atmospheric pressure in a simple storage bag, and is dispensed on demand by force of the outlet pump. The entire RO unit--storage bag, pump, filters, UV sterilizer, membrane and all--is preferably entirely integrally packaged in a compact and aesthetically pleasing cylindrically-shaped housing.

1993

John A. Houlihan: "Hot water recovery system" is patented by John A. Houlihan. Abstract: An on demand, remotely activated, electronically and electro-mechanically controlled, energy saving, water conservation, hot, water recovery system, which may be installed in residential and commercial structures having a pressurized water supply (11). The system is comprised of a dual chamber, dual hot water outlet, water heating reservoir (23), and a flow control and recovery apparatus (10), in fluid communication with a cold water supply (11) and hot water outlets (93-97). The system installs in new or existing structures, without alteration of the plumbing lines or electrical wiring.

John H. Hendrich: "Assembly and method for constructing a building" is patented by John H. Hendrich. Abstract: An assembly is provided for constructing a building, which can be used to construct a high rise building. A building assembly unit is prefabricated in a factory, and is transported to a construction site. The unit includes a floor member and a pivotably connected wall member, which may be an exterior or interior wall. Electrical wiring, plumbing, ventilation, doorways, windows, and so forth may be pre-installed in the factory. Each unit is configured to be installed on a support structure, which may be a high rise support structure. Each unit is connected to the support structure, and to a proximate unit.

John R. McDonald, et al.: "Gray water recycle system" is patented by John R. McDonald, Michael P. Henry and Ronald J. Steele. Abstract: A modular, retrofittable, and portable drain water recycle system, for installation into, and removal from, an existing host plumbing system having a host water supply, a sink, a tub or shower, a toilet, and a sewer. The modules include a drain fixture module, a system control module, and a storage tank module, all interconnectable. Gray water is collected from a tub, shower, or sink, by a drain fixture module, and is stored in a storage tank module for reuse in flushing a toilet. The drain fixture module and storage tank module are controlled by the system control module. Capacity can be altered by adding or removing storage tank modules. Different host systems can be accommodated by adding or removing drain fixture modules and system control modules.

Joseph A. Cavaness: "Composite building panel" is patented by Joseph A. Cavaness. Abstract: Provided is a composite building panel including, in accordance with a preferred embodiment, a planar concrete slab portion at the front and a plurality of elongated frame members at the rear. Each frame member includes a first end and an opposite second end that define a length therebetween, and a front side and a rear side which define a width therebetween which is less than the length. The front side of each frame member is imbedded in the concrete slab portion along the entire length of the frame member, and the rear side of each frame member is oriented opposite from the concrete slab portion.

Joseph Decker: "Tool for removing and inserting a plumbing fixture seal structure" is is patented by Joseph Decker.

Joseph P. Ismert and Frank J. Julian: "Hook shaped pipe hanger" is patented by Joseph P. Ismert and Frank J. Julian. Abstract: A pipe hanger is formed of an elongate stem joined to a flexible, curved, substantially semicircular lower hook portion. The stem has holes therethrough for nailing to a support beam and suspending a run of plumbing piping from the support beam. The hook portion is of commensurate size to the pipe and cradles the pipe in a suspended position. In a preferred embodiment, a tooth extending angularly, outwardly and downwardly from the portion of the stem adjacent to the hook portion cooperates with the hook tip so that there is a snap fit between the tooth end and the hook tip as the pipe is urged therebetween and into a retained, cradling relation in the hook portion.

Jurgen Humpert, et al.: "Leak shield for recessed valve" is patented by Jurgen Humpert, Bruno Heimann and Harald Dickel. Abstract: A shield is used in combination with a wall having an outer surface and formed with a throughgoing hole having an edge and with a plumbing fixture almost entirely recessed behind the wall surface and having a control part projecting forward through the hole past the surface. The shield is elastically deformable waterproof and is formed unitarily with a cup-shaped body generally surrounding the plumbing fixture and with an annular bellows-type cuff surrounding the control part and having a rear edge unitarily joined to the body and a front edge fixed to the wall surface at the hole edge.

Karl Rafeld: "Plumbing and heating pipe system for water supply purposes, made either completely or mainly of plastic material, especially of polypropylene" is is patented by Karl Rafeld.

Karl Sutherland, et al.: "Multi-functional valve with unitary valving member and improved safety" is patented by Karl Sutherland, Frederick J. Reinhart and Terry Sprague. Abstract: A pressure-responsive control valve is especially useful to control aspiration of fluids from a patient during a surgical procedure. The control valve includes features which control the aspiration suction level communicated to the patient, which prevent reverse flow positive pressure from communicating to the patient, which safely vents such a reverse flow positive pressure in the event it reaches a level jeopardizing the integrity of the valve or plumbing fixtures, and which prevents aspirated fluids from weeping from the valve into the surgical environment in the event that a positive pressure communicates to the inlet of the control valve.

Konrad Bergmann: "Plumbing fixture with passage choke having a knockout" is is patented by Konrad Bergmann.

Larry G. McKinney Sr: "Fluid assisted casting apparatus" is patented by Larry G. McKinney Sr. Abstract: An apparatus and method for automated casting of an item such as a plumbing fixture is disclosed. Female and male mold portions provide a spacing for molding the desired item between them. A fluid release system is operatively positioned inside one of the mold portions so as to assist in separating the formed item from a mold portion in a controlled and uniform manner so as to minimize damage to the cast item. In a preferred form, a liquid is ejected into the corners of a male mold. By diffusion the liquid travels to the periphery of the mold piece so as to drive the formed part off the mold.

Lawrence Livermore National Lab.: Sponsored research "Regenerative fuel cells for High Altitude Long Endurance Solar Powered Aircraft." Sponsored by: Lawrence Livermore National Lab., CA.; Department of Energy, Washington, DC. Written by F. Mitlitsky, N. J. Colella, B. Myers and C. J. Anderson. Abstract: High Altitude Long Endurance (HALE) unmanned missions appear to be feasible using a lightweight, high efficiency, span-loaded, Solar Powered Aircraft (SPA) which includes a Regenerative Fuel Cell (RFC) system and novel tankage for energy storage. An existing flightworthy electric powered flying wing design was modified to incorporate present and near-term technologies in energy storage, power electronics, aerodynamics, and guidance and control in order to design philosophy was to work with vendors to identify affordable near-term technological opportunities that could be applied to existing designs in order to reduce weight, increase reliability, and maintain adequate efficiency of components for delivery within 18 months.

Los Alamos National Lab.: Sponsored research "Effects of magmatic processes on the potential Yucca Mountain repository: Field and computational studies." Sponsored by: Los Alamos National Lab., NM.; Department of Energy, Washington, DC. Written by G. A. Valentine, K. R. Groves, C. W. Gable, F. V. Perry and B. M. Crowe. Abstract: Assessing the risk of future magmatic activity at a potential Yucca Mountain radioactive waste repository requires, in addition to event probabilities, some knowledge of the consequences of such activity. Magmatic consequences are divided into an eruptive component, which pertains to the possibility of radioactive waste being erupted onto the surface of Yucca Mountain, and a subsurface component, which occurs whether there is an accompanying eruption or not. The subsurface component pertains to a suite of processes such as hydrothermal activity, changes in country rock properties, and long term alteration of the hydrologic flow field which change the waste isolation system. This paper is the second in a series describing progress on studies of the effects of magmatic activity.

Lowell C. Schirado, et al.: "Quick connect coupling system" is patented by Lowell C. Schirado, James

L. Chambers and Richard H. Whitaker. Abstract: A male/female quick-connect system is provided which is adapted to sealingly couple to the opening of a container of liquid product. The female component of the system is adapted to couple to any standard 3/4" plumbing fitment and/or 1/4" ID standpipe and is self-venting so that any stock container can be used without modification. The male component which sealingly couples to the female component is provided with a barbed tip adapted to receive a variety of feed line sizes. A one-way elastomeric valve is disposed in the male member which only allows product to flow therethrough when the male component is coupled to a source of vacuum thereby preventing product from flowing back into the container.

Lynwood W. Swanson, et al.: "Secondary ion mass spectometry system" is patented by Lynwood W. Swanson, John M. Lindquist, Milton C. Jaehnig and Joseph Puretz. Abstract: A focused ion beam is directed toward a sample to be analyzed while iodine vapor is directed toward the sample. The iodine vapor, which is formed by heating solid iodine to a temperature of 30.degree. C. to 50.degree. C., aids in sputtering of material impinged by the ion beam and in enhancing the conversion of neutral to ionic sputtered species. A quadrupole mass analyzer is positioned for receiving secondary ions sputtered from the sample whereby chemical analysis is accomplished. The iodine may be initially handled in a solid state, exhibiting a low vapor pressure, and is then heated to moderate temperatures inside a focused ion beam system without presenting a toxic hazard or requiring external plumbing.

Manitoba. Manitoba Labour: Publication of "Manitoba Plumbing Code 1992. Book." Publisher: National Research Council of Canada (Ottawa). Published in 1993.

Merceret, Honor: Author of "Our plumbing, ourselves: a public bath house." Published in 1993.

Michael A. Erman: "Level" is patented by Michael A. Erman. Abstract: A hand tool for leveling operations includes level and plumb indicators in an elongated, linear support member, or body. Disposed on opposed ends of the support member are first and second telescoping extension members. By positioning the distal end of one extension member in a recessed point or line on a wall, commonly known as a "quirk", and using the level indicator, a point or a line on another adjacent wall at the same elevation, or height, may be precisely located. The opposed extensions may also be used with a ruler to precisely measure the vertical distance between a structure inaccessible by a conventional level, such as a doorway header, and the edge of an adjacent structure, such as a ceiling beam.

Michael Beals and Brian Marine: "Door frame assembly jig" is patented by Michael Beals and Brian Marine. Abstract: An assembly jig for bracing a metal door frame includes a pair of squaring braces that fit into diagonally opposite corners of metal door frame that square the door frame and a door-spreading brace that interacts with the squaring braces at a single point which properly spaces the side jambs of the door frame. The squared door frame may be plumbed with a pair of plumbing braces which attach to the floor by means of an anchor plate.

Michael R. Stoltenberg and Brian Neuhaus: "Plumbing trap water collection device" is is patented by Michael R. Stoltenberg and Brian Neuhaus.

National Association of Plumbing, Heating and Mechanical Services Contractors: Publication of "Members' reference book and buyers' guide - The National Association of Plumbing, Heating and Mechanical Services Contractors." Published in 1993.

National Board of Waters and the Environment: Sponsored research "Valtakunnallinen kaivovesitutkimus. Talousveden laatu ja siihen vaikuttavat tekijaet. (Nationwide rural well water survey. The quality of household water and factors influencing it)." Sponsored by: National Board of Waters and the Environment, Helsinki (Finland).; Ministry of Social Affairs and Health, Helsinki (Finland). Written by K. Korkka-Niemi, A. Sipilae, T. Hatva, L. Hiisvirta and K. Lahti. Abstract: The quality of water in 1 421 drinking-water wells was monitored in a nationwide well water study. Samples were taken once from all wells, and during three seasons from 421 wells. The wells were selected in such a way that me sample would be as representative as possible of the quality of the drinking-water in households' own wells in rural areas. The study comprised general water quality parameters, influence of sampling season, and factors related to the type, the condition and the pollution of the wells. In part of the well waters selenium, radioactivity and pesticides were determined. The effect of plumbing materials on the quality of water was also examined. (33 refs., 148 figs., 71 tabs.).

National Inst. of Standards and Technology: Sponsored research "Impacts: NIST Building and Fire Research Laboratory (Technical and Societal). - Special pub." Sponsored by: National Inst. of Standards and Technology (BFRL), Gaithersburg, MD. Written by N. J. Raufaste. Abstract: The Building and Fire Research Laboratory (BFRL) of the National Institute of Standards and Technology (NIST) is dedicated to the life cycle quality of constructed facilities. The report describes major effects of BFRL's program on building and fire research.

New York State Dept. of Health: Sponsored research "Public Health Assessment for Hertel Landfill, Plattekill. Ulster County, New York, Region 2. CERCLIS No. NYD980780779. - Final rept." Sponsored by: New York State Dept. of Health, Albany.; Agency for Toxic Substances and Disease Registry, Atlanta, GA. Abstract: The Hertel Landfill site is located in the Town of Plattekill, Ulster County, New York. On-site subsurface soils, surface water and sediment were sampled and found to be contaminated with volatile organic compounds (VOCs), semi-volatile compounds and inorganic compounds. Off-site downgradient surface water and sediment are contaminated with inorganic compounds. Several semi-volatile compounds and VOCs have also been detected in off-site downgradient sediment samples. On-site groundwater is contaminated with VOCs, semi-volatile compounds and metals. Water from an off-site drinking water supply well was contaminated with lead; however, confirmatory sampling indicates the source is from the household plumbing and not from the site.

Nicholas Kozumplik Jr. and Gerald M. Distel: "Air operated double diaphragm pump" is patented by Nicholas Kozumplik Jr. and Gerald M. Distel. Abstract: The design of an air operated double diaphragm pump provides improved assembly, mounting flexibility, multiple plumbing combination including check valves which allow the pump to be mounted in any position without effecting its ability to prime or pump. A two shell housing design provides an enclosure for the air motor and includes structural ribbing, internal baffling, and all connections are made on the end of the pump in line with the diaphragm centerline allowing the pump to be installed in any access in line with the plumbing system.

Oak Ridge National Lab.: Sponsored research "Construction of a Solid State Research Facility, Building 3150. Environmental Assessment." Sponsored by: Oak Ridge National Lab., TN.; Department of Energy, Washington, DC. Abstract: The Department of Energy (DOE) proposes to construct a new facility to house the Materials Synthesis Group (MSG) and the Semiconductor Physics Group (SPG) of the Solid State Division, Oak Ridge National Laboratory (ORNL). The location of the proposed action is Roane County, Tennessee. MSG is involved in the study of crystal growth and the preparation and characterization of advanced materials, such as high-temperature superconductors, while SPG is involved in semiconductor physics research.

Ontario New Home Warranty Program: Publication of "Introduction to residential plumbing for home builders." Publisher: The Program (Toronto). Published in 1993.

Ontario Training and Adjustment Board: Publication of "Plumbing in school curriculum." Prepared by the Plumbing College Curriculum Advisory Committee for the Ontario Training and Adjustment Board. Publisher: Queen's Printer, March (Toronto). Published in 1993.

Ontario. Buildings Branch: Publication of "Code and guide to Part 7 (plumbing) of the Ontario Building Code." Publisher: Ontario Buildings Branch, Ministry of Housing (Toronto). Published in 1993.

Parsons Brinckerhoff Facilities Services:

Sponsored research "Condition Assessment Survey (CAS) Program. Deficiency standards and inspections methods manual: Volume 8, 0.08 Mechanical, Book 2." Sponsored by: Parsons Brinckerhoff Facilities Services, Inc., Herndon, VA.; Department of Energy, Washington, DC. Abstract: Inspection methods presented for plumbing, fire protection, heating, cooling, and special items (drinking water cooling systems).

Paul J. Barker: "Shut-off valve for installation immediately downstream from a defective valve mounted into the compression-connection type of outlet of the defective valve" is patented by Paul J. Barker. Abstract: A trouble-shooting shut-off valve includes an inlet-tail-tube mountable directly into a compression-fitting outlet socket of a defective shut-off valve, thus positioning the trouble-shooting valve immediately downstream from the defective valve in line in series with the defective valve. An inlet-tail-tube fitting is mounted onto an upstream end of the valve housing as a component of the valve. This fitting has an axial bore forming an upstream extension of an inlet passage in the valve housing. The inlet-tail-tube projects axially from this fitting adapted for insertion directly into such a socket in the defective valve.

Piero A. Policicchio: "Dental prophylaxis and water conservation device" is patented by Piero A. Policicchio. Abstract: A dental prophylaxis and water conservation device for in-home use. The device includes a tank coupled to the household water supply line and adapted to receive water which causes air contained within the tank to be pressurized. The water and air from within the tank are connected by lines to a handpiece which discharges both mediums simultaneously. Water leaving the tank passes through a container having an abrasive material which is picked up by the water and also discharged. The tank is further coupled to a plumbing fixture, such as a shower head. This enables the tank to be used as a water conservation device by allowing cold water to be purged from a hot water line into the tank, and subsequently used to provide water to the plumbing fixture.

Randal V. Hoffmeyer: "Combination plumb or level and height setting instruments" is patented by Randal V. Hoffmeyer. Abstract: An instrument set for plumbing or leveling and relative height setting of members such as posts or beams, each instrument including orthogonal sides and a feature projecting from the top of one side allowing each instrument to be set atop a respective post with the orthogonal sides against the post and a rabbeted feature on the bottom of one side allowing the instruments to be set atop a beam. Bubble levels on the sides of at least one of the instruments enable plumbing of a post or leveling of a beam, and open topped sight tubes attached to each instrument and interconnected with a water filled hose enable height setting with the same instruments.

Richard J. Goughneour: "Fluid conducting joint" is patented by Richard J. Goughneour. Abstract: A swivel joint connecting articulable fluid conducting arm members of a plumbing assembly includes an inlet member matable with a first arm member and having an inlet fluid passage from the arm member to an inlet collar section. An outlet member is provided matable with a second arm member. The outlet member also defines an outlet fluid passage from the respective second arm member to an outlet member collar section. A fluid conducting shaft member is disposed through the inlet and outlet member collar sections so that the collar sections rotate about the longitudinal axis of the shaft. A bearing sleeve is concentric about the shaft so that the collar sections rotate about the bearing sleeve.

Robert A. Rauscher Jr: "Method for attaching metallic tubing to nonmetallic pressure vessel, and pressure vessel made by the method" is patented by Robert A. Rauscher Jr. Abstract: A method for making a pressure tank includes procuring a metallic feed pipe (12) with a substantially cylindrical outer surface (312), a bore (21), and, at an attachment end thereof, an annular ring (350) protruding from the cylindrical outer surface. A dissolvable mandrel (410) in the shape of the desired tank or pressure vessel is made. The mandrel includes a neck portion (412, 414) dimensioned to fit within the bore of the feed pipe. If necessary, the outer surface of the mandrel is rendered electrically conductive, as for example by metal sputtering or evaporation, or by electroless deposition.

Sanjeev Madan, et al.: "Process for the preparation of a composite structure comprising a ceramic enamel layer and polyurethane layers" is patented by Sanjeev Madan, Hans-Joachim Kogelnik, Majid Daneshvar, Richard S. Pantone and Jan L. Clatty. Abstract: A novel polyurethane prepared by reacting a) a specific polyol or specific polyol blend, b) an organic diamine, c) fillers, and d) a specific polyisocyanate is described. The invention also relates to the use of the polyurethane in the preparation of a composite structure wherein the polyurethane is applied to an adhesive coated ceramic enamel layer. The composites are eminently suitable for use in plumbing applications (e.g. as a bathtub).

The Centre: Publisher of "Small business profile for plumbing businesses for the financial year ended 30th June, 1991." Publisher: The Centre (Armidale, N.S.W.). Published in 1993.

Thomas J. Pogorzelski and Kevin B. Sinnett: "Disc brake caliper with auxiliary system to cool brake fluid" is patented by Thomas J. Pogorzelski and Kevin B. Sinnett. Abstract: A disc brake caliper with auxiliary system to cool brake fluid for use in a high performance automobile includes a brake caliper (12) and a cooling system (14). The brake caliper (12) has a housing (34), a first conduit (60), and a second conduit (74). The first conduit (60) conveys a hydraulic fluid to first and second bores (48, 50), whereby pistons received within the bores (48, 50) may be activated to press friction pads (22, 26) against a rotor (16) and provide a braking action. The second conduit (74) conveys a coolant through the housing (34) to a region proximal the first conduit (60). The cooling system (14) comprises the second conduit (74), a pump (94), and a radiator (96) connected in series via connective plumbing (92) to form a fluid circuit.

Wilkes, Michael: Author of "Basin plumbing dynamics: modelling flow in the Weald Basin, Southern England." Published in 1993.

William D. Guentzler: "Galvanic anode device and electrolysis control monitor" is patented by William D. Guentzler. Abstract: The use of a sacrificial anode in a plumbing system or in the cooling system of an internal combustion engine or the like to protect the system against the destructive effects of electrolysis caused by the many different metals employed in modern plumbing systems or engines is disclosed, along with several methods and apparatus for monitoring the condition of the sacrificial anode to indicate when replacement is needed for continued protection of the system. Physical, optical and electrical systems are taught, each designed to indicate the need for replacement of the anode in an easily discernable manner.

Woodson, Roger Dodge: Born in 1955, authored "National plumbing codes handbook." Publisher: McGraw-Hill (New York, N.Y.). Published in 1993.

1994

American National Standards Institute: Publication of "Safety requirements for plumbing." Secretariat MCA/NAPHCC Joint Task Force. Publisher: National Association of Plumbing-Heating-Cooling Contractors (Rockville, MD. Mechanical Contractors Association of America; Falls Church, Va.). Published in 1994.

Amtrol Inc: Publication of "Amtrol Inc. Residential Heating & Plumbing, Water System Products 1994." Published in 1994.

Ava Madison: "Portable cleaning device" is patented by Ava Madison. Abstract: A portable hand held cleaning device is adapted to receive various cleaning implements, such as bristle brushes, abrasive wheels, chisels, and the like, into a tool engaging member. The tool engaging member is preferably operable by a rechargeable battery to selectively rotate and/or reciprocate at varying speeds. The rechargeable battery is included in a housing. The tool engaging member is preferably displaceable to improve the efficiency of the cleaning device in hard to reach areas. The housing may further include plumbing and a pump for delivering fluid from a cleansing fluid container to a discharge proximate the cleaning tool engaging member.

Ballantyne, Brian Andrew: Born in 1959, authored "'This must be the place': plumbing a land ethic for the built environment: a thesis submitted for the degree of Doctor of Philosophy, University of Otago, Dunedin, New Zealand." Published in 1994.

Boyce, Robert: Author of "Plumbing: prerequisite modules for NVQ level 2." Publisher: Stanley Thornes (Cheltenham). Published in 1994.

California Building Standards Commission: Publication of "Uniform plumbing code. California plumbing code." Publisher: International Conference of Building Officials (Sacramento, CA: California Building Standards Commission; Whittier, Calif). Published in 1994.

Center for Fjernvarmeteknologi: Sponsored research "Mikrobiel vaerkst i fjernvarmeroer - en forundersoegelse. (Microbial growth in district heating pipes - preliminary investigation)." Sponsored by: Center for Fjernvarmeteknologi, Tastrup (Denmark). Written by H. D. Smidt. Abstract: Questionnaires on plants, supplementary and district heating water, connections and corrosion were sent to 332 Danish district heating plants. After analysis of the replies, 41 district heating plants were selected for interviews of which 39 took place. An investigation of microbial conditions of the water from 4 plants was carried out. Based on these investigations, it can be concluded that 10% of the plants have experienced the problem of steel corrosion and ca. 6% have experienced corrosion of copper containing sensors or soldering in connection with the latter. Interviews and a microbial investigation of the district heating water as well as the consumption of biocide in the water indicated that corrosion could be due to microorganisms.

Coleman Vickary: "Apparatus for lifting and tilting heavy containers" is patented by Coleman Vickary. Abstract: Apparatus is disclosed for engaging, raising and rotating tanks/cylinders which contain liquids or gases under pressure. The apparatus comprises a cradle rotationally mounted on an elevator housing. While the tank/cylinder is elevated, an auto turn linkage in one embodiment of the apparatus assists in turning the cradle assembly by engagement with an indexing mechanism. Once the tank has been rotated 90 degrees, the indexing mechanism is locked in place, the auto turn linkage is released, and evacuation plumbing is affixed to the tank. The tank is then manually inverted for evacuation of the liquid.

David L. Sordello: "System of plumbing for an over-the-road vehicle" is is patented by David L. Sordello.

Delmar Publishers: Publisher of "Pocket reference to plumbing and pipefitting calculations." Contributing authors, James Sullivan, William Callahan; contributors, Maurice O'Connell ... (et al.). Publisher: Delmar Publishers (Albany, NY). Published in 1994.

Dennis D. Palmer: "Sealing disc used in hydraulic testing of plumbing system" is is patented by Dennis D. Palmer.

Dept. of Environment and Land Management: Publisher of "Tasmanian plumbing code." Publisher: Dept. of Environment and Land Management (Hobart). Published in 1994.

Donald P. Freier and Andrew H. Matznick: "Vacuum breaker for faucets" is patented by Donald P. Freier and Andrew H. Matznick. Abstract: A faucet with a vacuum breaker for a pull-out spray head plumbing fixture is provided. The vacuum breaker is in the faucet housing and provides a guide for and surrounds an extendible and retractable hose connected to the pull-out spray head. The vacuum breaker has a flapper valve stretch fitted over a body member of the vacuum breaker. The body member also affords pivotal attachment of a spout. A tubular guide for the hose also provides a quick connect or disconnect feature.

Duncan, Justin: Author of "Plumbing technology." Published in 1994.

E & FN Spon: Publisher of "Plumbing and domestic heating 1995." Publisher: E & FN Spon (London). Published in 1994.

Floyd Cartwright: "Portable sofa and bathing unit" is patented by Floyd Cartwright. Abstract: A portable bathing unit for use in bathing bedridden patients is disclosed. The portable bathing unit includes a bath tub supported by a housing which is movably positionable in the proximity of a patient. Casters depend from the bottom of the housing to permit the portable bathing unit to be rolled in an upright posture. Additional casters are also attached to the rear of the housing which permit the portable bathing unit to be turned up on its rear and transported through narrow doorways. Water delivery and retrieval may be accomplished through the use of a submersible pump and a segment of conduit. Alternatively, a water delivery and retrieval may be accomplished through the use of an auxiliary faucet which is connected to an existing plumbing system.

Gianfranco Gobbi: "Universal clamp for supporting the wall mounted piping of external electrical, telephone or plumbing systems" is is patented by Gianfranco Gobbi.

Glenvale Publications: Publisher of "The Australian plumbing merchant." Publisher: Glenvale Publishers (Waverley, Vic). Published in 1994.

Goro Kambara: "Extended stroke linear actuator assembly" is patented by Goro Kambara. Abstract: An array of symmetrically disposed piston-cylinder assemblies may be utilized to produce oppositely directed movements along a single force axis. Plumbing between the various cylinders may be external or internal, or a combination thereof, the exact form depending upon the particular embodiment. The array may be fabricated as a unitized inter/plumbing configuration or from separate cylinders that are functionally retained about an inter/plumbing fixture.

Gulson, B. L., et al.: "Effect of plumbing systems on lead content of drinking water and contribution to lead body burden" appears in The Science of the Total Environment written by B. L. Gulson, A. J. Law, M. J. Korsch and K. J. Mizon. Published on April 29, 1994.

Hemp, Peter Addison: Author of "Installing & repairing plumbing fixtures." Publisher: taunton Press (Newton, CT). Published in 1994.

Holloway, David: Born in 1944, authored "The Which? book of plumbing & central heating." Publisher: Consumers' Association (London). Published in 1994.

Hometime: Publisher of "Plumbing (videocassette): preparation and installation." Hometime; producer/writer, Chris Balamut; director, Jeff Lyman. Publisher: Hometime (Chaska, MN). Published in 1994.

Institute of Plumbing: Publication of "Directory." Publisher: Institute of Plumbing (Hornchurch). Published in 1994.

Jack Navarez: "Post support with offset slanted stake and method for using same" is patented by Jack Navarez. Abstract: An anchoring device for retrofitting a possibly rot weakened wood post consisting of a slanted metal stake welded to a vertical attachment plate; where the device is bolted via the plate to the base area of the post above the ground; while the method includes digging an offset footing hole, then setting the bottom half of the stake in the footing hole with poured concrete after plumbing the post, temporarily bracing it, and mounting the device on it.

James P. Cowan: "Portable garden work station" is patented by James P. Cowan. Abstract: A portable wash basin stand for use outdoors that uses a common garden hose as a water connection between the stand and the nearest plumbing. The stand has a circular weighted base and four upright posts that support a sink. Arrayed on the upright posts are a number of bayonet mounts that can be used to support a variety of accessories including a garden umbrella, a paper towel dispenser, a paper cup dispenser, a soap dispenser, a working shelf and other useful accessories.

Jaye F. Wheeler and Glenn Sicard: "Automatic device for the detection and shutoff of excess water flow in pipes" is patented by Jaye F. Wheeler and Glenn Sicard. Abstract: A readily detachable automatic programmable water shutoff device for stopping the flow of excess water in plumbing pipes of a plumbing pipe system. This device requires no plumbing pipe system modifications for installation and use. The device comprises a detachable acoustic flow sensor which is placed externally on existing plumbing pipe, a detachable valve actuator which consist of a high torque motor attached to existing plumbing pipe valve stem, and a microprocessor based control circuit which a) monitors state of flow sensor, b) provides an operator control interface to the device, c) determines excess water flow conditions, d) provides an output signal to the high torque motor which shuts off the water for an excess water flow condition.

Jerome P. Downey: "Process for reducing lead leachate in brass plumbing components" is is patented by Jerome P. Downey.

Jim W. Horton and Harvel K. Crumley: "Metal wall stud" is patented by Jim W. Horton and Harvel K. Crumley. Abstract: A metal wall stud in the shape of an elongated open channel having pre-punched nail or screw holes and pre-punched passageways for electrical or plumbing facilities. Integral tabs extending beyond the ends of stud walls are foldable to provide connections to wooden plates or metal wall stud purlins in the construction framing. Split tabs integral with the bottom wall of the channel provide lateral stabilization, greater uplift loads, and the capability of being load bearing. A pair of studs have nesting capability to provide telescopic adjustability for walls in a vaulted ceiling room.

John D. Carroll Jr: "Energy and water saving laundry system" is patented by John D. Carroll Jr. Abstract: An energy and water conservation laundry mechanism which includes a plurality of automatic washing machines, a rinse water storage tank, plumbing which connects the storage tank to the each of the washing machines, and electrical controls which are tied into the existing control circuitry of the washing machines for selectively directing the flow of rinse water between the storage tank and the washing machines. The plumbing includes pumps and valves which enables rinse water, as stored in the storage tank, to be delivered to each washing machine at the beginning of a wash cycle and waste water from the wash cycle to be discharged into a conventional sewer line.

John Hughes: "Animal dross absorbent and method" is patented by John Hughes. Abstract: A composition and method of absorbing animal dross. In one embodiment, the composition comprises discrete particles (about 50 microns to about 3350 microns, preferably about 600 microns to about 3350 microns in size) of a non-compacted water-swellable bentonite clay that effectively absorbs animal dross and simultaneously agglomerates into a sufficiently large and stable mass, thereby permitting physical separation of the soiled and wetted water-swellable bentonite clay particles from discrete particles of the unsoiled and unwetted water-swellable bentonite clay even after partial drying of about 1 to about 24 hours at room temperature, without substantial sticking to animal paws and fur.

Joseph D. Robinson: "Plumbing adapter" is patented by Joseph D. Robinson. Abstract: A plumbing adapter for installation in series with a flexible conduit leading to a plumbing fixture, such as a toilet tank or a kitchen or bathroom sink. The adapter has a first end suitable for engagement in sealing relationship with the terminal end of the conduit and an opposite, second end configured to engage the coupling portion of the plumbing fixture in sealing relationship. A threaded side extension having an opening communicating with the water passage within the adapter is provided for coupling to an auxiliary appliance through which water is to be supplied.

Lovell C. Moore: "Ready-to-use copper pipe nipple apparatus" is patented by Lovell C. Moore. Abstract: A nonferrous nipple fitting apparatus and of the type that is preserved for future use in the field of plumbing. The nipple having two clean, xerotic surface recess fitting sections on its outer wall. A volume of inert gas has precluded oxidation of the recess fitting sections by surrounding the segment to be made into a nipple, before the fitting sections are established on the wall surface of the segment. A gas-impermeable bag surrounds the nipple and the volume of inert gas, after recess fitting sections are established on the pipe's wall surface within that volume. The apparatus provides a nonferrous pipe nipple fitting for solder-bonding, having clean, dry surface recess fitting sections that are preserved for future use.

Low-flow plumbing: Plumbing equipment that uses less water than was considered standard prior to January 1, 1994 (NAPHCC, 1992. Low flow plumbing products fact sheet. National

Association of Plumbing, Heating, and Cooling Contractors, Alexandria, VA).

M. Smith: "Mower hitch for lawn tractor" is patented by M. Smith. Abstract: A hitch attaches to a lawn tractor and draws two lawn mowers therebehind. The hitch includes a draw bar solidly mounted to the tractor, and a link for each towed mower, which mowers each include a bracket to the deck thereof. The links include plumbing tees perpendicularly arranged, so that universal joints are formed between the draw bar and the mowers. A third tee is provided at each bracket so that each mower may be individually tilted, as for enabling access to the underside while still ganged to the hitch. The draw bar, links, and third tee are made from readily available plumbing components. The resultant hitch is thus fabricated from readily available components, is durable, uncomplicated, and has wide flexibility in allowing for various attitudes of the mowers.

Mark A. Maniar: "Drain cleaning apparatus" is patented by Mark A. Maniar. Abstract: A drain cleaning system which utilizes a plumbing cable and nozzle assembly. A fluid-conveying hose is incorporated within a plumbing cable and a nozzle is affixed to the distal end of the cable and in communication with the hose. The nozzle includes a body having a rounded radius tip and a rotatably mounted ring having a plurality of radial jet passages formed therein. The ring and the body cooperatively define an annular passage therebetween. Pressurized water passes through the nozzle body and into the annular passage to produce a water bearing. The water is then discharged through the jet passages in the ring, causing the ring to rotate about the water bearing to produce a rotating spray of pressurized water.

Massey, Howard C.: Author of "Basic plumbing with illustrations." Publisher: Craftsman Book Co (Carlsbad, CA). Published in 1994.

Matthew L. Collins: "Wrench with tightening grip" is patented by Matthew L. Collins. Abstract: A unique and novel adjustable wrench including a fixed handle (10) and handle jaw (10C), a movable handle (12), pivoting about a dog (16) and assembled to a slide (18) by a pair of links (24). The wrench features parallel jaws and provides a significant mechanical advantage by multiplying and transferring the operator's force to an object to be held and/or turned. A set of unique holding plates (40 & 42), in the shape of an -U-, attached to fixed handle jaw (10C) and sliding jaw (18) by means of mounting bolts (44 & 46). Holding plates (40 & 42) may be removed and/or reversed, this enables the wrench to be adapted to various work situations including rough plumbing, soft metal, and reverse thread.

Miguel A. Suarez and Gilberto Avila: "Prefabricated bathroom walls" is patented by Miguel A. Suarez and Gilberto Avila. Abstract: A prefabricated polymer bathroom wall apparatus has a unitary molded wall section formed of a waterproof polymer and having a gridwork of interconnected molded frame portions forming a plurality of hollow cells therebetween and having a plurality of edges with one or more insets in the edges. Some of the molded frame portions are formed with elongated passageways therein to form prefabricated pipes in the wall section opening at the wall insets. Coupling members are attached to the ends of the passageways within the wall section edge insets whereby a lightweight prefabricated wall section can be attached to a wall for coupling to a building's plumbing and to plumbing fixtures.

Movie Release: The movie "Interior Plumbing" is released.

Murray Borod: "Hygienic spray apparatus" is patented by Murray Borod. Abstract: A hygienic spray bottle dispenses liquid through a discharge tube. The spray bottle includes an electrically powered pump for pressurizing the liquid; a discharge tube having a nozzle; a valve for dispensing the pressurized liquid; and a pickup tube extending to the bottom of the bottle. A rechargeable battery powers the pump. The discharge tube is configured to cooperate with a toilet bowl wall to allow the spray bottle to function as a portable bidet. The discharge tube has a sliding sleeve for selectively covering and uncovering liquid spray holes to vary the spray pattern or location. Alternatively, the discharge tube includes a flexible section to vary the orientation of the nozzle for douching.

Nibco, Inc: Publication of "Nibco, Inc. Plastic Plumbing Products: 1994." Published in 1994.

Oak Ridge Y-12 Plant: Sponsored research "Mercury detection with thermal neutrons." Sponsored by: Oak Ridge Y-12 Plant, TN.; Department of Energy, Washington, DC. Written by Z. W. Bell. Abstract: This report describes the work performed to design a gauge to detect mercury concealed within walls, floors, pipes, and equipment inside a building. The project arose out of a desire to decontaminate and decommission (D&D) a building in which mercury had been used as part of a chemical process. The building contains plumbing and equipment, some with residual mercury even after draining, sumps, and hollow walls. So that releases of mercury to the environment might be minimized during D&D activities, it was considered advisable to locate pockets of mercury that may have collected in concealed spaces so that they might be drained in a controlled fashion prior to the application of the wrecking ball or sledge hammer.

Office of the Massachusetts Secretary of State: Publisher of "Fuel gas and plumbing codes." Publisher: Office of the Massachusetts Secretary of State (Boston, Mass). Published in 1994.

Ohnemus, Stephen Patrick: Author of "A locational analysis of plumbing cooperatives." Published in 1994.

Plumbing Education Council of Texas: Publisher of "1994-1995 plumbers professional education journeyman, master and inspector." Publisher: Plumbing Education Council of Texas (Austin, Tex). Published in 1994.

Raymond J. Konger: "Duct chase frame for joists" is patented by Raymond J. Konger. Abstract: A duct chase frame is substituted for a portion of the length of a conventional wooden or metal floor joist to facilitate running hot or cold air ductwork, plumbing and even electrical wiring. The frame includes a pair of elongated metal channels of uniform cross-sectional configuration with two metal spacers spanning and maintaining a joist accepting separation between those channels. One of the spacers is generally U-shaped for receiving and cradling a lower edge of one end of a floor joist, and the other spacer has an inverted U-shape for engaging an upper edge of the floor joist in a location intermediate the joist ends. The inverted U-shaped support is located near a first end of the pair of metal channels and the U-shaped support is located intermediate the metal channel ends.

Richard C. Blaine: "Mobile pump and hose assembly deployment, decontamination, storage and transport system" is patented by Richard C. Blaine. Abstract: A mobile pump and hose assembly deployment, decontamination, storage.

Richard E. Clarke: "Seamless bathroom module for a marine vessel" is patented by Richard E. Clarke. Abstract: A prefabricated bathroom module for installation onto a deck of a marine vessel. The module having a floor sloped toward a drain assembly, a plurality of walls extending upward from the floor, and a ceiling attached to the top of the walls. The drain assembly has a drain trap arrangement with a drain line that extend from between the module floor and the deck of the vessel and connect to a drainage system of the vessel without penetrating through the deck. The module further having a plumbing system with water supply lines connected to the outside of the walls and routed to a common area, with control valves connected to the drain lines at the common area. An access panel mounted to a wall of the module adjacent to the control panels to provide a user easy access to the control valves.

Ripka, L. V.: Author of "Plumbing." Publisher: American Technical Publishers (Homewood, Ill). Published in 1994.

Robert W. Waterhouse: "Redundant joint structure and method" is patented by Robert W. Waterhouse. Abstract: Redundant joints for a wide variety of redundant-joint structures have three-way plumbing elbows (1, 5, 6) with coupling sleeves (2) into which two-way plumbing elbows (9, 13, 14) are inserted and rotated to form an infinite variety of angles of joining edges or sides of structural assemblies bordered by cylindrical beams (15) inserted into sleeves (12) in the two-way elbows. The three-way elbows can have different angles for particular structures than employed for conventional plumbing uses. For other structures, the three-way elbows have the same or similar angles as those employed for conventional plumbing.

Ronald Sproule: "Bleed valve for water supply for camping vehicle" is patented by Ronald Sproule. Abstract: A bleed valve apparatus for the fresh water system of a camping vehicle. The apparatus is interposed between a garden hose and the female hose coupling of the plumbing system of the camping vehicle. The apparatus includes a housing which contains three ends, one of which has a mating coupling for the camping vehicle plumbing system. A second end may be coupled to the garden hose. The third end is isolated from the other ends by a water valve which may be opened to allow the apparatus to serve as an outdoor faucet at the camping vehicle or to serve to allow water to drain from the camping vehicle plumbing when the user of the camping vehicle desires to disconnect from the external water system provided through the hose.

Smith, Lee: Born in 1935, authored "Plumbing technology: design and installation." Publisher: Delmar Publishers (Albany, N.Y.). Published in 1994.

Southern Building Code Congress International: Publisher of "Standard plumbing code." Publisher: Southern Building Code Congress International (Birmingham, AL). Published in 1994.

Steve H. Sachs: "Access panel assembly" is patented by Steve H. Sachs. Abstract: An access panel assembly with a door and multi-functional frame which prevents sagging and warping of the door from the frame, and which is more safely and easily installed in both new and existing building structures. Flush mounting of the door to either face of the frame is achieved by a symmetrical mechanism wherein the inner edge of all four sides of the frame opening contains a molded, shallow groove which is equidistantly located from the two faces of the frame. The door contains on its underside a plurality of molded tabs, wherein each edge of the door has one or more tabs located adjacent thereto. The molded tabs are resilient so that they deflect when the door is press-fitted into the frame from either face.

Stewart, Harper C.: Author of "75 year history of the United Association of Journeyman and Apprentices of the Plumbing and Pipe Fitting Industry: Local Union 741, Tucson, Arizona, 1918-1993." Publisher: The Local (Tucson, Ariz). Published in 1994.

The Association: Publisher of "Uniform plumbing code." International Association of Plumbing and Mechanical Officials. Publisher: The Association (Walnut, CA). Published in 1994.

Thomas Swierski: "Laser plumbing device" is patented by Thomas Swierski. Abstract: In a projected light plumb device which is buoyantly supported within a fluid-filled container on a float platform which is horizontally supported by the fluid, an improvement wherein the float platform is inclined upwardly from its outer diameter to its inner diameter on its lower surface which rests in the fluid to allow any developed air bubbles on the lower surface of the float platform to escape. Improvements also include a locator plate to align the container. The locator plant has apertures to view and align a locator mark on the surface on which the device is placed with indicia on the locator plate.

Todd C. Loschelder and Erwin F. Mikol: "Anti-siphon mixing valve" is patented by Todd C. Loschelder and Erwin F. Mikol. Abstract: A hot and cold water mixing valve for use with faucets, shower/tub controls and other plumbing fittings includes a sleeve having a hot water inlet and a cold water inlet spaced therefrom and an outlet axially spaced from the inlets. There is a stem movable within the sleeve to control water flow from the inlets to the outlet. There is a water passage between the exterior of the stem and the interior of the sleeve and there is an axially extending air passage within the stem having an outer end in communication with air at ambient pressure. There are air outlets in the stem intermediate its ends which connect the air passage with the exterior of the stem.

Walter Whipple III: "Refrigeration system with dual cylinder compressor" is patented by Walter Whipple III. Abstract: An energy-efficient refrigeration system includes a dual cylinder compressor and a compressor controller coupled to the compressor to control compressor capacity by selection of a predetermined refrigerant flow path through the compressor. The dual cylinder compressor includes first and second cylinders with respective first and second pistons that are horizontally opposed and coupled together by a fixed and non-pivoting connecting rod. The void volume of one cylinder is typically greater than the void volume of the other cylinder, and the compressor typically is a scotch-yoke drive apparatus or, alternatively, a linear voice coil drive apparatus.

Ward Lock: Publisher of "Plumbing and heating." Publisher: Ward Lock (London). Published in 1994.

Werner W. Kochte: "Container with internal liquid distribution port for holding equipment with internal passages during sterilization" is patented by Werner W. Kochte. Abstract: A microbial decontamination system includes a lower housing portion (10) which receives a removable tray (12). The tray (12) defines a cassette receiving basin, a pair of anti-microbial fluid outlets (28, 64) and a drain (50). A pump (54) and associated plumbing circulates the anti-microbial fluid from the drain through the pair of outlets. A cassette (B) has a lower portion (FIGS. 8-10) which is configured to match the tray's basin and an upper portion (FIGS. 5-7) which is received on the lower cassette portion in an airborne microbe blocking relationship. The cassette bottom portion has an inlet (32) which receives the anti-microbial fluid and a baffle plate (44) adjacent the inlet having a plurality of apertures (96) for distributing the anti-microbial fluid within the cassette.

Westinghouse Hanford Co.: Sponsored research "616 Nonradioactive Dangerous Waste Storage Facility -- Essential/support drawing list. Revision 2." Sponsored by: Westinghouse Hanford Co., Richland, WA.; Department of Energy, Washington, DC. Written by K. R. Busching. Abstract: This document identifies the essential and supporting engineering drawings for the 616 Nonradioactive Dangerous Waste Storage Facility. The purpose of the documents is to describe the criteria used to identify and the plan for updating and maintaining their accuracy. Drawings are designated as essential if they relate to safety systems, environmental monitoring systems, effluents, and facility HVAC, electrical, and plumbing systems. Support drawings are those which are frequently used or describe a greater level of detail for equipment, components, or systems shown on essential drawings. A listing of drawings identified as essential or support is provided in Table A.

William J. Lund: "Hydrothermal stabilizer" is patented by William J. Lund. Abstract: Plumbing apparatus is provided for reducing energy consumption of a hot water heater, the apparatus includes a tank and a buoyant piston movably disposed within the tank and having a perimeter slidably engaging an inside wall of the tank. Water entering a top of the tank pushes the buoyant piston towards a bottom of the tank and at a selected position, grooves are provide in an inside wall of the tank to enable entering water to pass the buoyant piston. When the apparatus is connected between a conventional hot water heater and a cold water source, the water heater is buffered from the cold water source for small draws of water from the hot water heater thus preventing such small draws of water from tripping the water heater thermostat.

William M. Good, et al.: "Cold header pierced valve stem" is patented by William M. Good, Junior W. Rhodes and Andrejs Pavuls. Abstract: A method of cold forming a plumbing and heating valve stem by providing a cylindrical blank workpiece, axially stamping the workpiece to circumferentially reduce and axially lengthen a portion of the workpiece, axially stamping the circumferentially larger portion to form a circumferentially enlarged head on the larger portion, while punching a central axial cylindrical cavity in the head to a depth no greater than the axial thickness of said head, and then axially punching the cylindrical axial cavity to a depth greater than the thickness of the head and also stamping a central cylindrical axial cavity into the opposite end, forming self tapping screw cavities. The larger portion is then provided with rolled threads.

Woodson, Roger Dodge: Born in 1955, authored "Plumbing contractor: start and run a money-making business." Publisher: TAB Books (Blue Ridge Summit, Pa.). Published in 1994.

1995

Akhileshwar R. Singh: "Plumbing fixtures and fittings employing copper-bismuth casting alloys" is is patented by Akhileshwar R. Singh.

Alex Mauerhofer: "Process and device for the contactless electronic control of the flow of water in a plumbing unit" is is patented by Alex Mauerhofer.

Amtrol Inc: Publication of "Amtrol Inc. Plumbing, Heating, Water Systems 1995." Published in 1995.

Association canadienne de normalisation: Publication of "Recommended practice for the installation of thermoplastic drain, storm and sewer pipe and fittings: plumbing products & materials." Publisher: Canadian Standards Association (Etobicoke, Ont). Published in 1995.

Ben-Zion Cohen and Eliyahu Gonen: "Modular building system" is patented by Ben-Zion Cohen and Eliyahu Gonen. Abstract: A modular building system including modules for a majority of structural elements making up a modem building. Modules include, floors, walls, elevator shafts, stairways, conduit assemblies. Facilities located on or off site are utilized to prefabricate most of the structural elements needed to construct a building. Finished floor modules are complete sections of floor including floor core, floor covering, insulation, ceiling beams and ceiling below. Wall modules include wall core, exterior wall covering, utility runs, wall beams and interior wall covering. Elevator modules include stackable elevator shells and guide tracks. Stairway modules include stackable stairway shells that may be stacked as many number of floors as needed.

Blower, G. J.: Author of "Plumbing: mechanical services. Bk. 1." Publisher: Longman Scientific & Technical (London). Published in 1995.

Brian C. Allen and James D. Simpson: "Pneumatic plug and method for hydrostatic testing of bathtub plumbing" is is patented by Brian C. Allen and James D. Simpson.

Building Officials and Code Administrators International, Inc: Publisher of "International plumbing code." Building Officials, Code Administrators International, International Conference of Building Officials, Southern Building Code Congress International. Publisher: Building Officials and Code Administrators International, Inc (Country Club Hills, IL). Published in 1995.

California Building Standards Commission: Publisher of "California plumbing code." Publisher: California Building Standards Commission (Sacramento, Calif). Published in 1995.

Canada Mortgage & Housing Corporation: Sponsored research "Homeowner Residential Rehabilitation Assistance Program: Standards for rehabilitation: A guide for RRAP technical resources and delivery agents." Sponsored by: Canada Mortgage & Housing Corporation, Ottawa. Abstract: The Homeowner Residential Rehabilitation Assistance Program provides financial assistance to owners of existing accommodation in need of major repair, or lacking basic facilties, in any of the following categories: Structural soundness, electrical system, plumbing, heating system, and fire safety.

Castán, Santiago: Translator of "Plumbing and central heating" by Mike Lawrence into Spanish ("Fontanería y calefacción"). Publisher: Gustavo Gili (Barcelona). Published in 1995.

Charles F. Brandel: "Hot water system" is patented by Charles F. Brandel. Abstract: A hot water plumbing system comprising a water heater, a delivery location, a delivery line delivering water from said heater to said delivery location, a riser located adjacent said delivery location and extending upward above the level of said heater, and a return line connected adjacent the upper end of said riser and inclined so as to extend gradually downward to an input located adjacent the bottom of said heater to provide a continuous flow of hot water within the system, which ensures immediate and constant delivery of hot water to the delivery location and prevents accumulation of sediment within the system and, hence, minimizes installation and maintenance costs and significantly reduces the amount of wasted water.

Clifford E. Chartier: "Apparatus for producing sheet waterfall for pool or spa" is patented by Clifford E. Chartier. Abstract: A self-contained module installed in the side walls or deck of a pool or spa is connected to the pool or spa plumbing system, and converts the turbulent water supply of the system to a laminar sheet of water which free falls into the pool or spa in a manner pleasing in sight and sound. Narrow, elongated spouts prevalent in the prior art have been reduced to a short, compact, economical and structurally stronger emitter owing to the provision of components including an apertured conduit, or "flute", traversing a relatively large manifold chamber open along an element.

Communications Electrical Electronic Energy Information Postal Plumbing and Allied Services Union: Publisher of "CEPU national." Publisher: Communications Electrical Electronic Energy Information Postal Plumbing and Allied Services Union (Carlton South, Vic). Published in 1995.

Dana F. Buccicone: "Plumbing valve" is is patented by Dana F. Buccicone.

Daniel Glenn Pretty: "Plumbing cleanout cover" is patented by Daniel Glenn Pretty. Abstract: A releasably mountable cleanout cover for releasable mounting onto a plumbing cleanout cap, having a protruding cap member, exposed within an aperture in a wall includes an aperture covering member having an exterior surface and an interior surface for covering the aperture in the wait, a hollow mounting tube rigidly mounted to and generally centered on, the interior surface and extending longitudinally and generally perpendicularly outwardly from the interior surface.

David L. Sordello and Carl A. Engstrom: "System of plumbing for recreational vehicles" is is patented by David L. Sordello and Carl A. Engstrom.

Dennis E. Bowman: "Refect water drain line installation system and apparatus for under sink reverse osmosis filter system" is patented by Dennis E. Bowman. Abstract: Reject waste water adapter coupling fitting, system and installation method for use with a household undercounter reverse osmosis (R/O) water filtration installation associated with an in-counter sink having a garbage disposer with its outlet connected by standard slip fit plumbing fittings to a sink drain trap plumbed to the household sewer system. The R/O reject waste water undercounter drain line is coupled into the sink drain trap in parallel drainage relation with the disposer outlet plumbing fittings by a baffle Tee plumbing fitting having first and second inlets perpendicular to one another with their input drainage liquid flow separated by an internal baffle.

Dept. of Business and Employment Health and Safety Organisation, Victoria;: Publisher of "10+ plumbing hazards: plumbers beware." Publisher: Dept. of Business and Employment Health and Safety Organisation, Victoria; (Melbourne). Published in 1995.

Dinosaur Nature Association: Publication of "The rivers of the Colorado River Basin - The plumbing of the Colorado River Basin." Publisher: The Association (Vernal, Utah). Published in 1995.

Domenic Luisi: "Backflow prevention device and vacuum breaker for kitchen plumbing" is is patented by Domenic Luisi.

Donald E. Army Jr., et al.: "Pressure regulation valve with integrated downstream pressure tap" is patented by Donald E. Army Jr., Brian G. Donnelly and John P. Nikkanen. Abstract: A baffle insert or sleeve is disclosed for the integration of the downstream pressure tap into a pressure regulation valve ("PRY") for an aircraft environmental control system ("ECS"). The purpose of this insert is to return the flow, disturbed by the pivoting disk of a butterfly valve, to a more normal distribution within the length of the valve body. This allows the PRV downstream pressure tap to be part of the valve, instead of it (along with additional plumbing) being located four more pipe diameters beyond the valve housing.

Frank-Thomas Luig and Roland Weiss: "Vented backflow preventer for hose-type faucet" is patented by Frank-Thomas Luig and Roland Weiss. Abstract: A plumbing fixture having a valve supplying water under pressure to an output and a hose outlet having an intake end has a vented backflow preventer having a housing separate from the valve and having an inlet port connected to the valve output and an outlet port connected to the hose intake end. A lower check valve in the housing has a lower seat, an upper seat, and a valve body of density greater than water movable between a lower position sitting on and blocking the lower seat and an upper position sitting on and blocking the upper seat. The housing is formed with an inlet passage leading from the inlet port to the lower seat and an outlet passage leading from between the seats to the outlet port.

Frederick B. Wyss and Joseph Harings: "Apparatus and method for eradicating zebra mussels in vessel raw water marine plumbing systems" is is patented by Frederick B. Wyss and Joseph Harings.

Frederick N. Lancia: "Bird feeding station" is patented by Frederick N. Lancia. Abstract: A bird feeding station is described which is formed principally from commercially available PVC plumbing fittings and pipe. Because of the overall light weight of the station, it may be supported from a patio block or the like. The system is modular, being able to accommodate a variety of feeder arrangements as well as seed dispensing arrangements. This modularity also provides an opportunity for configurations which are bird species specific due to a configuration which is achieved. By virtue of the use of PVC pipe, the stations are easily cleaned by the user inasmuch as they inherently incorporate somewhat straight-through passageways providing the functions of seed reservoir and seed dispensing.

Galvin, Patrick J.: Author of "Opportunities in plumbing and pipe fitting careers (computer file)." Patrick J. Galvin; foreword by Allen Inlow. Publisher: VGM Career Horizons (Lincolnwood, Ill., USA). Published in 1995.

George Sullivan: "Method and apparatus for draining plumbing lines" is is patented by George Sullivan.

Gerald W. Hall: "Building module providing readily accessible utility connections" is patented by Gerald W. Hall. Abstract: A smaller building module is comprised of two parallel frames and a water closet carrier disposed between the frames and adapted to support an off-the-floor water closet on each side of the parallel frames upon each of which a wall may be constructed. Waste conduit means, hot and cold water conduits and electrical lines extending, between the parallel frames provide ready access for connection to plumbing and electrical fixtures. Additionally, gas conduits, dryer vent conduits or other utility conduits or lines may be provided. Such building module is advantageously included in a larger building module comprised of two toilets, and one or more bath, shower, lavatory or other plumbing fixtures.

Gesellschaft zur Foerderung der Heizungs- und Klimatechnik m.b.H.: Sponsored research "Demonstration, messtechnische Analyse und Optimierung von kostenguenstigen Solaranlagen unter Einbindung energie- und wassersparender Nachheiz- und Sanitaertechnik. Schlussbericht. (Demonstration, analysis and optimization of low cost systems by integration of plumbing and pre-heating technics with low energy and water demand. Final report)." Sponsored by: Gesellschaft zur Foerderung der Heizungs- und Klimatechnik m.b.H., Hilden (Germany, F.R.). Written by F. A. Peuser, R. Croy, M. Brillinger, F. Ranft and H. Schaube. Abstract: A building and plumbing typology was worked out, on the basis of which typical refurbishing concepts could be carried out making use of energy and water saving projects. The testing of simple solar pre-heating systems showed that small systems with low solar heating costs are already available on the market today but that problems with the stability of plastic materials and the control of the collector circulating pumps have occured in some systems. The energy comparison between a conventional solar system and a Low Flow collector system only shows small advantages for the Low Flow plant for small-dimensioned systems (pre-heating systems). For system left angle ca. 15 m(sup 2) there are still no optimum components on the market.

Hamilton Standard: Sponsored research "Urine Pretreat Injection System. - Final Report." Sponsored by: Hamilton Standard, Windsor Locks, CT.; NASA, Washington, DC. Abstract: A new method of introducing the OXONE (Registered Trademark) Monopersulfate

Compound for urine pretreat into a two-phase urine/air flow stream has been successfully tested and evaluated. The feasibility of this innovative method has been established for purposes of providing a simple, convenient, and safe method of handling a chemical pretreat required for urine processing in a microgravity space environment. Also, the Oxone portion of the urine pretreat has demonstrated the following advantages during real time collection of 750 pounds of urine in a Space Station design two-phase urine Fan/Separator: Eliminated urine precipitate buildup on internal hardware and plumbing; Minimized odor from collected urine; and Virtually eliminated airborne bacteria.

Harald Philipp: "Divided box for valve controller" is patented by Harald Philipp. Abstract: An enclosure containing valves, batteries and electronic circuitry controlling the operation of an automatically actuated faucet includes a dividing wall slanted from the horizontal and separating an upper compartment, containing the valves, from a lower compartment containing the control electronics. Water from leaks in the top compartment (or water that runs down a pipe into the top of the box) runs down the slanted dividing shelf and drains from the box without contacting the electronic components. All the associated plumbing fittings are adjacent a top surface of the box so as to ease installation of the controller.

Heiner Monch: "Base body for plumbing fixtures" is is patented by Heiner Monch.

Heinz Graber: "Control cartridge for a single-lever mixer fitting" is patented by Heinz Graber. Abstract: In a plumbing assembly, a control cartridge for a single-lever mixer fitting is small enough to be installed into the mouth region of a discharge arm. The shut-off elements include a first control disk, which is fixed to the fitting housing and a second control disk, which can be rotated by an actuating lever. The control disks preferably consist of ceramic and have, in each case, two through-passages, one each for cold and hot water. Upon rotation of the fitting, first the cold-water through-passage and then hot-water through-passage are released, and, subsequently, the cold-water through-passage is throttled. With exclusively one rotary movement of the lever, the following flow conditions result: cold-mixed-hot.

Heinz-Dieter Eichholz, et al.: "Plumbing fixture with line-powered control unit" is is patented by Heinz-Dieter Eichholz, Werner Kleinhans and Hans-Peter Rudrich.

James F. Maxwell: "Prefab fiber building construction" is patented by James F. Maxwell. Abstract: Prefabricated panels are formed by compressing a fiber slurry which may be composed of waste fiber products such as waste paper, cardboard, straw, leaves and grass clippings. The slurry, which may contain waterproofing, fire retardants, anti fungal agents and insecticides, is poured into a press form which contains the framework of a roof panel, wall panel, ceiling panel or floor panel as well as electrical wiring, heating ducts, plumbing or any other desired component. The fiber slurry is compressed to at least 1/4 of its original volume forming a solid dense inner core. This inner core can be covered with wall board, wall board paper, stucco, plaster, cement or stone. A method for locking the panels together is also disclosed.

Jerauld G. Wright and Sidney K. Tissington: "Prefabricated building panel" is patented by Jerauld G. Wright and Sidney K. Tissington. Abstract: A prefabricated building panel comprises a wooden grid of crossing longitudinal and transverse studs which are notched to interengage at the crossing points, one array of studs having surfaces coinciding with one major surface of the panel and having opposed surfaces recessed from the opposite major surface of the panel and vice-versa. The studs which are made of standard dimension lumber provide adequate nailing surfaces on each of the major surfaces of the panel for attachment of finish sheeting such as drywall thereto after installation. The panel may include molded in situ insulation and provides on the inner side of the panel large longitudinally recessed channels through which electric wiring, plumbing and the like can be ducted.

Jergen Humpert, et al.: "Faucet with motion-detector on/off control" is patented by Jergen Humpert, Bruno Heimann and Christian Frankholz. Abstract: A plumbing fixture has a housing provided with a water inlet and formed with a water outlet and with a circuit pocket. This housing is secured to a support surface. An electrically operated valve in the body between the inlet and outlet has an electrical feed wire energizable for movement of the valve between a closed position blocking flow between the inlet and outlet and an open position permitting such flow. An insert fittable in the pocket is formed with a battery compartment holding a battery. A screw or the like fixed the insert in the pocket. An electrical circuit in the insert connected to the feed wire and to the battery opens the valve on detection of a solid object in front of the housing.

Jerome Warshawsky and Frank Antoniello: "Wall mount inlet stop system" is patented by Jerome Warshawsky and Frank Antoniello. Abstract: An improved inlet stop fixture for conventional hot and cold inlets to plumbing fixture which is threaded onto a male pipe thread with a nipple, to prevent a gap of uncontrolled length from the fixture to the wall. The improved inlet stop system includes a new intermediate element, namely a water inlet tube extension, which fits between the conventional pipe nipple and the valve fixture itself. The inlet tube extension includes an inlet coupling section, an O-ring collar, with an O-ring, and a fixture coupling threaded nipple at the far end. The water inlet tube extension is threaded onto the nipple that extends through the wall. Alternately, a non-threaded solder type connection water inlet tube extension may be connected to a non-threaded copper tube for a solder connection.

Jerry P. Gronwick and Leonard A. Koniewicz: "Adjustable tail ground joint" is patented by Jerry P. Gronwick and Leonard A. Koniewicz. Abstract: An adjustable plumbing conduit for connecting the inlet of a flush valve body and the outlet of a control valve wherein the flush valve body inlet has interior threads and the control valve outlet has exterior threads. The adjustable plumbing conduit includes an adjustable tail having an exterior thread on a portion thereof and a tapered nose which is in contact with an interior mating surface on the control valve outlet. There is an outward projection on the adjustable tail adjacent the tapered nose, which outward projection coacts with an inwardly directed shoulder of a coupling nut which is threaded onto the exterior of the control valve inlet and thereby holds the adjustable tail to the control valve.

Jimmy Cochimin and Richard J. Halsey: "Liquid pumping system with cooled control module" is patented by Jimmy Cochimin and Richard J. Halsey. Abstract: Apparatus comprising a flow carrier connectable in a liquid flow system including an electric motor-pump unit and a conduit for conveying a pumped liquid to a liquid utilization apparatus. The flow carrier is connectable in the conduit and includes an opening which exposes the liquid flowing through the carrier. A heat sink or cold plate is located on the carrier over the opening, the heat sink covering the opening and having a wet side exposed to the liquid. The heat sink further includes a dry side, and heat generating electrical control components are secured to the dry side. A sensor is also mounted on the heat sink and responds to a characteristic, such as the pressure, of the liquid.

John C. Kennedy: "Method for making a rotationally molded spa" is patented by John C. Kennedy. Abstract: A spa having a one-piece, rotationally molded shell defining a reservoir for containing water including at least three sidewalls connected by an interior footwell, at least three exterior sidewalls, a coping interconnecting the reservoir sidewalls and the exterior sidewalls, and a floor beneath the reservoir footwell and interconnecting the exterior sidewalls. Water is circulated within the reservoir by a plumbing system which is disposed within an interior space defined between the reservoir sidewalls, the exterior sidewalls, the coping, and the floor; the plumbing system including a plurality of jets extending through the reservoir sidewalls; a plumbing harness; and a pump for circulating the water from the reservoir into the jets.

John D. Carroll Jr: "Filter for laundry system having toridal shared filter elements" is patented by John D. Carroll Jr. Abstract: An energy and water conservation laundry mechanism which includes a plurality of automatic washing machines, a rinse water storage tank, plumbing which connects the storage tank to the each of the washing machines, and electrical controls which are tied into the existing control circuitry of the washing machines for selectively directing the flow of rinse water between the storage tank and the washing machines. The plumbing includes pumps and valves which enables rinse water, as stored in the storage tank, to be delivered to each washing machine at the beginning of a wash cycle and waste water from the wash cycle to be discharged into a conventional sewer line.

John Frederick Tryon: "Work and storage cabinet assembly having multiple identical cabinet units formed by rotational molding" is patented by John Frederick Tryon. Abstract: A rotationally molded cabinet assembly for storage of supplies or retail stock, the cabinet assembly including at least two cabinet units; where the cabinet units are adjoined side by side; where each cabinet unit includes: inner and outer polymeric shells; formed by rotational molding; where shells form multiple joined panels; and where the panels have at least two side panels, one back panel, and a bottom panel. The panels surround a hollow for containing within the hollow supplies or retail stock and an opening is formed in a front portion of the cabinet unit for access to the hollow for storing supplies or retail stock. The back panel of the cabinet unit has an opening for allowing access to electrical outlets, plumbing, and other resources which may be located behind the cabinet unit.

John J. Imre: "Refrigeration system using coldambient sources" is patented by John J. Imre. Abstract: The apparatus is composed of a vacuum panel insulated cabinet containing six mirrored cylindrical compartments served by transparent sliding doors and their internal space divided by a rotating disc shelf as well as steel rods positioned through the axis shaft of the disc at right angles. The compartments are cooled with water passing through water jackets that surround them, being pre-chilled by having the water coarse through an ice water bath via a coiled and finned tube in a lidded container. Cold air can also be used directly from outdoors to cool the compartments. A remoted powered cooler is held in reserve. In automatic defrost models the apparatus is integrated with the household hot water plumbing.

John R. Wilson: "Vandalproof control stop cap" is patented by John R. Wilson. Abstract: A vandalproof cap assembly for closing an access opening in a plumbing fitting includes a plastic sleeve formed and adapted to be normally non-removably attached to the plumbing fitting about the access opening. The plastic sleeve has a plurality of outwardly extending flexible projections. There is a cap with a smooth exterior and an interior recess which is snapped upon the sleeve so that the sleeve projections interlock with the cap recess. When so mounted the cap is freely rotatable relative to the sleeve, and can only be removed from the sleeve with a tool and specific knowledge as to use of the tool.

John W. Collins: "Plumbing apparatus" is patented by John W. Collins. Abstract: A plumbing device comprises a clamp 10 which is clamped around a "live" pipe 12 and which threadedly receives a cutter/valve 16 having cutter portions 30 and a valved passage 32. The cutter/valve 16 is screwed home to remove a section of pipe and to align the valved passage with the pipe. The device may then function as a stop-cock.

Johnson, Derek: Author of "Home plumbing: the complete guide to maintaining and updating domestic plumbing systems." Publisher: Haynes (Sparkford). Published in 1995.

Keith D. Kramer, et al.: "Brass alloys" is patented by Keith D. Kramer, Thomas R. Hoesly and Frederick F. Treul. Abstract: Reduced-lead yellow brass alloys are disclosed. The alloys comprise copper; zinc; an amount of bismuth effective to enhance castability of the alloys; and an amount of selenium effective to increase machinability of the alloy. Preferably, the alloys further include an amount of antimony effective to inhibit dezincification of the alloys.

Khol, Kris: Author of "Vented plumbing for livestock manure handling systems." Prepared by Kris Kohl, and Tom Greiner. Publisher: Iowa State University, University Extension (Ames, Iowa). Published in 1995.

Lawrence Berkeley Lab.: Sponsored research "Promoting plumbing fixture and fitting replacement: Recommendations and review for state and local water resource authorities." Sponsored by: Lawrence Berkeley Lab., CA.; Department of Energy, Washington, DC. Written by C. Dunham, J. D. Lutz and S. J. Pickle. Abstract: Lawrence Berkeley National Laboratory (LBNL) has prepared this report to facilitate compliance with the requirements of Section 123 of the Energy Policy Act of 1992 (EPACT). Section 123 requires the Department of Energy to issue recommendations for establishing state and local incentive programs to encourage acceleration of voluntary consumer replacement of existing water closets, urinals, showerheads and faucets with water-saving products meeting EPACT standards.

Leonard L. Miller Jr. and Tracy A. Presnell: "Locking arrangement for a plumbing connection" is is patented by Leonard L. Miller Jr. and Tracy A. Presnell.

Lisa M. Leighton: "Plunger device" is patented by Lisa M. Leighton. Abstract: A plunger device for forcing waste through a drain line of a plumbing fixture comprising an elongate, tubular member. Fluidly connected to the top end of the tubular member is a valve assembly which is adapted to have a water supply source fluidly coupled thereto. The valve assembly comprises a valve stem which is reciprocally movable between open and closed positions and adapted to block the flow of water from the water supply source into the tubular member when in the closed position.

Lytle, Elizabeth Stewart: Author of "Careers in plumbing, heating, and cooling (computer file)." Publisher: Rosen Pub. Group (New York). Published in 1995.

M. Fred Rose: "Variable torch apparatus" is patented by M. Fred Rose. Abstract: A collection of components which may be assembled into a variety of home, garden and patio-type torch configurations includes a torch portion having a fuel canister and a wick element, a vertical support or pole portion, and a base portion. The apparatus is preferably constructed from standard copper plumbing pipe and associated copper fittings.

Manfred Pawelzik, et al.: "One-hole mount mixing faucet" is patented by Manfred Pawelzik, Max Derr and Dieter Kahle. Abstract: A plumbing fixture has a housing defining a chamber and having a bottom wall forming an upper surface and formed with at least one inlet port opening at the upper surface. A cartridge assembly in the chamber having a bottom surface directly confronting the bottom-wall upper surface is formed with an inlet port opening on the bottom surface in line with the bottom-wall inlet port. An inlet conduit having an end fitting extending through the inlet port and into the inlet port is formed with an outwardly open circumferential groove generally level with the surfaces. A split and spreadable snap ring fitted to the groove bears on the floor.

Mark E. Chiffon, et al.: "Self cleaning drain system and modular plumbing system for a sterilizing apparatus" is is patented by Mark E. Chiffon, Kenneth J. Klobusnik and Anthony B. Ruffo.

Mark H. Naedler and Nathan L. Goldfein: "Vehicle brake system" is patented by Mark H. Naedler and Nathan L. Goldfein. Abstract: Disclosed is an air-applied, mechanically-held brake assembly and a vehicle air brake system employing the same. The air brake system typically includes a push-pull or hand-brake valve for park and emergency applications, a treadle valve for service applications, reservoirs of air under pressure, and other valving and plumbing. The brake assembly applies and releases the brake upon the supply and exhaust, respectively, of air from a first pressure chamber. The brake assembly locks and unlocks the brake in an applied position by the exhaust and supply, respectively, of air from a second pressure chamber.

Michael D. Steinhardt, et al.: "Plumbing nozzle" is patented by Michael D. Steinhardt, John A. Fiumefreddo and Michael J. Kurth. Abstract: A plumbing nozzle is disclosed that discharges a hollow cylinder of water. In a preferred form, the cylinder flows along a horizontal axis as the water is discharged from the nozzle. The nozzle has a core member with an angled wall surface which directs water against an inner wall surface of the nozzle. The inner wall encloses upon itself and has an outwardly diverging wall surface. The nozzle is particularly useful in conjunction with a bathing fixture with recirculating water.

1995

Miguel Pedreno Lopez: "Construction system for partition walls, walls and extradoses" is patented by Miguel Pedreno Lopez. Abstract: A system of construction based on the use of polystyrene boards for constructing partition walls as well as extradoses, these said boards being equipped with grooves for electrical and plumbing ducts, as well as for the formation of structural ribs, while their vertical edges are equipped with grooving and tonguing for their interconnection. Boards are put into place between the floor and ceiling, with the interposition of perimetrical perimeter strips made of the same material. Plaster with an additive is then used to coat the surfaces of the said boards as a finish which forms an adhesive paste.

Mike Le: "Three-dimensional optical levelling, plumbing and angle-calibrating instrument" is is patented by Mike Le.

NAHB National Research Center: Sponsored research "Steel Framed Residential Construction: Demonstration Homes." Sponsored by: NAHB National Research Center, Upper Marlboro, MD.; Department of Housing and Urban Development, Washington, DC. Office of Policy Development and Research. Written by W. R. Farkas. Abstract: The report describes the experience of two steel frame demonstration projects coordinated by the National Association of Home Builders. The demonstration built a large custom home in Raleigh, North Carolina, and a simpler, affordable home in Upper Marlboro, Maryland, both with light-gauge steel frames. Planning, materials, tools, and construction of different home components are described for both houses.

NASA: Sponsored research "Inflight Refill Unit for Replenishing Research Animal Drinking Water." Sponsored by: NASA, Moffett Field, CA. Ames Research Center. Written by P. D. Savage, M. L. Hines and R. Barnes. Abstract: This paper presents the design process and development approach for a method of maintaining sufficient quantities of water for research animals during a Shuttle mission of long duration. An inflight refill unit (IRU) consisting of two major subsystems, a fluid pumping unit (FPU) and a collapsible water reservoir (CWR), were developed. The FPU provides the system measurement and controls, pump, water lines, and plumbing necessary to collect water coming into the unit from the potable water system and pump it out into the RAHF drinking water tanks.

National Research Council Canada: Publisher of "National plumbing code of Canada, 1995." Issued by the Canadian Commission on Building and Fire Codes, National Research Council of Canada. Publisher: National Research Council of Canada (Ottawa, Ont). Published in 1995.

National Rural Community Assistance Program: Publisher of "Still: living without the basics: a report on the lack of complete plumbing that still exists in rural America." Publisher: National Rural Community Assistance Program (Leesburg, Va.). Published in 1995.

Pacific Gas and Electric Company: Publication of "Electric and gas service requirements architects and engineers, electrical contractors, plumbing contractors, city and county building inspectors, manufacturers of electrical equipment, PG & E employees." Pacific Gas and Electric Company. Publisher: The Company (San Francisco, CA). Published in 1995.

Plumbing Education Council of Texas: Publication of "1995-1996 plumber's continuing education program: volume II journeyman, inspectors and master plumbers." Publisher: Plumbing Education Council of Texas (Texas). Published in 1995.

Publication: Publication of "Housing of American Indians on reservations, plumbing." Published in 1995.

Raun A. Kopp: "Plastic valve with inlet conduit extension" is patented by Raun A. Kopp. Abstract: A water shut-off valve includes a valve body and inlet conduit molded out of a solvent weldable plastic such as CPVC. The inlet conduit has a threaded portion proximate the valve body to receive a nut used to secure the valve to a mounting bracket, and an integral extension at an outer end of the threaded portion having a smooth cylindrical surface which may be solvent welded to conventional plastic plumbing.

Richard Craig Paschal: "Dental treatment unit" is patented by Richard Craig Paschal. Abstract: A dental treatment unit and method for use by dentists and the like, the treatment unit including an isolated aseptic central core component with a positive pressure internal environment, and which contains a work area for a dental dispensing assistant, plumbing, dental mechanical and electrical components, dental equipment and controls, dental instruments, and dental supplies. The supply core component mechanically engages, conveniently accesses, and provides function to an attachable treatment module enabling a dental team to provide treatment to a patient who is physically separated from all dental materials and medicament containers, cabinet and drawer handles, instruments, and dental devices, thereby creating an aseptic environment heretofore nonexistent in the dental profession.

Robert E. Bridges and Archie C. Epes: "Modular structure" is patented by Robert E. Bridges and Archie C. Epes. Abstract: A modular structure consisting of three modular units, the center module being the primary module containing the mechanical components of the building, with plumbing, air conditioning and heating ducts, and electrical wiring in the slab floor structural foundation and door jambs. The primary module is completed at the factory. The major exterior walls, slab floor foundation panels, and ceiling/roof panels for all three modules are similarly manufactured in one piece. The major components of the side modules, consisting of the slab floor foundation panels, ceiling/roof panels and the exterior side walls, are all hinged so that they fold to the side and on top of the primary module.

Robert W. Boyer: "Wall stud" is patented by Robert W. Boyer. Abstract: An improved wall stud utilized in framing structures, the wall stud including core elements and insulative materials enclosed within C-shaped frame members. The walls studs can be aligned and secured in a metal track mounted on the top and bottom ends of the wall studs. The wall studs provide good insulation, support, and easy access for the installation of electrical and plumbing equipment.

Roger N. Anderson, et al.: "Method for identifying subsurface fluid migration and drainage pathways in and among oil and gas reservoirs using 3-D and 4-D seismic imaging" is patented by Roger N. Anderson, Albert Boulanger, Edward P. Bagdonas, Liqing Xu and Wei He. Abstract: The invention utilizes 3-D and 4-D seismic surveys as a means of deriving information useful in petroleum exploration and reservoir management. The methods use both single seismic surveys (3-D) and multiple seismic surveys separated in time (4-D) of a region of interest to determine large scale migration pathways within sedimentary basins, and fine scale drainage structure and oil-water-gas regions within individual petroleum producing reservoirs. Such structure is identified using pattern recognition tools which define the regions of interest. The 4-D seismic data sets may be used for data completion for large scale structure where time intervals between surveys do not allow for dynamic evolution.

Seal, G. Mark: Author of "The patient's guide to urology: plumbing problems in layman's terms." Publisher: High Oaks Pub. Co (Toledo, Ohio). Published in 1995.

Standards Association of Australia: Publication of "Methods of testing plastics and composite materials sanitary plumbing fixtures. Method 12, Determination of resistance to thermal shock of baths for ablutionary purposes." Published in 1995.

Statens Provningsanstalt: Sponsored research "Guide foer Ombyggnad av Vatrum. Rad och Tips Samt Litteraturgenomgang (Rebuilding of Bathrooms. Advices and Literature)." Sponsored by: Statens Provningsanstalt, Boras (Sweden). Energiteknik. Written by A. Ekstrand-Tobin, J. Fransson and I. Samuelson. Abstract: The first part contains a survey of important parts of the process to be considered: former damages and moisture problems, layout and need of changes, heating and ventilation, materials for walls and floor, installations, piping and plumbing, quality assurance and control. The second part is a detailed presetantion of reference documents. These documents have mainly Nordic origin. A reference list completes the report.

Stefan Hiesener: "Apparatus for operating a vacuum plumbing system in an aircraft" is is patented by Stefan Hiesener.

Steven H. Domansky: "Condensation line purging

device" is patented by Steven H. Domansky. Abstract: Condensation line purging devices and assemblies. The present invention relates to devices and assemblies for purging HVAC condensation lines. Such lines are relatively delicate, as opposed, for instance, to drain lines and plumbing systems. Accordingly, devices of the present invention include a body which is adapted to contain a conventional gas cylinder such as a 12 gram CO.sub.2 cylinder. The body is adapted to connect to a nozzle which in turn is connected to a connector that is attached to the condensation line. The body may be rotated onto the nozzle in a manner that controllably releases gas pressure from the gas cylinder into the condensation line so as to cause a pressure buildup that effectively purges the condensation line without breaching its seals or other discontinuities.

Sunset Pub. Corp: Publisher of "Basic plumbing." By the editors of Sunset Books; (book consultants, Richard Day, Don Vandervort). Publisher: Sunset Pub. Corp (Menlo Park, CA). Published in 1995.

Tesoriero, John: Author of "Plumbing rules made simple for high rise and multiple dwellings." Publisher: J & L Publications (Sydney, N.S.W.). Published in 1995.

The Association: Publisher of "Wisconsin Association of Plumbing, Heating, Cooling Contractors, 100 years, 1895-1995." Publisher: The Association (Menomonee Falls, WI). Published in 1995.

Time-Life Books: Publisher of "Plumbing." By the editors of Time-Life Books. Publisher: Time-Life Books (Alexandria, Va.). Published in 1995.

Timothy J. O'Brien: "Method for measuring the quantity of lead on the surface of a brass component" is patented by Timothy J. O'Brien. Abstract: A process for measuring the quantity of lead on the waterway surface of a brass component, for example a brass plumbing fixture, includes the steps of filling the brass component waterway with an aqueous solution of an acid which removes lead from the surface of the brass component. The acid solution is removed from the waterway after a time period which is sufficient to remove substantially all surface lead from the brass component, but which is insufficient for the acid to remove significant surface zinc and copper to expose surface lead. The quantity of lead per unit surface area of the brass component can then be determined by the use of the volume of the acid solution, the surface area of the brass component and the concentration of lead in the acid solution.

TMB Pub. Inc.: Publisher of "1995 engineered plumbing systems product directory and directory of manufacturers." Publisher: TMB Pub. Inc. (Northbrook, Ill). Published in 1995.

Victorio C. Rodriguez: "Portable toilet bowl ventilator" is patented by Victorio C. Rodriguez. Abstract: A portable fan apparatus is provided for ventilating toilet bowls by forced ventilation wherein air from the toilet bowl is exhausted by the fan via a tube that extends through the water trap formed by water in the trap formed partly by the bottom of the toilet bowl and partly by the drain portion of the toilet, thereby exhausting the foul air into the drain line of the building's plumbing system. The apparatus can be carried by a traveler from toilet to toilet, thereby to provide the desired ventilation for any toilet facility the traveler may visit.

Vincent Musso: "Quick release toilet tank valve" is patented by Vincent Musso. Abstract: A quick release connector enables replacement of a toilet tank valve by one having little, if any, knowledge of repair or skills relating to plumbing. The toilet tank valve includes a quick release connector coupling the toilet tank valve to a source of water within the toilet tank. The toilet tank valve may be quickly and easily replaced by manipulation of the quick release connector by the user's fingers without the necessity of mechanical tools or the like.

Washington: Publication of "Washington State building code: chapters 51-26 and 51-27: Uniform plumbing code and Uniform plumbing code standards." Publisher: Washington State Building Code Council (Olympia, Wash). Published in 1995.

Wes Delport: "Pressure-vacuum fluid handling system and method of removing and replacing engine coolant" is patented by Wes Delport. Abstract: A complete fluid handling system for automotive engine coolant that is installed within an automotive service center. The system delivers either new coolant in a 50% antifreeze--50% water ratio or recycled coolant also in a 50/50 ratio. The coolant is mixed in a new coolant delivery tank and is delivered under pressure to a service device at each service bay. The recycled coolant is also delivered to the services device at the service bays from a recycled coolant delivery tank under pressure. Recovery of coolant can be directed to either a waste holding tank or to a recycling tank. If directed to recycling tank the coolant is cleaned and treated to restore the coolant to the proper chemical balance.

William E. Loftus: "Building construction method" is patented by William E. Loftus. Abstract: A low cost building is made of modular parts in the absence of special tools. Light-in-weight wall blocks having a facade of conventional appearance include a thick, insulating mixture of a cementitious material, polystyrene, and organic fiber aggregates capable of retaining water. The blocks have interlocking top and bottom surfaces so that they are easily stacked to form walls. A floor is built by spanning foundation beams with floor trusses that have a key along their respective tops and by sliding modular floor panels between contiguous floor trusses, each floor panel having opposite edges that slidingly engage the keys of the floor trusses. A roof is made in a similar manner by sliding modular roof panels between contiguous roof trusses.

William J. Lund: "Hydrothermal stabilizer and expansion tank system" is patented by William J. Lund. Abstract: Plumbing apparatus is provided for reducing energy consumption and controlling increases in water pressure of a hot water heater. The apparatus includes a tank and a buoyant piston movably disposed within the tank and having a perimeter slidably engaging an inside wall of the tank. Water entering a top of the tank pushes the buoyant piston towards a bottom of the tank and at a selected position, grooves are provide in an inside wall of the tank to enable entering water to pass the buoyant piston. When the apparatus is connected between a conventional hot water heater and a cold water source, the water heater is buffered from the cold water source for small draws of water from the hot water heater thus preventing such small draws of water from tripping the water heater thermostat.

William Nattel and Serge Michaud: "Construction member protector plate unit" is patented by William Nattel and Serge Michaud. Abstract: Metal construction members or studs have a generally U-shaped profile, and can be provided with openings for cables, plumbing conduits and the like. Walls are constructed by attaching wallboard to vertically asserted studs. To protect cables etc. against accidental penetration by nails and screws, a protector plate unit has first and second protector plates for mounting adjacent outer faces of the metal stud. A mounting web extends between the protector plates. Securing means, for example a collar and tabs on the mounting web, engages the opening in the steel stud, to secure the protector plate unit in position, and to provide an internally smooth bushing.

1996

ACTRAC: Publisher of "(Certificate in Plumbing and Gasfitting)." Publisher: ACTRAC (Melbourne). Published in 1996.

American Society of Mechanical Engineers: Publisher of "Performance requirements for backflow protection devices and systems in plumbing fixture fittings." Publisher: American Society of Mechanical Engineers (New York, NY). Published in 1996.

Andrew B. Alaska: "Side-packed chromatographic column" is patented by Andrew B. Alaska. Abstract: The present invention describes a fixed volume, vertical flow chromatographic column. The column comprises a column member having an inner chamber for containing the particulate sorbent in a space surrounded by sidewalls and two flat frits, one on the top and one on the bottom. The sidewall has at least one dedicated packing port formed therein through which the sorbent may be packed into and unpacked from the column member. Upon the completion of the packing process, a plug is placed into the packing port flush with the inside surface of the sidewall. The frits are covered and supported by two lids.

The lids have plumbing ports formed therein through which a liquid sample enters and exits the column member.

Andrew Laird and Alex Laird: "Compactly-shipped site-assembled concrete forms for producing variable-width insulated-sidewall fastener-receiving building walls" is patented by Andrew Laird and Alex Laird. Abstract: Generally large, typically eight feet by two inches by ten or sixteen or twenty-four inches, sidewalls for modular concrete forms are easily, efficiently and economically produced by cutting and by routing sheet-type polymeric material, preferably polyurethane or expanded polystyrene foam. Metal connecting members are produced in standard sizes by cutting and bending sheet steel and/or wire. The sidewalls and connecting members are transported to a building site tightly and compactly in pieces, and then flexibly assembled into precision wall forms at the site with good efficiency at any scale. The wall forms so assembled define a cavity into which reinforcing steel rod, electrical and/or communications conduit, plumbing, etc., may be entered.

Argonne National Lab.: Sponsored research "D&D of the Experimental Boiling Water Reactor (EBWR)." Sponsored by: Argonne National Lab., IL.; Department of Energy, Washington, DC. Written by C. R. Fellhauer, L. E. Boling, T. J. Yule and S. K. Bhattacharyya. Abstract: Argonne National Laboratory has completed the D&D of the Experimental Boiling Water Reactor. The Project consisted of decontaminating and for packaging as radioactive waste the reactor vessel and internals, contaminated piping systems, miscellaneous tanks, pumps, and associated equipment. The D&D work involved dismantling process equipment and associated plumbing, ductwork drain lines, etc., performing size reduction of reactor vessel internals in the fuel pool, packaging and manifesting all radioactive and mixed waste, and performing a thorough survey of the facility after the removal of activated and contaminated material. Non-radioactive waste was disposed of in the ANL-E landfill or recycled.

Blower, G. J.: Author of "Plumbing: mechanical services. Bk. 2." Publisher: Longman (Harlow). Published in 1996.

British Columbia. Ministry of Social Services. Research, Evaluation and Statistics Branch: Publication of "Building and public works plumbing and heating program of study." Publisher: Le Ministère (Québec). Published in 1996.

Bruce R. Kohn, et al.: "Forced dilution system and method for emissions measurement systems" is patented by Bruce R. Kohn, Donald W. Bilsbarrow and Pradeep R. Tripathi. Abstract: The combination of ambient air, exhaust and premeasured calibration gases is used according to this invention in the analysis of either low or high pollutant concentration gases measured by a single range analyzer. By using ambient air as a diluent and employing its concentration values to generate the Reference Dilution Ratio, DR.sub.ref, iterative calculations are made to find the Raw Sample Concentration value, C.sub.raw. The gas diluting/mixing system includes pressure balanced infeed plumbing legs. Each of the legs feeds to respective flow restrictors and a common, downstream mixing "T" fitting. One leg is interconnected to the high concentration emission gas output from the sampling system and high concentration calibration gas.

BTL: Publisher of "The SDP push-fit plumbing system." Publisher: BTL (Porirua, N.Z.). Published in 1996.

Canadian Standards Association: Publication of "CPVC pipe, tubing, and fittings for hot and cold water distribution systems: plumbing products & materials." Canadian Standards Association; (technical editor: Solomon Ko; managing editor: Gary Burford). Publisher: Canadian Standards Association (Etobicoke, Ont). Published in 1996.

Clair L. Hopper: "Prefabricated modular invalid bathroom unit" is patented by Clair L. Hopper. Abstract: A prefabricated modular invalid bathroom unit for installation in a room which has a shower seat portion with a shower seat, a shower floor portion adjacent the shower seat portion for draining shower water, an upper shower wall portion detachably mounted on the shower seat portion which performs as a back-splash surround opposite the shower floor portion, and a commode portion for receiving a water closet which is joinable with the shower floor on the opposite side from the shower seat. The shower floor is provided with a door opening for wheelchair access. Water supply pipes and water drain pipes are carried by the shower unit and connected together between modular portions with conventional plumbing connectors, couplers and fittings.

Construction Engineering Research Lab.: Sponsored research "Control of Plumbosolvency in Building Plumbing Supplies. - Final rept." Sponsored by: Construction Engineering Research Lab. (Army), Champaign, IL. Written by V. F. Hock, H. Cardenas, K. W. Smothers and E. D. Zelsdorf. Abstract: Army installations must comply with the increasingly stringent drinking water quality standards enacted at the Federal level and enforced by state regulations. Much attention has focused on the costly remediations required when the allowable level of lead in drinking water is exceeded. This issue plays a significant role in the search for cost-effective ways to ensure that drinking water at Army installations meets all standards for quality and compliance with applicable laws. This study evaluated the effectiveness of three chemical treatments versus a control for inhibiting lead corrosion under a variety of water quality parameters in both the laboratory and field.

Cowles Creative Pub: Publisher of "Plumbing essentials." Publisher: Cowles Creative Pub (Minnetonka, Minn). Published in 1996.

David B. Cameron, et al.: "Sanitary toilet with integral water supply and manual flush assembly" is patented by David B. Cameron, John M. Antos and Charles L. Sargent. Abstract: A sanitary toilet system with an integral water supply and manual flush assembly for a recreational vehicle in which a flush water supply tank is provided adjacent a recreational vehicle wall with an inlet extending through the wall, thus eliminating plumbing within the vehicle between a water inlet and the supply tank. A manually operated piston pump is provided in which a clearance exists between the piston and the pump cylinder allowing water to flow past the piston during operation of the pump. This reduces the forces necessary to operate the pump in comparison to a piston in sealing relation to the cylinder.

David S. Matthews: "Pipe fitting alignment systems" is patented by David S. Matthews. Abstract: Alignment system and method for use by pipefitters. A portable hand tool having the appearances of a flashlight and the capability of projecting a collimated, coherent or otherwise directed, highly focused and narrow light beam is provided a coupling device on the end opposite the light emanation end, swivel capability about its elongate axis and bubble-type level devices. A targeting subsystem, for use with the light emanating tool, completes the alignment system. A portion of the targeting subsystem uses a vertically adjustable stand having a bracket useful both for alignment of piping and/or pipe supports, as well as for securing target placards.

Dennis Lunder: "Valve adapter locking system" is patented by Dennis Lunder. Abstract: An apparatus for attaching and securing a cap to a hose adapter used in connection with an RV waste removal valve assembly to prevent inadvertent sewer or waste spillage in the event of a failure of the primary locking components. The apparatus comprises two principal components, including a Y-branch plumbing fitting with a hose adapter incorporated at one end. On the outside surface of the hose adapter are a coupling pin and an adjacently located coupling tongue. The other component is a closure cap, which includes one or more generally L-shaped coupling arms.

Department of Energy: Sponsored research "Environmental assessment for effluent reduction, Los Alamos National Laboratory, Los Alamos, New Mexico." Sponsored by: Department of Energy, Washington, DC. Los Alamos Area Office. Abstract: The Department of Energy (DOE) proposes to eliminate industrial effluent from 27 outfalls at Los Alamos National Laboratory (LANL). The Proposed Action includes both simple and extensive plumbing modifications, which would result in the elimination of industrial effluent being released to the environment through 27 outfalls. The industrial effluent currently going to about half of the 27 outfalls under consideration would be rerouted to LANL's sanitary sewer system. Industrial effluent from other outfalls would be eliminated by replacing once-through cooling water systems with recirculation systems, or, in a few instances, operational changes would result in no generation of industrial effluent.

Dieter Katzer: "Sanitary article or plumbing fitting with a coated surface and a print image applied thereto and a process for making the same" is is patented by Dieter Katzer.

Douglas C. Burton: "A Pressing and a Method of and Apparatus for Making a Pressing" is patented by Douglas C. Burton. Abstract: A plumbing fitting comprising a first part being a pressing of sheet metal and a second part being a pressing of sheet metal, the first and second parts being connected together so that the first part provides a first limb and the second part provides a second limb of the fitting. A method of making a pressing including the step of taking a component having a first end part of tubular configuration of a first diameter and acting thereon to form at least the end part to a second, smaller diameter.

Edward A. Wicks: "Fire protection system and method using dual-purpose plumbing" is is patented by Edward A. Wicks.

Eric Nyenhuis, et al.: "Flood Control Device" is patented by Eric Nyenhuis, James Nyenhuis, Terry Sr. Simpkins and Terry J. Simpkins Jr. Abstract: A flood control device (200) which measures the volume of fluid delivered in a continuous steady flow to a house or building and which shuts off the fluid flow if a preset maximum limit is reached, indicating overly high consumption due to a leak, break or open faucet in the plumbing of the housing of building.

Eugene M. Brooks: "Tube fitting ratchet tool" is patented by Eugene M. Brooks. Abstract: Disclosed is a novel means for connecting and disconnecting fluid line couplings usually encountered in the automotive, refrigeration, and plumbing industries. The present invention comprises a common ratcheting handle adapted to receive a plurality of standard sized cogwheels. Independently, a cogwheel, having peripheral radially extending gear teeth and a central polygonal aperture intersected by a free opening is slidably positioned along a tubular conduit and onto a nut. The handle, having a cradle, is mated to the cogwheel and worked ratchet fashion to achieve a desired task.

Fabrizio Turco and Raffaella Turco: "Process and Chain of Installations for Completing and Finishing Hollow Bricks" is patented by Fabrizio Turco and Raffaella Turco. Abstract: Process and machines for completion and finishing of hollow bricks (10, 12) comprising an installation (35) for filling bricks with mortar, for grinding their surfaces and for drying, a finishing installation for trimming with milling of the four longitudinal edges of the bricks, for application of fluid mortar by spraying, for application of a fiberglass net and of plaster for surface finish, an installation for forming holes and channels to receive components for electrical and plumbing purposes and vertical components for anti-seismic reinforcements, the various installations being connected by conveyor belts (40-45), there being between one installation and another equipment for formation of packages of bricks and their transfer onto pallets.

Fareed-M. SalahUddin: "Element based foam and concrete wall construction and method and apparatus therefor" is patented by Fareed-M. SalahUddin. Abstract: A element based wall construction, process of modular construction and apparatus for constructing structures of spaced concrete cylinders and beams and foam insulating blocks. The wall construction includes spaced, vertical concrete cylinders interconnected by horizontal concrete beams, reinforced by centrally located reinforcing bars, with a pilaster projecting inwardly beyond the cylinders and beams to support roof and floor joists or trusses, and insulating foam blocks occupying the spaces between cylinders and beams and projecting outwardly beyond the cylinders and beams to define channels for mounting plumbing and electrical conduits and wiring beneath the sheet rock or siding which abuts the foam block surfaces.

Ford Oxaal: "Method and apparatus for producing a three-hundred and sixty degree spherical visual data set" is patented by Ford Oxaal. Abstract: The present invention is directed to an apparatus and method for producing a three-hundred and sixty degree spherical visual data set using at least one lens. The lens encompasses a field of view of not less than one-hundred and eighty degrees. The field of view is represented by a hemisphere defined by a half-space which is, in turn, defined by a first plane having an origin point through which a vertical axis of the plane extends. The apparatus includes a mounting support member and a plumbing device. The mounting support member positions at least one camera having the at least one lens. The mounting support member is aligned with the vertical axis and rotatable in first and second directions through at least one-hundred and eighty degrees from a first position to a second position.

Gabriel Lechuga: "Floor mounted water basin support" is patented by Gabriel Lechuga. Abstract: A water basin floor mounted support for holding a water basin, such as a floor mounted sink or bathtub in a position where it is to be mounted in the floor of a structure during the building of the structure. The floor mounted support comprises a carrier plate having an enlarged central opening designed to receive plumbing connected to the depending tub portion of the water basin. The water basin also has a peripheral flange which is to be mounted in the floor of the construction. A plurality of height adjustable legs hold support the support plate at a desired elevation and thereby stabilize the water basin during the actual fabrication of the floor, such as the pouring of a concrete floor.

Government of Cuba: Decree 211 of 9 August 1996 covers violations of regulations for aqueduct and plumbing public services. Defines the violations and provides for authorities to impose measures that solve the problems. Published in Gaceta Oficial on August 09, 1996.

Jeffrey R. Gordon and William B. Rose: "Pipe burst protection pressure relief apparatus for plumbing fixtures" is is patented by Jeffrey R. Gordon and William B. Rose.

Jerry Lovett: "Fluid storage and delivery system" is patented by Jerry Lovett. Abstract: A below-grade fuel delivery and storage system is constructed in the form of a fully vaulted system located under the dispenser area. The vault is made of concrete; and all of the plumbing, fill, vapor recovery locations and the bulk storage tank itself are located entirely within the vault. The fill pipes for tanks located within the vault extend through openings in the roof of the vault. Similarly, fuel delivery lines extend from the tanks upwardly through openings in the vault roof to dispensers located directly above the vault.

John E. Schommer: "Leak detection system for plumbing fixtures" is is patented by John E. Schommer.

John M. Mankins: "Testing of plumbing installations" is patented by John M. Mankins. Abstract: A method and apparatus for testing a plumbing system in a more dependable and cost-effective manner. During the rough-in plumbing phase of construction, the drain pipe leading from the plumbing system in a building to the city sewer main or main sewer line is positively sealed off by a test cap welded in the pipe at the location of the clean-out. Access to the test cap is maintained through the clean-out. Pressurizing the rough-in plumbing to test the same can then proceed knowing that if any leaks occur, they are in the branch plumbing on the building side of the test cap, and not at or in the test cap. Following successful completion of the initial test, the top-out plumbing job is completed, leaving the test cap welded in the clean-out or drain pipe.

John R. Alonso and Randy V. Cannady: "Apparatus for cleaning ducting" is patented by John R. Alonso and Randy V. Cannady. Abstract: A duct cleaning apparatus and method for cleaning and maintaining the interior of most types of ducts, including chimneys, air conditioning and heating ducts, dryer ducts, vents, plumbing and rain gutter ducts. The apparatus is made up of a flexible shaft connected to a cleaning brush or tool. The flexible shaft can be extended through the use of attached couplings to create an infinitely long cleaning apparatus. The cleaning brushes and tools are configured in a variety of sizes with differing configurations of bristled appendages for specific applications. At least some of the cleaning appendages are partially covered with a sleeve. In one embodiment, cleaning brushes are described for general cleaning and maintenance of ducts.

Joint Plumbing Apprentice & Journeyman Training, Inc: Publication of "Water supply: apprentice & journeyman training. Section G." Publisher: Joint Plumbing Apprentice & Journeyman Training (Washington, D.C.). Published in 1996.

Kenneth Lochbaum: "Stabilizer for aquatic exercise" is patented by Kenneth Lochbaum. Abstract: The stabilizer devices for aquatic exercising and a device for aquatic exercise are disclosed. The stabilizers may be fixed to the side walls or bottom of a container of water to hold a person in an exercising position. The stabilizers may be made of plastic plumbing pipe and fittings may be portable, supported on, or fixed permanently in position on a container of water. The stabilizers may be rigid or flexible, may be completely immersed in water.

Klaus Fink: "Process for distinguishing plumbing parts by the coatings applied thereto" is is patented by Klaus Fink.

Lawrence Livermore National Lab.: Sponsored research "National Ignition Facility subsystem design requirements laser and target area building (LTAB) SSDR 1.2.2.1." Sponsored by: Lawrence Livermore National Lab., CA (United States).; Department of Energy, Washington, DC. Written by P. Kempel and J. Hands. Abstract: This Subsystem Design Requirements (SSDR) document establishes the performance, design, and verification requirements for the conventional building systems and subsystems of the Laser and Target Area Building (LTAB), including those that house and support the operation of high-energy laser equipment and the operational flow of personnel and materials throughout the facility.

Malireddy S. Reddy and Syama M. Reddy: "Biochemical media system for reducing pollution" is patented by Malireddy S. Reddy and Syama M. Reddy. Abstract: A first media provides an oxygen inducer such as catalase, bound and stabilized in pellet form so as to dissipate slowly into aqueous surroundings. A second media provides an oxygen supplier such as a peroxide, stabilized by combination with a proteinaceous compound such as urea and bound in a matrix that limits oxygen release. The two media are combined in aqueous environment to generate nascent oxygen at a modulated rate such that the oxygen is efficiently absorbed into the surrounding aqueous environment, promoting growth of aerobic species and reducing biological pollution. Specific adaptations demonstrate benefits of use in shrimp or fish ponds, raw milk, fruit juice, fresh food, silage and animal feed, fertilizer, plumbing systems, and grease traps.

Mark Conrad Smith: "Apparatus and method for the formation of a bathtub or shower stall liner" is patented by Mark Conrad Smith. Abstract: Bathtub or shower stall liner vacuum forming system for the forming of a liner to be positioned over an existing bathtub comprises a bathtub liner vacuum machine, a plumbing apparatus and a lift for moving the plumbing apparatus. The bathtub liner vacuum machine comprises a frame member, a track member, an oven and a skirt forming member. The plumbing apparatus includes a conventional plumbing fixture, a manifold, mesh member and a vacuum pump. Upon positioning of the formable member within the frame member and skirt forming member, the frame member is rolled along the track member into the oven.

Marziani, Gianluca Berardi, Franco Galleria Mascherino: Publication of "Giuseppe Tubi e l'arte del tubo = (Joe Piper (friendly) plumbing)." A cura di Gianluca Marziani, con testi di Gianluca Marziani e Franco Berardi (Bifo) Joe Piper (friendly) plumbing. Publisher: Galleria Mascherino (Rome). Published in 1996.

Maug Hla Win, et al.: "Flushable premoistened personal wipe" is patented by Maug Hla Win, Mark Alan Burazin, Steven Alexander Engel, Bernhardt Edward Kressner, William Dee Lloyd and Walter Theodore Schultz. Abstract: A pre-moistened wet wipe provides functional wet strength in use, yet is dispersible if flushed down the toilet so that plumbing and sewage treatment facilities do not become clogged. A particular embodiment of the wipe consists of three uncreped through-air-dried tissue plies that are attached to each other by edge embossing. The two outer plies contain a wet strength agent to provide wet poke-through resistance to two large, centrally-located unembossed regions. The center ply contains no wet strength agent to aid in dispersibility. The embossing around the edges of the wipe further degrades the strength of the wipe in the embossed areas to assist in dispersibility when the wipe is flushed.

Melford L. Miller: "Method of providing increased access to temperature and humidity control systems" is patented by Melford L. Miller. Abstract: A plumbing assembly is disclosed that comprises an access panel which allows increased access to a temperature and humidity control system such as a heating or air-conditioning system. The access panel includes at least one valve for controlling the flow of a fluid and communicates with the first end of a first piping assembly. The second end of the first piping assembly communicates with a second piping assembly typically through a valve situated within the second piping assembly. The second piping assembly is part of a temperature and humidity control system and is generally in fluid communication with a heat transfer coil in the temperature and humidity control system.

Midgley, Mary: Born in 1919, authored "Utopias, dolphins, and computers: some problems in philosophical plumbing." Publisher: Routledge (London; New York). Published in 1996.

Monty Dale Lowella: "Wall-attached plumbing connector" is is patented by Monty Dale Lowella.

National Research Council Canada: Publication of "National construction codes (computer file) National building code of Canada National Fire Code of Canada National Plumbing Code of Canada National Farm Building Code of Canada." Publisher: National Research Council Canada (Ottawa). Published in 1996.

Norman J. Jaeckels and Randy O. Mesun: "Pump operated plumbing fixture" is patented by Norman J. Jaeckels and Randy O. Mesun. Abstract: A toilet has a pump to deliver selected quantities of water from a reservoir to a toilet bowl so as to effect a water savings. In one aspect, both the motor and pump are positioned in the reservoir to deliver water to both the rim and bowl portions. In another aspect, there are conduits connected between the basin, the rim and controls which are provided to deliver water to the rim and bowl either independently, simultaneously or in selective sequences. In alternative embodiments, a refill tube is connected to an intake conduit and the rim of the bowl to effect a water seal, a fail safe valve is connected to the supply conduit, a receptacle with a cleaning fluid and a pump is connected to the bowl and there are at least two receptacles for receiving waste.

North Carolina. State Board of Plumbing, Heating, and Fire Sprinkler Contractors: Publication of "Continuing education, 1997." State Board of Examiners of Plumbing, Heating, and Fire Sprinkler Contractors. Publisher: The Board (Raleigh, NC). Published in 1996.

NTS: Publisher of "Piping and plumbing." Publisher: NTS (Oslo, Norway). Published in 1996.

Ogle, Maureen: Author of "All the modern conveniences: American household plumbing, 1840-1890." Publisher: Johns Hopkins University Press (Baltimore, Md.; London). Published in 1996.

Parsons Engineering Science: Sponsored research "Operation and Maintenance Manual for Bioventing Pilot Testing Systems Spill Site Number 1, Building 457, and UST 702, Eaker Air Force Base, Blytheville, Arkansas." Sponsored by: Parsons Engineering Science, Inc., Denver, CO. Abstract: This Operations and Maintenance (O&M) Manual has been created as a guide for monitoring and maintaining the performance of the pilot-scale bioventing blower systems and vent well plumbing at Spill Site No. 1, Building 457, and underground storage tank (UST) 702, at Eaker Air Force Base (AFB), Arkansas. Bioventing is the forced injection of fresh air, or withdrawal of soil gas, to enhance the supply of oxygen in subsurface soils for in situ bioremediation. A blower system is used to inject air into the soil, thereby supplying fresh atmospheric air (with approximately 20.8 percent oxygen) to contaminated soils. Once oxygen is provided to the subsurface, existing soil bacteria aerobically break down fuel residuals.

Peter Pierre: "Under-sink hose retainer" is patented

by Peter Pierre. Abstract: A hose retainer for spray hoses that uses a "U" shaped hose retainer that has a hollow interior. The hose retainer is sized to hold a fully retracted sprayer hose. The sprayer hose can be attached to a sprayer nozzle or to a removable faucet sprayer, found on modern sinks. A flange secures the hose retainer under the counter top. If needed, brackets can be installed near the bottom of the hose retainer to provide additional support. In this way, the hose can be stored within the hose retainer, removed for use, and replaced without exposing the sprayer hose to any of the under-sink plumbing or items that may be stored there.

Peter Schmucki and Silvio Marti: "Plumbing fixture mounting device using a threaded rod with interrupted threads" is is patented by Peter Schmucki and Silvio Marti.

Plumbing Manufacturers Institute: Publication of "Plumbing Manufacturers Institute." Publisher: Plumbing Manufacturers Institute (Schaumburg, Ill). Published in 1996.

Prescher, Ray E.: Author of "National plumbing & HVAC estimator 1997." Publisher: Craftsman Book Co (Carlsbad, Calif). Published in 1996.

R.R. Brad Follett: "Boat lift" is patented by R.R. Brad Follett. Abstract: A boat lift for lifting a boat above the water adjacent to a wharf on a water bed comprises a wharf attachment mounted to the wharf above the water; a frame having a wharf end portion hinged adjacent to the wharf attachment; a footing seated on the water bed beneath the outer end portion of the frame; and scissor arms one having a top end portion which is hinged to the outer portion of the frame; the other having a top end portion which is hinged to the lower end portion of the upper scissor arm and a lower end portion which is hinged to the footing therebelow; and opening/closing means to alternatively fold the scissor arms together and open them to a straight in-line position.

Richard A. Minutillo: "Valve safety handle" is patented by Richard A. Minutillo. Abstract: A valve safety handle having a handle slidably attached to a valve stem. The handle incorporates a handle female spline sized to engage a valve stem male spline. The handle female spline is urged out of engagement with the valve stem male spline by means of a spring trapped between the handle and valve stem. The valve stem also has a valve stem key sized to slide into a handle lower recess keyway. Thus the handle may engage with the valve stem only after the handle has been rotated relative to the valve stem until the valve stem key aligns with the handle lower recess keyway, and the handle has then been translated relative to the valve stem against the spring until the handle female spline is engaged with the valve stem male spline.

Roy L. Matlock: "Golf grip washing device" is patented by Roy L. Matlock. Abstract: A golf grip cleaning device mounted on a support which is in turn mounted on a base. The base can be stationed at the tee box of the golf course or can be mounted on a golf car itself. For convenience and economics, the entire assembly can be made out of readily available PVC plumbing parts. The washer section includes a tube having a plug at the bottom end and a cap at the top end. The cap has an open mouth so that the golf club can be inserted into the tube. The tube is aligned vertically and has a series of brush rings stacked in the tube and spaced from each other by spacers inserted between each brush ring. The brush rings include bristles projecting radially inwardly toward the axial center of the tube with the brush tips terminating generally in a circular pattern.

Shigeyuki Matsumoto, et al.: "Coupling for drainage pipings" is patented by Shigeyuki Matsumoto, Shinobu Katoh, Keisuke Sugawara, Masao Kanazawa and Yutaka Yoshida. Abstract: A coupling for vertical connection in sewage plumbing used in tall and high-rise buildings, is disclosed. The coupling is equipped in its inside walls with a pair of vortical blades for descending sewage streams from the upper floors into the coupling to impinge on their top blade surface to flow sideways into a spiral flow down the coupling. The more intense vortex streams developed, the faster the streams fall along the plumbing. For a vortex generates a vertical column of upwardly moving ventilative air in the center of the sewage streams, smoothing the descent of the drainage. Moreover, the top and bottom blades are mounted at different levels of height inside the coupling, and circumferentially displaced to each other so as to form a V-shape as seen in the horizonal projection view.

Shin Tokui and Masaki Kohyama: "Multi-layer pipe" is patented by Shin Tokui and Masaki Kohyama. Abstract: A multi-layer pipe has an innermost layer formed of a butene polymer composition. At least one other layer is formed of a polyolefin resin composition comprising (A) 95-5 parts by weight of a polyolefin resin, (B) 5-95 parts by weight of a filler, and (C) 0.1-10 parts by weight per 100 parts by weight of components (A) and (B) combined of a modified polyolefin resin. This multi-layer pipe undergoes minimal elongation by heat so that it is free from troubles by thermal deformation even when high temperature fluid is passed therethrough, has high rigidity, and is thus suitable as plumbing for cold and hot water.

Specialists in Business Information, inc: Publication of "SBI market profile. Plumbing fixtures Plumbing fixtures." Publisher: Specialists in Business Information (New York). Published in 1996.

Standards Association of Australia. Committee WS/18, Copper and Copper Alloy Tubes for Plumbing and Gasfitting: Publication of "Copper tubes for plumbing, gasfitting and drainage applications." Publisher: Standards Association of Australia (North Sydney, N.S.W.). Published in 1996.

Stanley Berlin: "Modular work evaluation apparatus" is patented by Stanley Berlin. Abstract: A modular universal work evaluation apparatus to give therapists the ability to measure job task performance in the context of a variety of specific jobs or tasks. The invention generally comprises a main bench unit forming a walled semi-enclosure with a removable top, one or more simulated work evaluation stations enclosed within the main bench unit, and one or more work evaluation stations attachable to the main bench unit. All simulated work evaluation stations include a plurality of workable components for simulating specific job related tasks performed by the patient at work. The internal work evaluation stations include one or both of a simulated shoveling pit and/or a simulated engine block accessible by removing the removable top.

Texas Natural Resource Conservation Commission: Publication of "State of Texas approved plumbing fixture list." Prepared by Water Utilities Division. Published in 1996.

The International Association of Plumbing and Mechanical Officials: Publisher of "Uniform plumbing code." Publisher: The International Association of Plumbing and Mechanical Officials (Los Angeles, CA). Published in 1996.

Thomas J. Watson: "Plumbing fittings and method of packaging therefor" is is patented by Thomas J. Watson.

Treloar, Roy: Author of "Plumbing encyclopaedia." Publisher: Blackwell Science (Oxford; Cambridge, Mass). Published in 1996.

Walter Becker and Herbert Reinecke: "Plumbing fixture carrying drinking water comprised of a copper alloy" is is patented by Walter Becker and Herbert Reinecke.

Woodson, Roger Dodge: Born in 1955, authored "Builder's guide to residential plumbing." Publisher: McGraw-Hill (New York). Published in 1996.

1997

Allied Technical Services: Publisher of "Plumbing information system, master specification." Publisher: Allied Technical Services (Willowdale, Ont). Published in 1997.

Anthony L. James: "Plunger" is patented by Anthony L. James. Abstract: A plunger having a handle, an upper cylinder, a lower cylinder, and a nozzle. The bottom portion of the upper cylinder fits over the top portion of the lower cylinder. The handle may be grasped to push the upper cylinder down over the lower cylinder to force compressed air out through the nozzle, or to pull the upper cylinder up to create a vacuum to suck air and/or fluids up. Either compression or vacuum, or both, may be used to unclog drains in sinks, toilets, or other household plumbing fixtures. A disc shaped piston compresses the air inside the lower cylinder when the upper cylinder to which the piston is attached moves down, and creates a partial vacuum when it moves up. The piston is attached by a rod to the handle and the upper cylinder.

Anthony Stephen Hodgkinson: "Water diverting device" is patented by Anthony Stephen Hodgkinson. Abstract: A water diverting device (10,51,60,70,80,83,85,86,600,700) for directing leaking water from a plumbing fitting such as a tap having a body (50) and breech (100) mounted behind the wall to the front face (401) of the wall, the device including a sleeve (12,56,58), an inner flange (18), an outer flange (20), the arrangement being such that the inner flange (18) engages the breech (100) of the tap and the tap body extends through the sleeve and the outer flange (20) engages the front face (401) of a wall whereby water leaking from the connection between the tap body and a tap breech is directed by the device to the front face of the wall.

Anton J. Kolar and Jeffrey Hildebrand: "Self-closing solenoid operated faucet" is patented by Anton J. Kolar and Jeffrey Hildebrand. Abstract: A self-closing faucet includes a hollow body with a spout. The hollow body contains an integral plumbing sub-assembly that has a solenoid valve supplied by an inlet tube and connected to a spout tube that extends through the spout to an outlet opening at a remote end of the spout. An actuator assembly coupled to the housing includes a timer circuit that controls the solenoid valve to send water from the faucet for a predefined period of time. A switch triggers the timer circuit upon activation by a user operable mechanism on the faucet.

Argonne National Lab.: Sponsored research "Decommissioning of a research reactor in the USA: A case study from planning to site release." Sponsored by: Argonne National Lab., IL.; Department of Energy, Washington, DC. Written by L. E. Boing. Abstract: Argonne National Laboratory (ANL) has completed the D&D of the Experimental Boiling Water Reactor (EBWR). The project consisted of the decontamination and/or packaging as radioactive waste the reactor vessel and internals, contaminated piping systems, miscellaneous tanks, pumps, and associated equipment. The dismantling process involved the removal and size reduction of equipment and associated plumbing, ductwork, drain lines, etc. Size reduction of reactor vessel internals was performed in the fuel pool. All radioactive and mixed waste was packaged and manifested. A thorough survey of the facility was performed after the removal of contaminated and activated material. Non-radioactive waste was disposed of in the ANL landfill or recycled as appropriate.

Arkansas. Board of Examiners in Speech-Language Pathology and Audiology: Publication of "Annual report & mission statement." Publisher: Plumbing & Natural Gas Section, Division of Protective Health Codes, Arkansas Dept. of Health (Little Rock). Published in 1997.

Augustin Pavel: "Reverse osmosis membrane housing with integral wide-area check valve and shut-off valve, optional pressure gauge, and optional large-volume high-flow membrane cartridge" is patented by Augustin Pavel. Abstract: The cap to a reverse osmosis (R.O.) system membrane cartridge housing integrates both (i) a system automatic shut-off valve, and (ii) an improved check valve of such enlarged area and low pressure drop as typically gains 2-4 gallons per day in purified water output. The housing both reduces, typically from seven ports to five ports, and simplifies with hand-tightened quick fittings, the plumbing requirements of the R.O system. The housing fits a new and larger, typically 100+ gallon per hour, high-flow-rate R.O. membrane cartridge as well as myriad universal standard cartridges. A pressure gauge is optionally integrated.

B. Bernetiae Reed: "Device for sanitary tampon removal and disposal" is patented by B. Bernetiae Reed. Abstract: This invention comprises a mitten device for sanitarily removing a tampon from a body cavity of an individual and thereafter disposing of the tampon through the solid waste system as opposed to the plumbing system. The mitten is adapted to fit over a hand and wrist and has a front side and a back side. The mitten has an unitary finger portion, a partially detached index finger portion, a thumb portion, a mid-section, a cuff portion, an absorbent pad affixed to the mid-section on the front side of the mitten, and an adhesive tab. The unitary finger portion includes a grasping portion on the front side of the middle finger near the fingertip. In use the mitten is utilized to remove the tampon for disposal from an individual's body. The individual then makes a fist around the tampon.

Billy D. Pullam: "Interlocking stubs" is patented by Billy D. Pullam. Abstract: The present invention is a wall framing system comprising upper beams, lower beams and a plurality of studs secured to the beams via a securing system. The securing system comprising a plurality of apertures located within the upper and lower beams. The studs include flanges extending outwardly and perpendicularly from there lower ends. The flanges are received within the apertures for providing the studs to be in a secured and fixed position. The studs are preferably made of plastic and include apertures for allowing wiring, plumbing and conduits to extend through each stud.

Billy J. Hobbs and Philip A. Mulvey: "Water service box and connectors for PEX pipe" is patented by Billy J. Hobbs and Philip A. Mulvey. Abstract: A plumbing connector system having a recessed, in-wall water service box, at least one valve connected to the water service box, and connector fittings particularly adapted for use in connecting in-wall potable water supply lines made of Cross linked polyethylene (PEX) to appliances and fixtures such as washing machines, ice makers, sinks, and the like. A valve inlet extension having a barbed end is disclosed for use in releasably securing the valve to the water service box and for connecting the valve to the Cross linked polyethylene water supply line.

Blankenbaker, E. Keith: Author of "Modern plumbing." Publisher: Goodheart-Willcox (Tinley Park, Ill). Published in 1997.

Brent H. Larkin: "Plumbing tool for temporarily plugging a pipe" is is patented by Brent H. Larkin.

Brian Chagnot: "Post plumbing device" is patented by Brian Chagnot. Abstract: A post plumbing device has a pair of brackets connected by a threaded rod. Each bracket has a base having a selected length, a top, a bottom and four sides extending between the bottom and the top. A top flange is attached to the top and has a threaded bore passing through the flange, along an axis substantially parallel to the base. One bracket has a shorter side flange extending from a portion of one side of the base away from and substantially perpendicular to the bottom. A plurality of holes are provided in each base and the side flange to receive nails or screws. A threaded rod having a handle at its midpoint is threaded into the threaded bore of each of the brackets.

Butch Jones: "Method and device for attaching fittings to receptacle" is patented by Butch Jones. Abstract: An improved device and method for attachment of a plumbing fitting to a pipe or other drain receptacle is described in which the device has at least one elastomeric rib disposed about the outer circumference of the body of the device for forming a watertight seal against the interior wall of the drain receptacle. The ribs are angled in an axial direction opposite to the direction of insertion, allowing easy insertion into a drain receptacle, while causing a radial self-tightening force resisting movement in the direction of removal, and enhancing the seal. The device also allows lateral movement of the receptacle relative to the device, as well as expansion and contraction, without impairing the seal.

Daniel J. Parker and Mark H. Thesken: "Combination lawn/garden ornament and cremation container" is patented by Daniel J. Parker and Mark H. Thesken. Abstract: A combination lawn/garden ornament and cremation container comprises a decorative water fountain adapted to circulate water from a water source upwardly and to allow the water to cascade downwardly and an openable and closable compartment adapted to contain cremated remains of a deceased. The fountain includes a water reservoir, a pump and plumbing. The plumbing has a first end connected to the pump and has a second end open to atmosphere and located above the reservoir. The pump is operable to pump water from the reservoir upwardly through the plumbing. The openable and closable compartment comprises a bowl for receiving the cremated remains therein, the bowl being removably securable to the fountain.

1997

Daniel Rochette, et al.: "System for coupling operating equipment to a washer" is patented by Daniel Rochette, Michel Lemay, Yves-Andrebec Theriault, Michel Emond, Mario Duchaine, Ghislain Parent and Nathalie Thibault. Abstract: An operating system (20) for a washer (1) is mounted on a moveable trolley (52). The trolley carries all of the failure prone elements such as pumps (24, 28, 40) solenoid valves 80, electrical heaters (48), an electrical control circuit (50) and the like. Quick-release couplings (58, 59,60 62), between the operating system and plumbing associated with a washing chamber (10), allow the operating system to be quickly disconnected from and reconnected with the chamber. The trolley is then wheeled a distance away from the chamber, providing ready access to all the operating equipment for maintenance and repair.

Departments of the Army, and the Air Force: Publisher of "Plumbing." Publisher: Departments of the Army, and the Air Force (Washington, DC). Published in 1997.

Douglass E. Hughes: "Shower filter for chlorine removal and scale deposit prevention" is patented by Douglass E. Hughes. Abstract: Embodiments of a multi-purpose shower/tub filter unit are shown and described, the filter unit containing a chlorine-removal media and a scale-inhibiting media. The housing of the filter unit is adapted to attach universally to various water sources, such as a pipe or faucet and to a showerhead or hand-held spray unit. The filter unit preferably has an arm extending out from the main body of the filter unit, and the filter unit preferably extends upward and outward from the attachment point on the pipe or faucet.

Enzo L. Coltrinari, et al.: "Apparatus and method for inhibiting the leaching of lead in water" is patented by Enzo L. Coltrinari, Jerome P. Downey, Wayne C. Hazen and Paul B. Queneau. Abstract: A copper alloy plumbing fixture containing interdispersed lead particles coated non-continuously on a water contact surface to resist the leaching of lead into potable water systems. The leach resistant fixture is prepared by immersing conventional copper alloys in a bismuth nitrate solution, selectively and non-continuously coating the lead dispersoid particles on the water contact surface with bismuth, tin or copper.

Frederick J. Whiting, et al.: "Blanket cylinder throw-off device" is patented by Frederick J. Whiting, Thomas W. Orzechowski, Stanley Momot and Thaddeus A. Niemiro. Abstract: An improved throw off device for disengaging adjacent blanket cylinders (12) and (14) from each other and corresponding adjacent plate cylinders (16) and (18) is provided. The device includes pairs of bearing assemblies (28A), (28B), (30A) and (30B) that are mounted on the opposite ends of the journal (26) of each of the blanket cylinders (12) and (14). Each bearing assembly is defined by an inner race (36) and an outer race (38) having an eccentric bore in which the inner race is disposed. The device eliminates the need for a bearing sleeve.

Garry Schmidt: "Distribution header for potable water and hot water space heating" is patented by Garry Schmidt. Abstract: A water manifold is usable in the construction of a fluid-based heat-transfer system for space heating, the supply and distribution of potable water, and other applications. The water manifold is formed from a number of elements in a flexible manner, in that the elements are assembled as needed for a particular application. A plurality of manifold segments 100, each supporting a pipe directed away from a main pipe, transfer heat to a specific area, and may be be connected in a linear manner, as required by the design of the application. A cross tee segment 300 is attachable to the manifold segments, and may be used to support a thermometer unit 200, an automatic air vent or other apparatus. A spigot 400 is attachable to the cross tee segment, adjacent to the thermometer.

Gary K. Weise: "Plumbing apparatus" is patented by Gary K. Weise. Abstract: A bubble jet fitting for use in a spa provides for a lay-length short enough to allow its installation within a six-inch dam wall. The bubble jet fitting has an outlet portion which in one use provides for solvent welding within a standard size of PVC pipe. A pipe extender has end portions similarly sized and configured to solvent weld within end portions of adjacent pipe sections which are connected through the pipe extender.

Geological Survey: Sponsored research "Geologic Studies in Alaska by the U.S. Geological Survey, 1997. - Professional paper." Sponsored by: Geological Survey, Reston, VA. Written by K. D. Kelley. Abstract: Contents: Introduction; Geologic setting of Mississippi vein-breccias at the Kady Zn-Pb-Cu-Ag prospect: Plumbing system for a failed Sedex deposit; Chemical and isotopic data for rocks and ores from the Upper Traissic Greens Creek and Woewodski Island volcanogenic massive sulfide deposits, southeastern Alaska; Core lithofacies analysis and fluvio-tidal environments in the AK 94 CBM-1 well, near Wasilla, Alaska; Lower Paleozoic deep-water facies of the Medfra area, central Alaska; Alagogshak Volcano: A Pleistocene andesite-dacite stratovolcano in Katmai National Park; Gravity changes during the 26 years following the 1964 Alaskan earthquake; Metal cycling along the northwestern Seward Peninsula, Alaska: A possible natural cause of metal contamination in the Arctic.

Government of Honduras: Accord 058 of 9 April 1997 approves the Technical Standards for the Discharge of Water to Receptacles and Sanitary Plumbing. Published in Gaceta Oficial on April 09, 1997.

Hermann Moldenhauer: "Flow controls" is patented by Hermann Moldenhauer. Abstract: Flow controls that can be inserted in a liquid-supply line or in the accommodating bore of a plumbing fitting. The controls have an essentially cup-shaped mount with perforations through its bottom and a disk of resilient material fits into the perforations. At least the edge of the side of the disk facing the bottom of the cup has a conical bevel of 1.degree. to 5.degree. to the midplane of the disk and narrow ribs and/or sector-shaped webs that extend out essential radially at a prescribed angle around a prescribed circumferential angle.

Hsin-Chun Liao: "Toy submarine ballast system" is patented by Hsin-Chun Liao. Abstract: A ballast system for toy submarines comprises a plumbing device, a flexible bag, a piece of wire and a rod. The ballast system draws water in and forces water out by decompressing and compressing the flexible bag.

International Association of Plumbing and Mechanical Officials: Publisher of "Uniform plumbing code, 1997." Publisher: International Association of Plumbing and Mechanical Officials (Walnut, CA). Published in 1997.

International Code Council: Publisher of "International plumbing code 1997." International Code Council ... (et al.). Publisher: International Code Council (Country Club Hills, IL). Published in 1997.

James Andrew Smith, et al.: "Recirculating plumbing system" is patented by James Andrew Smith, John Ross Elliott and Michael E.S. Lawrence. Abstract: A water conservation and delivery system for a building includes a first subsystem for dispensing clean water from a faucet, a second subsystem for draining waste water from the vessel supplied by the faucet, and a third subsystem for recirculating clean water prior to dispensement back into the dispensing subsystem while the dispensing temperature and flow are adjusted.

James L. Caffrey: "Plumbing device and method" is patented by James L. Caffrey. Abstract: An improved device and method for plumbing a recirculating water pump into a hot water heating system, the water pump having a pair of connecting flanges on the inflow and outflow sides of the pump. The present invention includes a section of copper tubing which has one end flared, the flare preferably being at approximately right angles to the longitudinal axis of the tubing. Further, an installation flange is provided having a central hole and an inside face to be positioned against a corresponding face of a connecting flange of the recirculating water pump, the copper tubing being inserted through the central hole of the installation flange with the flared end positioned against the inside face of the installation flange.

James Melvin Devore and Charles Franklin Helms Jr: "Drain trap" is patented by James Melvin Devore and Charles Franklin Helms Jr. Abstract: A drain trap for a plumbing drainage system includes a drain pipe having an inlet end for fluid-connection to an area to be drained of liquid, and a discharge end. A drain cup is provided which includes a bottom wall and a side wall joined to the bottom wall. The side wall defines an open upper end which surrounds the discharge end of the drain pipe and is positioned within a portion of the drain cup to establish therebetween an annulus space to allow liquid flowing through the drain pipe to fill the drain cup and then overflow into plumbing associated with the drainage system. At least one pair of radially extending lugs are provided which are circumferentially spaced apart from one another about the drain pipe.

Jeff Bayley: "Waste and overflow drain adaptor device" is patented by Jeff Bayley. Abstract: An adaptor bushing for bathtub plumbing kits is disclosed. The bushing is adapted to be field securable into either a conventional sanitary tee or elbow fitting. In this way a kit is provided, having identical components, which may be connected in both a direct or indirect waste drain configuration, without any additional components being required.

Jeffrey R. Gordon and William B. Rose: "Compressed stopper channel bypass pipe burst pressure relief apparatus for plumbing fixtures" is is patented by Jeffrey R. Gordon and William B. Rose.

Jerome M. Gauthier, et al.: "Control board for controlling and monitoring usage of water" is patented by Jerome M. Gauthier, Nhon T. Vuong and Mark J. Sippel. Abstract: An apparatus and method for controlling plumbing fixtures includes an electronic control board having a microprocessor that accepts four inputs and produces four outputs. Inputs at other than the microprocessor's operating voltage are converted thereto. Outputs having different voltages are controlled by latching relays. The control board can be used with a Smart Sink that requires a sequenced hand washing. The control board can form a node on a network that monitors and controls the functions of multiple boards throughout a facility.

Jimmy Cochimin: "Clamp and cup securing strain gauge cell adjacent pressure transmitting diaphragm" is patented by Jimmy Cochimin. Abstract: Apparatus comprising a flow carrier connectable in a liquid flow system including an electric motor-pump unit and a conduit for conveying a pumped liquid to a liquid utilization apparatus. The flow carrier is connectable in the conduit and includes an opening which exposes the liquid flowing through the carrier. A heat sink or cold plate is located on the carrier over the opening, the heat sink covering the opening and having a wet side exposed to the liquid. The heat sink further includes a dry side, and heat generating control components are secured to the dry side. A sensor is also mounted on the heat sink and responds to a characteristic, such as the pressure, of the liquid. The sensor and the control components are operable to control the motor-pump unit.

John E. Hartman, et al.: "Hydraulic trim cylinder for marine stern drives and outboard motors" is patented by John E. Hartman, Paul M. Dadd and John T. Venaleck. Abstract: It is an object of the current invention to provide a trim cylinder that is cost effective; it is further an object of the invention to provide a cylinder that has few parts, less than one-third the number of parts of present art; it is further an object of the invention to provide a unique and simple check valve for operation as a shock absorber and further to provide passages integral of the extruded or molded body allowing plumbing to be attached at one end only of the cylinder; also to eliminate the plastic shroud which normally covers unsightly plumbing.

Joseph Cericola: "Combination tool" is patented by Joseph Cericola. Abstract: A new Combination Tool for use in measuring, leveling, squaring, and plumbing operations. The inventive device includes a housing adapted to encase a tape measure including an extendable and retractable tape and adapted to encase a laser source capable of projecting a visible light beam, wherein the extendable and retractable tape is extendable from the housing and the visible light beam is projectable from the housing perpendicular to the extendable and retractable tape. A horizontal bubble-leveling vial and a vertical bubble-leveling vial are mounted on the housing for leveling thereof in horizontal and vertical planes.

Kermit Crain: "Chambers for Promoting Surface Adhesion under Vacuum and Methods of Using Same" is patented by Kermit Crain. Abstract: In one aspect, the present invention provides a method of depositing a layer of surface coating material. The method is carried out in a vacuum chamber and comprises the steps of depositing a layer of surface adhesion promotion material on a surface of a substrate; and depositing a layer of a surface coating material on a surface of the layer of the surface adhesion promotion material so that the layer of surface coating material has an adhesion of greater than about 3.75 pounds per inch according to the hesiometry test. In another aspect, the present invention provides an article of manufacture. The article comprises a substrate, a layer of surface adhesion promotion material and a layer of a surface coating material.

Larry D. Brown and Kirt R. Hubbard: "Anti-rotation pipe locator and holder" is patented by Larry D. Brown and Kirt R. Hubbard. Abstract: An anti-rotation pipe locating and support device comprises a support and insert assembly that precisely locates and supports plumbing pipes relative to the structure of a building and prevents rotational movement of the pipes relative to the support. The support includes a support that can be fastened to the building structure and has one or more support openings for receiving the pipes. Inserts are used to receive and grip the pipes to secure them within the support openings with or without additional fastening techniques. Each support opening has at least one small tab which forms a lock with a slot provided in the insert, or is shaped to cooperate with a non-circular opening in the support to restrain the insert.

Larry K. Acker: "On-demand zone valve recirculation system" is patented by Larry K. Acker. Abstract: A zone valve hot water recirculation system in accordance with the present invention generally includes a hot water source, such as an electric or gas water heater, a conduit for enabling circulation of hot water from hot water source to one or more plumbing fixtures and recovery of water to the hot water source, a pump for accelerating delivery of hot water to the fixtures and, importantly, a zone valve for preventing flow of water into the hot water source during standby periods of the hot water source. A controller, which may include an electronic timer, is provided for causing the zone valve to open and close and the pump to start and stop.

Larry Lamore Jr: "Door and frame mounting enabling door hanger bolt assembly" is patented by Larry Lamore Jr. Abstract: For a prehung door unit of door and door frame, a locking assembly lock together the prehung door units irreversably until after permanent final installation, a portion of the assembly is removable from the door's latch bore through the doors lockset bore. The assembly achieves its benefits by thus allowing factory "bench" final settings of accurate door mounting parameters of plumbing and leveling fixed relationships relative to its mounting frame.

Larry R. Walters and Tim Balas: "Combination square, level and plumbing tool" is is patented by Larry R. Walters and Tim Balas.

Lawrence Berkeley National Lab.: Sponsored research "Tenant guidelines for energy-efficient renovation of buildings at the Presidio of San Francisco." Sponsored by: Lawrence Berkeley National Lab., Berkeley, CA (United States).; Department of Energy, Washington, DC. Written by J. L. Warner, D. Sartor and R. Diamond. Abstract: These Guidelines are intended to help current and future tenants of the Presidio work with designers and contractors to incorporate energy efficiency and sustainable practices into the renovations of the buildings. This guide is designed to complement the detailed Guidelines for Rehabilitating Buildings at the Presidio of San Francisco, available from the National Park Service. Energy efficiency yields benefits far beyond energy savings. Daylighting and efficient electric lighting, natural ventilation and cooling, and other conservation strategies improve tenant health, comfort, and productivity, while preserving the historical heritage of Presidio buildings.

Leonard E. Wager and Dana S. Marshall: "Deodorant holding device for a plumbing fixture" is is patented by Leonard E. Wager and Dana S. Marshall.

1997

Lester J. Skidmore and Paul J. Latino: "Reconstituted wood block modular building system" is patented by Lester J. Skidmore and Paul J. Latino. Abstract: A reconstituted wood block modular building system utilized to build at least a wall that includes a concrete slap, a plurality of anchor bolts, a plurality of vertically-oriented steel rods, a plurality of threaded sleeves, a plurality of reconstituted wood blocks, a plurality of elongated, slender, and rectangular-parallelepiped-shaped horizontal alignment keys, a plurality of elongated, slender, and rectangular-parallelepiped-shaped vertical alignment keys, and an adhesive. The plurality of reconstituted wood blocks are positioned horizontally side by side and are stacked vertically without being staggered.

Manuchehr Shirmohamadi: "Shower water automatic temperature controller" is patented by Manuchehr Shirmohamadi. Abstract: A self-contained unit 160 that rapidly and accurately senses, controls and maintains the temperature of water delivered to the user of a shower or bath. The invention allows a user to preset a desired water temperature using a manual control interface 60 and uses a sensor 10 located on (or within) the mixer outlet pipe 20 to measure the temperature of the mixed water being delivered to the user. The sensor produces an input signal that is used by a microprocessor 30 to calculate both derivative gain and proportional gain, and fuzzy logic may also be used by the microprocessor to produce an output signal, such that the system responds quickly and accurately to both quantum temperature changes and to the rate of temperature change.

Maug H. Win, et al.: "Water-Dispersible Wet Wipe" is patented by Maug H. Win, Mark A. Burazin, Steven A. Engel, Bernhardt E. Kressner, William D. Lloyd and Walter T. Schultz. Abstract: A premoistened wet wipe provides functional wet strength in use, yet is dispersible if flushed down the toilet so that plumbing and sewage treatment facilities do not become clogged. A particular embodiment of the wipe consists of three uncreped through-air-dried tissue plies that are attached to each other by edge embossing. The two outer plies contain a wet strength agent to provide wet poke-through resistance to two large, centrally-located unembossed regions. The center ply contains no wet strength agent to aid in dispersibility. The embossing around the edges of the wipe further degrades the strength of the wipe in the embossed areas to assist in dispersibility when the wipe is flushed.

Michael C. Dean: "Ink Jet Printer Cartridge Refilling Method and Apparatus" is patented by Michael C. Dean. Abstract: A refill apparatus for refilling a liquid for a printer includes a printer cartridge housing, a liquid refill bottle and an adapter piece to convert the printer cartridge housing. The printer cartridge housing has an interior compartment and a print head (22) to deliver the liquid to the computer printer. The refill bottle (102) contains the liquid and has a septum (118) covering an opening to deliver the liquid from the refill bottle (102) to the print head in the printer cartridge housing. The adapter piece is placed in the interior compartment of the printer cartridge housing for converting the printer cartridge housing to be connectable with the refill bottle. The adapter piece includes a base (146), a seat (148), a foot (158) and plumbing.

Michael J. Rutkowski and Jon R. Dunkin: "Feed control device for plumbing tools" is is patented by Michael J. Rutkowski and Jon R. Dunkin.

Michael Jerome Strzok: "High pressure plunger device" is patented by Michael Jerome Strzok. Abstract: An improved hand operated plunger for clearing drains and other plumbing fixtures of obstructions is disclosed. The hand operated plunger has two coaxial handles that help maintain a seal with the plumbing fixture during operation and check valves that direct hydraulic or pneumatic pressure to the obstruction through the application of hand force applied to the movable handle. In the event that one stroke of the handle does not dislodge the obstruction, a second or subsequent stroke may be applied without loosing all of the pressure developed from the first stroke. In one preferred embodiment, air is used to create pneumatic pressure that is applied to the obstruction through check valves and the pressure is increased by subsequent strokes of the movable plunger handle.

1997

Mietzner, S., et al.: "Efficacy of thermal treatment and copper-silver ionization for controlling Legionella pneumophila in high-volume hot water plumbing systems in hospitals" appears in American Journal of Infection Control written by S. Mietzner, R. C. Schwille, A. Farley, E. R. Wald, J. H. Ge, S. J. States, T. Libert, R. M. Wadowsky and S. Miuetzner. Published in December 1997.

Office of the Secretary of the Commonwealth: Publisher of "Commonwealth of Massachusetts fuel gas and plumbing code." Board of State Examiners of Plumbers and Gas Fitters. Publisher: Office of the Secretary of the Commonwealth (Boston). Published in 1997.

Ontario. Housing Development and Buildings Branch: Publication of "Code and guide for plumbing 1997: containing the Building Code Act and O. Reg. 403/97." Publisher: Ministry of Municipal Affairs and Housing, Housing Development and Buildings Branch, (Toronto, Ont). Published in 1997.

Paul F. Roth: "Latent heat actuated non-fogging shower mirror" is patented by Paul F. Roth. Abstract: A condensation free mirror to be used in a shower environment consisting of a mirror substrate and a means for detachably mounting the mirror to a shower wall. The mirror assembly is designed for optimum heat retention in order to provide a condensation free surface after being exposed to the warm shower stream. No internal plumbing, reservoirs, or anti-fog coatings are required to achieve a condensation free surface.

Peter Schmucki, et al.: "Framework, especially for fastening plumbing units" is is patented by Peter Schmucki, Silvio Marti and Alfred Mahler.

Phillip Dudley Loizeaux and Thai Ton: "Gatling jet" is patented by Phillip Dudley Loizeaux and Thai Ton. Abstract: A jet for use in spas and hydrotherapeutic reservoirs having a first set of nozzles aligned in a plane at the water entrance side of the jet and a second set of nozzles aligned one-to-one with the first set of nozzles at the water exit side of the jet. A chamber separates the two sets of nozzles and includes a slot which is used to introduce air into the fluid stream. The amount of air introduced into the chamber is controlled by the user by rotating the jet within its housing from a maximum air intake position to a "no-air" intake position, air being introduced through a slot surrounded by a rectangular seal structure. A housing is provided to mount the jet within the wall of a spa comprising a rear wall mounting, an end cap, and a front wall mounting.

Plumbing Education Council of Texas: Publisher of "Plumber's continuing education program, 1995-1996: Volume II journeyman, inspectors and master plumbers." Publisher: Plumbing Education Council of Texas (Austin, TX). Published in 1997.

Plumbing fixture: In most of Europe, garbage disposers are not used at all as the high load of organic matter in the waste water requires a higher capacity sewage treatment plant, since the increased organic matter requires additional oxygen and water to process. Instead, garbage is separated at the source, into compostable and other types of garbage and collected. Similarly, In the USA, there have been some political and environmental issues with garbage disposers. For many years, New York City had banned their use. The stated reason was the above-mentioned increased sewage treatment capacity, but many area residents also suspected that it was the garbage unions not wanting work taken away from them. The ban was rescinded on October 11, 1997. [WP]

Prescher, Ray E.: Author of "1997 national plumbing & HVAC estimator." By Ray E. Prescher; edited by Martin D. Kiley and Marques Allyn. Publisher: Craftsman Book Co (Carlsbad, CA.). Published in 1997.

Princeton Architectural Press: Publisher of "Plumbing:: sounding modern architecture." Edited by Nadir Lahiji and D.S. Friedman; with a preface by Ignasi de Solà-Morales. Publisher: Princeton Architectural Press (New York). Published in 1997.

Ralph B. Senninger: "Test closure plug for the trap bushing of a conventional T-fitting" is patented by Ralph B. Senninger. Abstract: A plumbing fitting comprising a test closure plug for the free end of a trap bushing mounted in the center port of a T-fitting constituting a part of a soil pipe and vent pipe assembly of a plumbing system the free end of the trap bushing is provided with an adapter having an adapter nut and washer. The washer is removed and the plug is inserted in the adapter opening. The plug is configured to close the adapter opening and make a seal therewith when held in place by the adapter nut. The plug enables pressure testing of the plumbing system or the maintenance of a head of water therein.

Richard E. Clarke: "Bathroom module accessible to wheeled assemblies" is patented by Richard E. Clarke. Abstract: A prefabricated bathroom module for receiving a wheeled assembly such as a wheelchair, a walker, a piece of wheeled cleaning equipment, or the like. In a preferred embodiment, the bathroom module includes two floor surfaces, a first one of which is adapted to receive liquids thereon. The first floor surface that receives the liquids is inclined toward the second floor surface so the liquid is directed toward this second floor surface. A drainage trough is positioned between the first and second floor surfaces for collecting the liquid from the first floor surface and for preventing liquid from moving between the two floor surfaces. The trough contains an aperture and drain for removing liquid collected in the trough.

Robert E. Bridges and Archie C. Epes: "Method of constructing a modular structure" is patented by Robert E. Bridges and Archie C. Epes. Abstract: A modular structure consisting of three modular units of approximately the same size, the center module being the primary module containing the mechanical components of the building, with plumbing, air conditioning and heating ducts, and electrical wiring in the slab floor structural foundation and door jambs. The primary module used to transport the entire structure is completed at the factory, requiring no further work at jobsite, with heating and cooling unit, hot water heater, cabinets and appliances, plumbing and light fixtures and accessories installed at the factory in permanent locations.

Robert Menzel: "Bathing enclosure for retrofitting bathrooms" is patented by Robert Menzel. Abstract: A prefabricated tub/shower enclosure, and a method for retrofitting a bathroom with same are disclosed. The enclosure consists of a molded shell having three walls, a tub portion, a ceiling and integral plumbing. In use, a portion of the tub/shower enclosure is cantilevered beyond the exterior wall of the house, allowing a larger-sized tub/shower enclosure to be incorporated into the bathroom than would otherwise be possible. The tub/shower enclosure is installed through an opening formed in an exterior wall of the house between interior framing members defining the bathroom.

Roland L. Ruetz, et al.: "Reduced lead bismuth yellow brass" is patented by Roland L. Ruetz, Jan V. Vojta and Donna L. Day. Abstract: Reduced lead bismuth yellow brasses are disclosed that are primarily useful for plumbing applications. Very low levels of grain refiners are used to increase dezincification resistance, to improve polishability, and for other desired characteristics. At least two grain refiners are selected from the group consisting of B, In, Ag, Ti, Co, Zr, Nb, Ta, Mo, Ga, Tl, and V. At least one of the grain refiners is selected from the group consisting of B, Ti, Co, Zr, Nb, Ta, Mo, Ga, Tl, and V and is between 0.0001% and 0.01% of the alloy. If Ag or In is a selected grain refiner, it is less than 0.25% of the alloy. Silver and gallium are preferred grain refiners.

Ronald William Jocher: "Plumbing wireless phones and apparatus thereof" is is patented by Ronald William Jocher.

Shelley L. Joe: "Process for the inhibition of leaching of lead from brass alloy plumbing fixtures" is is patented by Shelley L. Joe.

Standards Association of Australia: Publication of "National plumbing and drainage. Part 4.1, Hot water supply systems: performance requirements." Published in 1997.

Steve Norman Smeltzer: "Self-supporting reconfigurable hose" is patented by Steve Norman Smeltzer. Abstract: The reconfigurable self-supporting hose allows the user to select the position of the sprayer, as well as the direction of the water spray from the sprayer, or shower head. The position of the shower head and the direction of spray from the shower head can be adjusted to remain in the desired position until modified by the user. A self-supporting arm structure is selectively configurable along at least portions of its length to temporary fixed positions, the structure having a first end and a second end, and having a fluid transport path for transporting fluid from the first end to the second end. The first end of the arm structure is connected to the liquid source in fluid communication with the fluid transport path. The second end of the arm structure can be connected to a sprayer.

Steven C. Crow: "Single-Crystal Oxygen Ion Conductor" is patented by Steven C. Crow. Abstract: A single-crystal solid oxide material, rather than a polycrystalline ceramic, is used for electrolytic and fuel cell applications. For the electrolytic production of oxygen from carbon dioxide, a yttria-stabilized zirconia crystal (12) is coated with platinum electrodes and encased in a platinum structure, to provide a thermally stable electrolytic cell. A multilayered device (50) is constructed by stacking crystals (12) and spacers (56, 58, 60) in an alternating arrangement and by plumbing the active surfaces of the crystals in parallel through perforations drilled directly into the crystals, so that manifolding and sealing problems are minimized.

Thomas Acquaviva: "Paper conditioning system" is patented by Thomas Acquaviva. Abstract: A paper conditioner re-moisturizes paper immediately following fusing to restore paper temperature and moisture equilibrium and reduce curl. The paper conditioner has plumbing that includes a pump, supply lines, overflow lines, metering blade lines and return lines. A soaker hose is used to uniformly distribute conditioner agent to a wick. The soaker hose has pin-holes that are evenly spaced adjacent the wick. The wick is a high density material, such as, cotton that contacts and supplies the conditioner agent to metering rolls. These rolls contact donor rolls, which contact moisturizing rolls which contact the paper. Metering blades are used to remove excess conditioning agent from the moisturizing rolls.

Todd C. Loschelder: "Reversible extension nut for side spray escutcheons" is patented by Todd C. Loschelder. Abstract: A dual position fastener for use in attaching a plumbing fitting having an exteriorly threaded conduit to sink decks of varying thickness has an elongated, generally cylindrical body with an interior bore. The bore is threaded. There is a radial extension at one end of the elongated body with the radial extension having oppositely facing generally parallel surfaces, which surfaces are essentially normal to the axis of the bore. One of the parallel surfaces is at the end of the fastener, with the other of the parallel surfaces being axially spaced from the one end. Each radial surface is adapted to abut the underside of a sink deck when the fastener is used in attaching a plumbing fitting.

United Association of Journeymen and Apprentices of the Plumbing and Pipe Fitting Industry: Publication of "Pneumatic controls manual for United Association journeymen and apprentices." Publisher: The Association (Washington, D.C.). Published in 1997.

USDOE Assistant Secretary for Energy Efficiency and Renewable Energy: Sponsored research "Manufactured residential utility wall system (ResCore), overview." Sponsored by: USDOE Assistant Secretary for Energy Efficiency and Renewable Energy, Washington, DC (United States). Written by R. Wendt, C. Lundell and T. M. Lau. Abstract: This paper provides an overview of the design and development of a manufactured residential utility wall system referred to as ResCore. ResCore is a self-contained, manufactured, residential utility wall that provides complete rough-in of utilities (power, gas, water, and phone) and other functions (exhaust, combustion make-up air, refrigerant lines, etc.) to serve the residential kitchen, bath, utility, and laundry rooms. Auburn University, Department of Industrial Design faculty and students, supported by a team of graduate student researchers and the project's advisory team, developed the ResCore. The project was accomplished through a research subcontract from the US Department of Energy administered by the Oak Ridge National Laboratory.

Wallace Martin: "Joist bridging" is patented by Wallace Martin. Abstract: A joist bridge has a web extending between a pair of end members. The web has a straight edge and an edge having a central indentation. The indentation provides a space through which plumbing pipes, electrical conduits and wiring and the like can be run. The joist bridge is economical of material and is therefore relatively inexpensive to manufacture. An adhesive strip may be provided along the top of the joist bridge to bond the joist bridge to the flooring above.

Wentz, Tim: Born in 1953, authored "Plumbing systems: analysis, design, and construction." Publisher: Prentice Hall (Upper Saddle River, N.J.). Published in 1997.

William E. Ferguson and Leigh A. Morehouse: "Pop-up sprinkler housing" is patented by William E. Ferguson and Leigh A. Morehouse. Abstract: A pop-up-sprinkler housing has a cap sleeve (1) that slides adjustably into a base sleeve (2) having a base plate (3) with a fluid conveyance (4) that screws onto underground sprinkler plumbing (10) and into sprinkler shafts (8). A housing cap (11) on top of the cap sleeve has a sprinkler-shaft aperture (12) that is sized and shaped to allow ingress and egress of pop-up portions (13) of select sprinkler shafts and has cap-sleeve shoulders (14) that extend over the base sleeve and a support surface (15). Threaded fasteners are provided for attaching the fluid conveyance to the sprinkler shafts and to the underground sprinkler plumbing. A plurality of sprinkler adapters 31 are provided for adaptation to different sizes and types of pop-up sprinklers.

William J. Miller and Kenneth W. Nisley: "Slide out kitchen for motor homes and the like" is patented by William J. Miller and Kenneth W. Nisley. Abstract: A plumbing assembly is provided which is formed from a plurality of rigid pipe sections, connected between a movable sink and a relatively fixed fluid outlet. These pipe sections are joined together by swivel fittings that permit the pipe sections to rotate with respect to each other. In this manner, different distances between the sink and the fluid outlet are accommodated by a folding and unfolding motion of the plumbing assembly in a minimum of space behind the wall of an expandable portion of the room. Fluid supply lines for providing hot and cold water to the sink faucet can be mounted within the same spacial area by means of similar swivel fittings that create an offset parallelogram structure.

William W. Rowley: "Crosslinked overmolded plumbing tubes" is patented by William W. Rowley. Abstract: The invention described herein pertains generally to a crosslinked plumbing tube which has at least one overmolded end (e.g. nose cone or nut) attached thereto. In one aspect of this invention, the tube is more rigid than the overmolded component while in another aspect of the invention, the tube is more flexible than the overmolded component. In either embodiment of this invention, the tube provides an all-plastic waterway for a contained liquid or gas to flow through. The degree of flexibility is controlled independently controlling the density of the tube polymer and the overmolding polymer. In one aspect of the invention, the tube and the overmolding polymer are both partially crosslinked to independent first degrees prior to the overmolding process.

Wisconsin Univ.-Milwaukee.: Sponsored research "Development of lead-free copper alloy graphite castings. Annual report for the period January through December 1996. - PROGRESS REPT." Sponsored by: Wisconsin Univ.-Milwaukee.; Department of Energy, Washington, DC. Written by P. K. Rohatgi. Abstract: Centrifugal casting of Copper alloys containing graphite particles established the feasibility of making hollow cylindrical castings. In theses castings, the graphite particles are segregated to the inner periphery making them well suited for bearing applications because of the lubricity of the graphite particles. The recovery of graphite is found to be around 90%. Chemical analysis shows that the average concentration of graphite particles near the inner periphery is 13 vol.% (3.5 wt.%) and 16.3 vol.% (4.54 wt.%) for castings made from melts originally containing 7 vol.% (2 wt.%) and 13 vol.% (3.5 wt. %) graphite particles, respectively.

1998

Agre, P., et al.: "The aquaporins, blueprints for cellular plumbing systems" appears in The Journal of Biological Chemistry written by P. Agre, M.

Bonhivers and M. J. Borgnia. Published on June 12, 1998.

Allan Robinson and Dennis Ristvedt: "Disposable fluid control island" is patented by Allan Robinson and Dennis Ristvedt. Abstract: A disposable fluid control island for workers is made of a broad, shallow tray or flat open-topped container that is filled with a stiff mesh, grid, grille or net upon which workers may stand. Water, oil, blood and other liquids pass through the mesh easily and are retained in the tray. Workers are supported above the accumulated liquids by the support medium. The apparatus helps to keep the feet of workers dry, reduces the likelihood of slipping, and prevents liquids from dispersing. The disposable fluid control island is particularly well-suited for use during orthopedic surgical procedures, but can be used with other activities including plumbing repairs, handling of hazardous materials, and other medical procedures.

Allan S. Chace and Karl C. Huff: "Continuous filtration system using single pump, venturi, and flow control valve" is patented by Allan S. Chace and Karl C. Huff. Abstract: This invention is directed to filtration systems comprising a venturi, flow control valves, filter and pump. In one specific embodiment the flow control valve and venturi are combined hereinafter known as a CHUF. The CHUF may also contain concentrate release, and temperature, flow and two pressure sensors into a single structure. A continuous filtration system for liquid or gas applications is constructed by plumbing a CHUF to a pump and filter. The CHUF is constructed of plastic, stainless steel or other materials. Different plumbing to the CHUF positions the filter in either series, parallel, or series and parallel with a venturi and flow control valve resulting in different pressures and flows at the filter.

Anthony Cappuccio: "Method and system for forming walls" is patented by Anthony Cappuccio. Abstract: A method and system for forming walls includes a dual-wall cavity. A stud is formed of an outer flange, middle flange and inner flange arranged in an "E" shape configuration. An outer panel attaches to the outer flange, a middle panel attaches to the middle flange and an inner panel attaches to the inner flange. An outer cavity is formed between the outer panel and the middle panel. The outer cavity can be filled with a filler material for providing structural and insulation features. Thereafter, an inner panel attaches to the inner flange for providing an inner cavity. The inner cavity can be used to house utility materials such as plumbing, air ducts, heating and electrical.

Anthony J. DiBiagio, et al.: "Flexible plumbing assembly" is patented by Anthony J. DiBiagio, Gordon G. Hastings, Todd C. Krenelka and Thomas J. Ward. Abstract: A flexible plumbing assembly for use in a trailer with an extensible cabin having rigid plumbing that can be moved between a retracted position wherein the extensible cabin is substantially inside the trailer and an extended position wherein the extensible cabin is substantially outside the trailer.

Anton J. Kolar, et al.: "Advanced touchless plumbing systems" is patented by Anton J. Kolar, Andrew J. Paese, David J. Richter-O'Connell, Steven M. Tervo, Carter J. Thomas, William R. Burnett, David C. Shafer and Fred Judson Heinzmann. Abstract: The present invention is a system for controlling a plumbing fixture. The system includes at least two sensors, each sensor including a receiver, and a controller coupled to receive detection signals from the sensors and to generate a control signal in response to the received signals. An actuator is coupled to receive the control signal from the controller and couplable to the plumbing device to act on the bathroom device. The invention is also a method of controlling plumbing fixtures that includes receiving detection signals from a plurality of sensors in a central controller, selecting, in the central controller, which of a plurality of actuators attachable to the plumbing fixtures to operate and directing control signals to the selected actuator to operate the selected actuator.

Association of Plumbing & Heating Contractors: Publication of "Members' list." Association of Plumbing & Heating Contractors. Publisher: Association of Plumbing & Heating Contractors (Coventry). Published in 1998.

Barry J. Lake, et al.: "Reversible air conditioning and heat pump HVAC system for electric vehicles" is patented by Barry J. Lake, David Cleveland, David A. Barwin, Robert Bandeen and Arthur A. Naujock. Abstract: A pressure reducing assembly is provided for managing refrigerant flow in a reversible HVAC system. Refrigerant lines from the system heat exchangers connect to bi-directional ports of a pressure reducing assembly which converts the high pressure refrigerant flowing from one heat exchanger into pressure reduced refrigerant that flows to the other heat exchanger. The pressure reducing assembly converts bi-directional refrigerant flow from the heat exchangers into unidirectional refrigerant flow through a pressure reducing device. Refrigerant emitted from the pressure reducing device flows out of the pressure reducing assembly to the other heat exchanger.

Borg Hansen, et al.: "Spa Apparatus with Heat Transferring Hanging Interior Structural Liner" is patented by Borg Hansen, Rafael Gonzales and Roc V. Fleishman. Abstract: A heated therapeutic spa (10) which comprises a spa tub containing water and having plumbing attached thereto, the tub having a wall (13) which is a relatively good thermal conductor; a thermally efficient, insulating container comprising a load bearing outer wall (12), and a bottom wall (94); a plenum chamber (15) formed between the tub wall (13) and the container wall (12) and extending about the tub wall (13); a motor (17) and pump (18) supplying circulating water to the tub and extending in the plenum chamber; a fan (19) located to circulate air that converts heat from the motor into hot air exhausted into the plenum chamber.

BRANZ: Publisher of "Preventing noise in plumbing installations." Publisher: BRANZ (Porirua, N.Z.). Published in 1998.

British Columbia. Ministry of Municipal Affairs: Publication of "The British Columbia Building Code, 1998: Part 7, plumbing services." Publisher: Building Policy Section, Ministry of Municipal Affairs, Recreation and Housing; (Victoria). Published in 1998.

Bruce A. Cincotta and Damon L. Fisher: "Direct contact steam injection heater" is patented by Bruce A. Cincotta and Damon L. Fisher. Abstract: A direct contact steam injection heater includes a Mach diffuser having a plurality of steam diffusion holes in lieu of a coaxial steam nozzle. High velocity steam (i.e. choked flow) flows radially through the plurality of steam diffusion holes into a high velocity axial flow of liquid through a combining tube within the heater. An adjustably positionable cover over the steam diffusion holes in the Mach diffuser modulates the amount of steam added to the liquid by exposing the proper number of steam diffusion holes. This modulation is done at constant steam pressure without the use of an external steam control device. The arrangement facilitates thorough mixing of steam and liquid within the combining region.

BSI: Publisher of "Copper and copper alloys: plumbing fittings." Publisher: BSI (London). Published in 1998.

Bureau of the Census: Sponsored research "Census of Population and Housing, 1990. Summary Tape File 3A (STF 3A) (All States) (on CD-ROM). - Data file." Sponsored by: Bureau of the Census, Washington, DC. Abstract: This product contains sample data weighted to represent the total population. In addition, the file contains 100-percent counts and unweighted sample counts for total persons and total housing units.

Chyi-Yiing Wu: "Optical calibrating apparatus for emitting datum laser line" is patented by Chyi-Yiing Wu. Abstract: An optical calibrating apparatus includes: a laser illuminator (6) disposed in an eccentric adjusting sleeve (5), an inner inclined adjusting sleeve (4) within a jacket (3), an outer inclined adjusting sleeve (2) outside the jacket (3), and a cylindrical casing (1), in which a laser line is emitted by the illuminator (6) for checking levelling, plumbing and verticality and the laser line has been calibrated for a horizontality or a verticality by rotating the eccentric adjusting sleeve (4), the inner and outer inclined adjusting sleeves (4, 2) until the emitted laser line is aligned with a standard laser line emitted from a standard optical calibrator or aligned with a mark preset by a standard instrument.

Chyi-Yiing Wu and Lin Chin Hsiung: "Automatic optical plumbing instrument" is patented by Chyi-

Yiing Wu and Lin Chin Hsiung. Abstract: An automatic optical plumbing instrument includes: an objective telescopically mounted at a front portion of a telescopic housing adjacent to an object to be observed, an ocular telescopically mounted at a rear portion of the housing adjacent to an observer's eye, and a transparent plumbing protractor defining a plumbing line thereon and mounted in the housing between the objective and the ocular, whereby upon entrance of a vertical line (or plane) of the object into the instrument to form an image therein, a verticality of the vertical line (or plane) of the object can be checked whether the vertical line is aligned with the plumbing line marked on the protractor, thereby providing a plumbing instrument for calibrating a verticality of the object.

Clark, Mary Higgins: Author of "The body in the closet and plumbing for Willy more stories from the lottery winner." By Mary Higgins Clark; read by Frances Sternhagen. Publisher: Simon & Schuster, Inc (NY). Published in 1998.

Clatsop Community Coll.: Sponsored research "MERTS Field Research/Integrated Marine Technology Center- Construction of Building and Purchase of Related Equipment. - Final technical rept. Jun 97-Jun 98." Sponsored by: Clatsop Community Coll., Astoria, OR. Marine and Environmental Research and Training Station. Written by J. W. Wubben. Abstract: The MERTS Field Research/Integrated Marine Technology Center has been completed and equipped, providing a highly modern facility for the staging and support of research, as well as for industry-standard training in marine-related fabrication and maintenance. Successful project completion is evidenced by (1) the Certificate of Occupancy; (2) consulting engineer's certificate of compliance with plans, specifications, and the State Building Code; (3) final building inspection certificates indicating conformance to State electrical, plumbing, and mechanical codes; (4) complete list of equipment purchased; (5) documenting photos of completed building and selected equipment.

Crane Plumbing: Publication of "Crane Plumbing: 1998 / CR/PL L P." Crane Plumbing-Fiat Products Inc. Published in 1998.

Creative Pub. International: Publisher of "The complete guide to home plumbing: a comprehensive manual, from basic repairs to advanced projects." Publisher: Creative Pub. International (Minnetonka, Minn). Published in 1998.

David Jon Ludlow: "Plumbing and shell system for spa" is is patented by David Jon Ludlow.

David P. Crockett: "Wall unit structural system and method" is patented by David P. Crockett. Abstract: A wall-unit structural system has wall units (1) with insulating structural material (2) intermediate an exterior panel (3) for fixation of outside covering and an interior panel (4) for attachment of inside wall surfacing (5). Attachment ridges (6) are spaced apart on the interior panel to provide channels or vacancies between the attachment ridges for positioning of plumbing, electrical and other lines. Tie-down members (8) such as rebar are attached vertically to the wall units for securing the wall units to the footing (21) and for securing elevated tie-down structure (20) such as roofing and/or higher sections of wall units to secured wall units in accordance with applicable building regulations and design preferences.

Don W. Seiber: "Wilderness plumbing" is patented by Don W. Seiber. Abstract: A self-contained, portable, water heating system, adjustable in temperature comprising two duel use water proof bags, two water lines, a heater core and a shower head. The bags consists of a draw strap, a zipper, a rain flap, two flow valves each, one valve located on the bottom of the bags and one valve nearer the middle of the bags, a filler cap located on the top of the bags with an integrated air valve and grommets along the top of the bags. The bags are capable of having their forms altered to act as storage bags during transport containing all system components and other equipment; then to another form for use as water reservoirs. The bags are equipped with a zipper each by which this process is achieved.

Donald L. Werling and James A. Thomas: "Modular air tank assembly" is patented by Donald L. Werling and James A. Thomas. Abstract: A modular air tank assembly for a mobile vehicle such as a heavy duty highway tractor trailer truck and the process of assembling and installing the modular air tank assembly onto a vehicle. More specifically, the modular air tank assembly is comprised of two "J" shaped brackets, and one or two air tanks seated within the lower portion of the J-brackets and held in place by curved contour retaining elements. The modular air tank assembly may be assembled separate from the main vehicle assembly line and then brought to the line as a unit for installation. The modular assembly includes all tank-to-tank plumbing fittings, check valves, tank drain valves, and local drain valve operator strings which are installed to the assembly separate from the main vehicle assembly line.

Douglas E. Boyd, et al.: "Spectrophotometric analytical cartridge" is patented by Douglas E. Boyd, Jan B. Yates, Ronald Coleman, James Hutchison and Richard Riedel. Abstract: An analytical cartridge adapted for use in analyzing fluids for spectrophotometry. The cartridge includes a plumbing system composed of the cuvette and various wells or chambers which are interconnected by passageways. After introduction into the cartridge, liquid samples are separated (if necessary) and transported to a cuvette utilizing a sequential application of centrifugal force followed by pressurization of the system. The cartridge may be used in a wide variety of spectrophotometric procedures to measure the concentration of a wide variety of constituents in fluids, including bodily fluids which contain liquid and solid components.

Edwin Randall Harris: "Engineered structural modular units" is patented by Edwin Randall Harris. Abstract: A modular house is constructed with Engineered Structural Modular Units (EMSU's) made from Stucturally Engineered Oriented Strand Boards (SEOSB's). Unitized structures are formed from modular units comprising two SEOSB panels with internal webbing for floor, wall, ceiling and roof modules; and adapter units such as corner adapter units, U-channel adapters, alignment connectors, trim adapters, and roof support adapters. Window and door openings can be cut on-site during construction. Any insulation meeting local building code requirements can be installed on-site. Standard electrical, plumbing, and mechanical products and procedures can be used as required by local building codes.

Emanuel Szumer: "Post, Pipe and Sign Level" is patented by Emanuel Szumer. Abstract: A post level (10) including a pair of arms (12) pivotally attached to each other at a hinge (14), each arm (12) defining at least one level face (16) for plumbing a surface, and at least one bubble vial (24) mounted on at least one of the arms (12) on a surface (26) generally opposite to the at least one level face (16), wherein the arms (12) may be swung about the hinge (14) so as to be positioned generally parallel with each other with the at least one level vial (24) being between the arms (12).

Fang C. Chen, et all.: "Heat Pump Having Improved Defrost System" is patented by Fang C. Chen, Viung C. Mei and Richard W. Murphy. Abstract: A heat pump system includes, in an operable relationship for transferring heat between an exterior atmosphere and an interior atmosphere via a fluid refrigerant: a compressor (10); an interior heat exchanger (12); an exterior heat exchanger (14); an accumulator (16); and means for heating (18, 18', 18", 18'") the accumulator (16) and/or plumbing lines (25, 26, 27) in order to defrost the exterior heat exchanger (14).

Fiat Products, Inc: Publication of "Fiat Products, Inc. 1998 / CR/PL L P." Crane Plumbing-Fiat Products Inc. Published in 1998.

Frank Antoniello and Alex Maxim: "Combination check valve, shutoff and seal for thermostatic valve" is patented by Frank Antoniello and Alex Maxim. Abstract: A combination check valve, shutoff and seal cartridge is provided for a thermostatic valve, wherein the thermostatic valve includes hot and cold water inlets communicating with an ON/OFF/volume control and/or diverting water valve. The water output of the water volume control is then plumbed to a tub spout, faucet, showerhead or other plumbing device(s). The thermostatic valve has a body with both the cold water inlet and the hot water inlet, and a mixed temperature water outlet for mixed water of a predetermined temperature. Each inlet has respective ports accepting a corresponding combination check valve shutoff and seal cartridge. The cartridge has a housing with a spring therein.

Frank J. Cascia: "Automatic liquid chemical additive dispenser for recreational vehicle toilets" is patented by Frank J. Cascia. Abstract: An adapter for automatically dispensing any aromatic, deodorizing, cleansing, sanitizing fluid directly into the bowl of a recreational vehicle toilet as a result of operating either the bowl rinse or the bowl flush control. An apparatus adapted to toilets installed in recreational vehicles, travel trailers, an marine craft. Because it passively senses the presence of toilet inlet rinse water flow, the apparatus achieves its objective without making modifications to, and is totally independent of, the RV plumbing system. The adapter utilizes an electronic control unit which employs the electrically conductive property of water to detect the flush and the refill operations of the RV toilet.

Frank Kerr: "Prefabricated sink rough-in plumbing apparatus" is is patented by Frank Kerr.

Frederick Lee Simmons Jr. and Ron Ferrante: "UV reflective photocatalytic dielectric combiner having indices of refraction greater than 2.0" is patented by Frederick Lee Simmons Jr. and Ron Ferrante. Abstract: The invention relates to a transparent zero distortion photocatalytic dielectric combiner housing a series of hard durable thin films that reflect 98% of UV, with a plurality of dielectric layers having indices of refraction greater than 2.0 but otherwise is transmissive to light at all wavelengths. The photocatalytic dielectric combiner selectively reflects and concentrates UV from sources such as light fixtures or sunlight within a narrow range of wavelengths on the outer surface of the combiner element, promoting photocatalytic oxidation to decompose bacteria and contaminants, making surfaces the combiner is placed upon self-cleaning, self-sanitizing, and self-deodorizing. The invention is suitable for windows, counter tops, door hardware, plumbing fixtures, and the like.

Gerald L. Buhman: "Dowell rod inserter" is patented by Gerald L. Buhman. Abstract: A device for inserting rods into plastic forms comprising a frame, a plunger assembly coupled to the frame, an air cylinder assembly also coupled to the frame and to the plunger assembly, and a pneumatic plumbing assembly connected to the air cylinder assembly. The frame can be attached to a slipform paving or curbing machine. When actuated, the air cylinder assembly pulls the plunger along the frame. The plunger pushes a dowel rod resting in the frame along the frame and into a concrete member being extruded from the machine.

Gordon M. Smith and Kevin W. Lilie: "Bleed system" is patented by Gordon M. Smith and Kevin W. Lilie. Abstract: An improved bleed system for a double block and bleed plug-type valve which employ a safety check valve which automatically shuts off bleed system flow upon ruptures or upon an inadvertently open manual bleed valve during normal plug valve operation. An integral component combines the safety check valve and other bleed system components in a unitary device which is especially resistant to plumbing damage incidents.

Hazelton, Ron Time-Life Books: Publication of "Kitchen & bathroom plumbing." By the editors of Time-Life Books; with trade secrets from Ron Hazelton Kitchen and bathroom plumbing. Publisher: Time-Life Books (Alexandria, Va.). Published in 1998.

Heinrich Dettmann: "Valve combination" is patented by Heinrich Dettmann. Abstract: A valve combination is proposed for use in plumbing applications which is suitable as a replacement for conventional solenoid valves with a plunger armature. The valve combination consists of a main valve (10), embodied as a diaphragm valve, a servo valve (14) integrated into a cable connector head (12), and a fluidic coupling (16) between the cable connector head (12) and the main valve (10). The cable connector head (12) is provided with an electrical quick connector (18).

Hometime: Publisher of "Plumbing: preparation and installation." Publisher: Hometime (Chaksa, MN). Published in 1998.

Hong-Ming Cheng: "Reliable flush valve" is patented by Hong-Ming Cheng. Abstract: A flush valve includes.

James C. McGill: "Interface apparatus for adapting

a gas flow valve to a gas meter" is patented by James C. McGill. Abstract: A gas flow valve is adapted to mimic an existing plumbing arrangement between the gas flow meter 10 and inlet and outlet plumbing at a point of use. By providing a similar arrangement of mating parts and union nuts, the gas flow valve 20 can be easily and quickly installed between the inlet and outlet plumbing and the gas flow meter without having to replumb the plumbing. The gas flow valve 20 can either directly connect between both the inlet and outlet plumbing and the gas flow meter, or could connect between either the inlet or the outlet plumbing and the gas flow meter 10, with the other connection being provided either by the original connection between the gas flow meter and the plumbing or by an additional inserted pipe.

James E. Lowry: "Low pressure carbon dioxide fire protection system for semiconductor fabrication facility" is patented by James E. Lowry. Abstract: A fire protection system for a clean room semiconductor fabrication facility involves the use of a low pressure carbon dioxide source and a discharge system to extinguish fires detected in or near the tools. Each tool is plumbed with dedicated carbon dioxide suppression agent discharge plumbing. The system individually monitors each tool for fire, preferably using infrared radiation sensors and linear heat detection cable. A remote control panel responsive to the fire detectors controls the discharge of carbon dioxide suppression agent unless there is operator intervention.

James M. McKenna and John T. O'Keefe: "Multi-purpose plumbing and measuring apparatus" is is patented by James M. McKenna and John T. O'Keefe.

John A. Houlihan: "Selectable control energy and water conservation system" is patented by John A. Houlihan. Abstract: The system is unique in that a structure's plumbing lines are effectively routed, to stop energy and water waste, while adding little to construction cost. Water pressure to hot water supply (50) is controlled through a selectable flow control valve (10). A hot water manifold (3) and check valves 42 and 43 produce a dual line connection, between hot water manifold (3) and the hot water use area. In the water saver mode, positioning selectable flow control valve (10) causes pump (4) to draw water from distribution conduit (6), through selectable flow control valve (10), through cold water manifold (12) and solenoid valve (37) to hot water supply (50). Pump (4) causes hot water to fill distribution conduit (6), to the hot water use area.

John M. Mankins: "Plumbing tool" is patented by John M. Mankins. Abstract: A plumbing tool for providing a passageway through a blockage, such as a test cap or other blockage, in a fluid-carrying line. During the rough-in plumbing phase of construction, the drain pipe leading from the plumbing system in a building to the city sewer main in the street is positively sealed off by a test cap welded in the pipe at the location of the clean-out. Pressurizing the rough-in plumbing to test the same can then proceed knowing that if any leaks occur, they are in the branch plumbing on the building side of the test cap and not at or in the test cap. Following successful completion of the initial test, the top-out plumbing is completed, leaving the test cap welded in the clean-out or drain pipe.

John Richard Stracke Jr: "Multiple push protocol unifying system" is patented by John Richard Stracke Jr. Abstract: A unifying push framework in a computer network environment uses a plumbing approach wherein a "pipe" (producer) is created to interpret a specified push protocol. Push Universal Resource Locators (PURLs) (the streams) are delivered from a server across the computer network to each pipe that handles the specific protocol which interprets the protocol and delivers the stream to the subscribing client (consumer). Several pipes can be combined and clients can subscribe to several different protocols. These pipes are capable of delivering streams to multiple clients and are created dynamically as each client subscribes to different protocols. Filters are easily added and removed dynamically to or from the system to filter streams.

Joseph U. Han: "Universal connector" is patented by Joseph U. Han. Abstract: A plumbing connector is provided to communicate water between a wall valve and a toilet. An adapter is provided to facilitate a mating relationship between threads of a first configuration on the valve and threads of a second configuration on the connector. The adapter has a cylindrical configuration with outer threads mating with the connector, and inner threads mating with the valve. The adapter can be positioned within a cap associated with the connector so that no separate gaskets are required for sealing purposes. With the adapter, a single connector size can be inventoried to accommodate different thread configurations associated with the wall valve.

Klaus Fink and Inho Song: "Fabrication of zinc objects by dual phase casting" is patented by Klaus Fink and Inho Song. Abstract: A plumbing product is made by a dual phase casting process with a zinc-aluminum alloy having between 0.5%-4% or 6%-22% aluminum by weight. The alloy is shredded into chips and heated to liquid state, processed to a dual phase state and then injection molded to form the part. The part can be plated using conventional plating techniques.

Larimer County: Publication of "County of Larimer, Colorado Code Amendments to the 1997 Uniform Building Code, Uniform Mechanical Code, Uniform Plumbing Code." Publisher: The Commission (Fort Collins, Colo). Published in 1998.

LASRE: Five follow-on flights focused on the experiment; two were used to cycle gaseous helium and liquid nitrogen through the experiment to check its plumbing system for leaks and to check engine operation characteristics. The first of these flights occurred March 4, 1998. The SR-71 took off at 10:16 a.m. PST. The aircraft flew for one hour and fifty-seven minutes, reaching a maximum speed of Mach 1.58 before landing at Edwards at 12:13 p.m. PST. [WP]

Lepine, L. A., et al.: "A recurrent outbreak of nosocomial legionnaires' disease detected by urinary antigen testing: evidence for long-term colonization of a hospital plumbing system" appears in Infection Control and Hospital Epidemiology: the Official Journal of the Society of Hospital Epidemiologists of America written by L. A. Lepine, D. B. Jernigan, J. C. Butler, J. M. Pruckler, R. F. Benson, G. Kim, J. L. Hadler, M. L. Cartter and B. S. Fields. Published in December 1998.

Luis Cruz: "Sanitizing protector for drainage pipes" is patented by Luis Cruz. Abstract: A sanitizing protector for drainage pipes typically found below a sink, tub and other plumbing fixtures. The protector includes a housing with two connecting tubular ends. A tubular member is coaxially disposed within the housing and mounted at one end to one of the connecting ends. An annular channel is mounted to the internal surface of the cylindrical wall of the housing and the tubular member passes through without being in contact with it. A dispenser pump supplies an anti-bacterial, and optionally including a fragrance, liquid through a conduit that passes through the cylindrical wall to discharge the liquid in the annular channel.

Michael McCleskey: "Removable utility connection floor box and method" is patented by Michael McCleskey. Abstract: An improved floor box of the type commonly installed into the concrete floor of a facility for providing temporary connections to utilities is disclosed which may be removed and replaced without requiring either the demolition and subsequent reconstruction of the floor in which the improved floor box is installed or the replacement or repair of the utility lines located in the floor and connected to the improved floor box.

Michael Smith Kynett: "Pressure cleaning flow diverter" is patented by Michael Smith Kynett. Abstract: This invention provides a plumbing structure that functions as a highly convenient, flow diverter valve assembly. The flow diverter permits a user to routinely, rapidly, and repeatedly clean surfaces beneath the flow diverter using at least two intersecting streams of fluid. The first stream of fluid is a convention stream of fluid, such as, for example, an aerated stream of fluid from a sink spout. The second stream of fluid is an auxiliary stream of fluid that intersects the first stream of fluid. When a surface, such as the surface of a razor blade, is held in the area where the at least two streams intersect, any foreign matter on the surface, such as hair particles or shaving cream, is rapidly removed by the streams of fluid.

1998

Movie Release: The movie "Basic Plumbing II" is released.

National Risk Management Research Lab.: Sponsored research "Leaching of Metals from Household Plumbing Materials: Impact of Home Water Softeners." Sponsored by: National Risk Management Research Lab., Cincinnati, OH. Water Supply and Water Resources Div. Written by T. J. Sorg, M. R. Schock and D. A. Lytle. Abstract: A pilot plant study was conducted to evaluate the effects of household ion exchange softening on the leaching of metals from home plumbing materials. Phase I was conducted using a finished tap water having a hardness of 10 mg/L (as CaCO3) and a pH of 9.1 and Phase II was conducted using a ground water having a hardness of 300 mg/L (as CaCO3) and pH around 7.3. The pilot plant systems consisted of two pipe loop systems, each system having duplicate loops of lead pipe, copper-solder pipe, copper tubing, and brass faucets. One pipe loop system was used as a control system and was fed the source water and the second system was the test system and fed the same water softened with a houshold ion exchange water softener.

Northrup, Anthony: Author of "NT network plumbing: routers, proxies, and web services." Publisher: IDG Books Worldwide, Inc (Foster City, CA). Published in 1998.

Ontario Ministry of Municipal Affairs and Housing, Housing Development and Buildings Branch: Publisher of "Code and guide for plumbing, 1997: containing the Building Code Act and O.Reg. 403/97." Publisher: Ontario Ministry of Municipal Affairs and Housing, Housing Development and Buildings Branch (Toronto). Published in 1998.

Oswald P. Meli: "Plumbing compression fitting for connecting ends of pipe" is is patented by Oswald P. Meli.

Plumbing Products: United Arab Emirates: The population of the UAE reached 2.6 million in 1998.

Ralph B. Senninger: "Cover, spacer and plumbing installation assembly" is is patented by Ralph B. Senninger.

Rene Laulhe: "Actuator including a jack" is patented by Rene Laulhe. Abstract: An actuator including a jack having first and second pistons engaging a control rod, particularly for rotating the shaft of a fraction-of-a-turn plumbing device. The actuator can also include energy storage cartridges and/or damping members placed between the pistons. The energy storage cartridges can engage the first piston on one side and the second piston on the opposite side.

Richard Jack Young: "Apparatus and method for multipurpose residential water flow fire alarm" is patented by Richard Jack Young. Abstract: A multipurpose residential plumbing and fire sprinkler system or, more simply, a multipurpose piping system ("MPS") is a system for providing water to both domestic uses (e.g., showers, sinks, toilets) and to sprinklers for fire protection. The invention provides an apparatus and method for alarming when one or more sprinklers connected to the MPS are activated by a fire. The invention uses a water flow detector. In particular, the invention provides an apparatus and method for distinguishing typical domestic water flow from the flow caused by one or more sprinkler heads.

Richard Raya: "Bathing water pre-mixing system" is patented by Richard Raya. Abstract: A bathing water pre-mix system, for attaching to an existing plumbing system and supplying temperature regulated water to a user. A mixing tank has a hot water inlet and cold water inlet that is attached to the existing plumbing system. The mixing tank has at least one outlet for dispensing water from the mixing tank, preferrably through a shower head. A desired temperature control allows the user to set a desired water temperature. A pair of solenoid valves control water flow at the hot water inlet and cold water inlet in an attempt at achieving the desired water temperature within the mixing tank. A water level indicator informs the user about the water level within the mixing tank.

Rybaczyk, Peter: Author of "Novell's internet plumbing handbook." Publisher: Novell Press (San Jose, Calif). Published in 1998.

Smith, Christopher James: Born in 1951, authored "Practical plumbing." C. J. Smith and B. Curry. Publisher: Macmillan (London). Published in 1998.

1998

Sorg, Thomas J.: Author of "Leaching of metals from household plumbing materials: impact of home water softeners." By Thomas J. Sorg, Michael R. Schock, Darren A. Lytle. Publisher: National Risk Management Research Laboratory (Cincinnati, OH). Published in 1998.

Standards Association of Australia: Publication of "National plumbing and drainage. Part 3.1, Stormwater drainage: performance requirements." Published in 1998.

Standards Australia: Publisher of "AS/NZS 3500 national plumbing and drainage code seminar paper, workshop 23, October 1998." Publisher: Standards Australia (Homebush, N.S.W.). Published in 1998.

Steinert, M., et al.: "Regrowth of Legionella pneumophila in a heat-disinfected plumbing system" appears in Zentralblatt Fur Bakteriologie: International Journal of Medical Microbiology written by M. Steinert, G. Ockert, C. Luck and J. Hacker. Published in November 1998.

Steven D. Wilson: "Prefabricated concrete wall form system" is patented by Steven D. Wilson. Abstract: A prefabricated concrete wall form system which can be taken to a construction site, joined to other wall forms to form a wall, and filled with concrete. The wall form has an outer wall and an inner wall, each of which can be made from gypsum wall board, plywood sheathing, OSB sheathing, medium density overlay plywood, cement board, rigid foam board, exterior gypsum sheathing, steel siding, steel or aluminum sheet, or fiberglass panels. The outer and inner panels are braced by a series of horizontal, zigzag wires. Vertical wood strips having horizontal grooves corresponding to the wires are used to hold these wires in place.

Tamayo, José Luis: Translator of "Plumbing and heating" into Spanish ("Fontanería y calefacción"). Publisher: Ágata (Alcobendas, Madrid). Published in 1998.

Terry L. Mattoon: "Beam clamp" is patented by Terry L. Mattoon. Abstract: A beam clamp for attachment to a beam structure such as a side flange of an I-beam for suspending threaded hanger rods therefrom for installing plumbing and electrical apparatuses thereon. The beam clamp includes a generally C-shaped clamping member with a spaced apart pair of clamping arms and a connecting portion connecting the clamping arms together. The clamping arms of the clamping member define a space designed for receiving a portion of a beam structure therein. A first of the clamping arms has a threaded axial bore extending therethrough. A threaded bolt is threadably extended through the threaded axial bore of the first clamping arm into the space between the clamping arms of the clamping member.

Tesoriero, John: Author of "Plumbing rules made simple for domestic type dwellings." Produced by J & L Publications (John Tesoriero). Publisher: J & L Publications (Arncliffe, N.S.W.). Published in 1998.

Ulrich Morlok: "Assembling module for sanitary plumbing and method for manufacturing same" is is patented by Ulrich Morlok.

USDOE Assistant Secretary for Energy Efficiency and Renewable Energy: Sponsored research "Effects of plumbing attachments on heat losses from solar domestic hot water storage tanks. Final report, Part 2. - PROGRESS REPT." Sponsored by: USDOE Assistant Secretary for Energy Efficiency and Renewable Energy, Washington, DC (United States). Written by J. Song, B. D. Wood and L. J. Ji. Abstract: The Solar Rating and Certification Corporation (SRCC) has established a standardized methodology for determining the performance rating of the Solar Domestic Hot Water (SDHW) systems it certifies under OG-300. Measured performance data for the solar collector component(s) of the system are used along with numerical models for the balance of the system to calculate the system's thermal performance under a standard set of rating conditions. SRCC uses TRNSYS to model each of the components that comprise the system. The majority of the SRCC certified systems include a thermal storage tank with an auxiliary electrical heater. The most common being a conventional fifty gallon electric tank water heater.

Wesley Hodson: "Plumber's caddy" is patented by Wesley Hodson. Abstract: A plumber's caddy is disclosed which provides a holder for plumbing tools, fittings and supplies. An arm permits the caddy to be secured to a member such as a ceiling joist. The arm is jointed in one or more places such that the holder can move relative to the fastener. A swivel joint is disclosed which permits rotation and tilting of the holder relative to the fastener. Hangers are provided for hanging tools from the holder.

Winston R. MacKelvie: "Wastewater separator" is patented by Winston R. MacKelvie. Abstract: The present invention is a plumbing device for buildings that installs inline with a drainpipe to separates large solids component of wastewater from small solids and liquid components of said wastewater, thereby creating two separate output streams. The second stream of mostly liquid can be directed first to a heat exchanger and then to a sewer or wastewater recycling device. The large solids stream may be directed to a sewer or to a composter .

1999

Aaron E. Daniel: "Construction block" is patented by Aaron E. Daniel. Abstract: Right rectangular parallelepiped construction modules including a system of latitudinal tangs and grooves and inner and outer shoulders which cooperate to interlock stacked or staggered construction modules. The construction modules can also include reliefs in their tops, sides and bottoms for receiving rebar supports, electrical lines, plumbing lines, or other means.

Alberta. Plumbing, Gas, Electrical, Elevators, Boilers & Pressure Vessels Safety: Publication of "Statistics re: electrical incidents in Alberta, 1997-98." Publisher: Alberta Labour, Technical & Safety Services, Plumbing, Gas, Electrical, Elevators, Boilers & Pressure Vessels Safety (Edmonton). Published in 1999.

Armand Jean Goede: "Ozone generating system for laundries" is patented by Armand Jean Goede. Abstract: A system for generating water with predetermined amount of ozone dissolved and minimum entrained ozone. The system includes the use of an entrained gas separator assembly in series with the recirculating plumbing feeding and discharging ozone enriched water. The novel entrained gas separator assembly allows the water with dissolved ozone to pass through while extracting the entrained ozone for subsequent use or destruction. The entrained gas separator includes a secondary tank with an off gas valve for releasing the entrained gases including ozone. A cylindrical member with a helicoidal wall and centrally perforated tube defines a helicoidal path that forces the water down allowing the entrained ozone to pass through.

Association française de normalisation Centre scientifique et technique du bâtiment: Publication of "Plumbing for residential buildings: amendment A1 to the Specification book (NF P 40-201/A1) Travaux de bâtiment: Plomberie sanitaire pour bâtiments à usage d'habitation. Cahier des charges = Building works--Sanitary plumbing in residential buildings: Technical specifications = Bauarbeiten--Sanitärinstallationen in Wohngebäuden: Technische Vorschriften Building works--Sanitary plumbing in residential buildings: Technical specifications Bauarbeiten--Sanitärinstallationen in Wohngebäuden: Technische Vorschriften." Publisher: Association française de normalisation (Paris). Published in 1999.

Barbara Rodstein, et al.: "Quick Connect Mounting Apparatus for Water Spout" is patented by Barbara Rodstein, Joaquin Serrano and Ron Bowers. Abstract: An apparatus that provides for the quick and easy installation and removal of Roman Tub Spouts onto a water fitting comprising a water spout (24), a quick connect member (12), a trim escutcheon (14), a hub (16), a pair of deck nuts (18, 20) and a lock washer (22). The quick connect member (12) screws into a Tee fitting (26) in the plumbing system. The hub (16) screws into the base of the spout (24) and slidably engages the smooth end of the quick connect member (12). The trim escutcheon (14) is disposed between the spout (24) and hub (16) to provide support to the hub (16) and to conceal the hub (16) while providing decorative ornamentation to the apparatus.

Bradley Mann: "Termite-proofing system" is patented by Bradley Mann. Abstract: The present invention provides a pipe system for termite-proofing a sub-floor area of a structure having a foundation penetrated by at least one penetration comprising: (a) a primary tube system comprising tube(s) located substantially at or adjacent the perimeter of the building; (b) a secondary tube system comprising tube(s) adjacent at least one penetration; and (c) means for charging both primary and secondary tube system with insecticide. The tube systems comprise tubes perforated along a substantial portion of their length by a plurality of apertures of such size and spacing that insecticide flows through the apertures and infuses the adjacent ground. The penetrations may take the form of plumbing pipelines or load bearing members for a suspended slab or floor.

BRANZ: Publisher of "BRANZ plumbing & drainage guide." Publisher: BRANZ (Porirua, N.Z.). Published in 1999.

Brian K. Smith: "Plumbing fixture surface restoration process" is is patented by Brian K. Smith.

Britt Murphey and De Von Smith: "Water supply coupling with one-way valve for recreational vehicles" is patented by Britt Murphey and De Von Smith. Abstract: On a recreational vehicle, a water supply coupling is provided to permit the hookup of an external water supply to the plumbing of the recreational vehicle. The coupling selectively permits one-way flow into, but not out from, the plumbing, thereby maintaining the pressurized integrity of the plumbing system. The coupling has a movable check member which may be seated against an annulus to create a seal. In various disclosed embodiments, the check member may be a check ball, a mushroom-shaped check member having a hemispherical seating portion and a stem, and a two-piece check member.

Building Products: Chile: Imports of plumbing, sanitary fixtures and sanitary-ware totaled US$ 40 million in 1999.

Bulleyment, Alan: Author of "Plumbing & drainage guide." (writer and illustrator, Alan Bulleyment; editors, Margaret Mortlock, Celia Tatham). Publisher: BRANZ (Porirua (N.Z.)). Published in 1999.

Burns, Max: Born in 1948, authored "Cottage water systems: an out-of-the-city guide to pumps, plumbing, water purification, and privies." Publisher: Trade distribution by Firefly Books (Toronto, Ont.; Buffalo, N.Y. Cottage Life Books; Willowdale, Ont.; Buffalo, N.Y.). Published in 1999.

Canadian Commission on Building and Fire Codes: Publication of "National plumbing code of Canada, 1995: first revisions and errata." Issued by the Canadian Commission on Building and Fire Codes. Publisher: The Commission (Ottawa). Published in 1999.

Charles E. Eberling, et al.: "Spring brake actuator with integral biased double check valve for anti-compounding and roll-back protection" is patented by Charles E. Eberling, Andrew Marsh and William P. Amato. Abstract: A double check valve is integrally located in a spring brake chamber to reduce plumbing associated with a pneumatic brake system. Anti-compounding is provided by virtue of a bias pressure of approximately twenty to thirty psi between a pressure chamber of a service actuator and an operating chamber of a parking/emergency actuator. Likewise, vehicle roll-back is addressed since the transition from a service application to a park application assures that the service brakes are sufficiently applied until the spring brake becomes operative.

Craftsman Book Co: Publisher of "National plumbing & HVAC estimator, 2000." Publisher: Craftsman Book Co (Carlsbad, CA). Published in 1999.

Craig D. Lack and Peter R. Pratt: "Solder preforms with predisposed flux for plumbing applications" is is patented by Craig D. Lack and Peter R. Pratt.

Curry, B.: Author of "Installation tips. 2." Publisher: UK Copper Plumbing and Heating Systems Board (London). Published in 1999.

Dale J. Brisson and W. Scott Hammond: "Apparatus and method for installing prefabricated building system for walls roofs and floors using a foam core building pane" is patented by Dale J. Brisson and W. Scott Hammond. Abstract: A building assembly for efficiently and economically constructing walls and roofs for a building assembly that utilizes a prefabricated building panel. The prefabricated panels utilize miter-cuts when joined, form cores, interior and exterior walls, and roofs, when placed together. The walls are pre-formed, offsite according to the required size dimensions and then transported to the job site. The panels are made essentially of a expanded polystyrene panel having cores and channels. Each building panel also includes vertically disposed parallel voids that are approximately 4 in. in diameter, spaced approximately 2 to 4 ft. apart, and receive poured concrete and steel rebar to provide structural rigidity to the entire building assembly.

Daniel C. Shaw and Donald F. Bush: "Plumbing control system and method for prisons and push button therefor" is is patented by Daniel C. Shaw and Donald F. Bush.

David L. Fishel and Peter F. Payne: "Method of making an embossed, waterproof shower pan liner" is patented by David L. Fishel and Peter F. Payne. Abstract: A method for making a flexible, waterproof shower pan liner comprised of a water-insoluble thermoplastic sheet. The shower pan liner includes on at least one surface selected indicia such as product information or plumbing codes at regular intervals. The indicia are embossed into the shower pan liner thereby eliminating the need for a protective top coat. In the process for making the invention, the thermoplastic is heated, calendered, and thereafter embossed with the selected indicia while in a heated condition.

Dennis J. Gallant: "Modular patient room" is patented by Dennis J. Gallant. Abstract: A modular patient room includes a plurality of wall panels having various configurations and one or more plumbing units. The wall panels and plumbing units are connectable to each other to form the patient room. Each plumbing unit includes a water conduit and a water-using device that is connected to the water conduit. In some embodiments, the modular patient room includes modular patient service equipment that couples to the wall panels.

Dept. of Commerce, Bureau of the Census: Publisher of "1997 Economic Census. Construction. Industry Series. Plumbing, Heating, and Air-Conditioning Contractors." Publisher: Dept. of Commerce, Bureau of the Census (Washington). Published in 1999.

Dixon, Graham: Born in 1950, authored "The dishwasher manual: DIY plumbing, maintenance, repair." Publisher: Haynes (Sparkford). Published in 1999.

Donald D. Hudson: "Liquid soap mixer for showerheads" is patented by Donald D. Hudson. Abstract: The present invention is a Continuation-In-Part (CIP) of the originally filed U.S. Pat. application Ser. No. 08/820,751, and relates to the plumbing industry and more specifically to the personal showering portion of that industry, in which the device of the present invention is installed between the existing shower water delivery pipe and whatever showerhead the user may choose. The device of the present invention includes a liquid soap angled inlet elbow, screw in holding means on the top of the angled liquid soap inlet elbow to hold a standard liquid soap bottle with a on-off valve closure that releases the liquid into the water stream.

Douglas E. Boyd, et al.: "Electrochemical analytical cartridge" is patented by Douglas E. Boyd, Jan B. Yates and Ronald K. Coleman. Abstract: An electro-analytical cartridge adapted for use in analyzing fluids. The cartridge includes an electrochemical device that measures ionic activity using ion-specific electrodes. The cartridge further includes a plumbing system composed of the electrochemical device and various wells or chambers which are interconnected by passageways. After introduction into the cartridge, liquid samples are measured out and transported to the electrochemical device utilizing a sequential application of centrifugal force followed by pressurization of the system. Reference fluid is transported from a reference fluid well or reservoir to the electrochemical device for use in measuring ionic activity.

Economics and Statistics Administration: Sponsored research "Economic Census 1997: Manufacturing, Industry Series. Plastics Plumbing Fixture Manufacturing." Sponsored by: Economics and Statistics Administration, Washington, DC.; Bureau of the Census, Washington, DC. Abstract:

1999

The 1997 Economic Census - Manufacturing covers all manufacturing establishments with one or more paid employees. Manufacturing is defined as the mechanical, physical, or chemical transformation of materials or substances into new products. The assembly of components into new products is also considered manufacturing, except when it is appropriately classified as construction. Establishments in the manufacturing sector are often described as plants, factories, or mills and typically use power-driven machines and materials-handling equipment. Also included in the manufacturing sector are some establishments that make products by hand, like custom tailors and the makers of custom draperies.

Frederick C. Prue: "Adjustable additive injection unit for a marine toilet system" is patented by Frederick C. Prue. Abstract: A unit for injecting a disinfectant, deodorant or the like into the inlet stream of flushing water as it is pumped into the bowl of a tankless marine toilet. The injection unit is preferably constructed of commercially-available plastic plumbing components. The main body of the unit provides an additive reservoir which surrounds the flush water inlet pipe and is formed from a conventional plastic sanitary tee jointed fitted at each end with plastic size-reduction bushings. The two bushings connect the injection unit to the flush water inlet tubing and also support an interior flow pipe.

George De Jarlais: "Leach-protective coatings for water meter components" is patented by George De Jarlais. Abstract: A coated substrate for plumbing applications in which the leaching of metals into water contacting the substrate is significantly reduced, comprises an alloy having copper has a majority constituent and also comprising tin, zinc and lead; and a coating having a thickness in a range from 0.4 to 1.2 mils upon the substrate, the coating further comprising a mixture of an cationic epoxy resin material and a curing agent for said cationic epoxy resin material. The coating is preferably applied by electrodeposition and then cured by baking in an oven at approximately 400.degree. F. for about twenty minutes.

Gregory J. Corralejo: "Plumbing coupling and method of use" is is patented by Gregory J. Corralejo.

Gregory N. Castillo and Bradley E. Castillo: "Protective cover for plumbing fixtures" is is patented by Gregory N. Castillo and Bradley E. Castillo.

Gunter Veigel: "Water draining fixture with light guide illumination means" is patented by Gunter Veigel. Abstract: A water draining fixture (1) for plumbing applications with which light is introduced into a water jet (6) emanating from an outlet opening (5) of a fixture head (3), with a water conduit (4) guiding the water to the outlet opening (5), and with a light guide (8) guiding the light separate from the water conduit (4) from a light source located outside of the water draining fixture (1) up to exit out of at least one light outlet opening (19).

Hamilton, Gene: Born in 1943, authored "Plumbing for dummies." By Gene Hamilton and Katie Hamilton. Publisher: Idg Books Worldwide (Foster City, CA). Published in 1999.

Harold Ringlein, et al.: "Method of insulation and framing" is patented by Harold Ringlein, Alfred C. Ringlein and James Morgan. Abstract: A method of construction which produces an air tight structure which is capable of being insulated to high R values.

Hisashi Masuda and Shigeo Kubota: "Wavelength converter" is patented by Hisashi Masuda and Shigeo Kubota. Abstract: To obtain a laser beam the wavelength of 200 nm or less the repetition frequency of which is high, to reduce damage applied to mineral material such as synthetic fused silica, to extend the life of a stepper and others, to extend the life of laser parts without using toxic gas, to enhance the throughput of a stepper and others by enabling the compatibility of a high repetition frequency with the stability of a pulse, to realize an ultraviolet radiation source the whole of which is composed of a solid and to solve the problems of reliability, size, maintenance, a plumbing and others and sufficiently enhance reliability, the following procedure is taken.

Indiana. Dept. of Fire and Building Services: Publication of "Indiana plumbing code." Publisher: Indiana Dept. of Fire and Building

Services (Indianapolis, Ind). Published in 1999.

IT Corp.: Sponsored research "Streamlined Approach for Environmental Restoration Work Plan for Corrective Action Unit 329: Area 22 Desert Rock Airstrip Fuel Spill, Nevada Test Site, Nevada, Draft of Rev. 0." Sponsored by: IT Corp., Las Vegas, NV.; Department of Energy, Washington, DC. Abstract: This plan was prepared as a characterization and closure report for Corrective Action Unit (CAU) 329: Area 22, Desert Rock Airstrip (DRA) Fuel Spill identified in the Federal Facility Agreement and Consent Order (FFACO). The CAU, located on the Nevada Test Site, consists of one Corrective Action Site (CAS), 22-44-01, which encompasses an area contaminated by three recorded spills from a 25,000-gallon underground fuel storage tank. The tank was installed in 1980 and was imbedded in sand and gravel approximately 16 feet below the ground surface. Historically, the DRA consisted of a single runway, several portable buildings, two underground storage tanks containing aviation jet fuel, and plumbing to several refueling areas on the ramp.

Jackson, Albert: Born in 1943, authored "Collins plumbing and central heating." Publisher: HarperCollins (London). Published in 1999.

James M. Rogan: "Plumbing apparatus" is patented by James M. Rogan. Abstract: A kit for forming a plumbing apparatus for aiding in the snaking of drain pipes which kit includes a rubber cap having a cylindrical skirt, a circular clamp about the skirt, a snake rod receiving hole through the covered end of the cap and a flushing water tube also through the covered end of the cap. The cap can fit over and be tightened about a standard drainpipe, e.g. a 2 inch drainpipe, and adapters for coupling it to different standard sized (e.g. 11/2 inch) and different threading (male or female) are provided. The flushing water tube is connected to a flexible hose of sufficient length to run to the faucet of a sink when the cap is attached to that sink's drainpipe. A back flow protector (vacuum breaker) is incorporated at the free end of the hose.

Jean-Pierre Gustin: "Individual watering bowl with mulitdirectional connection of the type comprising a bowl and plumbing" is is patented by Jean-Pierre Gustin.

Jeffrey David Cohen: "Water flow monitoring system determining the presence of leaks and stopping flow in water pipes" is patented by Jeffrey David Cohen. Abstract: A water flow monitoring system for determining the presence of leaks in plumbing pipes having water flowing through the pipes under high pressure includes a flow monitor which is mounted to the pipe for sensing the flow of water through the pipe. A controller composed of a timer and/or accumulated volume meter associated with the flow monitor, to determine when the flow has continued for a preselected period of time, and/or when the amount of water has exceeded a preselected accumulated volume threshold, and logic components responsive to changes in flow rate. Upon detection of flow for the preselected period of time, and/or preselected accumulated volume threshold, a valve is actuated to stop flow through the pipe.

Joe D. Byles: "Non-circulating, rapid, hot tap water apparatus and method" is patented by Joe D. Byles. Abstract: Apparatus for attachment to a plumbing system having a warm water outlet, for rapidly delivering hot water through the plumbing system to the warm water outlet, comprising a diverter valve attachable to a building water pipe upstream of the warm water outlet for purging cold water from the water pipe, a diverter pipe section extending from the diverter valve, a back flow preventer in flow relationship with the diverter pipe section, and a flow control regulator in flow relationship with the diverter pipe section, whereby a small controlled flow of cold water may be diverted from the water pipe to thereby cause rapid delivery of warm water to the warm water outlet when actuated.

John D. McGhee: "Automatic mechanism for cut-off and drainage of under low-freezing ambient temperature conditions" is patented by John D. McGhee. Abstract: An automatic mechanism is provided for cutting-off water flow to a plumbing system of a house, an apartment, a business or the like, while at the same time draining water/plumbing systems when subjected to low/freezing ambient temperatures. The mechanism includes a valve body housing a reciprocal valve which is operative to place an inlet and an outlet in fluid communication while cutting off a drain port, and in a second position the inlet is closed and the outlet and the drain port are placed in fluid communication to drain the water system when the valve is shifted automatically under the influence of biasing means in reaction to low temperature sensing.

John F. Gleason: "Solid-sediment retainment plumbing trap" is is patented by John F. Gleason.

John M. Mankins: "Method and apparatus for testing plumbing installations" is is patented by John M. Mankins.

John Pinciaro: "Hydrotherapy jet system adapted for quick connection to air and water plumbing" is is patented by John Pinciaro.

Joseph P. Ismert: "Plumbing slider bracket and double ratchet arm pipe clamp assembly" is is patented by Joseph P. Ismert.

Kaoru Kumagai and Fumio Ohtomo: "Surveying instrument and plumbing device for plumbing surveying instrument" is is patented by Kaoru Kumagai and Fumio Ohtomo.

Karsten Laing and Nikolaus J. Laing: "Dual reservoir-based hot water recirculation system" is patented by Karsten Laing and Nikolaus J. Laing. Abstract: In a hot and cold water plumbing installation, a volume of hot water is first drawn from the hot water line and stored in an insulated reservoir. When the temperature of the water near the most distal location of the hot water line falls below a predetermined level, the contents of the insulated reservoir are reinjected back into that line to flush the cooled down water back into the water heater. A second reservoir is used between the water heater inlet and the cold water source to absorb the excess water resulting from the aforesaid reinjection and prevent hot water from being injected into the cold water line.

Keith Kaar Clayton: "Wash basin with protective water film" is patented by Keith Kaar Clayton. Abstract: A wash basin, as for a domestic bathroom, has normal inlet water faucet(s) and spigot(s) fitted at or above its top and a normal outlet or drain pipe at its bottom. The basin also has a peripheral inlet flow channel formed below its top rim, for creating a smoothly-flowing film of water cascading down the interior sides of the basin to the outlet. This flowing water film intercepts detritus such as shaving cream, toothpaste, and soap, preventing it from sticking to and soiling the interior of the basin. The basin preferably also has a peripheral overflow channel formed in its side wall adjacent but spaced from the peripheral inlet channel and communicating to the drain below any drain plug or stopper that may be used.

Klaus Grohe: "System of sanitary fittings" is patented by Klaus Grohe. Abstract: A system of sanitary fittings contains a connecting block having an identical construction for all the fittings and which can be connected to the water pipes of a plumbing system. The connecting block contains a joint face into which issue the through openings, which are connected to the pipe connections. The sanitary fittings are fitted to a functional block, which has a joint face cooperating with the joint face of the connecting block and channels emanating from said joint face.

Konrad Bergmann: "Sanitary fitting" is patented by Konrad Bergmann. Abstract: A sanitary fitting for attachment to a plumbing wall including a fitting body with a common supply housing, the common supply housing having an elongated shape with a hot water supply and a cold water supply which are positioned in a supply plane substantially perpendicular to the plumbing wall and a valve for closing and/or mixing water flowing through the sanitary fitting, the valve having an elongated shape and being located outside the supply housing underneath the supply plane and the common supply housing, where a lengthwise axis of the valve means extends substantially parallel to a lengthwise axis of the supply housing.

Kosyfas, Ioannis: Translator of "Plumbing Technology, Design and Installation" by Lee Smith into Greek, Modern (1453-) ("Technologia ydravlikon egkatastaseon: Meleti ke egkatastasi"). Publisher: Ion (Athina). Published in 1999.

Kurt H. Lundstedt: "Method and kit for retrofitting a plumbed eyewash station" is patented by Kurt H. Lundstedt. Abstract: A kit for retrofitting a plumbed eyewash station is provided. The plumbed eyewash station includes a basin and an outlet pipe mounted within the basin. Prior to retrofitting the plumbed station, the outlet pipe is used to dispense water delivered thereto by a facility's plumbing system. The retrofitting kit includes a nozzle support and a self-contained eyewash fluid delivery system. The fluid delivery system includes a portable container and a nozzle in fluid communication with the container. The portable container contains eyewash fluid. To retrofit the plumbed station, the nozzle support is mounted to the outlet pipe; the portable container is placed on a support surface above the nozzle support; and the nozzle is mounted to the nozzle support.

Lawrence, Mike: Author of "Plumbing & central heating." Publisher: Crowood (Marlborough). Published in 1999.

Maher I. Kelada: "Sequential air dissolved floatation apparatus and methods" is patented by Maher I. Kelada. Abstract: Sequential DAF apparatus and methods providing zero pool and nonmechanical waste material removal are disclosed which include a number of floatation tanks each arranged to operate either independently or sequentially, each tank has a conical shaped bottom with a centrally located port at the lowest vertical position of the tank, each tank is fitted with a number of valves and plumbing which allows an operator to fill each tank with waste water charged with dissolved air through the central port which is then retained during a floatation period to allowed waste material to separate from clarified water in the tank. Clarified water and waste material is removed from the bottom of the tank through the central port. Water clarity sensors are positioned in the tank near the central port.

Marc Frazier Baker: "Filter for an inkjet printhead" is patented by Marc Frazier Baker. Abstract: An ink jet printhead of an ink jet cartridge includes a filter plate that is downstream of the ink. Particularly, the filter plate is attached to the back of the heater chip of the printhead. The filter plate is in addition to a wire mesh filter that is disposed at the inlet of a plumbing standpipe that prevents particles which are shed from the ink reservoir from passing into the printhead chip assembly. The filter plate of the present invention prevents particles that originate in the plumbing standpipe channels below the wire mesh filter from clogging the bubble chambers of the heater chip of the printhead chip assembly. The filter plates are formed on a polymer sheet with a series of holes ablated using an eximer laser.

McNiven, James D.: Author of "Economic integration in the NAFTA zone: public policy, corporate strategy and plumbing." Publisher: Centre for International Business Studies, Dalhousie University (Halifax). Published in 1999.

Michael J. Peterson and Richard M. Russell: "Isolation block" is patented by Michael J. Peterson and Richard M. Russell. Abstract: A plumbing system for a pure water supply of a dialysis clinic includes an isolation block assembly to which the various purifying components can be quickly connected and disconnected. The isolation block assembly includes an isolation block which has both a supply passage and a discharge passage defined therethrough. A first self sealing quick connect part is connected to the supply passage outlet. A second self sealing quick connect part is connected to the discharge passage inlet. The purifying component may be connected to the isolation block assembly through the use of flexible conduits having complementary self sealing quick connect parts connected thereto, so that the flexible conduits may be connected to the quick connect parts of the isolation block assembly.

Mohammad J. El-Hibri and Barry L. Dickinson: "Plumbing articles from poly(aryl ether sulfones)" is is patented by Mohammad J. El-Hibri and Barry L. Dickinson.

Morinobu Shingaki: "Termite shielding structure of underground beams and a method for constructing the same" is patented by Morinobu Shingaki. Abstract: A floor mold slab 3 of reinforced concrete is uniformly assembled above sleeve crowns of underground beams 12 of mat foundations 1 of reinforced concrete, and underground beam piercing pipes 43, whose length is identical to a width of the underground beam 12, both pipe ends thereof being provided with connecting portions 433 for joints, are embedded and fixed within the underground beam 12 at the time of installing concrete for the mat foundations 1, and pipes 4 that are used for guiding plumbing for water, gas or other fluids or electric wiring cables are respectively connected to both pipe ends while the pipes 4 are extended indoor and outdoor.

Murray, John William: Born in 1972, authored "Simulation to assess plumbing and fire protection innovations." Published in 1999.

Oxmoor House: Publisher of "Basic plumbing." Publisher: Oxmoor House (Birmingham, Ala). Published in 1999.

Patrick DeLeFevre: "Method of designing a building for maximum compatability with modular forms" is patented by Patrick DeLeFevre. Abstract: A method is provided for specifying parameters for modular formworks from construction documents which define an original structure, in which the construction documents are either scanned or a CAD version is read out. From the scanned drawings or the CAD information, various elements of the structure to be built are identified and selected in an order specific to a particular modular construction system. After identification and selection, reference numerals are assigned for the selected parts or components, with the numbers representing a component of the building such as what floor is intended, walls, ceilings, and other structural components down to the placement of light switches, HVAC vents, drainage, sinks, and plumbing valves.

Paul L. Watson and Viola M. Watson: "Drain tube belt and shower pack kit" is patented by Paul L. Watson and Viola M. Watson. Abstract: After an operation, a drain tube or drain tubes may be placed in the patient's body. Sometimes the drain tube is sutured into the open end of the body and hangs from the body. After a mastectomy, the drain tube is often sutured into the body of the patient. The drain tube hangs downwardly and there is a collection bulb on the end of the drain tube to the discomfort of the patient. The applicant has devised a strap which fits around the abdomen and on the strap there is a pocket for receiving the drain tube and the collection bulb. The patient can walk and maneuver with less discomfort because the pocket and the strap are bearing some of the weight of the drain tube and collection bulb and provide proper drainage.

Plumbing Products: United Arab Emirates: The government has earmarked one billion dollars for the construction of new infrastructure projects and government, commercial, and residential buildings in 1999.

Plumbing Products: United Arab Emirates: The total market demand for plumbing products in 1999 is estimated at U.S.$ 262 million, an increase of eight percent over 1998.

Plumbing Products: United Arab Emirates: The next event is scheduled to take place at the Dubai World Trade Center on October 17-21, 1999.

Radoslav Sasha Rankovic: "Portable power plumbing plunger" is patented by Radoslav Sasha Rankovic. Abstract: The portable power plunger is for unclogging blocked drains in sinks, toilets, bath tubs and the like. The plunger has a main body having a reciprocating pump with a removable attachment mounted at its outlet lower end which is adapted to cover intimately over the waste water drain of a sink, toilet, or bath tub. The drain may be unclogged by operating the pump to dislodge the blockage and to dispose of it down the sewer. The pump is provided with a substantial back flow preventor such that the dirty water in the drain would not back into the pump to contaminate the latter. An integral injector pipe is also provided on the plunger.

Richard Shue and Michael Shue: "Vent pipe cover protective device" is patented by Richard Shue and Michael Shue. Abstract: A vent pipe cover protective device for a plumbing vent stack having a weatherproofing cover formed substantially of lead material permanently secured over the vent stack. The protective device completely covers the exposed surface of the weatherproof cover so as to prevent access thereto for chewing and consuming any of the lead material by rodents such as squirrels and rats. The upper end of the protective device includes an end piece having apertures such as provided by a screen or mesh material or a drilled plate which are of sufficient size to allow the free upward escape of sewer gas and which are sufficiently small in size so as to prevent, rodents, rats, and other critters such as roaches, birds and snakes from entering into the vent stack itself.

Rohr, U., et al.: "Four years of experience with silver-copper ionization for control of legionella in a german university hospital hot water plumbing system" appears in Clinical Infectious Diseases: An Official Publication of the Infectious Diseases Society of America written by U. Rohr, M. Senger, F. Selenka, R. Turley and M. Wilhelm. Published in December 1999.

Ronald J. Mastro: "Pipe coupler" is patented by Ronald J. Mastro. Abstract: Disclosed is a small space-saving two-part coupling system for attaching threaded pipes which is particularly suited for use in replacing broken valves, pipes or parts in existing plumbing systems where little space is available. The invention includes a pair of nuts with male extensions located thereon, each nut having a helically threaded axial bore therethrough, and exterior helical threads on the male extension. The bore of the first nut has R.H. threads, and the male extension of the first nut has L.H. threads. The bore of the second nut has L.H. threads, and the male extension of the second nut has R.H. threads. The nuts are designed to be coupled to each other using the L.H. threads, and coupled to an existing pipe system using the R.H. threads.

Ruth J. Bowden Wilcox, et al.: "Modular vacuum drainage system" is patented by Ruth J. Bowden Wilcox, Bjorn von Palffy, Tom Beatty, Doug Wallace, Mark Pondelick and Ian Tinkler. Abstract: A modular vacuum drainage system is provided which facilitates quick and easy installation in a building. The system includes a vacuum central housed in an enclosure and having interface connections located adjacent to a periphery of the enclosure to allow immediate access thereto. The vacuum central is sized to fit through standard doorway sizes, and is preferably housed in a soundproof enclosure so that the vacuum central may be installed in a room without requiring a separate mechanical room. The enclosure may be decorated to match the decor of the office, thereby providing an aesthetically pleasing appearance. A modular plumbing fixture is also provided which may be pre-fabricated off-site.

Safety Codes Council: Publisher of "Alberta private sewage system standard of practice 1999." Established by the Plumbing Technical council, Safety Codes Council. --. Publisher: Safety Codes Council (Edmonton, Alberta). Published in 1999.

Sandia National Laboratories: Sponsored research "Determining the Transfer Function for Unsteady Pressure Measurements Using a Method of Characteristics Solution." Sponsored by: Sandia National Laboratories (SNL), Albuquerque, NM, and Livermore, CA (United States).; Department of Energy, Washington, DC. Written by E. L. Clark, J. F. Henfling and D. D. McBride. Abstract: An inverse Fourier transform method for removing lag from pressure measurements has been used by various researchers, given an experimentally derived transfer function to characterize the pressure plumbing. This paper presents a Method of Characteristics (MOC) solution technique for predicting the transfer function and thus easily determining its sensitivity to various plumbing parameters. The MOC solution has been used in the pipeline industry for some time for application to transient flow in pipelines, but it also lends itself well to this application. For highly nonsteady pressures frequency- dependent friction can cause significant distortion of the traveling waves. This is accounted for in the formulation.

Scott M. Parker, et al.: "Rotary directional valve with integral load holding check" is patented by Scott M. Parker, Gregory F. Lantsberg and Peter R. Nelson. Abstract: A cartridge valve assembly (19) including a sleeve valve (49) fixed within a valve housing (17), and a spool valve (47) moveable both axially and rotatably within the sleeve valve. Rotation of an input (35,39) causes rotation of a cam member (43) and the spool valve, and the engagement of the cam member (43) with a cam surface (57) results in axial movement of the spool valve within the sleeve valve. The spool and sleeve valves define a neutral axial and rotational position (FIG. 5), and rotation from neutral in a first direction (FIG. 6) communicates fluid from an inlet port (21) to a first actuator port (25), and rotation from neutral in a second direction (FIG.

Standards Australia: Publisher of "Methods of testing plastics and composite materials sanitary plumbing fixtures: AS 3558.3:1999. Method 3, Determination of colour fastness." Publisher: Standards Australia (Homebush, NSW). Published in 1999.

Stanley L. Hansen: "Faucet assembly" is patented by Stanley L. Hansen. Abstract: An improved faucet assembly is provided which includes a standard valve assembly used in basic plumbing systems, and a spout which communicates with the valve assembly to deliver water to a desired area. The valve assembly includes a valve stem which serves as the means by which the flow of water through the valve assembly is controlled. A simplified knob or handle attaches to the valve stem by means of a spring member which minimizes rotational and longitudinal movement of the knob or handle with respect to the valve stem. The spring member may either be a D-shaped spring, or a flat spring, depending upon the specific type of movement which must be restricted with respect to movement between the knob or handle and the valve stem.

Steve D. Witcher: "Two unit dry stack masonry wall system" is patented by Steve D. Witcher. Abstract: A mason wall cementitious building block system comprising two lightweight dry-stackable block units and methods of using such units, including a wall unit and a corner/end unit, connected one to another in an interlocking fashion by means of male posts and female sockets, and variants on each of said units for capping the uppermost course of an assembled wall. The male posts angle rearwardly to define partial apertures, such that adjoining blocks define an aperture which extends vertically between the adjoined blocks for placement of vertical reinforcement, electrical and plumbing chase, and for the introduction of mortar or cement. The top surface defines a recessed cavity for placement of rebar when stacked.

Susan M. Geary: "Washing machine outlet box" is patented by Susan M. Geary. Abstract: A washing machine outlet box includes a housing having a bottom wall containing a first valve mount for a first shutoff valve of a first water supply line and a valve mount insert that forms a second valve mount for a second shutoff valve of a second water supply line. The valve mount insert is selectively positionable in any one of several openings in the bottom wall to accommodate the second water supply line. A drain pipe is connected to one of the openings in which the valve mount insert is not selectively positioned. A test cap forms a seal for the drain pipe opening. In this manner, the washing machine outlet box can accommodate different plumbing arrangements.

Thomas R. Brown, et al.: "Directional control valve and valve assembly in an asphalt distributor" is patented by Thomas R. Brown, Jeremey Heller and Patrick O'Brien. Abstract: A directional control valve having three positions controls the direction of flow through an asphalt distributor. The directional control valve is interposed between a pump and a feed line assembly to a spray bar. The directional control valve has a first position in which flow is recirculated through the pump, a second position in which flow is delivered to the spray bar and a third position providing for handspray and transfer operations. A pressure relief valve is provided for controlling return flow of asphalt from the spray bar to the tank. The pressure relief valve is open in spray bar circulation mode and is closed during a spraying mode. According to the preferred embodiment the directional valve and pressure relief valve are contained within a modular control valve assembly.

United States. Congress. House. Committee on Commerce: Publication of "EPCA regulation of plumbing supplies. Hearing, 106th Cong., 1st sess., on H.R. 623. July 27, 1999." Published in 1999.

Walter S. Bergquist, et al.: "Method and apparatus for casting a plumbing fixture" is is patented by Walter S. Bergquist, Frank P. Williams and Harold A. Teague.

William C. Smith: "Non-intrusive pressure/multipurpose sensor and method" is patented by William C. Smith. Abstract: Method and apparatus are provided for determining pressure using a non-intrusive sensor that is easily attachable to the plumbing of a pressurized system. A bent mode implementation and a hoop mode implementation of the invention are disclosed. Each of these implementations is able to non-intrusively measure pressure while fluid is flowing. As well, each implementation may be used to measure mass flow rate simultaneously with pressure. An ultra low noise control system is provided for making pressure measurements during gas flow. The control system includes two tunable digital bandpass filters with center frequencies that are responsive to a clock frequency. The clock frequency is divided by a factor of N to produce a driving vibrational signal for resonating a metal sensor section.

William D. Folsom: "Freeze-resistant plumbing system in combination with a backflow preventer" is is patented by William D. Folsom.

William W. Rowley: "Method for manufacturing crosslinked overmolded plumbing tubes" is is patented by William W. Rowley.

Yariv Porat, et al.: "System and Method for Monitoring Pressure, Flow and Constriction Parameters of Plumbing and Blood Vessels" is patented by Yariv Porat, Yoseph Tsaliah and Eyal Doron.

Yuuji Matsumoto, et al.: "Laser plumbing device, long member plumbing device and long member plumbing method" is is patented by Yuuji Matsumoto, Tatsusei Minami, Osamu Yoda and Akira Tanabe.

20th Century

Dunny: By the middle of the twentieth century, dunnies had become much less common as modern plumbing diminished the need to keep toilets at a distance from the house. They were still constructed occasionally up until the fifties and sixties, but these were typically brick buildings with flushing toilets. [WP]

Freetown Elementary School, Massachusetts: The Town of Freetown, Massachusetts operated between eight and one dozen small school districts throughout the 18th and 19th centuries, and well into the 20th century. These schoolhouses were typically of one or two rooms, were heated by woodstoves, and featured outhouses as their only form of plumbing. As part of the town's post-war planning, it was decided to construct a centrally-located elementary school for all the town's students. The central location was considered critical so as not to favor either of the town's villages (Assonet and East Freetown) as the two were historically strong rivals. [WP]

Pipe dream: A pipe dream is a fantastic hope that is generally regarded as being nearly impossible. The term derives from the opium pipe, which was popular in the early twentieth century. Such ideas usually need events to flow in just the right direction to be realized, as a plumbing pipe might. The probability of such a course, is extremely low. Misconceptions, obstacles unseen by the pipe dreamer, or simple ignorance of any issues involved are often disregarded. [WP]

Swartzendruber Amish: The Swartzendruber Amish are the result of a division that occurred in Holmes County, Ohio in the middle of the 20th century. There are five districts of Swartzendruber Amish in Holmes County and Wayne County. They are noted for their use of reflective tape in place of bright triangular slow moving signs for road travel, which they regard as too worldly. Like some other "Old Order" groups, they avoid the use of electricity and indoor plumbing. Swartzendruber Amish speak Pennsylvania German, and are considered a subgroup of the Old Order Amish, although they do not fellowship nor intermarry with more liberal Old Order Amish. [WP]

2000

Alan E. Kligerman and Sarah Rogers: "Oral rinse methods and compositions" is patented by Alan E. Kligerman and Sarah Rogers. Abstract: Methods of freshening and reducing acidity in both the mouth and the throat of a mammal, such as a human, include taking into the mouth an aqueous solution of calcium glycerophosphate (CGP) in an amount effective to reduce the acidity, maintaining the solution in the mouth, and swallowing the aqueous solution in order to freshen and reduce acidity in both the mouth and the throat. The methods are convenient for use at any place and any time and do not have the inconveniences and limitations of conventional oral rinse or oral hygiene methods, such as the need for proximity to private or public plumbing facilities.

Alvin B. See and Richard A. Mitchell: "Method, system and computer program product for self-draining plumbing for liquid-cooled devices" is is patented by Alvin B. See and Richard A. Mitchell.

American Society of Plumbing Engineers. Convention (18th: 2000: Nashville, Tenn.): Publication of "Technical proceedings of the 2000 ASPE Convention: engineering the future: October 28--November 1, 2000, Nashville, Tennessee." Published in 2000.

Andrew J. Machovsky: "Multi-purpose plumbing tool" is patented by Andrew J. Machovsky. Abstract: A multi-purpose plumbing tool includes first and second tubular sockets. A first end portion of each of the tubular sockets has four notches therein, extending inward from a first end of the tubular socket and spaced from each other on 90.degree. centers, for receiving complementary parts to be rotated and tightened or loosened by one of the sockets. Preferably, the second end portion of the second tubular socket can be removably mounted on the first end portion of the first tubular socket to rotate with the first tubular socket.

Angelo Bonomi, et al.: "Selective deleading process and bath for plumbing components made of a copper alloy" is is patented by Angelo Bonomi, Stefano Carrera and Giuliano Franzosi.

Armin J. Altemus: "Bidirectionally interlocking, hollow brick wall system" is patented by Armin J. Altemus. Abstract: A brick with, preferably, two or three cylindrical passageways running from top to bottom, a cylindrical passageway running from one end to the opposite end, two linear grooves at one end and two linear projections at the other end which are of identical shape, and annular projections centered around the bores at top and annular grooves centered around the bores at the other side which are of identical shape. These passageways intersect, the linear grooves are slightly larger than the linear projections, and the annular grooves are slightly larger than the annular projections. The linear projections and grooves are spaced apart from the end-to-end cylindrical passageway, run from top to bottom and are preferably designed with a break for ease of assembly.

Arthur Radichio: "Pipe freezer" is patented by Arthur Radichio. Abstract: A pipe freezing apparatus comprises a multi-cavity adapter and an evaporator adapted to be fitted therein. The present invention uses a multi-cavity adapter having from two to eight cavities to fit standard plumbing pipes in copper, steel and plastic, metric and US standard. The refrigeration evaporator fits into a cylindrical bore in the core of the radial multi-cavity array. The cavities are arrayed around the circumference of the bore. The adapter body that forms the array is of aluminum or the like. The coolant lines are elbowed at 90 degrees to the evaporator's longitudinal axis to facilitate attachment to the pipe in small or tight spaces and from the side of the pipe.

Austap Incorporated: Publisher of "Austap outlet: journal of the plumbing manufacturers group." Publisher: Austap Incorporated (Canberra). Published in 2000.

Burton, Jack L.: Author of "Domestic plumbing design." Publisher: Prentice Hall (Upper Saddle River, N.J.). Published in 2000.

Canadian Standards Association: Publication of "General instruction No.2: plumbing fixtures - originally published April 1999." Publisher: Canadian Standards Association (Etobicoke, Ont). Published in 2000.

CEPU: Publisher of "National plumbing occupational health & safety manual." Publisher: CEPU (Carlton South, Vic). Published in 2000.

Choudhury, Ifte: Author of "Water and plumbing." Publisher: Prentice Hall (Upper Saddle River, N.J.). Published in 2000.

Daniel D. Bell: "Self contained dental chair with integrated compressor and vacuum pump and methods" is patented by Daniel D. Bell. Abstract: The invention provides an exemplary modular dental chair system and methods for its use. In one embodiment, a compressor, vacuum pump, water reservoir, waste container and associated fittings, wiring, and plumbing are integrated into a dental chair. The compressor, vacuum pump, water reservoir, and waste container provide the services needed to perform dental procedures. Such a configuration allows the chair to be located and relocated without having to connect to facility centralized air, water, and waste.

David A. Potts: "Method and apparatus for treating leach fields" is patented by David A. Potts. Abstract: The functioning of the leach field of a septic tank type sewage system is maintained or rejuvenated by flowing air or other active gas through the system's conduits, for instance, leaching chambers or perforated pipes in stone filled trenches. Differential pressure created by an air mover forces air or other active gas to flow through the soil adjacent the conduits, to an extent sufficient to push water from any saturated soil and effect desirable aerobic biochemical conditions in the soil. In alternate embodiments, conduits may be pressurized or evacuated. Valves and other plumbing are provided to control air flow and enable continued function of the sewage system during air flow treatment.

David F. Friedman and Harry C. Friedman: "Compression stop and coupling wrench" is patented by David F. Friedman and Harry C. Friedman. Abstract: The present invention is an apparatus to facilitate the installation and replacement of mechanical devices, particularly plumbing compression fittings such as an angle-stop valve. The wrench has a first member that includes an open-end wrench and associated jaw surface and a hollow handle extending therefrom. A second member also includes an open-end wrench and a handle extending therefrom, the handle of the second member being of a diameter small enough to slidably fit within the handle of the first member. The handles of the first and second members preferably including mating means so as to enable the temporary locking of the two members for use and or storage of the two-piece wrench apparatus.

David L. Fishel and Peter F. Payne: "Embossed, waterproof lining and method of making the same" is patented by David L. Fishel and Peter F. Payne. Abstract: The invention relates to a flexible, waterproof shower pan liner comprised of a water-insoluble thermoplastic sheet. The shower pan liner includes on at least one surface selected indicia such as product information or plumbing codes at regular intervals. The indicia are embossed into the shower pan liner thereby eliminating the need for a protective top coat. In a process for making the invention, the thermoplastic is heated, calendered, and thereafter embossed with the selected indicia while in a heated condition.

David N. Bolinger and Edward J. Ross: "Adjustable scaffold used with concrete-receiving forms" is patented by David N. Bolinger and Edward J. Ross. Abstract: Walls of expanded polystyrene, concrete-receiving forms (referred to as insulated or insulating concrete forms or ICFs) need to be vertical while they are being filled with concrete and while the concrete is curing. An apparatus with a vertical member and a brace member is such that one person can erect it and use it to adjust walls of ICFs so as to be vertical or plumb. The apparatus is capable of being readily used with the forms of any manufacturer by being provided with asymmetrical brackets for detachably attaching the vertical member to a wall firmly, but not rigidly. The apparatus provides a support for a platform, or scaffold, for a person to stand on while guiding the concrete pouring and while plumbing the wall.

Dean B. Behlen: "Accessory for building construction" is patented by Dean B. Behlen. Abstract: A holder for use in building construction for holding anchor bolts, rebar, in-concrete plumbing, and the like, in predetermined positions during the pouring of concrete therearound.

Deryl Heil: "Slab plumbing system" is patented by Deryl Heil. Abstract: A plumbing system, a slab therewith and a bowl for a plumbing system have been invented, the bowl, in one aspect having an outer side wall, the outer side wall being generally cylindrical in shape with a hollow interior and having a height and a top opening, an inner wall, the inner wall being generally cylindrical and having a hollow interior, the inner wall having a top opening and a bottom opening and a height equal to or less than the height of the outer side wall, a bottom wall comprising a generally circular ring, the bottom wall having an outer edge contacting a lower edge of the outer side wall and an inner edge contacting a lower edge of the inner wall, the bottom wall spacing apart the outer side wall from the inner wall around a circumference of the bowl.

Diane Lark: "Contact lens kit and carrying pouch" is patented by Diane Lark. Abstract: A contact lens kit or pouch organizer for removably storing a plurality of accessories which are contained in separate containers such as lens solutions, contact lens themselves, a drain catcher and a mirror. The organizer includes a box-like container properly sized to accommodate the shape and size of the contact lens accessories intended to be placed therein. A container closure includes an upper flap intended to fold over an opening leading into the interior of a storage compartment and which closes with a snap fastener on a bottom flap which folds across the bottom of the container and folds upwardly to receive the snap fastener on the upper flap.

Donald M Pohler: "Self-contained toilet basin" is patented by Donald M Pohler. Abstract: A self-contained bathroom waste collection and disposal unit, having an access cover free of electrical and plumbing fixtures is disclosed. The unit includes a reservoir having an inlet and a sump opening. The sump opening is sized to receive a pump and a float mechanism therethrough. The sump opening is closed by a primary cover having venting, plumbing and electrical ports and an access cover. The access cover can be removed to access the enclosed sump, without interrupting the venting, plumbing or electrical connections.

Donald S. Kropidlowski: "Reference point locator for residential and commercial construction" is patented by Donald S. Kropidlowski. Abstract: A portable electronic reference point locator facilitates location of a reference point, located on one side of a structure (such as a wall, floor or ceiling), from the opposite side of the structure. The system is particularly useful when installing new electrical wiring or hardware, when installing new plumbing, or when performing other construction related tasks that require the location of one side of a structure to be determined relative to the other side of the structure. The system comprises a transmitter and a receiver. The transmitter is located at a position that defines the reference point, and includes an oscillator and an antenna that cooperate to generate and transmit an electromagnetic signal.

Einar Svensson: "Support structure for elevated railed-vehicle guideway" is patented by Einar Svensson. Abstract: A guideway and support structure (50) for supporting an elevated guideway (52) for a railed-vehicle (54) include individual unassembled components sized for easy transport. The components may be prefabricated with known materials and methods and transported to an installation site to be assembled together. The support structure (50) is preferably cantilevered and sized to support one or two vehicle guideways (52). The support structure (50) may include a pile foundation (56) for improved support during seismic activity and to facilitate installation on existing streets and sidewalks without covering or interfering with underground plumbing or utilities.

Eric James Lovelace and Bonnie Suzanne Schnitta: "Plumbing trap system" is is patented by Eric James Lovelace and Bonnie Suzanne Schnitta.

Eric S. Nordman, et al.: "Multi-channel capillary electrophoresis device including sheath-flow cuvette and replacable capillary array" is patented by Eric S. Nordman, John Shigeura, Albert L. Carrillo, David M. Demorest and Philip J. Wunderle. Abstract: A multi-channel capillary electrophoresis apparatus is disclosed. The apparatus includes a capillary array assembly comprising a plurality of capillaries, each capillary having a capillary outlet, and an outlet support for supporting the capillary outlets. The apparatus further includes a cuvette defining a receiving slot, a gap region, and a detection zone, where the receiving slot is adapted to removably receive the outlet support, and wherein when the outlet support is inserted into the receiving slot, the capillary outlets are positioned in the gap region in proximity to the detection zone, and a flow channel is formed by the outlet support and the receiving slot such that the flow channel is in fluid communication with the gap region.

Frankie Lee Carter: "Damage control leak pan" is

patented by Frankie Lee Carter. Abstract: The damage control leak pan designed to contain leaking water from defective plumbing. The leak pan contains the leaking water in it reservoir thereby preventing water damage. Said leak pan is utilized to prevent an array of damage created by water leaking into numerous areas, namely under bathroom and kitchen sinks. The leak pan is capable of being adjusted to fit into various sink areas by means of a perforated lip surrounding the upper edge of the reservoir. The leak pan solves many current problems associated with defective plumbing with and inexpensive and simple solution.

Gary H. Rebischke: "Flexible sink strainer and stopper" is patented by Gary H. Rebischke. Abstract: A combination flexible strainer and plug for use in conjunction with a drain opening of a plumbing fixture. The strainer comprising a substantially cylindrical portion constructed and arranged to extendingly engage the drain opening. The strainer having a bottom portion engaged to a lowermost portion of the substantially cylindrical portion, the bottom portion having a plurality of openings therethrough. The strainer having an annular ring engaged to an uppermost portion of the substantially cylindrical portion and outwardly extending therefrom, the annular ring constructed and arranged to form a seal with a portion of the plumbing fixture immediately adjacent to the drain opening. The plug comprising an upper surface, the upper surface and a lower surface.

General Accounting Office: Sponsored research "Water Infrastructure: Water-Efficient Plumbing Fixtures Reduce Water Consumption and Wastewater Flows. - Report to the Congress." Sponsored by: General Accounting Office, Washington, DC. Resources, Community and Economic Development Div. Abstract: Water-efficient plumbing fixtures, such as low-flow toilets and showerheads, first became generally available to American consumers in the late 1980s. Subsequently, under the Energy Policy Act of 1992, the Congress established uniform national standards for the manufacture of these fixtures to promote conservation by residential and commercial water users. Concerned about the potential implications of the proposed legislation, you asked us to examine the impact of the national water efficiency standards.

Gert J. Van Waveren: "Management System for Articles and Sticker Suitable for Use in Said System" is patented by Gert J. Van Waveren. Abstract: Management system for articles, in particular plumbing articles, which system is provided with a portable terminal, which terminal has been provided with a reading device for reading in the code applied on an article and with an input device for entering data, such as working hours and the like, with a main computer, the portable terminal being connectable to the main computer for transmitting read in article codes and the entered data, the main computer being provided with a stock management device having a stock file and an invoice device, and with a printer connected to the main computer.

Government of Honduras: Text of Regulation Governing the Use of Drinking Water, Sanitary Sewage, and Rain Drainage Systems for Urban Developments and Subdivisions, of 26 April 2000, was issued by the "Junta Directiva del Servicio Autonomo Nacional de Acueductos y Alcantarillados," the Board of Directors of the National Autonomous Service of Aqueducts and Plumbing, known by the Spanish acronym SANAA. Governs the relations between SANAA and urban developers, consultants, and individual construction companies in the development of housing and urban developments in relation to the construction and use of drinking water, sanitary sewage, and rain drainage systems. Provides for approval of designs, supervision of work, and many other pertinent matters. Contains several informational annexes. Published in Gaceta Oficial on April 26, 2000.

Gregory Stuart Cawthon: "Outdoor portable sink with plumbing connection" is is patented by Gregory Stuart Cawthon.

Gualberto Vallejo: "System for adapting a toilet for use as a bidet" is patented by Gualberto Vallejo. Abstract: A system for adapting a toilet for use as a bidet in a manner that easily adapts to different lavatory conditions and user preferences without requiring specialized plumbing. The system for adapting a toilet for use as a bidet includes a fluid distribution apparatus for mounting on the seat of a toilet, a forward spray apparatus for mounting on the seat in fluid communication with the fluid distribution apparatus for spraying a stream of fluid in a rearward direction from the front of the seat, and a rearward spray apparatus for mounting on the seat in fluid communication with the fluid distribution apparatus for spraying a stream of fluid in a forward direction from the rear of the seat. A coupling apparatus may be provided for coupling the fluid distribution apparatus to a faucet.

Guy T. Stoever, et al.: "Nestable fluid coupler" is patented by Guy T. Stoever, Jimmie Clifford and Gerard Restaino III. Abstract: The hydraulic coupler is used for connecting a valve to a tool used with a vehicle having a hydraulic pump and fluid communication with the valve through hydraulic plumbing. The hydraulic coupler comprises a coupler body having a base portion, a neck portion and a connector portion. The coupler body is two connector chambers in the connector portion which arc in fluid communication with two apertures, which when the hydraulic coupler is mounted on the valve, are in fluid communication with the valve. A connector assembly, typically of the quick-connect type, is mounted in each connector chamber and is configured to receive hydraulic plumbing to connect the valve to the tool. One embodiment provides that the coupler body is narrower than the valve on which it is mounted.

Heinz-Dieter Eichholz: "Accommodation for holding and connecting batteries" is patented by Heinz-Dieter Eichholz. Abstract: An accommodation for holding and connecting batteries, especially lithium batteries of the type ordinarily employed for photographic purposes, but in conditions where moisture constitutes a hazard, such as in electronically controlled plumbing fixtures. The accommodation is provided with a pocket-like envelope of elastomeric material with an inner surface that matches the outer surface of the battery to be accommodated therein and with an opening at one end to insert the battery therethrough and closed at the other end.

International Association of Plumbing and Mechanical Officials: Publication of "Uniform plumbing code." International Association of Plumbing and Mechanical Officials. Published in 2000.

International Code Council: Publication of "International plumbing code 2000." Publisher: International Code Council (Falls Church, Va.). Published in 2000.

invention: "A Conduit for Plumbing Fittings"

Jae K. Sim: "Automatic cleaning assembly for a toilet bowl" is patented by Jae K. Sim. Abstract: An automatic cleaning assembly for a toilet bowl includes a body member having an interior cavity therein for receiving a cleaning agent. An inlet is in communication with an interior of the body member and is connectable to a ball cock through a refill tube and an outlet is in communication with an interior of the body member and is connectable to an overflow pipe through a connecting hose. Furthermore, a cap is attached to the body member. The cap is free from apertures therethrough and sealed to said body member to form a sealed space at an upper portion of an interior of the body member. The sealed space ensures that a level of water within said interior cavity of said body member remains at a bottom of the cleaning agent to slowly dissolve the cleaning agent.

James Mantyla: "Replacement flange" is patented by James Mantyla. Abstract: There is provided replacement flange for attachment to a plumbing fitting having an inlet end, an outlet end attachable to a pipe and a pre-existing attachment groove. The replacement flange comprises a rim having a central opening. The central opening is sized and shaped to allow attachment of the rim to the inlet end while the outlet end is attached to the pipe. The flange also includes a lip projecting inwardly from the rim along a portion of a perimeter of the central opening. The lip is sized and shaped to engage a portion of the groove.

Jerome M. Arvin: "Plumbing workstation" is patented by Jerome M. Arvin. Abstract: A portable plumbing workstation used to install plumbing fixtures on sinks and to assemble tub/shower valve assemblies having a frame, a plurality of templates, the templates arrange and constructed to support at least one sink or tub/shower valve, the plurality of templates being interchangeable with one another and being pivotally carried on the frame for rotation about a horizontal axis, a releaseable lock for locking the template relative to the frame at selected angular positions about the horizontal axis, at least one sink retainer for securing a sink on the template such that when the template is at a first angular position, the sink can be inserted and secured on the template.

John M. Mankins: "Apparatus and method for testing plumbing system" is is patented by John M. Mankins.

John R. Sigman: "Apparatus for removing and installing plumbing flanges" is is patented by John R. Sigman.

Johnnie Robert Crean: "Recreational vehicles with expandable room" is patented by Johnnie Robert Crean. Abstract: A recreational vehicle having an expandable room wherein the room can be positioned in a retracted or deployed configuration. In the deployed configuration, the room expands inwardly into the main housing of the vehicle so as to enlarge the area of the room without displacing the fixtures and plumbing that are typically positioned adjacent an outer wall of the room. The room can be extended in conjunction with an exterior slide-out assembly wherein the deployed slide-out assembly creates a larger inner living space so as to accommodate the expanded room.

Jon Nimens: "Plumbing device" is patented by Jon Nimens. Abstract: The invention comprises a drain cleaning apparatus having a flexible forward tubular portion and a rigid real-ward tubular portion. The flexible portion is coupled to a drain pipe of a building connected to the sewer line, after the elbow connection between the drain pipe section and the drain in a sink in the building has been removed. The rearward tubular portion has a bowl with an open top and a spout is mounted over the bowl with a fluid connection connecting the spout to a spout of the faucet to fill the bowl and apparatus and drain pipe up to any blockage in the drain pipe.

Joseph P. Ismert, et al.: "Apparatus for supporting conduit between building members" is patented by Joseph P. Ismert, Victor M. Carr, Frank D. Julian, Arthur B. Hicks and Richard D. Thomas. Abstract: A plumbing slider bracket and ratchet arm conduit clamp includes a slider bracket with an inner bracket section which is telescopically received within an outer bracket section such that it is slidable back and forth within the outer bracket section to make an extendable slider bracket. Flexible tabs extending from either end of the slider bracket allow attachment of the bracket to an outer stud surface, or within the stud spacing in any desired orientation. Each ratchet arm conduit clamp is received by the slider bracket and is movable along the length of the slider bracket until a conduit is clamped therein.

Kenneth P. Nolan: "High pressure hose drop backflow/back siphonage preventers" is patented by Kenneth P. Nolan. Abstract: A backflow and back-siphonage preventer assembly, consisting of a ball valve and a double check valve backflow preventer with an atmospheric vent, provides isolation protection on high pressure plumbing supply lines, such as high pressure hose drops used for the washdown of equipment and facilities, e.g. in food processing plants. The backflow preventer includes a housing with an inlet, an outlet, and a drain outlet therebetween. A first valve is upstream of the drain outlet passage, and a second valve is downstream of the drain outlet, a sealing member moves between a first position in which the drain outlet passage is closed, and a second position in which the drain outlet passage is open.

Kevin M. Monk: "Hydraulic Services for Residential and Hotel Buildings" is patented by Kevin M. Monk. Abstract: The invention provides a hydraulic service system for multi-level buildings. The hydraulic service system includes a sanitary plumbing service, a hot water service and/or a cold water service for residential and hotel buildings, and optionally further includes a storm water drainage system, a gas service and/or a fire service.

Larry D. Brown and James B. Schell: "Bracket for securing pipes" is patented by Larry D. Brown and

James B. Schell. Abstract: A bracket supports tubing at a bend in the tubing. The bracket is curved, and has an open side into which the tubing is inserted into the bracket. Projecting lips or restraints extend into a portion of the opening through which the tubing is inserted, with the tubing being placed over lips to prevent the tubing from sliding out of the open side. A flange at one end of the bracket is notched to removably accept the edge of an opening in a plumbing strap, with a latch opposite the notch to releasably lock the flange to the strap. Preferably two or more spacers extend across the width of the bracket, with holes in the spacers sized to accept fasteners to nail the bracket to studs and keep the bracket from rotating about the fasteners.

Louisiana: Publication of "Louisiana State Plumbing Code: otherwise referred to as Chapter XIV, Plumbing, Sanitary Code, State of Louisiana, consisting of the 1994 Standard Plumbing Code as revised by the 1999 Louisiana Amendments." Publisher: State of Louisiana, Dept. of Health and Hospitals (Baton Rouge, La.). Published in 2000.

Marc F. Baker: "Filter for an Ink Jet Printhead" is patented by Marc F. Baker. Abstract: An ink jet printhead (16) of an ink jet cartridge includes a filter plate (30) that is downstream of the ink. Particularly, the filter plate is attached to the back of the heater chip of the printhead. The filter plate is in addition to a wire mesh filter (42) that is disposed at the inlet of a plumbing standpipe (40) that prevents particles which are shed from the ink reservoir from passing into the printhead chip assembly. The filter plate of the present invention prevents particles that originate in the plumbing standpipe channels below the wire mesh filter from clogging the bubble chambers of the heater chip of the printhead chip assembly. The filter plates were formed on a polymer sheet with a series of holes ablated using an eximer laser.

Mark A. Fisher: "Automatic bird feeder and waterer" is patented by Mark A. Fisher. Abstract: An automatic bird feeder and waterer includes both a food and a water reservoir therein, as well as dispensing areas for food and water supplied from the respective reservoirs. The water reservoir comprises a generally cylindrical container installed concentrically through the generally cylindrical food reservoir. The water outlet or dispensing portion is laterally offset by an upturned elbow, which also serves as the lowermost point of the assembly. The feed dispensers may include partial covers to preclude the feeding of larger non-flying animals (squirrels, etc.) therefrom. The device is supported by a rigid support extending downwardly from the elbow.

McIntyre Media Limited Meridian Education Corporation Advanced Productions: Publication of "Residential construction." Produced by Advanced Productions Residential electric wiring Plumbing Residential plumbing Masonry Residential masonry Electrical wiring. Publisher: distributed by McIntyre Media Inc., (Bloomington, IL: Meridian Education Corporation; Mississauga, ON). Published in 2000.

Meany, Terry: Author of "The complete idiot's guide to plumbing (computer file)." Publisher: Alpha Books (New York). Published in 2000.

Michael J. Hite and Lawrence P. Gillen: "Plumbing part installation and removal tool" is is patented by Michael J. Hite and Lawrence P. Gillen.

Midgley, Mary: Author of "Utopias, Dolphins and Computers: Problems in Philosophical Plumbing." Publisher: Routledge (London). Published in 2000.

Neil R. Bergstrom: "Portable spa construction" is patented by Neil R. Bergstrom. Abstract: A spa construction wherein a spa shell is supported and reinforced by a matrix of interlocking horizontal and vertical members attached to a base grid. The matrix supports the spa shell through contact with only two regions of the spa--namely the bar top and footwell areas. The construction eliminates the necessity to encase the shell in structural foam and facilitates ready access to spa plumbing.

Office of Health Services and Environmental Quality: Publisher of "Louisiana state plumbing code, 2000 edition (otherwise referred to as) chapter XIV plumbing, Sanitary code, State of Louisiana, consisting of the 1994 standard plumbing code revised by the 1999 Louisiana amendments." Publisher: Office of Health Services and Environmental Quality (Baton Rouge, La.). Published in 2000.

2000

Olf Woldach and Matthias Graf: "Plumbing Element for Sanitary Objects" is patented by Olf Woldach and Matthias Graf.

Ontario. Ministry of Municipal Affairs & Housing: Publication of "Objective-based codes: a consultation on the proposed objectives, structure and cycle of the National and Ontario Building Codes (including plumbing), October 16, 2000 to January 15, 2000." Publisher: The Ministry (Toronto). Published in 2000.

Paul A. Phillips, et al.: "Soft drink dispensing machine with modular customer interface unit" is patented by Paul A. Phillips, Ellen Sandor O'Brien, Alfred A. Schroeder and William A. Edwards. Abstract: A customer interface unit for a beverage dispensing machine facilitates configuration and assembly of the machine and reduces the amount of time required to fill orders for new equipment. The customer interface unit for soft drink machines of the disclosed embodiment facilitates reconfiguration of the machine and permits nozzles and associated plumbing to be added, removed, repositioned, repaired, or exchanged while in the field. These goals are accomplished by way of a modular construction which facilitates assembly and reconfiguration. The disclosed customer interface unit also includes a nozzle arrangement which facilitates visualization of the dispensing position by the customer, thereby minimizing the possibility of spillage.

Paul W. Painter: "Epicycloidic inductrial cleaning system" is patented by Paul W. Painter. Abstract: An industrial parts cleaning system including immersion and spraying which provides epicyclic parts movement (a plurality of revolutions per rotation, wherein the revolution is supersposed the rotation), rotating spray which synchronously follows the parts rotation, and a purge system for evacuating from the common plumbing the respective wash or rinse solution of a current cycle before commencement of the next cycle.

R. Stuart Holden, et al.: "Universal multi-path control valve system" is patented by R. Stuart Holden, Richard E. Marzec and Frank Pieters. Abstract: A universal multi-path control valve system includes at least two sets of outlets controlled by a single on/off operator. A compact design allows the control valve system to save space in the compact areas where plumbing fixtures are typically installed. The control valve system is constructed entirely of molded plastic components. Fittings supplied with the control valve system allow for customized installation according to the needs of the installer. Appliances may be easily added or removed using threaded connections on the valve and fittings supplied as part of the control valve system.

Ralf Mantel and Werner Lorch: "Protective device for sanitary fittings" is patented by Ralf Mantel and Werner Lorch. Abstract: A protective device for a sanitary fitting contains a covering, which during installation steps is mounted such that outlets of the fitting are sealed in pressure-resistant manner and/or are interconnected. This sealed covering is connected by separable means to a cylindrical skirt, which surrounds the fitting and/or the fitting part. After the installer tests the house plumbing and completes the wall surface, the covering is removed again from the sanitary fitting or the part thereof. As desired, it is also possible to remove the skirt or leave it in the wall. For this purpose the skirt is attached to the sealing part of the covering by easily separated ridges.

Rich F. Simpson and Francisco Hinojosa Jr: "Pool/spa waterfall apparatus with an interchangeable outlet cap" is patented by Rich F. Simpson and Francisco Hinojosa Jr. Abstract: The present invention provides a new waterfall apparatus water reservoirs such as pools, spa's and the like. It comprises a manifold having a water inlet connected to the a water supply, preferably the water supply from the reservoir's plumbing. The manifold has internal baffles to remove turbulence from the water, which is then directed to a spillway water outlet. The spillway has a through slot that allows water to flow out from the manifold. It also has a removable outlet cap which forms the water into a particular waterfall shape. Another embodiment of the invention for spas, has a tubular body and a outlet that is in the form of a longitudinal slot in the body. The outlet cap is then mounted in the slot.

Robert C. Sandness: "Apparatus for cleaning out

drain pipe obstructions" is patented by Robert C. Sandness. Abstract: An assembly useful in directing a narrow water stream against an obstruction inside drain plumbing includes an exteriortubular housing within which a spray wand may be telescopically received. A resilient seal is engaged to the free end of the wand, for capture between the tubular housing and the surface around the drain plumbing openings. The other end of the wand is connected across a valve to a source of water at pressure to be ejected through an axial drilling in the free end towards the obstruction. The lateral edge of the tubular housing may include cut-outs to allow manipulation of the valve handle once the valve is secured to the housing.

Ronald P. Doyle: "Biometric identification and thermostatic control method and system for temperature-sensitive water delivery in home plumbing systems" is is patented by Ronald P. Doyle.

Selwyn Reed: "Waste assembly allowing adjustable fitment of a floor waste or appliance" is patented by Selwyn Reed. Abstract: A floor or ground surface waste assembly for receiving floor or appliance generated waste including a waste body (1) defining a waste collecting receptacle (2).

Shea, Kevin Bruce: Author of "Frequency of plumbing fixture use through audio sampling." Published in 2000.

Sloan, Robert: Author of "Aunt Ethel's plumbing and other tales (sound recording)." Publisher: R.L. Sloan (Morehead, KY). Published in 2000.

Standards Association of Australia: Publication of "National plumbing and draining code. Part 5., Domestic installations." Published in 2000.

Standards Australia International Limited: Publication of "National plumbing and drainage. Part 5, Domestic installations." Published in 2000.

Stead, Kevin: Author of "Plumbing." Publisher: Arnold (London). Published in 2000.

Steve Occhiogrosso: "Pressure washer" is patented by Steve Occhiogrosso. Abstract: An pressure washer enclosure capable of high pressure spraying with all pumps and chemicals enclosed for the protection of personnel and security of the chemicals. An external curbside control panel allows the operator to control the amount and concentration of the fluid emissions. A sealed plumbing arrangement minimizes chemical storage, handling and exposure. The enclosure has provisions for related cleaning equipment including a ladder rack accessible from the exterior of the housing.

Steven E. Lewis, et al.: "Plumbing tool" is patented by Steven E. Lewis, Franklin D. Lewis and David Littlefield. Abstract: A versatile stopcock tool for installation of and adjusting flow in stop boxes for water, oil, gas and the like fluid materials. The tool is long with folding handles, has a telescopic shaft for storage and portage, and has specific heads for different functions. A flashlight can be removably clamped on the shaft.

Tatsusei Minami: "Plumbing device for plumbing and connection of a long member" is is patented by Tatsusei Minami.

Terry M. Abel and Thomas A. Velez: "Electrical drive system for rocket engine propellant pumps" is patented by Terry M. Abel and Thomas A. Velez. Abstract: A liquid propellant supply system (10) according to the invention is electrical in nature and avoids the need for a gas generator and a turbine assembly. In particular, the system (10) includes an electrical power source (12), a controller (14) and a motor (18) for driving the pump (20). The electrical power source (12) provides electrical power sufficient for high power, limited duration applications such as for launch vehicle applications. For launch vehicle applications, the power source (12) is preferably capable of providing very high power for at least 60 seconds. A number of different types of electrical power sources may be employed in this regard. For example, the power source (12) may include high energy density batteries, supercapacitors, or counter rotating flywheels.

Thomas N. Corso and Colleen K. Van Pelt: "High-throughput parallel liquid chromatography system" is patented by Thomas N. Corso and Colleen K. Van Pelt. Abstract: A high-throughput liquid chromatography system capable of parallel separations for increased sample throughput is described. The system comprises valves allowing for the use of multiple liquid chromatography columns and a single injector and pumping system while also minimizing extraneous plumbing and hardware. The system is capable of injecting individual samples and directing them to one of a multiplicity of columns followed by selective output to a detector. The system described allows for up to 16 columns, but the number may vary according to the application. The system may be run in an isocratic or gradient mode.

Timothy James Culver and Brian Paul Goodman: "Method and apparatus for providing alignment particularly in construction tasks" is patented by Timothy James Culver and Brian Paul Goodman. Abstract: A projection apparatus for projecting the axis of a plumbing fixture or an existing opening in a construction member onto a remote member, for locating an opening to be made in the remote member, has a body having at least a first cylindrical portion with a first diameter ending in a shoulder, the first cylindrical portion having an axis, and a laser pointer constrained in a cavity of the body such that the laser, when activated, projects along the axis. The apparatus is useful for projecting a center point from a plumbing fixture onto a remote member, such as for vent installation, and for aligning openings in construction members for pipes and other conduits.

Treloar, Roy: Author of "Plumbing: heating and gas installations." Publisher: Blackwell Science (Malden, MA). Published in 2000.

United States. General Accounting Office: Publication of "Water infrastructure: water-efficient plumbing fixtures reduce water consumption and wastewater flows: report to congressional requesters." United States General Accounting Office. Published in 2000.

Vernon R. Walcker: "Apparatus for installing a door frame" is patented by Vernon R. Walcker. Abstract: An apparatus for installing door frames which comprises at least two template members and at least three apertures on each template member. To provide horizontal adjustment means between said at least two template members, at least one elongated member may be joined approximately normal to each of said at least two templates. Said at least one elongated member may comprise at least one tongue member and at least one groove member, said at least one tongue member may be slidably positioned within said at least one groove member. To provide means for plumbing said template members, at least one screw may be positioned within said at least one template member.

Vincent M. Zarbo: "Adjustable plumbing connector and method" is is patented by Vincent M. Zarbo.

Vincent Wai Lau: "Portable spa" is patented by Vincent Wai Lau. Abstract: A spa pool assembly has a pool that has an enclosing wall defining an interior. The assembly further includes a jet nozzle unit removably coupled to the enclosing wall and positioned in the interior, the jet nozzle unit housing a plumbing system and at least one jet nozzle. The assembly further includes a control unit that houses a pump that is coupled to the jet nozzle unit. Alternatively, a pump unit is removably received inside a channel provided in the wall and has a jet nozzle that is directed at the interior of the pool when the pump unit is received inside the channel. The jet nozzle unit, the control unit, the pump unit and the pool are separate modular units that can be assembled together quickly and conveniently.

Walter Pitsch: "System and method of plumbing installation" is is patented by Walter Pitsch.

Woodson, Roger Dodge: Born in 1955, authored "International and uniform plumbing codes handbook." Publisher: McGraw-Hill (New York). Published in 2000.

Yukinori Ikemiya, et al.: "Cutting-free bronze alloys" is patented by Yukinori Ikemiya, Hideki Yoshimura, Kenji Sugiyama, Kunio Nakashima, Masao Hosoda, Wataru Yago and Kazuyuki Inagaki. Abstract: A cutting-free bronze alloy which is substantially free of lead contains 1 to 13 wt. % of tin, not larger than 18 wt. % of zinc, 0.5 to 6 wt. % of bismuth, 0.05 to 3 wt. % of antimony, not larger than 1 wt. % of phosphorus, less than 0.4 wt. % of lead, and the balance being copper. The alloy may further contain 0.1 to 3 wt. % of nickel. When 3 to 8 wt. % of tin and 6 to 10 wt. % of zinc are present, the alloy is particularly suitable for use as a plumbing faucet and fixture. Likewise, when 8.5 to 13 wt. % of tin and not larger than 1 wt. % of zinc are present, the alloy is suitable for use as a sliding member.

2001

Afghanistan - News: December 15, 2001 — **Headline:** U-S Embassy in Kabul to Reopen. **Excerpt:** The State Department has announced the U-S embassy in Kabul, Afghanistan will reopen Sunday for the first time in 12 years. U-S special envoy to Afghanistan, James Dobbins, will officially re-inaugurate what will, for now, be called the U-S liaison office. ... But they say it needs significant repairs, especially with the electric and plumbing systems.

Alfred Eichinger: "Combination plumbing fixture and bracing implement" is is patented by Alfred Eichinger.

Anthony G. Ingram, et al.: "Travel trailer" is patented by Anthony G. Ingram, Marion B. Johnson and Terry L. Harkins. Abstract: A travel trailer has a two-level chassis supporting at least two discrete floor sections at at least two different heights above the ground with at least one of those floors having a bathroom portion being supported by an upper chassis beam. In a preferred embodiment, the chassis has a substantially horizontal forward upper portion and a substantially horizontal rearward lower portion, and an upper floor is secured to the upper portion and a lower floor is secured to the lower portion with an intermediate floor positioned below the upper edge of the upper portion of the chassis to a height intermediate that of the upper and lower floors. In an alternative preferred embodiment, the intermediate floor is suspended below the upper chassis portion.

Anthony Prisco: "Toilet ventilation system" is patented by Anthony Prisco. Abstract: Disclosed is a ventilation device for removing offensive odors from within and near the toilet bowl, incorporating a modular asymmetrical exhaust airway to permit retrofitting onto a variety of toilet designs. The device may be used with a specially-designed toilet seat containing an internal duct and air outlets on its lower surface, or it may be used with a standard toilet seat by drawing gases from the bowl, through the space between the seat and the rim of the bowl, yet above the flood rim level specified in many plumbing codes. The invention also includes an easily disassemble design for sanitary cleaning.

Bureau of Construction Codes: Publisher of "Michigan plumbing code: incorporating the 2000 edition of the International Plumbing Code." Publisher: Bureau of Construction Codes (Lansing, Mich). Published in 2001.

California Building Standards Commission: Publication of "2001 California plumbing code: California code of regulations, Title 24, Part 5." Publisher: California Building Standards Commission (Walnut, CA: International Association of Plumbing and Mechanical Officials; Sacramento, CA). Published in 2001.

Carlos Guerra: "Inert gas fusion analyzer" is patented by Carlos Guerra. Abstract: A single pass analyzer includes multiple infrared sensors, a catalytic converter, a scrubber and a thermal conductivity cell all coupled in series to provide a single pass (i.e., one sample) analyzer which allows for fast analysis, allows for the speciation of hydrogen samples, requires no purging between different sample types, utilizes a single carrier gas, and eliminates molecular sieves and Shutze converters. The resultant analyzer provides improved quicker results with less plumbing (i.e., gas conduits and valving) in a single instrument.

Cary Gloodt: "Hand-held shower system with inline adjustable temperature/pressure balanced mixing valve" is patented by Cary Gloodt. Abstract: A bathtub plumbing system including a hand-held shower controlled by a compact pressure balanced, volume and temperature controlled mixing valve. The pressure-balancing valve is installed in a bathtub plumbing set having a hand-held shower accessory. The pressure balancing valve receives hot and cold water from hand-held shower water feed pipes coupled to the main hot and cold water inlet pipes, respectively, located upstream of the respective hot and cold water control valves used to supply water to the main faucet. The hand-held shower hot and cold feed pipes are each hydraulically connected to a first respective hot and cold water inlet of a compact pressure-balancing valve. The hand-held shower is hydraulically connected to the outlet of the pressure-balancing valve by a flexible hose.

Charles W. Sawyers: "Plating rack" is patented by Charles W. Sawyers. Abstract: A plating rack is provided and is adapted, for example, for use in connection with a physical vapor deposition system for plating components such as plumbing fixtures. The plating rack is adapted to be contained within a plating chamber and includes an elongated main support member. Secured to the elongated support member is a series of axially spaced component support assemblies with each component support assembly adapted to receive and hold an array of components to be plated. Respective components support assemblies are configured such that they include an open side that permits the entire component support assembly to be laterally moved into engagement with the main support member where the component support assembly can be secured thereto.

Christopher L. Cunningham: "Laser leveler" is patented by Christopher L. Cunningham. Abstract: A laser tool is designed to indicate and align measurements, preferably holes to be drilled for hangers that support plumbing and electrical piping, without the need for the use of a tape measure. The laser tool contains an angled base with magnets that allow the tool to remain steady on a pipe. Also included in the base is a bubble level, indicating and allowing the user to balance the tool in relation to the pipe. The laser of the tool is connected to the base by means of a swivel device, so that the user is capable of moving the laser at an angle to obtain additional measurements that are level and aligned with the original measurement for a hole.

Claus D. Zieger: "Spa shower and controller" is patented by Claus D. Zieger. Abstract: Systems and method for providing automated control over both water and temperature and pressure for a plurality of shower heads or other sources of water. The automated systems and methods for providing automated control over both water pressure and temperature make use of three distinct modules which comprise an input and display unit, and electronic processing unit, and the mechanical plumbing control unit. The electronic processing unit receives signals from the input and display unit and translates the received signals into the appropriate control signals for the mechanical plumbing control unit. A user is able to control the output water temperature from each of the shower heads or water sources as well as the individual water pressure from each of the shower heads or water sources.

Critchley, M. M., et al.: "Biofilms and microbially influenced cuprosolvency in domestic copper plumbing systems" appears in Journal of Applied Microbiology written by M. M. Critchley, N. J. Cromar, N. McClure and H. J. Fallowfield. Published in October 2001.

Dennis Roberts, et all.: "System and Method of Connecting Pieces of Plumbing" is patented by Dennis Roberts, Robert Nytko and Dale Hansen.

Eiler Torstensen: "Door framing apparatus and method of use" is patented by Eiler Torstensen. Abstract: A method and apparatus 10 for installing and trimming a plurality of wooden mounting blocks 110 within a roughed out door frame 100 to prepare the roughed out door frame to 100 to receive a finished door frame: wherein, the apparatus 10 includes a pair of vertical standard units 11 11' connected together by a pair of horizontally adjustable spreader units 12 12' that are adapted to cooperate with one another to conform to the outside dimensions of the finished door frame; wherein, each of the vertical standard units 11 11' is provided with a plurality of router templates 27 and means for plumbing each vertical standard unit relative to one of the vertical studs 101 101' in the roughed out door frame 100.

Einar Svensson: "Y-shaped support structure for elevated rail-vehicle guideway" is patented by Einar Svensson. Abstract: The invention is a support structure for a railed-vehicle that includes individual, unassembled components sized for easy transport. In one embodiment, the support structure includes curved columns integrally-formed with a base, the columns imparting a curved, Y-shaped configuration to the support structure. The components may be prefabricated with known materials and methods and transported to an installation site for assembly. The support structure is preferably sized to support one or two vehicle guideways. The support structure may include a pile foundation for improved support during seismic activity and to facilitate installation on existing streets and sidewalks without covering or interfering with underground plumbing or utilities.

Emmanuel Szumer: "Measuring and Leveling Device and Method of Using Same" is patented by Emmanuel Szumer. Abstract: A measuring and leveling device constructed with bubble vials for leveling which are movable to the precise point of application, with the measuring scale situated on a surface so constructed as to allow the scale to be located directly against and parallel to the surface to be measured. The device serves for both measuring and leveling tasks in one tool, and is constructed including a body portion provided with a ruler for measuring distances between points, in which the measuring scale is marked on a surface which tapers to a flat edge as in a conventional ruler.

Erich D. Slothower: "Spout with Vacuum Breaker Protection" is patented by Erich D. Slothower. Abstract: Disclosed herein is a plumbing spout (10) that has back flow protection. The spout (10) positions a check valve vacuum breaker (40) underneath a up knob (12) in a plug assembly (33). The spout (10) provides back flow protection even though it has no fluid control valve for controlling flow through to the outlet.

Evelin Weiss, et al.: "Kitchen appliance with a cooktop receptacle provided in a work surface" is patented by Evelin Weiss, Horst Stedron, Michael Muskalla and Bernd Schultheis. Abstract: A kitchen appliance with a work surface made of a temperature-resistant plastic material or composite plastic material, which has a cooktop receptacle. To reduce the installation effort for use in a row of kitchen appliances, a kitchen sink has cutouts for associated plumbing fixtures and a control panel receptacle is embodied in the work surface, besides the cooktop receptacle. Splash guard edges with support receptacles for support elements for kitchen utensils, kitchen utensil deposits and/or kitchen utensil supports are formed on the work surface.

Garry E. Clark: "Electric valve universal retrofit configuration having misalignment correction" is patented by Garry E. Clark. Abstract: A retrofittable electric valve operating mechanism is provided which can be attached to an existing manual valve configuration while still allowing the manual feature of the valve to be utilized in two different manners. The configuration includes features which allow for certain misalignment of elements lying along the drive path, and can be installed without disturbing the existing plumbing associated with the valve.

Gerald T. Lyons: "Plumbing assembly for hydronic heating system and method of installation" is is patented by Gerald T. Lyons.

Gerard P. Guertin Jr: "Plumbing connection and disconnection system and method" is is patented by Gerard P. Guertin Jr.

Government of Mexico: Rules of Operation for programs of hydroagricultural infrastructure, drinking water, plumbing, and sanitation under the "Comision Nacional del Agua," the National Water Commission, were issued on 14 March 2001 by the "Secretaria de Medio Ambiente y Recursos Naturales," the Secretariat of the Environment and Natural Resources. Table of contents specifies the numerous programs covered by these Rules. Published in Diario Oficial on March 14, 2001.

invention: "Plumbing Installation"

John Hatrick-Smith: "A Pre-Plumbed Shower Door System" is patented by John Hatrick-Smith. Abstract: A shower door system in knocked down from including.

John M. Harmeling: "Multiple level floor flange apparatus and associated method" is patented by John M. Harmeling. Abstract: A floor flange apparatus for use with a plumbing fixture positioned on a floor surface includes a conduit section having a fixture end and a drain end and defining a bore therethrough. The conduit section is adapted to be coupled to a drain pipe proximate the drain end and to be coupled to a plumbing fixture proximate the fixture end for draining water from the plumbing fixture. A flange is positioned proximate the fixture end of the conduit, and the flange is configured to engage a plumbing fixture and couple the fixture to the conduit section. Elevation structures extend from the flange and are configured for interfacing with a floor surface to elevate the flange above the floor surface.

John Tsai: "Plumbing device for a basin drainage" is is patented by John Tsai.

John W. Cantrell: "Drain assembly and sink" is patented by John W. Cantrell. Abstract: A drain assembly is provided that eliminates the need for reconfiguring of existing plumbing during installation of a deep-sink assembly while maintaining a suitable working height. The drain assembly including a hollow body, a valve within the body and a mount to operably connect the valve within the hollow body. The hollow body includes an inlet, an outlet, and an inner wall positioned between the inlet and the outlet. A fluid path enters the inlet of the body in a first direction and is diverted to a second direction substantially perpendicular to the first direction by the inner wall. The diverted fluid path exits the body moving in the second direction. The mount is located at least partially within the outlet.

Johnnie Crean: "Recreational vehicles with walk-in closet" is patented by Johnnie Crean. Abstract: A recreational vehicle having an expandable room wherein the room can be positioned in a retracted or deployed configuration. In the deployed configuration, the room expands inwardly into the main housing of the vehicle so as to enlarge the area of the room without displacing the fixtures and plumbing that are typically positioned adjacent an outer wall of the room. The room can be extended in conjunction with an exterior slide-out assembly wherein the deployed slide-out assembly creates a larger inner living space so as to accommodate the expanded room wherein the expanded room comprises a walk-in closet.

Jorg Hansen, et al.: "Metal-plastic multilayer pipe having form stability for plumbing and hydronic heating" is is patented by Jorg Hansen, Reinhold Freermann, Alfred Feldkamp and Franz-Josef Riesselmann.

Juergen Fleig and Juergen Meier: "Valve seal for a valve upper part, particularly for a water instrument or fitting" is patented by Juergen Fleig and Juergen Meier. Abstract: Sealing device for a valve upper part (18) comprised of a valve housing (20) and a spindle (22) rotatable therein, in particular for plumbing fixtures. The sealing device is comprised of a base disk (32) fixedly associated with the valve housing (20) and a control disk (34) which lies rubbing against the base disk and controlling the water flow through the valve upper part (18). The base disk (32) and control disk (34) are produced from ceramic or ceramic type material. A sealing surface of the base disk (32) facing away from the control disk is held urged against a sealing ring (36) of rubber or rubber like material.

La Vaughn Williams: "Plumbing snake diverting apparatus" is is patented by La Vaughn Williams.

Lance Michael Sweeney, et al.: "Insulated backflow device cover" is patented by Lance Michael Sweeney, Tara Denise Sweeney and Daniel LeRoy ZumMallen. Abstract: A semi-rigid cover for insulating exposed plumbing structures, such as above ground backflow devices, against freezing when exposed to subfreezing temperatures. The device includes an insulative bag and a removable outer cover that is placed over the insulative bag. The insulative bag and outer cover are closed on three sides and open on a fourth. The device also includes a plurality of securing structures, such as grommets, to facilitate securing the device to the plumbing structure with padlocks, combination locks, zip ties and the like. The device further includes a sealing structure, such as a strip of hook and loop fastener, placed along the open edge to facilitate sealing the device about the plumbing structure to minimize drafts into the interior of the device and to exclude pests.

Leonard J. Burns, et al.: "Top mount plumbing fixture" is patented by Leonard J. Burns, Nicholas A. Mascari and Martin Zummersch. Abstract: A plumbing fixture adapted to be installed from the top side of a sink deck through a sink deck opening includes a housing having a body portion which is adapted to extend through the sink deck opening and below the sink deck when mounted. The housing has a shoulder which is adapted to seat on the sink deck when mounted. There is a collar slidably movable on the body portion and of a size to pass through the sink deck opening. A threaded bore is in the collar and an unthreaded bore is in the housing shoulder, and a threaded member extends through these bores, with rotation of the threaded member from above the sink deck moving the collar axially along the housing body portion.

Mark David Hubbard and Thomas Lee Kendall: "Pipe protector and support" is patented by Mark David Hubbard and Thomas Lee Kendall. Abstract: An elongated strap has a plurality of openings sized to hold plumbing pipes extending through the openings. The openings have a periphery that undulates so the periphery extends on opposing sides of the strap to increase the periphery in contact with the pipe along the longitudinal axis of the pipe. A fluid-tight pipe cover releasably connects to further openings in the strap. The pipe cover has a first, open end sized to fit over the pipe. The open end has projections cooperating with the further openings to releasably fasten the cover to the strap. The cover has a closed, distal end that extends beyond the distal end of the pipe during use of the device.

Matthew G. Weir, et all.: "Flexible Hanger Strap Composite" is patented by Matthew G. Weir, M. D. Moore Iii, W. R. Hursey, J. R. Sheppard, Eric J. Knauss and Philbrick Allen. Abstract: A flexible composite fabric is a triple layer material for hanging ductwork, plumbing, and the like, wherein a layer of scrim material is sandwiched between a layer of non-woven material and a layer of metallized film. In a preferred embodiment, a tri-directional polyester scrim fabric is attached to a carded web polyester non-woven fabric using a thin layer of polyvinyl alcohol adhesive. On an opposite side of the scrim, an aluminized, 48 gauge polyester film is attached using a thermoplastic resin. The aluminized film imparts some additional strength to the composite, and provides a pleasing aesthetic feature, as the composite appears in a shiny, metallic color.

Michael W. Johnson, et al.: "Plumbing system test fitting" is patented by Michael W. Johnson, Gregory L. Sesser and Richard E. Schaupp. Abstract: A plumbing test fitting for insertion in a plumbing drain or pressure fluid distribution system includes a body with two spaced-apart lateral ports formed thereon and opening into a central bore of the body. One of the ports is adapted for receiving a hose bib for connection to a source of test fluid and the other port is provided for withdrawing a flexible diaphragm from the interior of the body with a pull member extending through the other port. The flexible diaphragm is retained in the body during a pressure or leakage test of the plumbing system and is removed after completion of the test by tearing the diaphragm away from a supporting rim part.

Michigan. Bureau of Construction Codes Michigan. Dept. of Consumer & Industry Services: Publication of "Michigan Plumbing Code: incorporating the 2000 edition of the International Plumbing Code." Michigan Department of Consumer & Industry Services, Bureau of Construction Codes. Publisher: International Code Council (Lansing, Mich). Published in 2001.

Moen: Sponsored research "Lifetime of Shine." Sponsored by: Moen, Inc., Morth Olmsted, OH.; NASA, Washington, DC. Abstract: Moen Incorporated identified a market need for more durable polished brass plumbing fixtures. NASA's Glenn Research Center is a leader in surface coating technology, which enhances the physical properties of a wide range of materials. The collaborative efforts of Glenn and Moen resulted in a new polished brass finish called LifeShine(R). Based on testing results generated at NASA Glenn, Moen was able to manufacture an affordable, polished brass finish that is as durable as chrome, and resists deterioration. LifeShine is guaranteed to resist normal wear and tear and is even scratch-resistant to cleaning products as abrasive as steel wool.

National Research Council Canada: Publication of "User's guide - National plumbing code of Canada 1995." Issued by the Canadian Commission on Building and Fire Codes. Publisher: National Research Council (Ottawa). Published in 2001.

NSF International: Publication of "NSF listings: plumbing and related products." Publisher: NSF International (Ann Arbor, Mi.). Published in 2001.

2001

Nytek Publishing: Publisher of "Plumbing & HVAC product news Plumbing & HVAC product news Heating, ventilation, air conditioning, refrigeration." Publisher: Nytek Publishing (Toronto). Published in 2001.

Paul Andrew Doyen: "Plumbing sink trap" is patented by Paul Andrew Doyen. Abstract: A plumbing sink trap having a rotatable actuating knob for rotating a sweeper bar through 360.degree. The sweeper bar forms a part of the U-shaped path for waste water. Rotation of the sweeper bar removes obstructions in the U-shaped path.

Prince Sultan Air Base: One new project is the construction of the Wing Operations Center for the US Air Force, Prince Sultan Air Base, Saudi Arabia. The single story pre-engineered building is constructed on concrete footings and is inclusive of electrical system with standby generator and transfer panel, plumbing, water and sewer systems, alarm system and a specialized HVAC and filtration system. It includes administrative space with finishes throughout and with raised flooring in some areas for computer and communications cabling. Tentative date for issuance was 8 June 2001. Tentative date for receipt of proposals was 24 July 2001. Construction period was approximately 8 months. [WP]

Publication: Publication of "Home plumbing." Handyman Club of America. Published in 2001.

Ricardo O. Gray: "Mounting assembly for plumbing control fitting" is is patented by Ricardo O. Gray.

Richard Young: "Apparatus for flow detection, measurement and control and system for use of same" is patented by Richard Young. Abstract: An improvement flow sensor of the type having inlet and outlet ports, a moving plate unit for moving in response to fluid flow through the sensor, a sensor unit for sensing the movement of the moving plate and creating a signal related to its location, and biasing unit for biasing the plate towards the inlet ("base elements"). One improvement comprises the moving plate composed of a magnetizable material and the sensor unit comprised of a steel sensor disposed adjacent to a path traveled by the moving plate for sensing the location of the moving plate.

Rick Rahimzadeh and John Hanna: "Dual size plumbing end cap" is is patented by Rick Rahimzadeh and John Hanna.

Robert L. Cooper and Robert G. Schultz: "Modular vacuum and low pressure valve assembly" is patented by Robert L. Cooper and Robert G. Schultz. Abstract: A modular valve assembly of this invention includes individual valve units and components, which can be selectively combined to form an integrated multi-port, multi-way valve assembly that is operated by a single common linear actuator is disclosed. The modular design of this invention is facilitated by the construction of valve housings and valve components of the individual valve units and assemblies of common plumbing pipes and fittings, such as, tee joints, threaded couplings, bushings and reducers.

Robert M. Vila: "Extendible p-trap dishwasher waste port" is patented by Robert M. Vila. Abstract: The present invention 10 discloses a p-trap 12 for commercial and residential plumbing systems wherein the p-trap 12 has an enlarged portion at 46 for receiving a drainpipe 20 and has a threaded port 22 to receive a pressure hose 16 for a dishwasher 14 waste line. Also disclosed is a deflection shield 24 disposed in operative connection to the threaded port 22 so as to direct waste water 50 downwardly away from the sink 18. The present invention 10 further includes a plurality of multiport PVC pipe fittings in various configurations to provide greater flexibility when plumbing.

Ruben Montalvo: "Pressurized plunger apparatus" is patented by Ruben Montalvo. Abstract: A pressurized plunger apparatus for cleaning drains and other plumbing fixtures of obstacles. The pressurized plunger apparatus includes a pressurizable handle assembly that has an air valve for releasing the compressed air into a chamber area of a plunger member when the device is depressed onto a drain, thereby forcing the compressed air into the plumbing system and clearing the debris.

Rudolf Broghammer and Thomas Kieninger: "Device for Producing Carbonated Drinking

Water" is patented by Rudolf Broghammer and Thomas Kieninger. Abstract: A device for producing carbonated drinking water comprises a mixing device (1), with which carbon dioxide is supplied to the water. This mixing device (1) has a microstructure (9), and said microstructure (9) is assigned to a Peltier element of a cooling device (5). The mixing device (1) provided with the microstructure (9) can be integrated inside a plumbing fixture (16) of a water basin (17) in order to produce carbonated drinking water.

Rudolph V. Ricci: "Plumbing stop valve and method of use" is is patented by Rudolph V. Ricci.

Russell E. Gwynn: "Toilet removal and transportation apparatus" is patented by Russell E. Gwynn. Abstract: A collapsible apparatus is disclosed for lifting and transporting objects, such as toilets and similar plumbing fixtures. The toilet lifter has a support structure and a strap system attached thereto. The support structure has three vertical legs with wheels on the bottoms and horizontal support structures connecting the legs at the tops. The strap system includes a loop strap that engages a bowl of the toilet and rear straps that engage a back or middle portion of the toilet. The strap system is supported by the support structure above the toilet in use and passes across a pivot point on the support structure to raise and lower the toilet. The straps are connected to a toilet, and the strap system is retracted to lift the toilet.

Simon J. Wilson and Howard J. Birch: "Plumbing Fixtures and Plumbing Fitment System" is patented by Simon J. Wilson and Howard J. Birch.

Spain, Bryan J. D.: Author of "Spon's estimating costs guide to plumbing and heating: project costs at a glance." Publisher: Spon Press (London; New York). Published in 2001.

Sunset Books: Publisher of "Sunset complete home plumbing." Publisher: Sunset Books (Menlo Park, Calif). Published in 2001.

Terry L. Miller, et al.: "Fuel conditioning module for reducing air in a fuel injection system" is patented by Terry L. Miller, Phillip M. Hall and Jeffrey L. Castleman. Abstract: Over aeration of fuel has been identified as a problem in some fuel injection systems. For instance, engineers have learned that it is desirable to reduce the amount of air in the fuel circulation plumbing of a pump and line fuel injection system in order to reduce timing retardation of the fuel injection and avoid engine power loss. A fuel conditioning module addresses this problem by separating out the air from the fuel before reaching the fuel injectors. The fuel conditioning module includes an inlet cavity separated from an outlet cavity by a baffle. An inlet passage opens to the inlet cavity, and an outlet passage opens to the outlet cavity at locations elevationally below the top of the baffle.

Thomson, James A.: Author of "2002 National plumbing & HVAC estimator." Publisher: Craftsman Book Co (Carlsbad, CA). Published in 2001.

Timo Anttalainen, et al.: "Waste water collection arrangement" is patented by Timo Anttalainen, Raimo Astikainen, Pentti Koskela, Ilkka Seppa , Veikko Laisi, Pertti Paatalo and Rauno Virtanen. Abstract: A waste water collection arrangement for combining the waste water discharge of several different plumbing fixtures includes a water receiving trap having a chamber in which water is received to provide a gas-tight seal. At least two inlet assemblies deliver waste water to the chamber and at least one outlet assembly discharges water from the chamber. The chamber has a lid part through which the inlet assemblies pass at least substantially perpendicular to the lid part. The inlet assemblies are mounted on the lid part so as to be movable as required to desired positions for connection to waste water conduits. The chamber is essentially isolated from the ambient air.

Ulrich Reiter: "Method for producing a tin film on the inner surface of hollow copper alloy components" is patented by Ulrich Reiter. Abstract: A method for producing an inner tin film on the surface of plumbing components, such as those made of red brass or yellow brass, for drinking water supply. The lead content on the inner surface of the hollow component parts is first reduced by treatment with an acid-based aqueous reducing solution. For this purpose, chloride-free and sulfate-free, non-oxidizing hydracids may be used. The hollow component parts are subsequently chemically internally tinned.

Wendell B. Colson, et al.: "Cladding system and panel for use in such system" is patented by Wendell B. Colson, Lee A. Cole and Jason T. Throne. Abstract: A cladding system for walls or ceilings of a building structure consisting of a panel or panels that are sectioned so as to provide a variety of aesthetics. The sections in the panel may be joined along articulated lines of joinder so that an entire panel comprised of a plurality of sections can be expanded or retracted to either cover or selectively expose the wall or ceiling across which the system is mounted. The sections in a panel may be cellular and may thereby form a honeycomb-type panel, and the materials from which the panels are made may vary between being rigid, flexible, hard, soft, flat, reflective, and the like.

William D. Folsom: "Multiple plumbing vent apparatus" is patented by William D. Folsom. Abstract: An apparatus for venting several plumbing pipes through existing roof openings made for existing ventilation systems, including turbine ventilators, roof ventilators, ridge ventilators and hip ventilators. The plumbing vent apparatus has two sides, a bottom and two removable end caps. End caps for use with a ridge ventilator or hip ventilator have slots for fitting around the ridge rafter. The apparatus is mounted in the roof opening made for the ventilation system, which is installed above it. When used with a ventilation system which has a ridge or hip rafter, the apparatus can be configured to have mounting flanges along the top of the sides for attachment to the roof decking, or can have mounting flanges along the slots on the end caps for attachment to the rafter.

William T. Comer: "Method and system for isolating water pressure from an appliance" is patented by William T. Comer. Abstract: A method and system for isolating water pressure from appliance water connections provides protection from structural damage due to bursting of flexible hoses that connect an appliance to a rigid plumbing water supply. The system includes at least one electrically controllable valve, a connection for coupling the valve to a water supply connection, a connection for attachment to the appliance water supply hoses and an interface for receiving a signal from the appliance control system. An appliance may provide an interface connection for coupling to a control connection on the system, or the system may be connected to existing electrical terminals within a standard appliance that control internal solenoid valves.

Woodrow James Tucker: "Pipe support apparatus" is patented by Woodrow James Tucker. Abstract: Apparatus for supporting the pipes of a plumbing system during the construction of a cement building structure. More specifically, apparatus which is attachable at one end to a form board and at another end to a pipe in order that the position of the pipe be maintained during a concrete pouring operation.

Woodson, Roger Dodge: Born in 1955, authored "Plumbing: tips, data, and rules of the thumb." Publisher: McGraw-Hill (New York). Published in 2001.

Yip, C. C., et al.: "A novel approach for the fixation of enucleated eyes during microsurgical procedures using common household plumbing accessories" appears in Ophthalmic Surgery and Lasers written by C. C. Yip, W. J. Heng, K. G. Au Eong and V. S. Yong. Published in March - April 2001.

2002

Aldo Giusti: "Low lead release plumbing components made of copper based alloys containing lead, and a method for obtaining the same" is is patented by Aldo Giusti.

Alfred I. Pan: "Flex Based Fuel Cell" is patented by Alfred I. Pan. Abstract: A fuel cell uses porous metal layers (104) attached on a flex substrate (101, 102) for delivery of liquid fuel (110) to the active catalytic areas on the anodic side. The flex substrate may form an enclosed package (130) such that the liquid fuel can be contained in the enclosed volume and the air can freely exchange with the cathode side of the fuel cell without the need of microchannels and plumbing for mass transporting both fuel and oxygen to the active catalytic area. The porous metal provides a large surface area for the catalytic reaction to occur.

Ali Heydari Monfarad: "Field replaceable packaged refrigeration heat sink module for cooling electronic components" is patented by Ali Heydari Monfarad. Abstract: A field and/or customer replaceable packaged refrigeration heat sink module is suitable for use in standard electronic component environments. The field replaceable packaged refrigeration heat sink module is self-contained and is specifically designed to have physical dimensions similar to those of a standard air-based cooling system, such as a fined heat sink or heat pipe. As a result, the field replaceable packaged refrigeration heat sink module can be utilized in existing electronic systems without the need for board or cabinet/rack modification or the "plumbing" associated with prior art liquid-based cooling systems.

American Society of Plumbing Engineers, Inc: Publisher of "Plumbing systems & design: official publication of the American Society of Plumbing Engineers." Publisher: American Society of Plumbing Engineers, Inc (Chicago, IL). Published in 2002.

Bill Spiegel: "Flex port base for swimming pool and spa heat pumps" is patented by Bill Spiegel. Abstract: An elevating system for a heat pump through which plumbing may be installed to permit multiple configurations of the plumbing the system consisting of a base having a floor and four sides, the floor having two holes to accommodate the inlet and outlet pipes of the heat pump and a selection of two or four holes in the sides forming an empty space beneath the floor.

Blower, G. J.: Author of "Plumbing: mechanical services." Publisher: Prentice Hall (Upper Saddle River, NJ). Published in 2002.

Brian G. Provencher: "Self-adhesive gasket" is patented by Brian G. Provencher. Abstract: A self-adhesive gasket having a pressure sensitive adhesive on one side or on both sides can be used in place of plumbers putty to seal sinks to countertops, faucets to sinks, and strainers and pop ups to sinks and tubs. The gasket is preferably preformed from a flexible cellular plastic, preferably a closed cell urethane foam. The gasket may be used in a multitude of plumbing application to form a liquid seal.

Canadian Standards Association: Publication of "Plumbing fixtures." Publisher: Canadian Standards Association (Mississauga, Ont). Published in 2002.

Chuying Li: "Laser plumbing and leveling instrument which adjusting height of horizontal line" is is patented by Chuying Li.

Claude Ragot: "Programmable Device for Liquid Distribution" is patented by Claude Ragot. Abstract: The invention relates to a liquid distribution device comprising means of actuating (8) other means (7) which trigger at least one electromagnetic valve (2). The aforementioned trigger means (7) comprise a magnetic sliding piece (14) which can slide, under the effect of the actuation means (8), on a complementary element (2a) of the electrovalve (2) in order to open and close same. The inventive device is characterised in that said actuation means (8) comprise means of connecting with the trigger means (7) which can be de-activated. The inventive device can be used in any system that requires a controlled supply of liquid, such as bathroom plumbing, hydraulic machines, etc.

Connecticut - News: March 20, 2002 — **Headline:** Hartford, Connecticut, Honors Katharine Hepburn. **Excerpt:** Hartford, Connecticut, has long celebrated novelist Mark Twain, who lived in the city for much of his life. Now, Hartford is also saluting its "favorite daughter," the legendary actress Katharine Hepburn, who was born in the city and still lives in Connecticut. Hartford Stage recently presented the world premiere of Tea at Five a one-woman play starring Kate Mulgrew as Ms. Hepburn. It shows two slices of her career: as a young, 31-year-old "struggling" actress; and later, as a 76-year-old Hollywood icon. Now, Hartford residents would like to see more recognition of the city's role in shaping one of America's finest actresses. Katharine Hepburn's performance in the comedy Philadelphia Story is just one of the four films for which she won an Academy Award. University of Hartford President Walter Harrison says the feisty movie star helped transform the depiction of women in film. ... "Around the perimeter of the backyard here -

which abuts the Hartford golf club - used to be some perennial plantings, which I'm slowly trying to grow back. If you take a close look, you'll see some old plumbing. I imagine it was not a typical thing for a sprinkler system to run along the exterior, all along the walls. But it was there," he explains. "The valves are in the basement too. And if you could turn them on, I'm sure [it leads to] some automatic watering system. I wonder how it worked; it certainly doesn't work anymore."

Critchley, Michelle Marie: Born in 1974, authored "Biofilms in copper plumbing systems: sensitivity to copper and chlorine and implications for corrosion." M. M. Critchley, N. J. Cromar, N. McClure and H. J. Fallowfield. Publisher: I. W. A. Publishing (London). Published in 2002.

Darrell Price: "Presealed system" is patented by Darrell Price. Abstract: Presealed System device for walls, floors and roofs. The Presealed System device forms pre-selected openings in floors and walls and roofs in buildings and/or houses and/or during remodeling projects for allowing plumbing pipes and/or electrical conduits to pass therethrough. The devices include stacked or side by side PVC type sleeves with an inwardly protruding portion of a resilient member such as a t cross-sectional shaped washer separating the sleeves from one another. The resilient member also includes a rearwardly extending portion which extends into the walls and floors that can have ridges thereon, and additional portions which are adjacent to exterior sides of the sleeves.

Delaware - News: March 24, 2002 — **Headline:** Hi-Tech Mini-Sub Seeks Delaware Aqueduct Leaks. **Excerpt:** Before becoming Commissioner of the New York City's Department of Environmental Protection the agency which oversees all the city's reservoir and water systems, among other things, Joel A. Miele Senior often marveled at the technical accomplishment the Delaware Aqueduct represents. "Unfortunately, you can't look at it," he pointed out. "It's not that simple because it's essentially buried below the ground deep in the rock that underlies the watershed area and the path from the watershed area down into the City of New York. It's essentially a large hole in the rock." The Delaware Aqueduct is also a very long hole in the rock. Completed in 1945, its 135-kilometer length makes it the longest continuous tunnel ever built. It is over four meters in diameter. However, recent tests showed the aqueduct is leaking about 136 million liters of water every day, a full two percent of its output. While no major rupture is anticipated for at least twenty years, Commissioner Miele decided the time to repair it is now. "It just disturbed me as an environmentalist and as an engineer that this quantity of water would be being lost," he said. But finding and repairing the leaks will not be easy. "It's not very accessible," Mr. Miele observed. "I mean, if you have a plumbing leak in your building or in an office building or even if we have a leak in the street, we dig up a hole in the street, we find the leak, we shut off the water at both ends, we put a clamp on it, we replace a piece of pipe, we close the street and we go on. This thing, again, is 300 meters below the ground in solid rock. There's no way to get at it from the outside and it's got a lot of water flowing in the inside. So it's not your normal plumbing repair." **Author:** Adam Phillips.

Dennis Baldwin and Debra Baldwin: "Plumbing plunger support and storage device" is is patented by Dennis Baldwin and Debra Baldwin.

Dennis E. Bowman: "Reject water drain line installation system and apparatus for under sink reverse osmosis filter system" is patented by Dennis E. Bowman. Abstract: Reject waste water adapter coupling fitting, for use with a household undercounter reverse osmosis (R/O) water filtration installation associated with an in-counter sink with its outlet connected by standard slip fit S/J plumbing fittings to a sink drain trap plumbed to the household sewer system.

Dennis Klein: "Mixed gas generator" is patented by Dennis Klein. Abstract: The present invention is a device, which generates a hydrogen and oxygen gas, preferably used for welding. The hydrogen and oxygen gas is generated by an electrolyzing process. Electrolyte is pumped into the hydrogen-oxygen generator where the gas is separated from the electrolyte by applying a direct current voltage across the generator. Oxygen is formed in one part, hydrogen in the other and then combined to form the gas. As the gas is generated, pressure is built up. When the pressure reaches an operating pressure, the gas is pumped via the plumbing system into the electrolyte reservoir, through a filtering process, and stored in a gas reservoir that is connected to a supply line. In operation the supply line is attached to a torch.

Donald P. Freier: "Water Spout with Removable Laminar Flow Cartridge" is patented by Donald P. Freier. Abstract: A water spout is capable of providing laminar flowing fluid from a wall-mounted or faucet fixture body (10).

Edward Archie McCulloch: "Composite building material and panels made therefrom" is patented by Edward Archie McCulloch. Abstract: A composite material that is formed into basic structural panels that can be subsequently assembled into the floors, walls, roof trusses, and roofs of buildings by unskilled labor having access to basic tools is disclosed. Thus, basic shelter, low-cost houses and various other structures, such as schools, churches, clinics, and storage facilities may be constructed to address the need for such structures in economically-distressed countries with large populations. The building material for the panels is a molded polymer composite, made from either homogeneous or non-homogeneous materials.

Frank C. Bien: "Applicator Assembly for Application of Adhesives, Sealants and Coatings" is patented by Frank C. Bien. Abstract: A melter, mixer and applicator system (10) for applying coating or sealing compositions is disclosed. An internal combustion engine (18), such as a diesel engine, is used to provide the motive force necessary to operate many or all of the components of the system (10). A tank (26) surrounded by an internal heating system is provided for melting a first material, such as asphalt. An insulated cabinet (44) is provided and heated from heat generated by the internal heating system. The plumbing configuration (120) for the system is disposed within the heated cabinet (44) for mixing the material heated within the tank (26) with an additional material fed to the plumbing configuration (120) by a proportioner pump (110).

Frank Perla: "Water delivery device and method of forming same" is patented by Frank Perla. Abstract: A plumbing part in the form of a water delivery device is comprised of a protective liner through which potable water can flow. The protective liner is in the form of one or more lengths of stainless steel tubing and is encased in a casting of a desired material, such as bronze or brass. Fittings required to attach the water delivery device to sinks, bathtubs or other water sources and to allow for insertion of various aerators and other flow devices are also encased in the casting. The various fittings are pre-assembled to the liner prior to casting to ensure a water-tight seal between the liner and the fittings prior to casting.

Frederick E. Coffman: "Domestic hot water distribution and resource conservation system" is patented by Frederick E. Coffman. Abstract: A domestic water distribution system that continuously delivers heated water to one or more hot water faucets. The system utilizes a convective return loop from the desired faucets, which is regulated by a flow control device. The control device is specifically designed to allow unhindered flow during circulation without allowing reverse flow when a faucet is opened. The flow control device has an easily accessible handwheel adjustment that is used to select the three modes of operation and the flow rate. These modes are called: HELD-ON, HELD-OFF, and NORMAL-OPERATION. With the first two modes being used to fill and flush the system as is necessary with new installation and recreation vehicles.

Gerardo R. Pardo and Alberto J. Pardo: "Anti-splash guard" is patented by Gerardo R. Pardo and Alberto J. Pardo. Abstract: An anti-splash guard to enclose the open upper portion of a toilet bowl to shield and contain liquid and matter splashing from the interior thereof when attempting to unclog or dislodge debris from the plumbing when using a plunger including an upper elongated handle and a lower plunger member, the anti-splash guard comprising a cover with or without an upper opening to receive a portion of the upper elongated handle therethrough and a lower opening to receive a portion of the toilet bowl such that when the anti-splash guard is operatively mounted on the toilet with the lower plunger member disposed therein liquid and matter is shielded and contained when splashed therefrom when the plunger is used to dislodge debris from the plumbing.

Government of Taiwan: The amendment of 18 December 2002 applies to the Running Water Law and adds additional articles 93-1, 93-2, 93-3, 93-4, 93-5, 93-6, repeal articles 15, 37, revises articles 2, 3, 4, 6, 10, 11, 12-1, 13, 14, 25, 26, 27, 30, 31, 32, 35, 38, 39, 42, 46, 49, 55, 58, 59, 60, 81, 107, 108, 110 and 112. The essential points are: 1)That due to streamlining of the Taiwan provincial government, it no longer acts as the competent authority under this law. 2)To repeal articles 15 and 37, the former regards the Taiwan provincial government may borrow money from the running water enterprises to set up a running water circulation foundation, and the latter deals with an existing running water enterprise prior to taking effect of this law shall, within six months after taking effect of this law, file with the provincial (city) competent authority for granting concessions. 3)That the central authority governing running water shall, in conjunction with the central authorities governing environmental protection and health, enact regulations governing running water quality standards. 4)To indicate the activities that shall be prohibited or restricted in the water quality and quantity protection areas. 5)To impose administrative penalties on a plumbing contractor for violation of the stipulations listed under articles 93-1, 93-2 and 93-3, the penalties include warning, suspension of business, and nullification of business license. 6)To impose administrative penalties on a plumber for violation of the stipulations listed under articles 93-4, 93-5 and 93-6, the penalties include warning, and suspension of working. 7)To impose fines on a plumbing contractor for violation of aforesaid items 5 and 6, and impose fines on an unlicensed plumber, or a plumber whose license having been nullified. Published in The Gazette of the Office of the President on December 18, 2002.

Graham M. Teal: "Flushable bowl protecting liner" is patented by Graham M. Teal. Abstract: A flushable bowl protecting liner for reducing the need for manual cleaning by providing a barrier between the bowl of the toilet and solid waste. The flushable bowl protecting liner includes a barrier material that is flat and rigid when dry and rendered flexible when in contact with water. In its' dry state the liner may set into a toilet bowl above the water level. As solid waste is deposited onto the material the moisture would allow the material to wrap about the waste material. By reason of the barrier's design pattern of radial incisions the waste would be fully enclosed. The material would provide not only a barrier to prevent the deposit of solid waste on the toilet bowl but a low friction package that would prevent plumbing blockages.

Harry Kazanjian and Margaret Kazanjian: "Hydro-energy conversion system" is patented by Harry Kazanjian and Margaret Kazanjian. Abstract: A hydro-energy conversion system that comprises a hydraulic turbine rotor, a turbine housing that is rotatably connected to the hydraulic turbine rotor and a turbine cover that is detachably connected to the turbine housing. A mounting flange is connected to the turbine housing. An input plumbing fitting is connected to the turbine housing. An output plumbing fitting is connected to the turbine housing. A generator is coupled to the hydraulic turbine rotor.

Henkenius, Merle: Born in 1950, authored "Plumbing Book: basic, intermediate & advanced projects." Publisher: Crabtree Publishing (Upper Saddle River, N.J.). Published in 2002.

Henry H. Holzgrefe: "System and method for measuring ventricular function" is patented by Henry H. Holzgrefe. Abstract: A system and method for measuring ventricular function in an isolated, perfused heart using an intraventricular balloon connected to a plumbing circuit containing a fluid, the plumbing circuit including (a) a valve for selectively opening the plumbing circuit to (i) atmospheric pressure or (ii) a pressure control circuit of a pressure control apparatus or (b) a pressure control apparatus which can be selectively connected to the plumbing circuit, including the steps of establishing a base pressure by (1) opening the valve to atmospheric pressure or the pressure control circuit or (2) operating the pressure control apparatus, after equalization of the pressure within the intraventricular balloon with the base pressure.

Homer F. Savard, et al.: "Modular animal boarding system" is patented by Homer F. Savard, Daniel E. Blackburn and Gary Silvis. Abstract: A modular, double-height animal boarding system which can be installed inside a building having limited headroom while permitting persons up to six feet in height to enter lower runs without stooping. The boarding system has a lower section divided into plural lower runs, each lower run having a rear wall and a door that opens outwardly away from the rear wall. At least one upper section is supported above the lower section and is divided into plural upper runs. The upper runs have doors that open onto a catwalk.

Icon Group Ltd: Publisher of "The 2000-2005 world outlook for misc plastic prod exc bottles & plumbing." Publisher: Icon Group Ltd (San Diego, Calif). Published in 2002.

International Code Council: Publisher of "International plumbing code commentary 2000." Publisher: International Code Council (Falls Church, Va.). Published in 2002.

Jackson, Albert: Born in 1943, authored "Popular mechanics home how-to: Plumbing and heating." Publisher: Hearst Books (New York). Published in 2002.

James C. Barnitz: "Method of Delivering Liquid Through Cerebral Spinal Pathway" is patented by James C. Barnitz. Abstract: Provided is a method of delivering a physiologically acceptable liquid into the cerebral spinal pathway at high flow rates : initiating flow into a ventricular catheter, through a cerebral spinal pathway, and out a lumbar outflow catheter with the patient in a supine position and using a first flow rate, wherein a positive first value for an outlet pressure is maintained in plumbing from the lumbar outflow catheter ; and increasing flow to a second flow rate greater than the first in conjunction with decreasing the outlet pressure to a second, negative value.

Jay D. White: "Vehicle Axle Vent Tube" is patented by Jay D. White. Abstract: A vent tube for hollow axles of heavy-duty vehicles such as semi-trailers releases built-up air pressure from the wheel hub and axle while preventing ingress of contaminants into the axle and hub. The vent tube includes a tubular portion preformed from a flexible material into a generally coiled configuration. The tubular portion is biased to the coiled state so that when stretched about the axle and released, it firmly grips the axle without the need for fasteners. One end of the tubular portion includes fitting for plumbing into the axle and the opposite end includes a one-way check valve such as a duck bill.

Jean-Marie Tandart: "Expansion Tool Device for Socket Pliers" is patented by Jean-Marie Tandart. Abstract: The invention concerns an expansion tool device for pliers used for producing sockets at the ends of pipes (T) made of plastic material or the like use in plumbing systems.

Jerome M. Arvin: "Plumbing workstation" is is patented by Jerome M. Arvin.

John B. Coffey and Walter G. Kaiser: "Water monitoring system" is patented by John B. Coffey and Walter G. Kaiser. Abstract: A water monitoring and control system adapted for residential and commercial use automatically shuts off the water supply after a predetermined period of time, whether the flow is intentional or unintentional, thereby preventing damage from leaks and other malfunctions. The system also gives an indication of all water flow ranging from normal usage to leakage of a few drops and large flow, as would typically occur due to a break in the plumbing system. The system is easily bypassed in the event of power outages. In terms of hardware, the main components of the system include a normally closed water shut-off valve, preferably solenoid-operated.

John Pinciaro: "Hydrotherapy jet system having fluid line quick connector adapted for multiple sizes of jet fixture bodies and other plumbing fittings" is is patented by John Pinciaro.

John R. Wilson and Steven R. Oliver: "Control stop cap friction ring" is patented by John R. Wilson and Steven R. Oliver. Abstract: A cap assembly for closing an access opening in a plumbing fitting includes a cap for rotatable attachment to the plumbing fitting, with the cap having an interior surface which faces the plumbing fitting. There is an elastomeric friction ring positioned between the cap interior surface and the plumbing fitting, which friction ring has a plurality of circumferentially spaced projections facing and in contact with the plumbing fitting. The projections are formed and adapted to require less torque when the cap is rotatably attached to the plumbing fitting than when said cap is rotatably removed from the plumbing fitting.

Kenneth R. Cornwall: "Hub seal firestop device" is patented by Kenneth R. Cornwall. Abstract: A firestop device (10) and firestop assembly for use in a plumbing system (100) installed in a structure to prevent the transmission of smoke and fire through the plumbing system. The firestop device includes a housing (12) with a connector (14) and intumescent material (16) mounted in the inner passageway (12C) of the housing. The firestop device is intended to be mounted over the hub portion (50B) of a plumbing fitting (50). When the housing is heated, the heat is transferred to the intumescent material which expands. As the intumescent material expands, the material crushes the conduit (102) extending through the firestop device and completely blocks the inner passageway (10C) of the firestop device which prevents smoke and fire from moving through the firestop device.

Larry R. Kondas and Robert N. Sanford: "In ground hose well" is patented by Larry R. Kondas and Robert N. Sanford. Abstract: A corrosion resistant enclosure adapted to be recessed below the ground which allows a covering lid to be placed about an opening at the upper end of the housing substantially parallel to the surrounding terrain. The housing is preferably cylindrically shaped, having a larger diameter at the bottom than at the top. However, the housing may take any desired shape, such as rectangular, elliptical, cubic, etc without departing from the intended scope of the invention. The housing also includes a supply of pressurized water which is hooked up to the supply of water previously utilized for the above-ground stored garden hose through any conventional plumbing arrangement.

Maine - News: January 13, 2002 — **Headline:** Portland, Maine, is New Refugee Haven. **Excerpt:** Large American cities, such as New York, Los Angeles, Chicago and Miami, attract most of the immigrants and political refugees in this country. But in the past decade or two, some smaller cities have seen a steady growth of the foreign-born population. The coastal city of Portland, in the north-eastern state of Maine, is one of them. During the 1990s, Maine admitted more than 7,000 immigrants and resettled more than 4,000 refugees. Most of them live in and around Maine's largest city, Portland. ... "In fact, in the last 15 years, Portland has enjoyed a remarkable renaissance, a sort of rebirth of its downtown area and lot of that can be credited to immigrants families, not just refugees, but to immigrant families who have come and bought up houses that nobody else wanted," said Mr. Ward. "Again, many, many, many immigrants and certainly many refugees bring skills like carpentry, plumbing, electrical work. They can do the stuff themselves, you know, so they are not afraid to buy a house that is a little dilapidated and make it look good."

Martin S. Laugesen: "A Disposable Absorptive Article" is patented by Martin S. Laugesen. Abstract: The present invention concerns a disposable article for absorbing a liquid, wherein the article has a substantially non-liquid permeable layer forming an outer packaging surface of the article, and an absorptive material, wherein the outer packaging surface surrounds at least one side of the absorptive material, and wherein said outer packaging surface further includes an opening, through which liquid can pass into the absorptive material. The invention also relates to a method of producing an article and the use of said article in for example the plumbing business, as a drip absorbent, as a residual liquid absorbent, and as a condensate absorbent.

Massachusetts - News: June 17, 2002 — **Headline:** Used Building Materials Grow More Popular. **Excerpt:** It's said that one man's trash is another man's treasure. That's especially true in the used building supply trade, where cast-offs from one re-decorated home or office might fit perfectly into another. Landfills in Massachusetts are becoming saturated with rejects from house renovations. So some local entrepreneurs have come up with a solution to the environmental problem, while also making home improvement more affordable. A sprawling suburban home in Northampton, Massachusetts is going through a major renovation that includes a new kitchen, bay windows and modern fixtures. "We're always taking out windows and doors and cabinets and all sorts of things in perfectly good condition, or at least restorable condition, but can't be used on a construction site, said contractor Nelson Shifflet, who adds that on large projects, his crew can end up with 5-10 tons of perfectly usable materials to throw away. "Previously we would not have a source for these, and we can't store them in our warehouse." he said. "We just end up with a warehouse full of stuff that we took to the landfill anyway, and that's just a shame to see that happen." Now Mr. Shifflet has a way to ease his environmental conscience, and save money on dumping fees. He takes his clients' rejects to the Re-Store, a new business in nearby Springfield that re-sells used building supplies. Set in an industrial section of the city, the store is filled with shutters, sinks, bathtubs, cabinets and vinyl replacement windows - most priced at about half the retail value. Store manager Holly Milton-Benoit says there's something for everyone. "Right now we're in the lighting and plumbing department, and we carry all different types," she said. "In chandeliers, we'll have something that ranges from ultra-modern with large globe lights and silver droops, to something a little more ornate, like a three-tiered tobacco-stained fixture that would be great for someone with high ceilings."

Michael Brent Ford: "Method and system for controlling a household water supply" is patented by Michael Brent Ford. Abstract: A method and system for controlling a household water supply provides protection of structures and fixtures from water damage due to plumbing failure or other causes. The household water supply is shut-off in conformity with a determination that the household is unoccupied and thereby provides automatic protection from water damage.

Michael James McCrea and Dave Brown: "Refrigerator door mounted water dispensing assembly" is patented by Michael James McCrea and Dave Brown. Abstract: A portable water dispensing module is mounted to a refrigerator door inner liner. The liner has side walls with aligned vertically spaced module supports. The water dispensing module comprises a reservoir having a fill chamber located above a main reservoir. The fill chamber has a lid that has an opening closed by a cap. The reservoir supports the fill chamber and has side walls with anchoring supports that releasably and matingly engage with the module supports on the liner side walls to mount the water dispensing module against the liner walls. A lower recessed portion of the front wall of the reservoir protects a spigot, mounted into the recess, from inadvertent contact with a user.

Michael W. Minnick: "Plumbing fixture supply assembly" is patented by Michael W. Minnick. Abstract: A valve outlet assembly for mounting to a building structure and adapted to interconnect a water supply line to a plumbing fixture or an appliance. The outlet assembly has a housing enclosure, an exterior cover and alignment and mounting assemblies which cooperate with the housing structure. A valve structure is mounted in the housing to a conduit fitting which extends through a housing wall. The valve structure is constructed and arranged to receive a water line extending to the appliance. The housing enclosure has opposing alignment and mounting assemblies which provide for various securement options to position the valve outlet assembly within a building wall.

Napier, J. A.: "Plumbing the depths of PUFA biosynthesis: a novel polyketide synthase-like pathway from marine organisms" appears in Trends in Plant Science written by J. A. Napier. Published in February 2002.

National Inst. for Occupational Safety and Health: Sponsored research "Fatality Assessment and Control Evaluation (FACE) Report: Career Fire Fighter Dies from Injuries When Stationary Fill Tank Becomes Over-Pressurized and Suffers Catastrophic Failure in California, July 10, 2002." Sponsored by: National Inst. for Occupational Safety and Health, Cincinnati, OH. Div. of Safety

Research. Abstract: On July 26, 2001, a 36-year-old male career fire fighter (the victim) was killed when filling the water tank of a new engine. On July 28, 2001, the U.S. Fire Administration notified the National Institute for Occupational Safety and Health (NIOSH) of this incident. A safety and occupational health specialist (SOHS) from the NIOSH Fire Fighter Fatality Investigation and Prevention Program investigated the incident from August 7-10, 2001. The NIOSH investigator met with the fire department chief, the battalion chief, a representative of the California Department of Forestry and Fire Protection, and a representative of the company that provided maintenance for the stationary fill tank involved in the incident.

Nelson, Thomas Erle: Author of "Designing plumbing and drainage systems for a solar powered house." Published in 2002.

New York: Publication of "Plumbing code of New York State." New York State Department of State, Division of Code Enforcement and Administration. Publisher: New York State Dept. of State (Falls Church, VA: International Code Council; Albany, NY). Published in 2002.

New York - News: July 8, 2002 — **Headline:** Kris Delmhorst Presents Her Latest CD, Five Stories. **Excerpt:** Kris Delmhorst grew up in Brooklyn, New York, studying classical cello, and playing with folk singers and jazz bands. She made her way to the folk music hub of Boston in 1996 and has quickly taken her place among the most-promising of the new generation of songwriters with her newest CD Five Stories. "Broken White Line" is one of 11 original songs on Five Stories, Kris Delmhorst's second CD. The music community was quick to make room for the newcomer when she first stepped on stage in 1995. Today, she is selling out the northeast's largest venues and playing over 150 shows a year in clubs, coffee houses, festivals and theaters across the USA. ... A desire to explore led her to a job on a farm in rural Maine after graduation, where she lived in a little log cabin having neither electricity nor plumbing. She said her goal was to get as far away from her growing up experiences as she could think of. **Author:** Katherine Cole.

Niles H. Singer: "Adjustable shower system" is patented by Niles H. Singer. Abstract: An adjustable shower system for providing multiple showerheads in various locations within a shower without requiring additional plumbing. The adjustable shower system includes a plurality of tubes having opposing female couplers, a plurality of connecting tubes having opposing threaded ends for threadably receiving the female couplers, a control valve fluidly connected to the connecting tube, a showerhead fluidly connected to the control valve, a plurality of suction cups attached to the connecting tube and the tubes, and an end cap attached to that distal threaded end of the last connecting tube. A first tube is fluidly connected to the existing shower pipe within a shower stall by simply removing the existing shower head.

North Carolina. Building Code Council: Publication of "North Carolina plumbing code: 2000 International plumbing code with North Carolina amendments." North Carolina Building Code Council and North Carolina Dept. of Insurance. Published in 2002.

Oswald Peter Meli: "Connection for a water meter" is patented by Oswald Peter Meli. Abstract: A pipe loop (10) for fitting a water meter (12) to a plumbing installation includes a pipe coupling having an adapter (20) with an inlet (22) and an outlet (24) and being adapted to be connected in a straight length of pipe (14) in the plumbing installation, the adapter (20) defines a seat formation (26) between the inlet (22) and outlet (24).

Parker, Philip M.: Born in 1960, authored "The 2002 world market forecasts for imported sanitary, plumbing, heating, and lighting fixtures." Publisher: Icon Group Ltd (San Diego, Calif). Published in 2002.

Paul A. Sommerfeld Sr: "Air gap cleaning method" is patented by Paul A. Sommerfeld Sr. Abstract: A method of cleaning an air gap in a plumbing fixture by removing the cap from a counter table access and inserting a flexible wire brush into a hose connecting the counter-top access to the drain opening.

Paul Joseph Candela: "Water leak mitigation system" is patented by Paul Joseph Candela.

Abstract: A water leak mitigation device comprising a power supply, a building systems interface, a plumbing interface, and a monitoring device is provided. The monitoring device produces a primary input to the building systems interface. Upon receipt of the primary input, the building systems interface instructs the plumbing interface to restrict water flow to the associated building. Upon receipt of a secondary input produced by a building device when the building device requires water for operation, the building systems interface instructs the plumbing interface to resume the flow of water to the building so as to permit the operation of the building device.

Phinney, Dennis: Author of "The Daniel Boyle Engineering code finder for building and construction: building codes, fire codes, plumbing codes, mechanical codes, electrical codes, public works standards." Publisher: BNi Building News (Irvine, Calif). Published in 2002.

Pinede Publishing: Publisher of "Plumbing, heating & air movement news." Publisher: Pinede Publishing (Barton Turn, Barton-under-Needwood, Staffordshire). Published in 2002.

Rachel Carson - News: September 18, 2002 — **Headline:** Visiting the Homestead of a Landmark Environmentalist. **Excerpt:** In 1962, a controversial book about the environmental and human health dangers of chemical pesticides sparked a major shift in public thinking about the environment. The book was Silent Spring. Its author was Rachel Carson. ... The Carson house had no indoor plumbing or heat. But there was a piano in the parlor where Maria Carson Rachel's mother gave piano lessons and in Maria Carson's upstairs bedroom stand a small coal stove and an old foot-powered sewing machine. **Author:** Rosanne Skirble.

Ricardo O. Gray, et al.: "Combined faucet and drain assembly" is patented by Ricardo O. Gray, Jeffrey L. Mueller, Perry D. Erickson and Mark F. McMullen. Abstract: A combined faucet and drain system can be installed primarily from above the basin. The faucet includes a quick-connect fastening assembly with a threaded sleeve bolt that also doubles as a life rod guide. A spring-biased toggle fastener threads onto the sleeve bolt and collapses when inserted through an installation opening from above the basin. It then automatically unfolds and engages an undersurface when the sleeve bolt is turned. The drain assembly is mounted in a drain opening of the basin and includes a movable stopper guide that can be used during installation to align the drain flange to the drain body from above the sink. A method of installing a combined faucet and drain assembly to a plumbing fixture is also disclosed.

Rice - News: April 5, 2002 — **Headline:** Rice Genome Deciphered, Could Help Ease Global Hunger. **Excerpt:** In an achievement that promises to help ease global hunger, two papers published Thursday in the journal "Science" describe the genetic blueprints of two varieties of rice. Experts say the development stands to improve a crop that feeds more than half the world's people. It could have other benefits as well. Rice is the food staple for approximately 67 percent of the world's population. Like many crops, the grain is subject to the whims of nature, including draught, disease, and gnawing insects. ... Another possibility, according to Purdue University's Jeff Bennetzen, is plumbing the rice genome for information for his area of study - corn. "Rice and wheat and barley and corn all have very similar genes... They have only diverged from a common ancestor from 50 to 70-million years," he says.

Robert D. House: "Lockable railing trough" is patented by Robert D. House. Abstract: The present invention is to a lockable railing trough. The railing trough may have end panels, forming a bin. The locking mechanism comprises a mechanically separate item from the trough. The trough or bin may be hung on a railing, perhaps on a man lifter, by a hook portion of the trough or bin and locked there with the locking mechanism, which engages the trough or bin and not the railing. The trough or bin may hang on the inside of the railing or on the outside of the railing. Matched pairs of troughs and/or bins may be arranged in saddle-bag fashion, with their hook portions overlapping over the railing. A plurality of bins and troughs may be used on a plurality of railings on a single man lifter.

2002

Robert G. Garber: "Single cartridge filter housing" is patented by Robert G. Garber. Abstract: A single cartridge filter housing assembly for the filtration of etching liquids, deionized water, slurries and other liquids used in the semiconductor, pharmaceutical and chemical industries. It comprises a bottom housing and a top housing with an O-ring in between and a nut ring engaging top and bottom housings in order to compress the O-ring thus forming a sealed cavity for the cartridge. The bottom housing holds the nose of the cartridge in a concentric recess and holds the cartridge top centered by several radial protrusions in its mouth. An inlet and an outlet at the bottom of the bottom housing for the liquid to be filtered are coaxial for easy plumbing connections.

Robert J. Schindler, et al.: "Night light for plumbing fixtures" is is patented by Robert J. Schindler, Srianath K. Aanegola, Greg E. Burkholder, Frank P. Dornauer, Mitchell J. Hart, Kerry D. Moore, James T. Petroski and Tomislav J. Stimac.

Roger Harper: "Plumbing flood control system" is patented by Roger Harper. Abstract: A control system for stopping a plumbing-related flooding situation in a building includes at least one sensor for accumulating water and producing a low voltage electrical control signal when sufficient water is accumulated. An actuating system receives the control signal and in turn routes 110 volt current to an electrically activated valve located in a main feed conduit of the plumbing system. The reopening of the valve is achieved by a manually operated electrical switch.

Russia - News: June 3, 2002 — **Headline:** St. Petersburg's Mariinsky Hospital in Continuous Operation for 200 Years. **Excerpt:** The northern Russian city of St. Petersburg is racing to restore its historic buildings, palaces and monuments in time for its 300th birthday celebration next year. City officials are vowing they will also upgrade infrastructure and such things as schools and hospitals. Looking through the wrought-iron fence, one might easily mistake this for an old theater or a small palace. The exterior paint is faded and the facade crumbling, but the building still exudes grandeur with its graceful white columns. ... Nurse Baranovskaya admits the hospital is in need of repairs. "The floor, plumbing, lighting we wish it were better," she said. "We wish things worked properly. We wish we had enough cold and hot water, we wish the sinks and toilets would not leak. We hope things do not fall off the ceiling ... you can see this leak in the ceiling; it happened when we had a lot of snow on the roof. The building is very old [so] of course, it is very difficult."

Saunders, N. M.: Author of "Sprinklers for houses: combination domestic plumbing and fire sprinkler systems: BRANZ design guide." Publisher: BRANZ (Porirua City, N. Z.). Published in 2002.

Shawn D. Bush: "Retrofit for mechanical combination plumbing fixture" is is patented by Shawn D. Bush.

Shea, Kevin Bruce: Author of "Plumbing fixture patterns through audio sampling." Published in 2002.

Standards Australia International Limited: Publication of "Air admittance valves (AAVs) for use in sanitary plumbing and drainage systems." Published in 2002.

Steven G. Dvorak: "Combination air gap for dish washer and soap dispenser" is patented by Steven G. Dvorak. Abstract: A structure is mounted on a sink top or counter top between a dishwasher discharge line and a vented plumbing line to provide an anti-siphon feature for a household dishwashing machine. The structure also includes in combination a pump-type soap dispenser. The pump-type soap dispenser includes a push-actuated pump to pump liquid soap from a reservoir bottle, and the pump slides into and out of a mounting collar for ease of removal to facilitate refilling the reservoir bottle.

Texas. Sunset Advisory Commission: Publication of "Texas State Board of Plumbing Examiners: Sunset staff report." Publisher: Sunset Advisory Commission (Austin, Tex). Published in 2002.

Thompson, Kay: Born in 1911, authored "Kay Thompson's Eloise takes a bawth." Drawings by Hilary Knight; additional plumbing by Mart Crowley. (Eloise takes a bawth). Publisher: Simon & Schuster Books for Young Readers (New York;

London). Published in 2002.

Travis G. Funseth and Kent Alvin Klemme: "Sprayer flood tip and nozzle body assembly" is patented by Travis G. Funseth and Kent Alvin Klemme. Abstract: A nozzle assembly includes a plastic, one-piece flood tip that attaches directly over the bayonet connector of a nozzle body. The nozzle body is of the diaphragm type for reduced weight, cost and complexity but modified to increase flow capacity. In one embodiment, a 90-degree bayonet is provided on the nozzle body turret, and other bayonet selections are also available on the turret for flat fan spray patterns. In a second embodiment, a conventional radially extending bayonet pattern is provided, and the flood tip itself is fabricated with a 90-degree turn. The plumbing system utilized for high spray rate applications with the flood tip is the same as for lower rate spraying using a different tip mounted on other bayonet connector on the turret.

U.S. - News: October 10, 2002 — **Headline:** Astronauts Assemble New Parts to Space Station in Space Walk. **Excerpt:** U.S. astronauts lengthened the international space station's new backbone Thursday. They added another section of aluminum girder, work that employed the station's robot arm and two spacewalkers. The girder is a 15 meter long, 13 metric ton framework that is packed with several kilometers of tubing and wiring to support cooling, power, and data relay equipment for future research laboratories. ... Then two Atlantis spacewalkers began the process of connecting plumbing, optical fiber, and electrical lines to bring the truss to life. They also unlatched two big radiators from their launch position to put them in the best position to release heat.

Uleses Alba: "Ventilated commode device, kit and method of using" is patented by Uleses Alba. Abstract: A new and improved ventilated commode device, kit and method of using is disclosed for using the device in removing odorous vapors from the immediate vicinity of the device into a sewer line. The ventilated commode device comprises a seat having a plurality of input vent holes fluidly communicating to an internal air passageway and terminating with an output vent hole positioned at the rear portion of the seat. The device also comprises a hinge having an air pathway fluidly connected to the output vent hole of the seat and fluidly connected to a hollow chamber in a toilet bowl. The hollow chamber comprises an air pump which actively moves the captured odorous vapors from the hollow chamber into the rear portion of the waste water drainage network of the toilet.

United States - News: January 20, 2002 — **Headline:** Concrete Goes to College. **Excerpt:** Mix sand, and water, and powdered stone called "cement," and what do you get? As humans have known since the Roman Empire, you get concrete. In the United States alone, concrete work accounts for one-third of the $250 billion construction industry. A university in the southern state of Tennessee is mixing sand, water, cement, and four full years of classes and producing the world's first college degree in "concrete management" Like plumbing, hairdressing, and carpentry, pouring concrete is blue-collar work. But Middle Tennessee State University, in the little city of Murfreesboro near the state capital of Nashville, offers a full, four-year concrete curriculum.

United States - News: February 17, 2002 — **Headline:** John Glenn Remembers Friendship 7. **Excerpt:** February 20 marks the 40th anniversary of John Glenn's historic Friendship Seven flight. Peter King looks back at the mission that first put an American astronaut into orbit. When Marine Colonel John Glenn became the first American in orbit 40 years ago, he was no longer just the son of an Ohio plumber. He had become one of the most celebrated Americans in history. "That wasn't something I was concentrating on at all, I can guarantee you," said Mr. Glenn. "I was just trying to get trained as well as I could to do the job. We thought it was important for the country. It wasn't a self interest thing as much as it was for the country because remember we were in the depths of the Cold War then." ... Forty years after Friendship 7, John Glenn says he tries to keep his historic role in perspective. On his desk sits one of his father's old, oily plumbing wrenches - to remind him, he says, of where he came from. Framed images from his astronaut days and his career in Washington are constant reminders of just how far he's gone.

United States - News: June 10, 2002 — **Headline:** Mob Boss John Gotti Dies in Prison. **Excerpt:** Convicted mob boss, John Gotti, 61, died in a U.S. federal prison Monday. Correspondent in reports Gotti was the head of one of the most notorious crime families in the United States. Gotti was serving a life sentence for murder and racketeering when he died of throat cancer. The former mob boss was the head of New York's Gambino crime family, one of the city's most powerful mafia rings. Gaining national attention as a "criminal" celebrity, he was seen as one of the most notorious gangsters in the nation. Although Gotti tried to pass himself off as a plumbing supply salesman, he was convicted in 1992 of racketeering and six killings. One of his victims included the former mob boss, "Big Paul" Castellano, whom he succeeded as "head of the family."

United States - News: July 25, 2002 — **Headline:** Western US Tries to Cope With Worst Drought in 100 Years. **Excerpt:** The Western United States is undergoing a major drought, and a looming water shortage threatens to make conditions worse in coming years. Regional officials are working on a plan to avert a crisis. Water-hungry Los Angeles is a case in point. Last winter's rainy season was the driest on record in the city. And water supplies from the Colorado River, which provides 17 million residents of Southern California with two-thirds of their water, could be cut by half unless regional officials can work out a plan involving better water-sharing and conservation. They have until the end of the year to do that. ... Los Angeles water official Dennis Underwood notes conservation also involves persuading property owners to eliminate grass lawns and use desert plants like cactus in their yards. And he says local official are encouraging the use of low-flow washing machines and toilets. "We're also looking at institutions, like older hotels, that if you're retrofitting some of the plumbing fixtures, showerheads, all of that makes a big difference," he said. **Author:** Mike O'Sullivan.

United States - News: November 23, 2002 — **Headline:** Do It Yourself: Home Improvement in 20th Century America. **Excerpt:** Before the 1900s, few American homeowners gave much thought to making home improvements themselves; any painting, building, or remodeling was left to a professional hired to do the job. Today, home improvement is a multi-billion dollar industry with approximately one third of all American homeowners embarking upon some kind of home improvement every year. The trend toward the "home-owner-as-handyman" began about a century ago, says National Building Museum curator, Chrysanthe Broikos. She says that's when wealthier people with more leisure time began to take an interest in home improvement as a hobby. "For example, in the late 1890's, woodworking became very popular and it's ornamental, not structural at all. It's not finishing off the basement or adding a garage," she says. "It's a design feature. So woodworking was one of the main ways that people gained confidence, maybe build a stool or a flower box or something that allows you to take on something bigger." The exhibit, "Do It Yourself: Home Improvement in 20th Century America", is presented as a real house under construction, where visitors can walk through rooms and witness the evolution of tools and projects through time. A 19th century foot-powered scroll saw used to carve intricate wood designs resembles a kind of sewing machine, and marked the beginning of the woodworking craze. By the 1930's, electric appliances and indoor plumbing fueled the push to modernize bathrooms and kitchens.

United States. Congress. Office of Compliance: Publication of "Plumbers Local 5, United Association of Journeymen and Apprentices of the Plumbing and Pipe Fitting Industry of the United States and Canada and Office of the Architect of the Capitol; International Brotherhood of Electrical Workers, Local 26 (v.) Office of the Architect of the Capitol." Publisher: Office of Compliance. Publisher: Washington, DC (LA 200, John Adams Building, 110 Second Street, S.E.): Office of Compliance. Published in 2002.

Vermont - News: January 25, 2002 — **Headline:** Dateline: Home Health Care in Vermont. **Excerpt:** The American population is aging rapidly. Health care experts say that means there will be a huge increase in the demand for long-term care in the next twenty to thirty years. Since the 1960s, much of that care has been provided in nursing homes. But today, more and more elderly Americans are choosing to remain home, getting help from a variety of health care providers in their community. The number of Americans getting government aid for home-based care has grown dramatically. One place to observe the the trend among the elderly to stay out of the nursing home is in the northeastern state of Vermont. Helen Hill waves to a familiar face as she makes her way through a nursing home in Rutland, Vermont. She used to be an administrator here. These days she's a case manager with the Southwestern Vermont Council on the Aging. Ironically, a big part of her job now is to help people avoid nursing homes. She does that by helping them apply for benefits, fuel assistance, food money or prescription drug coverage. She also helps people design home-based health care plans, which are paid for by the state as part of its Medicaid waiver program. That's what she is setting up for Dorothy and George Walsh. ... "We have a bathroom upstairs and a bathroom downstairs but nothing on the first floor," she said. "So we bit the bullet and took out a home equity loan and we created this bathroom, and what you see is a total of $8,000, plumbing, heating, carpenter work electrician and so forth."

Walter S. Bergquist, et al.: "Apparatus for casting a plumbing fixture" is is patented by Walter S. Bergquist, Frank P. Williams and Harold A. Teague.

William C. Tarr: "Swimming pool plumbing water/debris barrier device and method" is is patented by William C. Tarr.

William D. Freeman: "Sink support shell apparatus and method of making a protective sink support shell" is patented by William D. Freeman. Abstract: A sink support shell apparatus and method of making a sink support shell are provided. The sink support shell apparatus is a shell shaped to be compatible with the sink that is to be placed in the sink support shell. The sink support shell includes a rim for mounting the shell either above or below the countertop level. The shell further includes an overflow/vent channel and stand-off in the base for attaching the shell to the necessary plumbing fixtures to allow for drainage of the water from the sink. The overflow/vent channel is formed in the material of the shell and allows water to flow down the channel to be drained by the attached plumbing fixtures as well as air to be vented to reduce suction noise.

Woodson, Roger Dodge: Born in 1955, authored "Plumbing instant answers (computer file)." Publisher: McGraw-Hill (New York). Published in 2002.

Y-12 National Security Complex: Sponsored research "Continuous Holdup Measurements With Silicon P-I-N Photodiodes." Sponsored by: Y-12 National Security Complex, Oak Ridge, TN.; Department of Energy, Washington, DC. Written by J. A. Williams, D. E. Smith and M. J. Paulus. Abstract: We report on the behavior of silicon P-I-N photodiodes used to perform holdup measurements on plumbing. These detectors differ from traditional scintillation detectors in that no high-voltage is required, no scintillator is used (gamma and X rays are converted directly by the diode), and they are considerably more compact. Although the small size of the diodes means they are not nearly as efficient as scintillation detectors, the diodes' size does mean that a detector module, including one or more diodes, pulse shaping electronics, analog-to-digital converter, embedded microprocessor, and digital interface can be realized in a package (excluding shielding) the size of a pocket calculator.

2003

Allen D. Hertz: "Plumbing valve cover for avoiding interference with faucet hose" is is patented by Allen D. Hertz.

Andrew Webb and Michael Meagor: "Measuring Apparatus with Tape Measure and Pendulum for Plumbing" is patented by Andrew Webb and Michael Meagor.

Anthony M. Bootka: "Automatic water shut off system to prevent overflow of a plumbing device" is is patented by Anthony M. Bootka.

Anthony Warning: "Stowable sink for a vehicle" is patented by Anthony Warning. Abstract: A sink assembly for use on a vehicle that in one embodiment includes a mounting frame with an opening for mounting the sink assembly to the vehicle. The sink assembly also includes a door that is movable relative to the mounting frame and a sink top connected to the door. The sink top has a sink bowl with a drain, and is movable between a stowed position when not in use or when the vehicle is traveling to an operational position for use of the sink assembly. The sink assembly also includes at least one attachable plumbing apparatus that is connectable to a fluid source. The sink assembly may further include a storage container for storing the plumbing apparatus when not in use or when the sink top is in the stowed position.

Arkansas Division of Protective Health Codes: Publisher of "Arkansas plumbing code." Publisher: Arkansas Division of Protective Health Codes (Little Rock, Ark). Published in 2003.

Blackaby, Susan: Author of "Plant plumbing: a book about roots and stems." Written by Susan Blackaby; illustrated by Charlene DeLage. Published in 2003.

California - News: September 23, 2003 — **Headline:** Californians Seek to Right an Old Wrong for 'Repatriated' Mexican Americans. **Excerpt:** During the Great Depression of the 1930s, federal authorities and various state and local governments illegally deported or "repatriated" an estimated one to two million Mexicans and Mexican-Americans. The official reason was to free up jobs for so-called "real" Americans. Yet despite the massive scale of the decade-long campaign, it's not recorded in many history books and has largely been forgotten. Emilia Castaneda was born in Los Angeles in 1926. Her brother was born here, too. One day, when she was nine years old, she came home from school and her father said the family had to leave for Mexico. Right away. … Professor Balderrama says everyone in the plaza that day was shipped straight to Mexico, with no word to their families. For many, it was the beginning of a second-class existence, vilified by Mexicans as repatriados - repatriated ones - with work hard to find, meals scarce and no electricity or plumbing.

Centre for Science and Environment: Publisher of "Plumbing the rights." TVE; series editor, Robert Lamb. Publisher: Centre for Science and Environment (New Delhi, India). Published in 2003.

Christoph Weis and Hermann Grether: "Jet Regulator" is patented by Christoph Weis and Hermann Grether. Abstract: A jet regulator (1) has a jet regulator housing (2), which can be inserted into a plumbing spout fitting, and has at least one circular seal (6) placed on the jet regulator housing (2). Said seal effects a sealing between the jet regulator housing (2) on one side and the spout fitting on the other. The jet regulator (1) also comprises a component, which is located on the inflow side, extends over the clear spout opening, and which is joined while forming one piece to at least one seal that effects a sealing between the jet regulator housing (2) and the spout fitting.

Danny Heflin: "Recessed water faucet" is patented by Danny Heflin. Abstract: A recessed, frostproof water faucet having a tubular stem connected to a pivot plumbing unit connected to a subsurface water line through the rear wall of a box-like recess unit. A slider connector connects the water faucet tubular stem and the access panel or lid of the recess unit. The lid pivots on hinges and as one lifts the lid, the faucet is lifted by the slider connector from a horizontal storage position to a vertical locked position for use, the slider connector being connected to a faucet flange and sliding along grooves in tracks mounted along the inner side of the lid. A sliding hinge locks the lid upright, sliding downward along the upper end of the rear wall.

David W. Baarman and Eric K. Bartkus: "Automatic Shut-Off for Water Treatment System" is patented by David W. Baarman and Eric K. Bartkus. Abstract: A water treatment system including an automatic shut-off control valve (16). The system preferably includes inflow and outflow sensors (12, 14) that monitor flow through the system and a pressure sensor (22) that senses back pressure in a downstream plumbing system. If the sensors sense different flows, a leak in the system is assumed and the control valve (16) is closed. In one embodiment, the flowing back pressure is monitored by the pressure sensor to detect leaks in the plumbing system. In another embodiment, the valve (16) is closed after a specific volume of water flow is sensed and the pressure sensor (22) measures static back pressure in the plumbing system to detect a leak.

Davis, Karen Ann: Born in 1979, authored "Investigation of reverse plumbing in rotary seals." Published in 2003.

Dennis R. Hughes and Kevin M. Field: "Rooftop Water Heater" is patented by Dennis R. Hughes and Kevin M. Field. Abstract: A water heater adapted to be positioned outside of a building and to interface with the plumbing system of the building. The water heater includes a water storage tank adapted to store water outside of the building, a means for heating the water in the tank, a base member supporting the tank outside of the building, and a plurality of water pipes communicating with the water tank. The water heater also includes a manifold that is mounted to the base member and includes a plurality of pipe unions adapted to interface between the plumbing system and the plurality of pipes to provide cold water to the tank and to remove heated water from the tank for use in the building.

Edwin Kewish and Fred J Kewish III: "Automatic adjustable trap priming valve" is patented by Edwin Kewish and Fred J Kewish III. Abstract: An automatic adjustable trap priming valve includes a housing through which inlet water to a frequently used plumbing fixture flows; a diverter member which extends across the housing, the diverter member providing an interior passageway which communicates with a delivery line leading to a floor drain trap and a side opening which communicates with the interior passageway, the opening facing a downstream side of the diverter member; a needle valve in the interior passageway for adjusting the flow of water through the opening to the interior passageway in the diverter member and to the delivery line, and a flap for opening and closing the diverter member opening.

Frederic M. Newman and Richie D. Sites: "Automatic flood prevention system" is patented by Frederic M. Newman and Richie D. Sites. Abstract: A flood prevention system includes a double-latching solenoid valve that shuts off a water supply line in response to a moisture sensor detecting a leak in a plumbing system. The double-latching feature provides the solenoid's plunger with two positions of equilibrium. This minimizes electrical power consumption so that the flood prevention system can be battery operated. To minimize a buildup of hard water deposits, the valve includes a flexible diaphragm and is cycled periodically regardless of whether flooding occurs. The sensor includes multiple methods of mounting to a floor.

Geyser: Geysers are fragile phenomena and if conditions change, they can 'die'. Many geysers have been destroyed by people throwing litter and debris into them; others have ceased to erupt due to dewatering by geothermal power plants. The Great Geysir of Iceland has had periods of activity and dormancy. During its long dormant periods, eruptions were sometimes humanly-induced---often on special occasions---by the addition of surfactants to the water. Inducing eruptions at Geysir is no longer done, as the forced eruptions were damaging the geyser's special plumbing system. Following an earthquake in Iceland in 2000 the geyser became somewhat more active again. Initially the geyser erupted about eight times a day. As of July 2003, Geysir erupts several times a week. [WP]

Hong Kong - News: April 17, 2003 — **Headline:** Researchers Say Plumbing Helped Spread of SARS in Hong Kong. **Excerpt:** Researchers have concluded that plumbing in a Hong Kong high-rise helped spread Severe Acute Respiratory Syndrome to hundreds of people. Hong Kong officials blame faulty pipes for the high number of cases of Severe Acute Respiratory Syndrome in one apartment high-rise. Secretary for Health Yeoh Eng-kiong says most residents in the Amoy Gardens complex probably picked up the virus in their bathrooms, that large amounts of human waste carrying the virus went into the sewage system and leaked into apartments connected by toilet pipes.

Howard M. Allenbaugh, et al.: "Air-burst Drain

Plunger" is patented by Howard M. Allenbaugh, David M. Turchik and Gerard G. Adelmeyer. Abstract: An affordable plumbing device (10) that uses a compressed gas and a burst disk (24) having a relatively even surface of substantially uniform thickness to produce a sudden discharge of energy to forcibly act against any obstruction that may interfere with the proper function of a drain. The plumbing device (10) has a cylindrical chamber (22) for receiving the compressed gas and may generally take the shape of a plunger, which is flexible to use and is easy to store. A portion of the chamber (22) forms a receiving chamber with the burst disk (24) for harnessing and directing the energy of the compressed gas to clear a drain.

International Association of Plumbing and Mechanical Officials: Publication of "Uniform mechanical code." Publisher: International Association of Plumbing and Mechanical Officials (Ontario, Calif). Published in 2003.

Jackson, Albert: Born in 1943, authored "Collins complete plumbing & central heating: fix it yourself and save money - from changing a washer to installing a shower." (authors, Albert Jackson & David Day). Publisher: Collins (London). Published in 2003.

James Joseph Zaput: "Recondensing superconducting magnet thermal management system and method" is patented by James Joseph Zaput. Abstract: Heater duty cycle (the active pressure control circuit) in recondensing superconducting magnet systems is monitored to determine total thermal system performance, to minimize non-zero boil-off operation, and to reduce maintenance costs. Undesirable conditions, such as a degrading cold head, plumbing leaks, and so forth, may be detected earlier by monitoring heater duty cycle. Appropriate service intervals may be determined and cryogen or helium losses may be reduced. The technique provides earliest possible identification of failures related to such variables, as well as, facilitates isolation of the root cause of the problem.

John Hatrick-Smith: "Pre-plumbed shower door system" is patented by John Hatrick-Smith. Abstract: A shower door system in knocked down from including.

John R. Gilbert and Manish Deshpande: "Implementation of Microfluidic Components in a Microfluidic System" is patented by John R. Gilbert and Manish Deshpande. Abstract: A system and method for integrating microfluidic components in a microfluidic system enables the microfluidic system to perform a selected microfluidic function. A capping module includes a microfluidic element for performing a microfluidic function. The capping module is stacked on a microfluidic substrate having microfluidic plumbing to incorporate the microfluidic function into the system.

Joseph D. Rippolone: "Plumbing tool and method for repairing a pipe therewith" is is patented by Joseph D. Rippolone.

Lawrence Berkeley National Lab.: Sponsored research "Mantle Helium and Carbon Isotopes in Separation Creek Geothermal Springs, Three Sisters Area, Central Oregon: Evidence for Renewed Volcanic Activity or a Long Term Steady State System." Sponsored by: Lawrence Berkeley National Lab., CA.; Geological Survey, Menlo Park, CA. Written by M. C. van Soest, B. M. Kennedy, W. C. Evans and R. H. Mariner. Abstract: Cold bubbling springs in the Separation Creek area, the locus of current uplift at South Sister volcano show strong mantle signatures in helium and carbon isotopes and CO(sub 2)/(sup 3)He. This suggests the presence of fresh basaltic magma in the volcanic plumbing system. Currently there is no evidence to link this system directly to the uplift, which started in 1998. To the contrary, all geochemical evidence suggests that there is a long-lived geothermal system in the Separation Creek area, which has not significantly changed since the early 1990s. There was no archived helium and carbon data, so a definite conclusion regarding the strong mantle signature observed in these tracers cannot yet be drawn.

Mark R. Turner and Stephen J. Beagley: "Slide Rails" is patented by Mark R. Turner and Stephen J. Beagley. Abstract: Methods and apparatus of and for mounting slide rails (2), stood off from surfaces are disclosed. The method comprises the steps of mounting a first stand-off (1) to a surface by use of a fastener (5) and a taper-lock assembly

(17, 18) by attachment into the surface and expansion of the taper-lock against the interior of the first stand-off (1), locating an end of a rail (2) into the first stand-off (1), locating the other end of the rail (2) into a second stand-off (1a), and then mounting the second stand-off (1a) to the surface by use of a fastener (5) that, within said second stand-off (1a), passes through the rail (2) and into said surface. Apparatus comprises the finished slide rail assembly, the components thereof (in combination, assembly, disassembly or otherwise).

Massey, Howard C.: Author of "Illustrated guide to the international plumbing & fuel gas codes." Published in 2003.

Medical Research: "Inadequate plumbing systems probably contributed to SARS transmission" appears in Releve Epidemiologique Hebdomadaire / Section D'hygiene Du Secretariat de la Societe des Nations = Weekly Epidemiological Record / Health Section of the Secretariat of the League of Nations. Published on October 17, 2003.

Michael A. Joyce: Born in Northridge, California, Joyce works as a plumbing consultant. A resident of Cary since 1993, Joyce was elected to his first term on the Cary Town Council in 2003 as an at-large representative. Although his office is officially non-partisan, Joyce is affiliated with the Republican Party. [WP]

NAHB Research Foundation: Sponsored research "Performance Comparison of Residential Hot Water Systems. Period of Performance: January 30, 2001 through July 29, 2002." Sponsored by: NAHB Research Foundation, Inc., Upper Marlboro, MD.; National Renewable Energy Lab., Golden, CO. Written by J. Wiehagen and J. L. Sikora. Abstract: This report by the NAHB Research Center is a continuation of past Renewables and Energy Efficiency Program (REEP) technical efforts sponsored by the National Renewable Energy Laboratory (NREL) through 1999 and 2000. This work was undertaken to verify the estimated energy savings for hot water systems. The test results presented here support water heating energy savings reported in 2001. Results of weekly performance testing and annual simulations of electric water-heating systems are presented.

New Mexico - News: July 3, 2003 — **Headline:** Solitude: An Inner Journey. **Excerpt:** Many people are missing out on the pleasures of silence amid the bustle of modern life, according to a new book called Stillness: Daily Gifts of Solitude by author Richard Mahler. The travel writer took an inner journey in rural New Mexico to rediscover some ancient wisdom. Most of us are accustomed to constant stimulation, from the background noise of conversation to the blaring commercials of television and the ringing of cellular phones. Even a quiet lull of a few seconds' duration can be disconcerting. ... "I lived on a very, very remote ranch in conditions that are extremely unusual in the United States now, no electricity, no running water, no indoor plumbing, no radio, no television, no telephone, no e-mail," he says. "Basically [I had] a wood stove for heat, propane for cooking, an outhouse for bodily functions. And I lived there completely alone for three-and-a-half months. **Author:** Mike O'Sullivan.

New Mexico. Construction Industries Division of the Regulation and Licensing Department: Publication of "2003 New Mexico plumbing code: (Title 14 NMAC Chapter 5 and 8 effective 07/01/04)." State of New Mexico, Construction Industries Division. Publisher: The Division (Santa Fe, NM). Published in 2003.

New York - News: March 26, 2003 — **Headline:** 'Gangs of New York' Neighborhood Echoes with History. **Excerpt:** Gangs of New York was one of the most seen and talked-about films of the year, garnering 10 Oscar nominations. The movie focuses on clashes between Irish immigrants and so-called "nativists" in the volatile "Five Points" neighborhood of New York City. Today, the intersection near the site of the World Trade Center suggests nothing of the poverty and violence that reigned here in the 19th century. Even the street names have changed. ... By the 1920s, when Herbert Asner wrote the book that inspired Gangs of New York, the Sixth Ward had changed. The swampy land on which the Five Points was built was filled in. Homes had indoor plumbing. People had steady jobs. And the Irish gangs were gone, replaced by another of film director Martin Scorsese's favorite subjects, the

Italian Mafia.

Oliphant, R. J.: Author of "Causes of copper corrosion in plumbing systems." Publisher: Foundation for Water Research (Marlow). Published in 2003.

Ontario. Ministry of Municipal Affairs and Housing: Publication of "Changes to the plumbing provisions of Ontario Building Code (Ontario Regulation 304/03): questions and answers." Published in 2003.

Plumbing Industry Commission: Publisher of "Recycled water plumbing guide." Publisher: Plumbing Industry Commission (Camberwell, Vic). Published in 2003.

Robert A. Oropallo and Anthony Oropallo Jr: "Plumbing fitting cover cap retention system" is is patented by Robert A. Oropallo and Anthony Oropallo Jr.

Scheuring, Amy: Author of "Sex: more than a plumbing lesson: teaching your kids sexual values." Published in 2003.

Scott H. Pryne: "Polyvinyl alcohol plug for plumbing applications" is is patented by Scott H. Pryne.

Scottish and Northern Ireland Plumbing Employers' Federation: Publication of "Yearbook and directory of members." Scottish & Northern Ireland Plumbing Employers' Federation. (Year book and directory of members (Scottish and Northern Ireland Plumbing Employers' Federation)) (SNIPEF yearbook). Publisher: Burrows Communications (Wallington (106 Stafford Rd., Wallington, Surrey SM6 9AY)). Published in 2003.

Sebastian J. Maerkl, et al.: "Microfluidic Large Scale Integration" is patented by Sebastian J. Maerkl, Todd A. Thorsen, Xiaoyan Bao, Stephen R. Quake and Vincent Studer. Abstract: High-density microfluidic chips contain plumbing networks with thousands of micromechanical valves and hundreds of individually addressable chambers. These fluidic devices are analogous to electronic integrated circuits fabricated using large scale integration (LSI). A component of these networks is the fluidic multiplexor, which is a combinatorial array of binary valve patterns that exponentially increases the processing power of a network by allowing complex fluid manipulations with a minimal number of inputs. These integrated microfluidic networks can be used to construct a variety of highly complex microfluidic devices, for example the microfluidic analog of a comparator array, and a microfluidic memory storage device resembling electronic random access memories.

Standards Australia International Limited: Publication of "Plumbing and drainage. Part 2, Sanitary plumbing and drainage." Published in 2003.

Stenvinkel, P., et al.: "Coronary artery disease in end-stage renal disease: no longer a simple plumbing problem" appears in Journal of the American Society of Nephrology: JASN written by P. Stenvinkel, R. Pecoits-Filho and B. Lindholm. Published in July 2003.

Tai Kien: "Plumbing tool" is patented by Tai Kien. Abstract: A plumbing tool and its method of use are disclosed wherein the plumbing tool includes a tube for insertion into a pipe beyond an area of such pipe that is to be soldered, such tube having an inflatable balloon structure at one end thereof. After the tube is inserted in the pipe and the balloon structure is positioned at the location where fluid stoppage is desired, the balloon structure is inflated to allow for soldering operations to be completed. A water bypass can be disposed within such tube for directing any fluid flow to the exterior of the pipe.

Taylor, G. L.: Author of "Plumbing pocket codes: international residential code." C.L. Taylor. Published in 2003.

Treloar, Roy: Author of "Plumbing encyclopaedia." Publisher: Blackwell Pub (Oxford, UK; Malden, MA). Published in 2003.

United States - News: March 23, 2003 — **Headline:** Old-Time Wares for a New Wartime. **Excerpt:** The fear of a terrorist attack on the United States has Americans buying duct tape and plastic sheeting. Army surplus stores have been selling emergency preparedness kits containing potassium-iodide pills and hooded suits, for protection against possible contamination by biological or chemical weapons. But, some Americans are thinking beyond the immediate threat, they are preparing to live without modern "necessities" like electricity and indoor plumbing. A hardware store in Kidron, Ohio has seen a boom in its catalog and store business from people who want non-electric goods such as kerosene lamps and 190-liter rainwater drums. Natalie Walston visited the store that typically caters to the Amish community in three neighboring states. It's Thursday afternoon and, in Kidron, that means auction day. The streets are crowded with black, horse-drawn Amish carriages, and farmers in pickup trucks pulling livestock in long trailers.

United States - News: August 30, 2003 — **Headline:** New Book Shows Appreciation for Scouting. **Excerpt:** Take a hike in any American wilderness area during the summer, and there's a good chance you'll find a group of Boy Scouts. Since it began in Britain nearly a century ago, Scouting has revolved around camping, canoeing and other outdoor activities - the kinds of activities New York Times writer and editor Peter Applebome avoided for much of his life. He was drawn into the organization after his son Ben joined a troop in Chappaqua, New York. In his book Scout's Honor: A Father's Unlikely Foray into the Woods, Peter Applebome describes how he acquired a new appreciation for the outdoors and for Scouting. ... "On my honor, I will do my best, to do my duty, to God and my country..." ... "I was not a Boy Scout as a kid. I never camped," he said. "I never made fire over anything other than a gas grill. I believe God made indoor plumbing for a reason. But when we moved from Atlanta to New York five years ago, I was racked with pangs of modern dad guilt that I was uprooting my son from his good friends in Atlanta, so I found him a Scout troop. And then to go the extra mile I figured, 'Well, I'll get slightly involved.'"

Uv, A., et al.: "Drosophila tracheal morphogenesis: intricate cellular solutions to basic plumbing problems" appears in Trends in Cell Biology written by A. Uv, R. Cantera and C. Samakovlis. Published in June 2003.

Virginia. Dept. of Housing and Community Development: Publication of "Indoor Plumbing Rehabilitation Loan Program program year 2004." Department of Housing and Community Development. Publisher: Dept. of Housing and Community Development (Richmond, Va.). Published in 2003.

World Health Organization. Director-General's Office. Communications Office: Publication of "Inadequate plumbing systems likely contributed to SARS transmission." Publisher: World Health Organization. Published in 2003.

Zervos, Sara: Author of the electronic resource "Housekeeping and plumbing: the investability of emerging markets." Sara Zervos and Jeppe Ladekarl. Published in 2003.

2004

Branson, Gary D.: Author of "Solving home plumbing problems." Publisher: Firefly Books (Buffalo, N.Y.). Published in 2004.

Bridgewater, Julian: Author of "Home plumbing: the complete handbook." Publisher: New Holland (London). Published in 2004.

Casey, Michael: Born in 1959, authored "Code check plumbing: a field guide to the plumbing codes." Michael Casey, Redwood Kardon, and Douglas Hansen; illustrated by Paddy Morrissey. Published in 2004.

David Mathew: David Mathew was born in Wagga Wagga and spent several years at boarding school in Sydney. Following completion of a plumbing apprenticeship in Wagga Wagga, David moved to the Gold Coast in 2004. [WP]

Dept. of Consumer & Business Services, Building Codes Division: Publisher of "Notice to the following licensees - boiler, electrical, elevator, plumbing, pressure vessel, effective July 1, 2004, OAR 918-030-0200 visible identification badge: a new law passed by the 2003 legislature requires you to wear your trade license when you are on the job site unless wearing it would create an unsafe condition." Publisher: Dept. of Consumer & Business Services, Building Codes Division (Salem, OR). Published in 2004.

Edwards, Sally: Author of "In good hands: plumbing in Western Australia from settlement to the 21st century." Text by Sally Edwards and Margaret Robertson. Publisher: Master Plumbers and Gasfitters Association of Western Australia (Maylands, W.A.). Published in 2004.

Finland - News: December 28, 2004 — **Headline:** International Products Get a Localized Makeover. **Excerpt:** The world has embraced some of America's most popular board games, such as, Scrabble, Monopoly, and Trivial Pursuit. A board game called Cranium is a relative newcomer - just 6 years old. But Cranium company co-founder Richard Tait is on a crusade to take his line of products global. He says, "Whether you're an 8 year old kid in America or an 8 year old kid in Finland, putting on decoder goggles and solving clues is fun." ... "I know personally being Scottish and looking at the British game, when you're sculpting beans on toast, or impersonating Sean Connery...that's a great British moment," says Mr. Tait, "and I know that playing those games, people are going to have a different response and more fun." ... Mr. Henes says the modern-day field of localization took off in the 1980's with the software industry. Companies like Microsoft and Lotus translated screens and user manuals into dozens of languages, including Arabic and Chinese. But the business analyst says the early efforts were ugly, like building a house without thinking about the plumbing. "You have to go in and tear up the walls, the floors, and re-install plumbing," says Mr. Henes, "a very messy, costly, lengthy exercise that often was not completely satisfactory when everything was done." **Author:** Cathy Duchamp.

Galeno, Joseph J.: Author of "Plumbing estimating methods: includes standard plumbing & fire protection systems, special systems including medical gas & glass piping." Joseph J. Galeno and Sheldon T. Greene. Publisher: reed Construction Data (Kingston, MA). Published in 2004.

Gore Saravia, Nancy: Publication of "Plumbing the brain drain." Published in 2004.

Government of Taiwan: The amendment of 30 June 2004 applies to the Running Water Law. The essential points are: 1)To specify that the central competent authority shall impose fees for exploiting surface and underground water in the area of protecting water's quality and quantity, and the central competent authority shall, in conjunction with other concerned authorities enact regulations governing imposition of the fees; that the fees may be included in the water resource-related fund and earmarked for certain particular purposes by the central competent authority. (Article 12-2) 2) To set forth provisions governing formation of the water resource-related fund. (Article 12-3) 3)That due to the streamlining of the Taiwan provincial government, it shall be no longer the competent authority under this law. (Article 41) 4)To specify that a household shall preferentially make use of the water saving devices bearing a water saving badge. (Article 50) 5)To specify that the planning, designing, overseeing and verifying of the sizable engineering of running water facilities shall be certified by a licensed technician of running water facilities. (Article 56) 6)To specify that the central competent authority shall set up a water rates deliberation board in charge of adjusting water rates. (Article 60) 7) To specify that the central competent authority shall set the amount for national's basic water consumption, and shall encourage the private sector to research and develop technical skills of water saving. (Article 60-1). 8)To specify that a plumbing contractor shall only start up business after becoming a member of the plumbing-related guild (Article 93). Published in The Gazette of the Office of the President on June 30, 2004.

Halabi, Abdel Philpott, Clifton Dyt, Robyn: Publication of "Pete's Plumbing: an accounting practice set." Abdel Halabi, Robyn Dyt, Clifton Philpott. Publisher: McGraw-Hill Ryerson (Toronto). Published in 2004.

Iraq - News: June 21, 2004 — **Headline:** Power Shortages Pose Huge Problems for New Iraq. **Excerpt:** Restoring stable electricity supplies in Iraq had been a top priority for U.S.-led coalition authorities since the fall of Saddam Hussein's regime in April 2003. But efforts to turn the lights back on, and keep them on, have not been easy. In Najaf in south-central Iraq, American and Iraqi frustration over the lack of a solution to the power shortages is climbing, along with soaring summer temperatures. For the past week, locally hired workers have been busy repairing walls, replacing doors and windows, and installing electrical outlets and plumbing systems at the Abrar primary school in one of the poorest areas of Najaf. **Author:** Alisha Ryu.

J & L Publications: Publisher of "Plumbing rules made simple for domestic type dwellings." Produced by J & L Publishers (John Tesoriero). Publisher: J & L Publishers (Kellyville, N.S.W.). Published in 2004.

Jeff Patchell Pty. Ltd: Publisher of "Plumbing and mechanical connection." Publisher: Jeff Patchell Pty. Ltd (Hawthorn, Vic). Published in 2004.

Ladekarl, Jeppe: Author of "Housekeeping and plumbing: the investability of emerging markets." Jeppe Ladekarl and Sara Zervos. Publisher: World Bank, Financial Sector Operations and Policy Dept (Washington, D.C.). Published in 2004.

Lewis, Jerre G.: Author of "How to start and manage a plumbing service business: a practical way to start your own business." By Jerre G. Lewis and Leslie D. Renn. Publisher: Business & Professional Pub (Interlochen, MI). Published in 2004.

Madias, J. E.: "The impact of systemic BP on coronary blood flow and infarct size during reperfusion therapy for acute myocardial infarction: refinements beyond the plumbing" appears in Chest written by J. E. Madias. Published in April 2004.

McConnell, Charles: Author of "The home plumbing handbook." Publisher: Thomson Delmar Learning (Clifton Park, N.Y.; (London)). Published in 2004.

Meridian Education Corp;: Publisher of "Plumbing: rough-in & final (videorecording (DVD))." A production of Meridian Educational Corporation. Publisher: Meridian Education (New Jersey). Published in 2004.

National Plumbing Regulators Forum: Publisher of "Plumbing code of Australia." (produced by the National Plumbing Regulators Forum). Publisher: National Plumbing Regulators Forum (Camberwell, Vic). Published in 2004.

Ontario. Ministry of Municipal Affairs: Publication of "Building Code changes: plumbing fixtures and hot water temperature (Regulation 23/04): questions and answers." Published in 2004.

Renner, R.: "Plumbing the depths of D.C.'s drinking water crisis" appears in Environmental Science & Technology written by R. Renner. Published on June 15, 2004.

Scientists - News: January 30, 2004 — **Headline:** New Water-Saving Technologies Create Business Opportunities. **Excerpt:** Scientists say large parts of the world will face a water crisis sometime in this century, as supplies of fresh water dwindle. Conservation efforts and new technologies have created opportunities for some businesses. A report by the United Nations Educational, Scientific, and Cultural Organization says two billion people in 48 countries will face a water shortage by the middle of this century. That is a best-case scenario. The international agency says that unless pollution is reduced and water sources protected, as many as 7 billion people could lack the water they need for drinking and sanitation. ... James Krug of Falcon Waterfree Technologies says his company's sales are expanding in East Asia, where public rest rooms are being modernized to them more hygienic, while water-saving devices are promoting conservation and saving users money. He adds that Northern Europeans, already conservation leaders, are also showing interest in such environmentally friendly plumbing products. **Author:** Mike O'Sullivan.

Sierra Leone - News: June 2, 2004 — **Headline:** Sierra Leone to Begin Long-Awaited War Crimes Trials. **Excerpt:** The U.N.-backed war crimes court in Sierra Leone begins its long-anticipated trials on Thursday to bring to justice those accused of committing atrocities during the country's decade-long civil war. Former pro-government militia leaders will be the first to be tried. Just a week before the court was to begin its sessions, workers were trying to finish the new 120-seat courtroom. The building is shaped like the scales of justice. ... "Here we have one man per cell, we could very well have put three per cell very easily," he said. "They have good ventilation, screening up on the windows, bug spray to help keep the mosquitoes down, they got a table, chairs and they got their personal belonging in their cell, the only downside no toilet in the cell, no indoor plumbing, so you have to get a bucket."

Spon Press: Publisher of "Spon's estimating costs guide to plumbing and heating: unit rates and total project costs." Publisher: Spon Press (London; New York). Published in 2004.

Standards Australia: Publisher of "Heated water systems." (compiled by the Plumbing Industry Commission). Publisher: Standards Australia (Camberwell, Vic. Plumbing Industry Commission; Sydney). Published in 2004.

United States - News: July 23, 2004 — **Headline:** New Book Rates US Presidents. **Excerpt:** The 13th president of the United States, Millard Fillmore, is credited with the installation of indoor plumbing in the White House and virtually nothing else. With the race for the White House in full swing, Sheryl Swenson explores the qualities that make presidents great leaders, or greatly forgettable. President Bush and John Kerry are on the campaign trail, each trying to convince American voters that they possess the qualities to best lead the nation. But do they?

Wade A. Burdick and Gary M. Bowman: "Dynamic Sealing Arrangement for Movable Shaft" is patented by Wade A. Burdick and Gary M. Bowman. Abstract: A dynamic sealing arrangement for preventing leakage of a fluid along a shaft includes multiple seals and pressurized barrier sealarit. According to one aspect, at least three seals are arranged along the shaft with pressurized barrier sealant between the first and second seals and a collection area is provided between the second and third seals to collect any leakage that might occur. Collected leakage, if any, is ported to an output port. According to another aspect, a unitary seal block member is provided that supports the dynamic sealing arrangement for the shaft and defines a piston chamber and a drilled passageway connecting the piston chamber and barrier sealant pressurization chamber between two seals.

Warren, St. Croix County, Wisconsin: The town first developed local government in November 2004, and contracts with St. Croix County for electricity, plumbing, communications, garbage disposal and schools. [WP]

Weissman, K.: "Plumbing new depths in drug discovery" appears in Chemistry & Biology written by K. Weissman. Published in June 2004.

Woodson, Roger Dodge: Born in 1955, authored "2003 International Plumbing Codes handbook." Publisher: McGraw-Hill (New York: London). Published in 2004.

World Toilet Organization Summit in Beijing - News: December 3, 2004 — **Headline:** Beijing to Upgrade Public Toilets in Time for Olympics. **Excerpt:** Beijing is undergoing massive renovation in preparation for the 2008 Olympic Games, and one area receiving considerable attention is the city's public toilets, which have a reputation for being below international standards. At the recent World Toilet Organization Summit in Beijing, the government vowed to have the privies in pristine shape by the time visitors begin pouring in for the games. About 400 delegates gathered for the World Toilet Organization's annual summit, including town planners, environmental and hygiene experts and toilet designers. On a bright and sunny day, we set out for a guided tour of Beijing's updated WCs. … The city's traditional-style homes rarely have indoor plumbing, so the public toilets see a great deal of daily use. A lack of maintenance means hygiene standards are low. To tourists used to more cleanliness, they are a scene from someone's worst nightmare.

2005

American Society of Mechanical Engineers: Publication of "Plumbing waste fittings." American Society of Mechanical Engineers; Canadian Standards Association. Publisher: Canadian Standards Association (New York, NY: American Society of Mechanical Engineers; Mississauga). Published in 2005.

Blankenbaker, E. Keith: Author of "Modern plumbing." Publisher: Goodheart-Willcox Co (Tinley Park, IL). Published in 2005.

Boyce, Robert Piper: Author of "Plumbing: a practical guide for level 2." Publisher: Nelson Thornes (Cheltenham). Published in 2005.

Calear, Adrian: Author of "Captain's log: adventures of sanitary engineering in the good ship G & L Plumbing." By Adrian Calear from the diaries of George Calear. Publisher: Adrian Calear (North Fitzroy, Vic). Published in 2005.

Cauldwell, Rex: Author of "Remodel plumbing." Publisher: taunton Press (Newtown, CT). Published in 2005.

China - News: June 1, 2005 — **Headline:** Development Threatens Traditional Way of Life in Beijing's Ancient Alleyways. **Excerpt:** On a sunny afternoon, a rickshaw passenger explores the alleyways around Beijing's Tiananmen Square. These narrow streets, or hutongs in Chinese, have been around for more than seven centuries. Here, close-knit communities live in traditional one-story courtyard homes. On this day, groups of people sit on stools on the street - playing cards or Chinese chess. Outside one home, a visitor receives an enthusiastic welcome from an elderly woman. ... There are problems with the hutongs: most are overcrowded and the aged buildings are often in poor repair and lack modern plumbing. **Author:** Siska Silitonga.

Connection Magazines: Publisher of "Plumbing connection." Publisher: Connection Magazines (Notting Hill, Vic). Published in 2005.

Cory, Steve: Author of "Plumbing 1-2-3: expert advice from The Home Depot." Publisher: Meredith Books (Des Moines, IA). Published in 2005.

Hawaii. Dept. of Commerce and Consumer Affairs Regulated Industries Complaints Office: Publication of "Report of the task force on the Electrical and plumbing licensing laws." Prepared by the Regulated Industries Complaints Office, Department of Commerce and Consumer Affairs, State of Hawaii. Publisher: Regulated Industries Complaints Office, Department of Commerce and Consumer Affairs (Hawaii). Published in 2005.

Hometime: Publisher of "Hometime how-to guide to plumbing & electrical." Publisher: Hometime (Chaska, MN). Published in 2005.

Institute for Career Research: Publisher of "Your career in plumbing (netLibrary e-books)." Publisher: Institute for Career Research (Chicago). Published in 2005.

International Code Council: Publisher of "International plumbing code 2003." Publisher: International Code Council (Country Club Hills, IL). Published in 2005.

Joyce, Michael D.: Author of "Residential construction academy: plumbing." Publisher: Thomson/Delmar Learning (Clifton Park, NY). Published in 2005.

Leslie M.: Author of "Plumbing problem," published in Science of Aging Knowledge Environment: SAGE KE, vol. 2005, no. 38, p. nf75, on September 21, 2005.

Levash, Chris: Born in 1980, authored "2005 Solar Decathalon: domestic hot water and plumbing design." By Chris Levash and Patrick Yost. Published in 2005.

Muscroft, Steve: Author of "Plumbing." Publisher: Elsevier/Newnes (Amsterdam; Boston). Published in 2005.

National Research Council of Canada. Canadian Commission on Building and Fire Codes: Publication of "National plumbing code of Canada, 2005." Issued by the Canadian Commission on Building and Fire Codes, National Research Council of Canada. Publisher: Institute for Research in Construction, National Research Council Canada (Ottawa). Published in 2005.

Nejsum L.N.: Author of "The renal plumbing system: aquaporin water channels," published in Cellular and Molecular Life Sciences: CMLS, vol. 62, no. 15, p. 1692-706, in August 2005.

Ontario. Ministry of Training, Colleges and Universities: Publication of "Employers awarded for improving Ontarians' skills: apprenticeship training means better careers, stronger economy (includes backgrounder): (keywords: Brouwer Plumbing & Heating, Regent Car Star Collision, RHO-CAN Machine & Tool Company, Thompson Electric (Seeley's Bay))." Published in 2005.

Peru - News: February 8, 2005 — **Headline:** Peruvian Student Goes from Machu Picchu to Yale. **Excerpt:** Peruvian student Cesar Moran had both educational and personal reasons for coming to the United States to study for a masters degree in environmental management. "I was born in Lima, Peru," says Mr. Moran, now a senior and in his last semester at Yale University in New Haven, Connecticut. "Lima is a city on the coast...in the middle of a desert. The reason I wanted to come to the United States was to attend this school." He calls the Yale School of Forestry and Environmental Studies "a very open school and broad minded school.". ... Because of his interest in environmental issues, Yale allowed Cesar Moran to plan a visit this past November to China. "I organized a trip to go to the World Toilet Summit in Beijing," he says, "in which we discussed issues like dry sanitation and water issues and health issues. Toilets have lots of issues -- green design for example, accessibility toilets, new technologies in toileting, plumbing systems, etc. It is a very broad theme that nobody really talks about.". **Author:** Marsha James.

Plumbing, Gasfitting and Drainlaying Industry Training Organisation: Publisher of "ITO newsletter." Plumbing, Gasfitting and Drainlaying Industry Training Organisation Ltd. Publisher: Plumbing, Gasfitting and Drainlaying Industry Training Organisation (Wellington, N.Z.). Published in 2005.

Rosenberg, Paul: Author of "Plumbing professional reference." Publisher: pal Publications (Pottstown, PA). Published in 2005.

Saucyer, Jean-Robert: Translator of "Plumbing" by Plomberie into French ("techniques de construction étape par étape"). Publisher: Modus Vivendi (Montréal). Published in 2005.

TAFE Frontiers: Publisher of "Certificate III in Plumbing: (materials for six core competencies) BCPCM2001A BCPCM2002A BCPCM2003A BCPCM2004A BCPCM2005A BCPCM2006A." Publisher: TAFE Frontiers (Melbourne). Published in 2005.

Taylor, Gil L.: Born in 1954, authored "Plumbing and piping inspection notes (computer file): inspecting commercial, industrial, and residential properties." Publisher: McGraw-Hill (New York). Published in 2005.

Tesoriero, John: Author of "Plumbing rules made simple: sanitary plumbing & drainage for high rise & multiple dwellings." Publisher: J & L Publications (Kellyville, N.S.W.). Published in 2005.

Thomson, James Allen: Born in 1961, authored "2006 national plumbing & HVAC estimator." Publisher: Craftsman Book Co (Carlsbad, CA). Published in 2005.

Tunuguntla A., Yerra L.: Authors of "The renal patient with cardiovascular disease--no longer a simple plumbing problem," published in Tennessee Medicine: Journal of the Tennessee Medical Association, vol. 98, no. 8, p. 395-6, 399, in August 2005.

2006

Asia - News: November 30, 2006 — **Headline:** Paris Conference Takes Comprehensive Look at World Environment. **Excerpt:** Here are some estimates you may not want to hear: By 2050, up to two billion people may be affected by desertification, much of it due to climate change. In less than 20 years, up to two billion people may face water shortages. Air pollution kills more than 1.5 million people in Asia annually. These are among many grim statistics supplied by scientists and environmentalists, who gathered at a recent meeting in Paris to look at the future of the human species - and of our planet. ... That is a particularly good lesson, Biswat says, for cities like New Delhi and Bangkok, where up to 60 percent of public water never reaches consumers because of mismanagement and poor plumbing.

California. Dept. of Housing and Community Development: Publication of "Recirculated draft environmental impact report, adoption of regulations permitting statewide residential use of chlorinated polyvinyl chloride (CPVC) plastic plumbing pipe without first making a finding of potential premature metallic pipe failure due to local water or soil conditions." (prepared by Dept. of Housing and Community Development). Publisher: State of California, Dept. of Housing and Community Development (Sacramento, CA). Published in 2006.

Cauldwell, Rex: Author of "Plumbing." Publisher: taunton Press (Newtown, CT). Published in 2006.

Clarke G.K.: Author of "Glaciology: ice-sheet plumbing in Antarctica," published in Nature, vol. 440, no. 7087, p. 1000-1, on April 20, 2006.

Committee on Uniformity of Plumbing and Drainage Regulations in New South Wales:

Publication of "New South Wales code of practice: plumbing and drainage." Produced by Committee on Uniformity of Plumbing and Drainage Regulations in NSW. Publisher: Dept. of Energy, Utilities and Sustainability (Sydney, N.S.W.). Published in 2006.

Connection Magazines: Publisher of "WPR: World plumbing review." Publisher: Connection Magazines (Notting Hill, Vic). Published in 2006.

Dixon, Graham: Born in 1950, authored "The washing machine manual: DIY plumbing, fault-finding, repair and maintenance of most commonly used domestic washing machines." Publisher: Haynes (Sparkford). Published in 2006.

Griffin, David: Born in 1963, authored "Plumbing 101: 25 repairs & projects you really can do." Publisher: Creative Pub. International (Chanhassen, Minn). Published in 2006.

Henkenius, Merle: Born in 1950, authored "Plumbing: complete projects for the home." Publisher: Creative Homeowner (Upper Saddle River, N.J.). Published in 2006.

Institute for Research in Construction, National Research Council Canada: Publisher of "National fire code of Canada 2005, National plumbing code of Canada 2005, parts 4,5 and 6 of the National building code of Canada 2005: seminars." Publisher: Institute for Research in Construction, National Research Council Canada (Ottawa). Published in 2006.

Liu Z., Lin Y.E., Stout J.E., Hwang C.C., Vidic R.D., Yu V.L.: Authors of "Effect of flow regimes on the presence of Legionella within the biofilm of a model plumbing system," published in Journal of Applied Microbiology, vol. 101, no. 2, in August 2006.

Morabito, Natasha: Author of "The ladies' loos: from plumbing to plucking, a practical guide for girls." Publisher: Friday (London). Published in 2006.

Phinney, Dennis: Author of "Code finder for building and construction building codes, fire codes, plumbing codes, mechanical codes, electrical codes, public works standards, water and wastewater standards." Publisher: BNi Building News (Irvine, Calif). Published in 2006.

Plumbassist: Publisher of "Labour rates for plumbing contractors: a guide to the labour costs of plumbing works." Publisher: Plumbassist (Narellan, N.S.W.). Published in 2006.

Plumbassist Pty. Ltd: Publisher of "Australian plumbing cost guide: guide to current costs of plumbing & drainage works." Publisher: Plumbassist Pty. Ltd (Narellan, N.S.W.). Published in 2006.

Plumbing, Gasfitting and Drainlaying ITO Ltd: Publisher of "First for news." Recruitment Taskforce; Administered by the Plumbing, Gasfitting and Drainlaying ITO Ltd. Publisher: Plumbing, Gasfitting and Drainlaying ITO Ltd (Wellington, N.Z.). Published in 2006.

The Dept: Publisher of "Draft environmental impact report, adoption of regulations permitting statewide residential use of chlorinated polyvinyl chloride (CPVC) plastic plumbing pipe without first making a finding of potential premature metallic pipe failure due to local water or soil conditions." State of California, Department of Housing and Community Development. Publisher: The Dept (Sacramento, Calif). Published in 2006.

Thomson, James Allen: Born in 1961, authored "2007 national plumbing & HVAC estimator." Publisher: Craftsman Book Co (Carlsbad, CA). Published in 2006.

United States - News: July 25, 2006 — **Headline:** Small Loans Make a Big Difference. **Excerpt:** A growing number of not-for-profit groups in the United States are providing the capital to help people break out of poverty. They're making business start-up loans of as little as $500. It's called micro-lending. In America's Pacific Northwest, for example, single moms, refugees and ex-convicts are using these small loans to start a wide range of enterprises. … The playful scene is a far cry from where the 34-year-old was a few years ago. Then, the freshly minted college grad was barely making a living. She scraped by as a part-time dog walker. Her idea for getting ahead was to borrow enough money to start a pet photography business. … Micro-lenders around the Northwest have backed a wide range of new enterprises - from a plumbing franchise to an organic vegetable farm to a catering business.

Western Australia. Plumbers Licensing Board:

Publication of "Plumbers Licensing Board strategic plan 2006-2009: working towards a competent and professional plumbing industry in Western Australia." Published in 2006.

Woodson, Roger Dodge: Born in 1955, authored "2006 international plumbing codes handbook." Publisher: McGraw-Hill (New York). Published in 2006.

World Health Organization: Publication of "Health aspects of plumbing." Publisher: World Health Organization. Published in 2006.

World Plumbing Council: Publisher of "Health aspects of plumbing." World Health Organization and the World Plumbing Council. Publisher: World Plumbing Council (Geneva: World Health Organization). Published in 2006.

2007

Beaumont, Tony: Author of "Plumbing." Publisher: New Holland (London). Published in 2007.

Blower, G. J.: Author of "Plumbing: mechanical services." Publisher: Pearson Prentice Hall (Harlow). Published in 2007.

California Building Standards Commission: Publication of "2007 California plumbing code: California code of regulations, Title 24, Part 5." Publisher: California Building Standards Commission (Ontario, Calif. International Association of Plumbing and Mechanical Officials; Sacramento, CA). Published in 2007.

China - News: July 17, 2007 — **Headline:** British Rail Slowdown Tied to Copper Thieves. **Excerpt:** The global price of the refined metal has risen five-fold since 2001 and hovers at about $7,500 a metric ton. British police say they believe the stolen copper is sold to scrap yards, then on to smelters, and is transported to China by ship. … "It goes into construction, air conditioners, plumbing tubes, telecom cables, computer circuits, computers, electronics, white goods, all of those across the board are using little pieces of copper."

Government of Taiwan: The amendment of 3 January 2007 applies to the Sewerage Law. Article 21 specifies that householders' sewage facilities shall be installed by a plumbing contractor; that plumbers hired by the contractor shall be a licensed technician, and shall have undergone training courses held by the central competent authority; that the central competent authority shall enact regulations governing the management of plumbing contractors. Published in The Gazette of the Office of the President on January 03, 2007.

Iraq - News: March 22, 2007 — **Headline:** US Officials: Iraq Reconstruction Beset With Problems But Improving. **Excerpt:** "The inspector general's report is full of discouraging examples of key facilities that suffered from poor design, sloppy construction, inadequate quality control," he explained. "One example: plumbing was so poorly installed at the Baghdad Police College that dripping sewage not only threatened the health of students and instructors, it could [also] affect the structural integrity of the building." Levin was speaking at a hearing of the Senate Homeland Security and Governmental Affairs Committee. Among those testifying was Major General Ronald Johnson of the U.S. Army Corps of Engineers, who insisted that, despite problems, progress has been made in Iraq. **Author:** Michael Bowman.

Iraq - News: April 29, 2007 — **Headline:** US Auditors Find Seven Iraqi Reconstruction Projects Crumbling. **Excerpt:** Two leading U.S. newspapers report American auditors have found that seven Iraq reconstruction projects declared successes by the U.S. government are no longer operating as designed. The New York Times and The Washington Post report Sunday that out of eight projects inspected, seven were suffering from things such as lack of proper maintenance, electrical and plumbing problems, or expensive equipment going unused.

Iraq - News: April 30, 2007 — **Headline:** Iraqi Hospital Struggles to Maintain US-Funded Improvements. **Excerpt:** The U.S. government paid a contractor $6 million 800,000 in 2005 and 2006 to modernize the facility. Contractors installed new floors and plumbing, set-up new boilers and air conditioning units, and added some modern hospital equipment like an incinerator and an oxygen delivery system. Stuart W. Bowen, Jr. is the special inspector general for Iraq Reconstruction. **Author:** Barry Newhouse.

Jefferys R.: Author of "Plumbing HIV

pathogenesis," published in Research Initiative, Treatment Action: RITA, vol. 12, no. 2, p. 36-8, in Winter 2007 .

Kardon, Redwood: Author of "Code check complete: an illustrated guide to building, plumbing, mechanical, and electrical codes." Redwood Kardon, Douglas Hansen, Michael Casey; illustrated by Paddy Morrisey. Publisher: taunton Press (Newtown, CT). Published in 2007.

Long J.W.: Author of "Architectural design, interior decoration, and three-dimensional plumbing en route to multifunctional nanoarchitectures," published in Accounts of Chemical Research, vol. 40, no. 9, p. 854-62, in September 2007.

Muscroft, Steve: Author of "Plumbing: for Level 2 Technical Certificate and NVQ." Publisher: Newnes (Oxford). Published in 2007.

New Mexico - News: October 30, 2007 — **Headline:** How to Build a House With Bales of Straw. **Excerpt:** It was a cold winter in Santa Fe, New Mexico, in the early nineteen eighties. Athena Swentzell was a student in college there. She owned some property. She wanted her own place to live in but she did not have much money to build a house. The usual building materials of wood, concrete and brick were too costly. So she decided to try to build a house using big rectangular bales of straw, the waste material that remains after wheat and other grains are harvested. She covered the outside of the small house with a cement plaster to keep the straw dry. Miz Swentzell had never seen or heard of a house built of straw. She thought she had invented the idea and was surprised how livable it was. Later she learned that straw bale houses have been built since the late eighteen hundreds after a machine was invented to form the dry straw into bales. And she learned there are straw bale houses in many countries throughout the world. ... People learn the methods of building with straw bales. They learn that the straw must be kept completely dry or it will not last. They learn how to put in electricity and plumbing. And they learn how to build roofs that will keep rain from the walls.

Ohio: Publication of "Ohio plumbing code, 2007." Publisher: International Code Council (Country Club Hills, IL). Published in 2007.

Ontario. Ministry of Municipal Affairs and Housing. Building and Development Branch: Publication of "2006 Ontario Building Code overview training courses: plumbing - all buildings - 2007: participant's manual." Publisher: Building and Development Branch, Ministry of Municipal Affairs & Housing (Toronto). Published in 2007.

Patterson, Terry L.: Author of "Illustrated guide to the 2006 international plumbing and sewage codes." Publisher: McGraw-Hill (New York). Published in 2007.

Pearson Education Australia: Publisher of "Basic plumbing services skills: addresses 9 AQF level 2 core units of competence within the Plumbing and Services Industry Training Package (BCP03)." TAFE NSW South Western Sydney Institute. Publisher: Pearson Education Australia (Frenchs Forest, N.S.W.). Published in 2007.

Rosenberg A., Tremper K.K.: Authors of "Plumbing the limits of low tidal volumes for acute lung injury," published in Critical Care Medicine, vol. 35, no. 10, p. 2451-3, in October 2007.

Shannon S.C.: Author of "Osteopathic medical education in 2007: plumbing the depths with the questions we ask," published in The Journal of the American Osteopathic Association, vol. 107, no. 3, p. 105-6, in March 2007.

South Western Sydney Institute of TAFE: Publication of "Basic plumbing services skills: addresses nine AQF level 2 core units of competence within the Plumbing and Services Industry Training Package (BCP03)." TAFE NSW South Western Sydney Institute. Publisher: Pearson Education Australia (Frenchs Forest, N.S.W.). Published in 2007.

Standards Australia: Publisher of "Polybutylene (PB) plumbing pipe systems: AS 5082.1:2007: metric series. Part 1, Metric polybutylene (PB) pipes for hot and cold water applications." Publisher: Standards Australia (Sydney, NSW). Published in 2007.

Thomas Delmar Learing: Publisher of "Significant changes to the International plumbing code, International mechanical code, and International fuel gas code, 2006 edition." Publisher: Thomas

Delmar Learing (Clifton Park, NJ). Published in 2007.

United Nations - News: November 15, 2007 — **Headline:** Africa Faces Urban Challenges. **Excerpt:** Africa is the world's fastest urbanizing continent. According to a recent United Nations report, some urban centers are growing at an annual rate of more than 4.5 percent. But many experts who see urbanization as an engine for economic growth warn that unchecked expansion could create new problems for the region. ... But this trend is not unique to Africa. More than three-billion of the world's people already live in cities and the United Nations expects the number to surpass five-billion by 2030. But most analysts say that Africa, which is one of the world's most underdeveloped regions, is the least equipped to meet the demands of its growing urban population. ... To do that, most analysts say, authorities in African cities must provide their citizens with basic services and job opportunities. But many African cities have aging infrastructures that cannot support additional expansion. According to the United Nations, at least one-quarter of African city dwellers do not have access to electricity. Fewer than 45 percent have indoor plumbing and waste disposal poses major health risks in many urban centers. **Author:** Aida F. Akl.

Veit B.: Author of "Plant biology: plumbing the pattern of roots," published in Nature, vol. 449, no. 7165, p. 991-2, on October 25, 2007.

Yamamoto K., Kakutani N., Yamamoto A., Mori Y.: Authors of "A Case Study on the Effect of Storage of Advanced Treated Water in a Building's Plumbing System on Trihalomethane Levels," published in Bulletin of Environmental Contamination and Toxicology, vol. 79, no. 6, p. 665-9, in December 2007.

Yewdell J.W.: Author of "Plumbing the sources of endogenous MHC class I peptide ligands," published in Current Opinion in Immunology, vol. 19, no. 1, p. 79-86, in February 2007.

2008

Smith, Lee: Born in 1935, authored "Plumbing technology: design and installation." Lee Smith, Michael A. Joyce. Publisher: Thomson Delmar Learning (Clifton Park, NY). Published in 2008.

License for Wikipedia Entries

The GNU Free Documentation License does not apply to entries in the public domain, used under commercial license, or under copyright. For each entry or "Document" (as defined below) used from www.wikipedia.org the GNU Free Documentation License applies, the text of which is provided here. To retrieve the original Wikipedia article via the internet, use the url www.en.wikipedia.org/wiki/HEADWORD where "HEADWORD" is the headword provided before the entry. For example, a Wikipedia article for "Apple Pie" is http://en.wikipedia.org/wiki/Apple_Pie. Note that expression words are separated by underscores (e.g. Apple_Pie). Electronic backup copies of these articles are available from www.websters-online-dictionary.org; type the headword into the search box to locate the backup. Paperback versions of this book are being printed on demand, in unknown quantities. ICON Group International, Inc. makes no warrantees with respect to any of the content in this book.

Text of the GNU Free Documentation License

Version 1.2, November 2002; Copyright (C) 2000,2001,2002 Free Software Foundation, Inc. 51 Franklin St, Fifth Floor, Boston, MA 02110-1301 USA. Everyone is permitted to copy and distribute verbatim copies of this license document, but changing it is not allowed.

0. PREAMBLE

The purpose of this License is to make a manual, textbook, or other functional and useful document "free" in the sense of freedom: to assure everyone the effective freedom to copy and redistribute it, with or without modifying it, either commercially or noncommercially. Secondarily, this License preserves for the author and publisher a way to get credit for their work, while not being considered responsible for modifications made by others. This License is a kind of "copyleft", which means that derivative works of the document must themselves be free in the same sense. It complements the GNU General Public License, which is a copyleft license designed for free software. We have designed this License in order to use it for manuals for free software, because free software needs free documentation: a free program should come with manuals providing the same freedoms that the software does. But this License is not limited to software manuals; it can be used for any textual work, regardless of subject matter or whether it is published as a printed book. We recommend this License principally for works whose purpose is instruction or reference.

1. APPLICABILITY AND DEFINITIONS

This License applies to any manual or other work, in any medium, that contains a notice placed by the copyright holder saying it can be distributed under the terms of this License. Such a notice grants a world-wide, royalty-free license, unlimited in duration, to use that work under the conditions stated herein. The "Document", below, refers to any such manual or work. Any member of the public is a licensee, and is addressed as "you". You accept the license if you copy, modify or distribute the work in a way requiring permission under copyright law. A "Modified Version" of the Document means any work containing the Document or a portion of it, either copied verbatim, or with modifications and/or translated into another language. A "Secondary Section" is a named appendix or a front-matter section of the Document that deals exclusively with the relationship of the publishers or authors of the Document to the Document's overall subject (or to related matters) and contains nothing that could fall directly within that overall subject. (Thus, if the Document is in part a textbook of mathematics, a Secondary Section may not explain any mathematics.) The relationship could be a matter of historical connection with the subject or with related matters, or of legal, commercial, philosophical, ethical or political position regarding them. The "Invariant Sections" are certain Secondary Sections whose titles are designated, as being those of Invariant Sections, in the notice that says that the Document is released under this License. If a section does not fit the above definition of Secondary then it is not allowed to be designated as Invariant. The Document may contain zero Invariant Sections. If the Document does not identify any Invariant Sections then there are none. The "Cover Texts" are certain short passages of text that are listed, as Front-Cover Texts or Back-Cover Texts, in the notice that says that the Document is released under this License. A Front-Cover Text may be at most 5 words, and a Back-Cover Text may be at most 25 words. A "Transparent" copy of the Document means a machine-readable copy, represented in a format whose specification is available to the general public, that is suitable for revising the document straightforwardly with generic text editors or (for images composed of pixels) generic paint programs or (for drawings) some widely available drawing editor, and that is suitable for input to text formatters or for automatic translation to a variety of formats suitable for input to text formatters. A copy made in an otherwise Transparent file format whose markup, or absence of markup, has been arranged to thwart or discourage subsequent modification by readers is not Transparent. An image format is not Transparent if used for any substantial amount of text. A copy that is not "Transparent" is called "Opaque". Examples of suitable formats for Transparent copies include plain ASCII without markup, Texinfo input format, LaTeX input format, SGML or XML using a publicly available DTD, and standard-conforming simple HTML, PostScript or PDF designed for human modification. Examples of transparent image formats include PNG, XCF and JPG. Opaque formats include proprietary formats that can be read and edited only by proprietary word processors, SGML or XML for which the DTD and/or processing tools are not generally available, and the machine-generated HTML, PostScript or PDF produced by some word processors for output purposes only. The "Title Page" means, for a printed book, the title page itself, plus such following pages as are needed to hold, legibly, the material this License requires to appear in the title page. For works in formats which do not have any title page as such, "Title Page" means the text near the most prominent appearance of the work's title, preceding the beginning of the body of the text. A section "Entitled XYZ" means a named subunit of the Document whose title either is precisely XYZ or contains XYZ in parentheses following text that translates XYZ in another language. (Here XYZ stands for a specific section name mentioned below, such as "Acknowledgements", "Dedications", "Endorsements", or "History".) To "Preserve the Title" of such a section when you modify the Document means that it remains a section "Entitled XYZ" according to this definition. The Document may include Warranty Disclaimers next to the notice which states that this License applies to the Document. These Warranty Disclaimers are considered to be included by reference in this License, but only as regards disclaiming warranties: any other implication that these Warranty Disclaimers may have is void and has no effect on the meaning of this License.

2. VERBATIM COPYING

You may copy and distribute the Document in any medium, either commercially or noncommercially, provided that this License, the copyright notices, and the license notice saying this License applies to the Document are reproduced in all copies, and that you add no other conditions whatsoever to those of this License. You may not use technical measures to obstruct or control the reading or further copying of the copies you make or distribute. However, you may accept compensation in exchange for copies. If you distribute a large enough number of copies you must also follow the conditions in section 3. You may also lend copies, under the same conditions stated above, and you may publicly display copies.

3. COPYING IN QUANTITY

If you publish printed copies (or copies in media that commonly have printed covers) of the Document, numbering more than 100, and the Document's license notice requires Cover Texts, you must enclose the copies in covers that carry, clearly and legibly, all these Cover Texts: Front-Cover Texts on the front cover, and Back-Cover Texts on the back cover. Both covers must also clearly and legibly identify you as the publisher of these copies. The front cover must present the full title with all words of the title equally prominent and visible. You may add other material on the covers in addition. Copying with changes limited to the covers, as long as they preserve the title of the Document and satisfy these conditions, can be treated as verbatim copying in other respects. If the required texts for either cover are too voluminous to fit legibly, you should put the first ones listed (as many as fit reasonably) on the actual cover, and continue the rest onto adjacent pages. If you publish or distribute Opaque copies of the Document numbering more than 100, you must either include a machine-readable Transparent copy along with each Opaque copy, or state in or with each Opaque copy a computer-network location from which the general network-using public has access to download using public-standard network protocols a complete Transparent copy of the Document, free of added material. If you use the latter option, you must take reasonably prudent steps, when you begin distribution of Opaque copies in quantity, to ensure that this Transparent copy will remain thus accessible at the stated location until at least one year after the last time you distribute an Opaque copy (directly or through your agents or retailers) of that edition to the public. It is requested, but not required, that you contact the authors of the Document well before redistributing any large number of copies, to give them a chance to provide you with an updated version of the Document.

4. MODIFICATIONS

You may copy and distribute a Modified Version of the Document under the conditions of sections 2 and 3 above, provided that you release the Modified Version under precisely this License, with the Modified Version filling the role of the Document, thus licensing distribution and modification of the Modified Version to whoever possesses a copy of it. In addition, you must do these things in the Modified Version:

A. Use in the Title Page (and on the covers, if any) a title distinct from that of the Document, and from those of previous versions (which should, if there were any, be listed in the History section of the Document). You may use the same title as a previous version if the original publisher of that version gives permission.

B. List on the Title Page, as authors, one or more persons or entities responsible for authorship of the modifications in the Modified Version, together with at least five of the principal authors of the Document (all of its principal authors, if it has fewer than five), unless they release you from this requirement.

C. State on the Title page the name of the publisher of the Modified Version, as the publisher.
D. Preserve all the copyright notices of the Document.
E. Add an appropriate copyright notice for your modifications adjacent to the other copyright notices.
F. Include, immediately after the copyright notices, a license notice giving the public permission to use the Modified Version under the terms of this License, in the form shown in the Addendum below.
G. Preserve in that license notice the full lists of Invariant Sections and required Cover Texts given in the Document's license notice.
H. Include an unaltered copy of this License.
I. Preserve the section Entitled "History", Preserve its Title, and add to it an item stating at least the title, year, new authors, and publisher of the Modified Version as given on the Title Page. If there is no section Entitled "History" in the Document, create one stating the title, year, authors, and publisher of the Document as given on its Title Page, then add an item describing the Modified Version as stated in the previous sentence.
J. Preserve the network location, if any, given in the Document for public access to a Transparent copy of the Document, and likewise the network locations given in the Document for previous versions it was based on. These may be placed in the "History" section. You may omit a network location for a work that was published at least four years before the Document itself, or if the original publisher of the version it refers to gives permission.
K. For any section Entitled "Acknowledgements" or "Dedications", Preserve the Title of the section, and preserve in the section all the substance and tone of each of the contributor acknowledgements and/or dedications given therein.
L. Preserve all the Invariant Sections of the Document, unaltered in their text and in their titles. Section numbers or the equivalent are not considered part of the section titles.
M. Delete any section Entitled "Endorsements". Such a section may not be included in the Modified Version.
N. Do not retitle any existing section to be Entitled "Endorsements" or to conflict in title with any Invariant Section.
O. Preserve any Warranty Disclaimers.

If the Modified Version includes new front-matter sections or appendices that qualify as Secondary Sections and contain no material copied from the Document, you may at your option designate some or all of these sections as invariant. To do this, add their titles to the list of Invariant Sections in the Modified Version's license notice. These titles must be distinct from any other section titles. You may add a section Entitled "Endorsements", provided it contains nothing but endorsements of your Modified Version by various parties--for example, statements of peer review or that the text has been approved by an organization as the authoritative definition of a standard. You may add a passage of up to five words as a Front-Cover Text, and a passage of up to 25 words as a Back-Cover Text, to the end of the list of Cover Texts in the Modified Version. Only one passage of Front-Cover Text and one of Back-Cover Text may be added by (or through arrangements made by) any one entity. If the Document already includes a cover text for the same cover, previously added by you or by arrangement made by the same entity you are acting on behalf of, you may not add another; but you may replace the old one, on explicit permission from the previous publisher that added the old one. The author(s) and publisher(s) of the Document do not by this License give permission to use their names for publicity for or to assert or imply endorsement of any Modified Version.

5. COMBINING DOCUMENTS

You may combine the Document with other documents released under this License, under the terms defined in section 4 above for modified versions, provided that you include in the combination all of the Invariant Sections of all of the original documents, unmodified, and list them all as Invariant Sections of your combined work in its license notice, and that you preserve all their Warranty Disclaimers. The combined work need only contain one copy of this License, and multiple identical Invariant Sections may be replaced with a single copy. If there are multiple Invariant Sections with the same name but different contents, make the title of each such section unique by adding at the end of it, in parentheses, the name of the original author or publisher of that section if known, or else a unique number. Make the same adjustment to the section titles in the list of Invariant Sections in the license notice of the combined work. In the combination, you must combine any sections Entitled "History" in the various original documents, forming one section Entitled "History"; likewise combine any sections Entitled "Acknowledgements", and any sections Entitled "Dedications". You must delete all sections Entitled "Endorsements."

6. COLLECTIONS OF DOCUMENTS

You may make a collection consisting of the Document and other documents released under this License, and replace the individual copies of this License in the various documents with a single copy that is included in the collection, provided that you follow the rules of this License for verbatim copying of each of the documents in all other respects. You may extract a single document from such a collection, and distribute it individually under this License, provided you insert a copy of this License into the extracted document, and follow this License in all other respects regarding verbatim copying of that document.

7. AGGREGATION WITH INDEPENDENT WORKS

A compilation of the Document or its derivatives with other separate and independent documents or works, in or on a volume of a storage or distribution medium, is called an "aggregate" if the copyright resulting from the compilation is not used to limit the legal rights of the compilation's users beyond what the individual works permit. When the Document is included in an aggregate, this License does not apply to the other works in the aggregate which are not themselves derivative works of the Document. If the Cover Text requirement of section 3 is applicable to these copies of the Document, then if the Document is less than one half of the entire aggregate, the Document's Cover Texts may be placed on covers that bracket the Document within the aggregate, or the electronic equivalent of covers if the Document is in electronic form. Otherwise they must appear on printed covers that bracket the whole aggregate.

8. TRANSLATION

Translation is considered a kind of modification, so you may distribute translations of the Document under the terms of section 4. Replacing Invariant Sections with translations requires special permission from their copyright holders, but you may include translations of some or all Invariant Sections in addition to the original versions of these Invariant Sections. You may include a translation of this License, and all the license notices in the Document, and any Warranty Disclaimers, provided that you also include the original English version of this License and the original versions of those notices and disclaimers. In case of a disagreement between the translation and the original version of this License or a notice or disclaimer, the original version will prevail. If a section in the Document is Entitled "Acknowledgements", "Dedications", or "History", the requirement (section 4) to Preserve its Title (section 1) will typically require changing the actual title.

9. TERMINATION

You may not copy, modify, sublicense, or distribute the Document except as expressly provided for under this License. Any other attempt to copy, modify, sublicense or distribute the Document is void, and will automatically terminate your rights under this License. However, parties who have received copies, or rights, from you under this License will not have their licenses terminated so long as such parties remain in full compliance.

10. FUTURE REVISIONS OF THIS LICENSE

The Free Software Foundation may publish new, revised versions of the GNU Free Documentation License from time to time. Such new versions will be similar in spirit to the present version, but may differ in detail to address new problems or concerns. See http://www.gnu.org/copyleft/. Each version of the License is given a distinguishing version number. If the Document specifies that a particular numbered version of this License "or any later version" applies to it, you have the option of following the terms and conditions either of that specified version or of any later version that has been published (not as a draft) by the Free Software Foundation. If the Document does not specify a version number of this License, you may choose any version ever published (not as a draft) by the Free Software Foundation.

How to use this License for your documents

To use this License in a document you have written, include a copy of the License in the document and put the following copyright and license notices just after the title page: Copyright (c) YEAR YOUR NAME. Permission is granted to copy, distribute and/or modify this document under the terms of the GNU Free Documentation License, Version 1.2 or any later version published by the Free Software Foundation; with no Invariant Sections, no Front-Cover Texts, and no Back-Cover Texts. A copy of the license is included in the section entitled "GNU Free Documentation License". If you have Invariant Sections, Front-Cover Texts and Back-Cover Texts, replace the "with...Texts." line with this: with the Invariant Sections being LIST THEIR TITLES, with the Front-Cover Texts being LIST, and with the Back-Cover Texts being LIST. If you have Invariant Sections without Cover Texts, or some other combination of the three, merge those two alternatives to suit the situation. If your document contains nontrivial examples of program code, we recommend releasing these examples in parallel under your choice of free software license, such as the GNU General Public License, to permit their use in free software.

Index

C

D

E

F

G

I

J

K

L

M

N

Q

R

S

T

U

V

W

X

Y

Z

Made in United States
Orlando, FL
02 December 2022

25419994R00128